D0213158

Society and the Promise to David

Society and the Promise to David

The Reception History of 2 Samuel 7:1–17

William M. Schniedewind

New York Oxford

OXFORD UNIVERSITY PRESS

1999

Oxford University Press

Oxford New York
Athens Auckland Bangkok Bogotá Buenos Aires Calcutta
Cape Town Chennai Dar es Salaam Delhi Florence Hong Kong Istanbul
Karachi Kuala Lumpur Madrid Melbourne Mexico City Mumbai
Nairobi Paris São Paulo Singapore Taipei Tokyo Toronto Warsaw

and associated companies in
Berlin Ibadan

Published by Oxford University Press, Inc.
198 Madison Avenue, New York, New York 10016

Oxford is a registered trademark of Oxford University Press

Library of Congress Cataloging-in-Publication Data
Schniedewind, William M.
Society and the promise to David : the reception history of
2 Samuel 7:1–17 / by William M. Schniedewind
p. cm.
Includes bibliographical references and index.
ISBN 0-19-512680-7
1. Bible. O.T. Samuel, 2nd, VII, 1–17—Criticism,
interpretation, etc.—History I. Title.
BS1325.2.S38 1999
222'.4406—dc21 98-36495

1 3 5 7 9 8 6 4 2

Printed in the United States of America
on acid-free paper

Preface

Written words seem to talk to you as though they were intelligent, but if you ask them anything about what they say, from a desire to be instructed, they go on telling you just the same thing forever. And once a thing is put in writing, the composition, whatever it may be, drifts all over the place...

—Plato to Phaedrus

We are socially conditioned. I am no exception. The present study is the result of a long interest in the influence of society on interpretation. The interest in this subject goes back to my days as an undergraduate at George Fox University where I was challenged to think socially. It was there that I was led—somewhat inadvertently—into the study of the world of the Bible. This volume also reflects years that I spent rambling around Israel and studying historical geography with Anson Rainey and James Monson, who constantly reminded me "to think with my feet on the ground." It was especially wandering about in Jim's Land Rover that I began to envision the world of ancient Israel. Finally, the present study was shaped by my teachers at Brandeis University, particularly, Michael Fishbane who inspired me to imagine the world and Marc Brettler who honed my critical skills. I have picked up so much from so many that I sometimes think my work might be likened to a pack rat. Hopefully, there is something original in the way that I have pulled it all together. Michael Fishbane was an inspiration for much of what I have done here, although I developed his inner-biblical approach with my own particular sociohistorical twist. He kindly read the manuscript, offered insights, and encouraged me to move in my own directions. Marc Brettler carefully read the manuscript and offered innumerable suggestions that immeasurably improved the manuscript. I wish to thank Ben Sommer, Marv Sweeney, and Michael Rosenbaum for their insights into Isaianic literature, intertextuality, and social dynamics. James Monson was a sounding board for whatever geopolitical insights may be found. Anson Rainey, Sy Gitin, Andy Vaughn, Anne Killebrew, Steve Rosen, Gabi Barkay, and John Monson sharpened my thinking in several areas dealing with the archaeology of ancient Israel. I wish to express special thanks to John Monson who offered me his expertise in archaeology, stimulating discussion, and his friendship. Steve Weitzman stimulated my thinking on issues of theory and method. Daniel Smith-Christopher was a sounding board and fount of insight on the application of sociological methods and the problems of cultural exegesis.

Colleagues at UCLA have often sharpened my perceptions on issues. In particular, I wish to thank Antonio Loprieno and Arnold Band for their stimulating discussions on literary theory, Liz Carter for her archaeological insights, and Richard Leventhal for his critiques of archaeology. My students were constantly subjected to my ruminations on the Promise to David and Israelite society and contributed in many ways. New technologies, particularly the ANE discussion list administrated by Charles Jones at the Oriental Institute, have also provided a simulating source. This forum has frequently broadened the horizons of my methodological reflections and sharpened my perceptions of problems.

The present study could not have come to fruition without the support of a number of academic institutions. First and foremost, the Department of Near Eastern Languages and Cultures at UCLA and its chair Antonio Loprieno deserve special mention. They facilitated a half year in Jerusalem in the summer and fall of 1996 in order to work. In Jerusalem I had the support from the Hebrew University where I was a visiting scholar. The research for this book already begin in Jerusalem when I was a post-doctoral fellow at the Albright Institute for Archaeological Research in 1992-1994. The excellent library of the Ecole Biblique and the facilities of the Albright Institute for Archaeological Research provided the ideal conditions for research and writing.

The translations of biblical texts are usually my own, though I have tried to follow the NRSV or the NJPS versions where appropriate. Likewise, translations of other near eastern and early Jewish literature are my own unless otherwise stated. I have made an effort to place Hebrew only in parentheses and to translate in all places in order to make the work accessible to those who do not read Hebrew. Transcriptions of Hebrew into the roman alphabet are likewise simplified. In deference to other religious traditions I have adopted the spelling YHWH for the tetragrammaton and use the conventions BCE and CE for the traditional BC and AD.

From start to finish this project has seen the birth of my two lovely daughters, Tori and Mikaela. I wish I could say that this project has in no way deprived them of the attention they deserve. My wife has sacrificed so unselfishly that she scarcely realizes the debt I owe her. This study is dedicated to her in the hope that I might not forget also.

W. M. S.

Jerusalem
December 1997

Contents

Abbreviations, ix

1 *Reading the Promise to David*, 3
- Society and Interpretation: A Reception Theory Approach, 5
  - The Diachronic Aspect: Inner-Biblical Discourse, 7
  - The Synchronic Aspect of Interpretation: Historical Moments, 10
  - The Social Function of Literature, 13
- Significance of This Study, 14

2 *Forging a Common Ideology: Origins of the Promise*, 17
- State Formation and the United Monarchy, 18
  - Archaeological Evidence for the Emergence of a State, 19
  - Stages of State Formation, 22
  - Near Eastern Parallels to State Formation, 24
- Transition to State Religion, 26
- Forging a Common Ideology: The Promise to David, 28
  - 2 Samuel 7:1–17: A Promise to David, 29
  - Early Royal Liturgies, 40
- The Promise as Early Political Literature, 46

3 *Kingdoms in Crisis: Vindicating the Promise*, 51
- Jerusalem in the Late Eighth Century BCE, 52
- Social Anthropology of Jerusalem's Urbanization, 55
- Biblical Texts in the Context of Rapid Social Change, 58
  - Proto-DtrH: A Hezekian Historical Composition, 59
  - Isaiah ben Amoz, 61
  - Amos and the "Fallen Hut of David," 63
  - Hosea and "David Their King," 65
  - Psalm 78:67–72: God Rejects Shiloh but Chooses Jerusalem, 66
  - Psalm 2: An Enthronement Liturgy for the Sons of David, 69
- Vindication and Revitalization of the Davidic Dynasty, 70

4 *Josianic Reforms: A New Place for the Promise*, 72
- The Sociopolitical Context of the Late Judaean Monarchy, 72
- The Rise of Literacy and Social Formation, 74
- "The People of the Land" (*'Am Ha'aretz*): A Rural Judean Politic, 77
- Rapid Social Change and New Religious Movements, 80
- Josianic Reformers Recontextualize the Promise (Dtr^1), 82
  - 2 Samuel 7:13a: "He Shall Build a House for My Name," 83
  - Citations of the Promise within Dtr^1, 85
  - *EXCURSUS:* 4QKgs for 1 Kings 8:16, 89
  - Allusion to the Promise in Dtr^1: The Lamp of David, 91
  - Allusion to the Promise in Dtr^1: The "Sure House," 92

Psalm 89:19–37 [MT, 20–38]: Citation and Revision, 93
Religion and Interpretation, 96

5 *"By the Waters of Babylon": The Promise Fails*, 98
Exile and Crisis, 98
The Psychology of Exile and Mass Destruction, 100
The Supposed Inviolability of Zion, 104
When Prophecy Fails, 105
Reading a Promise in Crisis, 106
The Exilic Deuteronomic Readers (Dtr^2), 106
Psalm 89:38–52: Lamenting the Promise, 111
"Second" Isaiah, 114
Rationalizing the Promise, 117

6 *In Persia's Shadow: Restoring the Promise*, 119
The Colonial Empire and the Satrapy of Yehud, 119
Demography and Settlement Patterns, 120
The Economy of Persian Yehud, 122
Literature of the Restoration Program, 124
EXCURSUS: The Dating of Chronicles, 125
The Chronicler's Reading of the Promise, 128
Zechariah 6:12–13: An Allusion to the Promise, 134
MT Jeremiah 33:14–22: Davidic Dynasty and Levitical Priesthood, 135
2 Chronicles 6:41–42: YHWH's Physical Presence in the Temple, 137
Politics of the Return, 138

7 *Second Temple Judaisms Read the Promise*, 140
Alexandrian Diaspora: Acculturation and Identity, 141
The Alexandrian Greek Translation of the Promise to David, 144
Palestinian Judaisms of the Late Second Temple Period, 152
The Promise in the Wisdom of Sirach: Pre-Hasmonean Judaism, 152
Psalms of Solomon 17, 153
The Qumran Sect, 155
Messianisms in the Late Second Temple Period, 165

8 *The Legacy of the Promise to David*, 168

Notes, 173

Bibliography, 206

General Index, 223

Index of Passages, 226

Abbreviations

AB	*Anchor Bible*
ABD	*Anchor Bible Dictionary*
ANET	*Ancient Near Eastern Texts*, 3rd ed. Edited by J. Pritchard. Princeton: Princeton University Press.
AO	Der Alte Orient, Leipzig
ATANT	Abhandlungen zur Theologie des Alten und Neuen Testaments, Zurich
BA	*Biblical Archaeologist*
BAR	*Biblical Archaeological Review*
BASOR	*Bulletin of the American Schools of Oriental Research*
BBR	*Bulletin of Biblical Research*
Bib	*Biblica*
BibOr	*Biblica et Orientalia*, Rome
BIOSCS	*Bulletin of the International Organization for Septuagint and Cognate Studies*
BJS	*Brown Judaic Studies*
BN	*Biblische Notizen*
BWANT	Beiträge zur Wissenschaft vom Alten und Neuen Testament, Stuttgart
BZAW	Beihefte zur *Zeitschrift für die Alttestamentlichye Wissenschaft*, Giessen/Berlin
CAH	*Cambridge Ancient History* I-II, London: Cambridge University Press, 1972–75
CBQ	*Catholic Biblical Quarterly*
CD	*Cairo Geniza, Damascus Document*
CRINT	*Compendia Rerum Iudaicarum ad Novum Testamentum*, Assen: Van Gorcum, 1974 ff.
CTM	*Concordia Theological Monthly*
DJD	*Discoveries in the Judaean Desert*
DSD	*Dead Sea Discoveries*
EI	*Eretz Israel*
EJL	*Early Judiasm and Its Literature*
ESI	*Excavations and Surveys in Irael*
FOTL	*Forms of Old Testament Literature*
HAT	Handbuch zum Alten Testament, Tübingen
HKAT	Handkommentar zum Alten Testament, Göttingen
HSM	*Harvard Semitic Monographs*
HSS	*Harvard Semitic Studies*
HTR	*Harvard Theological Review*
HUCA	*Hebrew Union College Annual*
ICC	*International Critical Commentary*
IEJ	*Israel Exploration Journal*

IES	*Israel Exploration Society*
JAAR	*Journal of the American Academy of Religion*
JBL	*Journal of Biblical Literature*
JESHO	*Journal of the Economic and Social History of the Orient*
JJS	*Journal of Jewish Studies*
JNES	*Journal of Near Eastern Studies*
JNWSL	*Journal of the Northwest Semitic Languages*
JQR	*Jewish Quarterly Review*
JSJ	*Journal for the Study of Judaism*
JSNTSS	*Journal for the Study of the New Testament Supplement Series*
JSOT	*Journal for the Study of the Old Testament*
JSOTSS	*Journal for the Study of the Old Testament Supplement Series*
JSP	*Journal for the Study of Pseudepigrapha*
JSPSS	*Journal for the Study of Pseudepigrapha Supplement Series*
JSS	*Journal of Semitic Studies*
JTS	*Journal of Theological Studies*
KHAT	Kurzgefasstes exegetisches Handbuch zum Alten Testament, Leipzig
NCBC	New Century Bible Commentary
NEAEHL	*New Encyclopedia of Archaeological Excavations in the Holy Land*, edited by E. Stern. Jerusalem/New York: Israel Exploration Society/Carta/Simon & Schuster, 1993.
OBO	Orbis biblicus et orientalis
OTG	*Old Testament Guides*
OTL	*Old Testament Library*
PEQ	*Palestine Exploration Quarterly*
RB	*Revue Biblique*
RQ	*Revue de Qumran*
RSR	*Religious Studies Review*
SBLDS	*Society of Biblical Literature Dissertation Series*
SBLMS	*Society of Biblical Literature Monograph Series*
SBS	Stuttgarter Bibelstudien, Stuttgart
SBTSS	*Studies in Biblical Theology Supplement Series*
ScrHier	*Scripta Hierosolymitana*, Jerusalem
SEA	*Svensk Exegetisk Årsbok*
SHANE	*Studies in the History of the Ancient Near East*
SJOT	*Scandinavian Journal for the Old Testament*
SWBAS	*Social World of Biblical Antiquity Series*
TA	*Tel Aviv*
TynBul	*Tyndale Bulletin*
VT	*Vetus Testamentum*
VTSup	*Supplements to Vetus Testamentum*
WTJ	*Westminister Theological Journal*
ZA	*Zeitschrift für Assyriologie*, Leipzig/Berlin
ZAW	*Zeitschrift für Alttestamentlischen Wissenschaft*
ZThK	*Zeitscrift für Theologie und Kirche*, Tübingen

Society and the Promise to David

1

Reading the Promise to David

And my servant David shall be their prince forever. –Ezekiel 37:25

No text was ever written to be read and interpreted philologically by philologists.
–Walther Bulst

God promised David an eternal kingdom. What happened to it? It was read and reread over the course of centuries by a multitude of audiences and under widely divergent social and political conditions. The changing face of the Promise to David reflects the changing faces of those who read and passed it on. This book is a study of those readers and their interpretations. It follows the reception and transformations of the Promise to David in 2 Samuel 7:1–17 from the inception of the Hebrew monarchy until the dawn of Christianity. Throughout this historical adventure, societies reshape the Promise through reading and rewriting, and at the same time societies are constituted through these activities. To understand the interpretations of the Promise at various historical moments, we must begin by placing them in the societies in which they belong and which they address. This is the proper task of a literary history of the Promise to David.

The Promise to David is, perhaps, one of the most central texts to both Jewish and Christian traditions. It has continually captured the imagination of both academics and apocalyptists. Consequently, the choice of this text is shaped not just by its obvious importance to the emergence of the Davidic dynasty, but even more because of what it became after the demise of the Davidic line. The Promise to David was a constitutional text. That is, it was an idea and also a text through which Israel would define itself as a nation, as a people, and as a religion. In this respect, it functioned something like the Magna Carta or the Declaration of Independence. Certain texts have the power of engendering a national identity. The Promise to David became such a text. It has been argued that "the 'Davidic covenant' represents the thinking of only one (and, I think, a very small) faction in ancient Israel."[1] This was perhaps true at one early moment in the history of the Promise. Yet, the Davidic Promise grew in importance and prestige. The idealization of the Davidic kings as well as the Jerusalem temple were already firmly situated within the Promise by the late Judaean monarchy. So much so, in fact, that the destruction of these institutions precipitated something of a constitutional crisis during the Babylonian exile. In the end, it outlived the Davidic line itself and transcended the temple. The Promise was incarnated in the eschatological expectations of the Qumran community, the early Christian church, and restorative Judaism—and, its drawing power persists.

The present literary history restricts itself to explicit interpretations of Nathan's prophecy in 2 Samuel 7:1–17 up the end of the Second Temple Period in 70 CE. This arbitrary stopping point may be justified because the destruction of the Jerusalem Temple marks a seminal transition in Jewish history. I have chosen to further circumscribe the present study by focusing on *explicit* citations, even though this text spawned an enormous variety of literary allusion and became the focus of a larger literary complex. This choice may be justified because it sets limits on an otherwise amorphous intellectual discourse. Two particular themes from the Promise in 2 Samuel 7:1–17 will be traced through their explicit textual transformations: (1) the Davidic kingdom and (2) the Solomonic temple. The dynastic question might first be posed as follows: Did YHWH promise the kingdom to David's sons, or just to David's son Solomon? An ancillary question asks how conditional was the Promise. Was it really to be forever? An eternal Promise had enormous ideological import, but would present serious situational problems. A primary catalyst for different understandings of the temple would be the question in 2 Samuel 7:5: "shall you build a house for me to dwell in?" Did this undermine the whole concept of the temple, or just David as its builder? Another focal point in the literary history will be the referent of the "place" (מקום) in 2 Samuel 7:10. Does it refer to the land where God would settle his people or the temple where God himself would rest? Must the place be local, or could it encompass the entire earth? Might it refer to an eschatological "place"—the eternal kingdom and temple of God? These questions vexed ancient readers and continue to haunt modern ones.

A literary history of 2 Samuel 7:1–17 is an enormous project. It would be unmanageable if it were not carefully circumscribed. I am primarily interested in outlining only the literary history of the Promise and, even more importantly, a particular approach to literary history informed by Reception Theory (see the following section). Along these lines, I have tried to limit references to secondary literature. Furthermore, by following *only* explicit citations and transformations of the Promise, this study is further circumscribed. For example, the Promise to David is part of the much larger Zion tradition—a tradition I will touch on at points but which is not the focus of this study. The present study is narrowly interested in 2 Samuel 7:1–17 and the sociopolitical contexts that shaped its reading throughout history. By narrowing the focus, I am also able to consider more carefully the relationship between society and reading. It shall become clear, however, that the Promise to David is an organic part of a much larger social discourse; a small part of that discourse can be glimpsed in the pages that follow.

Society and Interpretation: A Reception Theory Approach

Literature and its reading are products of society at particular historical moments. This thesis engenders the present study. The pages that follow trace the reading of the Promise to David (i.e., 2 Sam 7:1–17) *through history* and *in society.* Over the course of history, a discourse concerning the meaning and significance of the Promise grows, develops, and evolves. To properly understand the meaning and significance of the Promise at any particular historical moment, we have to understand its place in a continually evolving discourse. By analogy, the interpretation of the United States Constitution or the Declaration of Independence have had a fascinating history. What does the right to bear arms mean? What does it mean that "all men are created equal"? The answers to these questions are a reflex of the discourse between text and society. To make sense of this discourse, we must understand the social and political contexts which shaped the audiences who read these texts—or, in the present case, the Promise to David. To be sure, it is a perilous task to reconstruct the sociopolitical context of reading, but it is also an essential task. The sociopolitical contexts in which the Promise was read were dramatically different. They included both the emergence of a state and its collapse. The Promise was read both within the structure of an independent state and outside it. It was interpreted both by insiders and by outsiders. It was shaped by both oral and literate societies. Its interpretation reflects the ebb and flow of a millennium of Jewish history.

A literary approach that serves as a heuristic model for the present literary history is reception theory (or *Rezeptionsästhetik*) as articulated by Hans Robert Jauss.[2] Reception theory argues that for outlining literary history more attention needs to be given to the reader than to the writer. Jauss writes,

> The method of the history of reception is essential for the understanding of literary works which lie in the distant past. Whenever the writer of a work is unknown, his intent not recorded, or his relationship to source and model only indirectly accessible, the philological question of how the text is "properly" to be understood, that is according to its intention and its time, can best be answered if the text is considered in contrast to the *background* of the works which the author could expect his contemporary public to know either explicitly or implicitly. [emphasis added][3]

Although Jauss applied his approach quite narrowly, its applicability to the present study should be readily apparent, not only because the problem of authorial intent is so elusive in literature from the "distant past" like the Bible but also because the present study examines specifically the *interpretation* of literature, which is a reflex of its reception. Interpretation primarily reflects the audience, not the author. It is underscores *reception*, not *intention*. Reception theory looks at literature as a barometer of society rather than of just an individual. Although literature is the creation of authors, these authors are framed as readers within a social and historical context and as part of the ongoing dialectic of reading texts.

Traditional literary approaches—whether they be formalist, new critical, Marxist—have tended to focus on the writer and the text. The audience for whom the literature was destined plays a limited role. In formalist approaches, the audience is relevant only in so much that they can follow the lead of the writer or the text. They discover the techniques, perceive the forms. The audience need only have the critical tools of the philologian or historian. Yet ancient texts were not written for philologians or historians. Jauss points out that such approaches deprive literature of its social function: its reception and influence. Jauss writes,

> The historicity of literature as well as its communicative character presupposes a dialogical and at once processlike relationship between work, audience, and new work that can be conceived in the relations between message and receiver as well as between question and answer, problem and solution.[4]

By "historicity" Jauss refers not to literature's veracity but its relationship to particular social and political contexts over time. Time inevitably poses questions, challenges, and problems for literature. New works arise that respond to these questions and pose solutions to emerging problems. Reception theory studies this discourse. Reception theory thus conceived can play an important role, especially when we study the literary history of the Promise to David.

A central concept for Reception theory is the readers' "horizon of expectations" (or *Erwartungshorizont*)—that is, the cultural, social, political, and literary expectations of a text's readers in the historical moment of its appearance. These expectations are the basis on which a text is received and a new text is produced. Jauss outlines three issues that need to be addressed to recover a text's reception history: (1) diachronic, or the ordering of the individual work in its literary series; (2) synchronic, or the relation of the work to its particular historical moment; and (3) the social function, or the relationship of the immanent literary development to the general process of history. In the present study these three aspects are explored through inner-biblical discourse, reconstruction of historical moments, and the use of social theory, respectively.

Reception theory is not without its shortcomings. The most significant criticism of Jauss's work is the inclusive definition of the readers' "horizon of expectations." This generalization is subject to the regular critique of all generalizations. In a useful survey of reader-oriented literary theories, Susan Suleiman notes, "Jauss's notion of the public and its expectations does not allow for enough diversity in the *publics* of literary works at a given time."[5] Ideally, this makes it necessary to multiply the "horizon*s* of expectations." Jauss' theory was originally developed for and applied to relatively modern readers. Multiplying the horizons of expectations poses a greater obstacle when we speak of ancient readers. To start with, there is the problem of dating texts in order to identify the historical moment of the readers. Then, we have to struggle to understand their social contexts. The multiplication of the horizons of expectations will be most acute in the late Second Temple period. The explosion of Jewish sects in the Second Temple period is striking when compared with the preexilic and exilic periods.[6] This, however, is as much a result of sources as it is a reflection of different social realities. The Diasporas did create a much broader spectrum of social contexts. For example, there were seminal differences between the sociopolitical context of Jews writing in Alexandria and Jerusalem. But even within Palestine significant differences existed between, for example, Jerusalem, Galilee, and Khirbet Qumran. These are only the most obvious differences. The more we appreciate these particular contexts, the better we may apprehend different audiences' reading of texts. We must be careful, however. The multiplication of readers' horizon*s* of expectations can quickly devolve into a Reader-response model that emphasizes the individuality of each reader in a particular social context and historical moment.[7] I would argue that the benefit of generalizing about readers' horizon of expectations justifies the necessary backgrounding of the individual. It is essential to literary history.

The Diachronic Aspect: Inner-Biblical Discourse

The diachronic ordering of a work in its literary series contextualizes the historical position and significance of the work. In Jauss's words, "The new text evokes for the reader (listener) the horizon of expectations and rules familiar from earlier texts, which are then varied, corrected, altered, or even just reproduced."[8] Literature does not exist apart from its organic connection to its literary series. In this respect, the chain of the literary series is critical to understanding a text in any particular historical moment because this chain is part of the readers' horizon of expectations and thus informs each new reading. Although we may complain that it is difficult to recover this literary series, it is nevertheless a critical task. The present study analyzes a series of interpretations of the Promise to David stretching over the course of a millennium. Separate chapters are devoted to each moment in the literary series, but their full import cannot be understood without reference to developing discourse. Biblical criticism has tended to focus on the extremes of this literary series, that is, either the origins of the tradition or its final form. Source criticism, for example, has been fixated on the urtext to the almost complete negligence of the text's final form. New criticism and canonical criticism, by contrast, have virtually dismissed literary history in their devotion to the text's final form. Often lost in between these extremes is the sense of text as part of an ongoing discourse.

The stages in the literary series have come to the fore in recent studies in *inner-biblical exegesis*. The seminal work by Michael Fishbane, *Biblical Interpretation in Ancient Israel*, has particularly drawn our attention to a vast network of textual interplay within the Hebrew Bible.[9] For this it has garnered almost unanimous kudos. The study of inner-biblical exegesis has successfully avoided the pitfalls of the traditional disciplines of historical criticism—namely, source and redaction criticism. These traditional approaches use a formal model that sees an evolutionary growth in the literary tradition. The approach of inner-biblical exegesis, however, envisions an ongoing dialogue in a manner not unlike Reception theory's emphasis on the process of reception which relates each new text to a "succession of texts that forms the genre."[10]

Inner-biblical exegesis and early Jewish interpretation have been one of the more visible areas of recent biblical research. Although Fishbane's work is the most encompassing, many scholars have contributed more focused studies. Yair Zakovitch, for example, traces the concept of the exodus in the Bible.[11] In tracing a specific seminal theme, Zakovitch's work is most similar to the present study;

however, the restriction of his study to the biblical canon (while not without justification) is historically artificial. The canon is a much later fixation and the limitation of the canon should apply only within a later religious context. By contrast, James Kugel's *In Potiphar's House: The Interpretative Life of a Biblical Text* and more recently *The Bible As It Was* transcend the historical accident of canon. No doubt studies on inner-biblical exegesis, early Jewish interpretation, and intertextuality will remain one of the hottest areas of research.

Recent studies of inner-biblical exegesis and Fishbane's work in particular have not been without their critics. Lyle Eslinger, for instance, has rightly pointed out that the term *inner-biblical exegesis* too narrowly describes the interplay of biblical texts, and he offers the term *inner-biblical allusion* in its stead.[12] *Allusion*, however, is far too weak and encompassing a term to be used meaningfully. Eslinger's attempt to jettison the term *exegesis* reflects his largely ahistorical interests. For those whose interest is merely in the "literariness" of the textual interplay in biblical literature, the term *allusion* will suffice. Certainly, it is easy to criticize the critical judgments which a historical model necessarily makes.[13] There is, however, a broad consensus that biblical literature was produced over the course of a long period of time—at least 500 if not 1000 years. Although historical judgments do have to be made to discuss this diachronic development, it is hardly credible to dismiss Fishbane's work with the cavalier argument, "You cannot discuss the qualities of diachronic interpretation in the detailed way that Fishbane does if you are not sure which way the literary connection points."[14] To be sure, historical critical judgments are just that—judgments—but they are not necessarily baseless judgments.

The question of terminology does highlight one weakness in Fishbane's study—namely, its reliance on a textual model. To be sure, this model is necessitated to a great extent by the nature of the evidence—that is, textual. Certainly later Jewish interpretation is primarily textual. Yet, early Israel was primarily an oral culture, and the transition to a literate culture did not begin until the late Judaean monarchy (see further chapter 4). Walter Ong, in his classic study on orality and literacy, notes, "Orality-literacy theorems challenge biblical study perhaps more than any other field of learning."[15] This challenge has been taken up in Susan Niditch's recent book, *Oral World and Written Word*, but there is still room much more reflection on the orality-literacy dynamic.[16]

Along these lines, one criticism of inner-biblical exegesis—namely, that it has relied too heavily on a rabbinic model—has some merit. Ultimately, the term *inner-biblical exegesis* is misleading because it implies a purely textual relationship. By contrast, the term *inner-biblical allusion* minimizes or ignores the historical substance of an evolving discourse. As the literary theorist Mikhail Bakhtin has stressed, a text can have no meaning in and of itself. Bakhtin writes, "The literary process is part of the cultural process and cannot be torn away from it."[17] For these reasons, the term *inner-biblical discourse* seems especially apt. It acknowledges that although the literature we read is textual, the relationship between textual artifacts is not purely textual: it is part of an ongoing cultural discourse. The attraction to tracing a literary history of the Promise to David comes from the central place it occupied in the cultural discourse of ancient Israel and early Judaism.

Traditional analyses of biblical texts have come under considerable criticism in recent years from both within and outside the discipline, and for good reason.[18] Even a short survey of the source and redaction analyses of 2 Samuel 7:1–17 betrays a bewildering array of opinions. The very foundations of traditional critical approaches must be shaken by the inability to arrive at any consensus, however slight, in these matters. Yet, even the most ardent critics of traditional biblical criticism will admit that biblical narratives used sources. It is difficult—even for the most passionate advocates of new literary approaches—to completely dismiss the historical criticism of the last century of biblical scholarship. In the end, there is consensus that at least *some* of the unevenness in biblical narratives is due to the use of sources, the editing of texts, or redactions. That is, *biblical literature reflects a historical process*. Once we admit this premise, the only question is whether the reader is interested in that process. If we are interested in literary history, then we are thrown back into the problem of editors, redactors, and sources. The present study maintains that the historical process informs the reading of biblical literature. Ultimately, it is this retrospective of the long history of reading that can serve to frame our own peculiar readings of the Promise to David.

Texts that deal with issues of vital importance to a community specifically or humanity generally attract redaction, supplementation, and editorial glossing. This study unashamedly employs traditional literary analyses to texts to recover the sources, redactional stages, and editorial additions. At the same time, it is quite critical of some of the methods and conclusions of these approaches. Nevertheless, striking proof for the long development of biblical tradition has come from the study of inner-biblical discourse. We should hardly be surprised that certain texts like the Promise to David were continually reworked and reinvented. As long as the issues a text treats remain vital, it will continue to attract further elaboration in the form of redaction, editing, glossing, and complete rewriting. Even after a text becomes canonical, it is not immune to these operations as the various Qumran texts dealing with the Torah illustrate (e.g., 11QTemple, Reworked Pentateuch, Genesis Apocryphon).[19] The exegetical ruminations and transformations within biblical literature fundamentally justify historical criticism, even if they do not exonerate all its excesses.

What methodology is there for identifying redactions and editorial hands? First of all, editors and redactors stand in a conscious line of literary tradition. Their work is not covert. It is marked.[20] The most prominent techniques include deitic markers (e.g., הוא), inclusios, chiastic citation (i.e., Seidel's Law), and the *Wiederaufnahme* (i.e., repetitive resumption).[21] An obvious indicator of multiple sources is doublets. For example, the two accounts of Sennacherib's campaign in 2 Kings 18:13–15 (// Isa 36:1) and 18:16–19:37 (// Isa 36:2ff.) are simply a case of multiple sources. They are not two separate campaigns but rather two separate sources joined with a temporal phrase, "at that time" (בעת ההיא, 2 Kgs 18:16), which introduces the second source.[22] Any redaction analysis must begin with the premise that units, sources, or insertions are marked editorially. Any identification of sources, redactional layers, or editorial additions based on thematic or linguistic arguments alone will be hopelessly subjective and ultimately circular. Second, the importance of a *literary* tradition as opposed to an *oral* tradition must be stressed. The types of source and redaction analyses stressed here depend on a literate culture; these types of analyses simply cannot be performed on literature that derives primarily from an oral setting.

This study is structured diachronically as chapters on the reading and interpretation of the Promise to David. The whole is more than the sum of its parts because each successive chapter augments and adapts an ongoing dialogue in ancient Israel and early Judaism about the meaning of the Promise to David for the community.

The Synchronic Aspect of Interpretation: Historical Moments

The present study also highlights a synchronic aspect of interpretation—namely, that literature must be understood with reference to its particular historical moment. I begin with the premise that all literature has a historical particularity. Jauss emphasizes "the possibility and necessity of uncovering the historical dimension of literary appearances in synchronic cross-sections."[23] Ultimately, a diachronic analysis such as inner-biblical discourse must stop and consider the historical moments to fully appreciate "the history-making moments and epochal caesuras."[24]

The reconstruction of historical moments would be hopelessly circular if it depended entirely on biblical literature. In short, it would mean reconstructing a historical context from the same literature that is being interpreted through the framework of that reconstructed historical context.[25] Archaeology and other Near Eastern literature, however, offer some respite to the endless circularity. Through the archaeologist's spade, we acquire an independent witness to the historical moments of ancient Israel. In the Near Eastern texts, we gain another witness of these moments. These two witnesses then serve as additional controls in historical reconstruction.

Archaeology is not ideal for illuminating events. It is good at describing processes. It is particularly adept at illuminating social, cultural, and religious contexts of periods. One of the problems of the old biblical archaeology was its obsession with the connection between biblical events and the archaeological record.[26] To take a parade example, John Garstang's excavations at Jericho were essentially aimed at discovering the walls that had fallen before Joshua. It actually is no better when archaeologists attempt to disprove events. Ultimately, the strength of archaeology is its ability to illuminate social processes. We are fortunate that Syro-Palestinian archaeology has increasingly concerned itself with the cultural and social processes within which literature arises and in which reading takes place.[27] It is to this strength that the present study will turn to archaeology. The study of the literary history of 2 Samuel 7:1–17 is unconcerned with events per se. Rather, we need to understand the general social, cultural, religious and political setting in which literature was read and produced.

Additionally, the physical environment—particularly, geography—is a fundamental yet often neglected force in shaping ancient Israelite history and society.[28] Geography is quite deterministic, and as such it should inform historical investigation. An obvious example is the geography of the kingdoms of Israel and Judah. The northern kingdom lay on the crossroads of the great trade routes of the Near East, between Egypt and Mesopotamia, between the Mediterranean and the Desert. Judah was perched in the southern mountains, bypassed by much of the commerce and conflict. The classic study by George Adam Smith summed up the situation picturesquely noting that Judah "has no harbours, no river, no trunk-road, no convenient market for nations on either side. . . . The whole plateau stands aloof, waterless, on the road to nowhere."[29] Smith observed, by contrast, that the northern part of Palestine "is as fair and open as the southern is secluded and austere, and their fortunes correspond. . . . The more forward to attract, the more quick to develop, Samaria was the less able to retain."[30] Ultimately, the physical character of the land shapes its history and its literature. The geopolitical dynamics of Palestine will be one of the surest guides in reconstructing its historical moments.

The political setting is perhaps the most critical part of the investigation of the historical moment. A weakness of literary treatments of biblical literature is not just the lack of diachronic perspective; even more than this, they deprive the Hebrew Bible of its social and political contexts. In this respect I have great sympathy for the attempt by Joel Rosenberg to infuse a literary reading of the biblical narrative with "political import." Rosenberg argues that "the makers of biblical literature . . . were deeply preoccupied with the nature of Israel's political community and were interested in the premises of political existence, addressing themselves to readers who thought about such things as leadership, authority, social cohesiveness, political order, rebellion, crime, justice, institutional evolution, and the relation of rich and poor."[31] Rosenberg's critique focuses equally on traditional source critics and more recent literary critics. For example, he observes, "Gunn [in *The Story of King David*] makes the political dimensions of the King David story an incidental bonus in its unfolding as art, just as the historical investigators of the story made its artistic brilliance an incidental bonus in its unfolding as history."[32] Newer literary approaches seem to assume that the oft proclaimed literary brilliance of biblical literature is unrelated to its interaction with the cultural, political, and religious milieu in which it was written. The brilliance of biblical literature begins with its relation to particular sociopolitical contexts.

Unfortunately, Rosenberg's emphasis on the political dimensions of the biblical narratives still takes a narrow synchronic view of the literature. For example, while admitting that the classic study by Leonard Rost "is substantial enough to imply a complicated pattern of traditionary accretion and infixing," he still recites the mantra of newer literary critics:

> The problems arise when a critic attempts to determine which texts are the "leaders" in the process, and which are the "followers." Is a folkloric or archival fragment infixed to a narrative cycle by the narrative author, or is it an addendum by a later editor or redactor, humbly annotating what is, by then, an ancient and venerable story with a long history of transmission? Here, we find ourselves in an area of decision where caprice and fashion tend to rule . . . .[33]

As I have already stated, I do not find a complete dismissal of historical criticism convincing. The political and cultural institutions of Israel were not static. There were many different political contexts. For preexilic Israel (which Rosenberg claims to deal with) these would minimally include the formation of the state and the Davidic dynasty, the divided and competing kingdoms, the fall of the north in the wake of the rise of the Assyrian empire, and the Josianic reformations (which followed the waning of the Assyrian empire). For the purposes of the present book, we may add additional contexts: exilic Israel, the return to the Persian province of Yehud, the Greek-speaking Jewish Diaspora in Alexandria, and various disenfranchised Jewish groups in Palestine before the destruction of the Second Temple in 70 CE. The political dimensions of literature written in each milieu must be radically different. Each unique political context informed the reading of the Promise to David in a particular way.

Finally, a note of caution is in order given the complicated problem of reconstructing social and political contexts from the distant past. In the present case, extensive space must be devoted to culling the limited sources to reconstruct reasonable contexts for literature. The results of recent archaeological studies have provided a much more extensive and firmer set of data for reconstructing ancient Israel. To a lesser extent, additional textual discoveries also continue to aid the historian's work. Even with these new resources, we must still fall back on the cautious words of the historian Robert Fogel:

> A judge and jury, indeed, would go mad if they had to decide cases on evidence which will often seem more than satisfactory to the historian. But there is no escape; the historian, if he is to interpret at all, will try and convict on evidence which a court would throw out as circumstantial or hearsay. The victims of the historical process have to seek their compensation in the fact that history provides them with a far more flexible appellate procedure. The historian's sentences are in a continuous condition of review; few of his verdicts are ever final.[34]

The deficiencies of our verdicts—which are only an inescapable product of the human condition—cannot absolve us from making decisions. If we are to properly understand the literary history of the Promise, we must recover something of the social and political settings that informed its ongoing reinterpretation. To our advantage, it is easier to reconstruct sociopolitical processes than it is to determine the particularities of events. The present work is primarily concerned with *intellectual* history and *perceptions* of realia as they concern the Promise to David. Ultimately, the act of reading is shaped by a complex symbiosis between the audience's perception of the moment and realia itself. Thus, biblical literature (like all literature), infused though it must be with ideology, still reflects a *perception* of the world. Part of our task is to re-create the contexts of reading in order to understand something of the import of those readings in their particular historical moments.

The Social Function of Literature

Jauss's final category highlights "the predominantly social, or society-forming function of literature"—a subject of increasing interest in recent studies on biblical literature. Jauss writes, "The social function [of literature] becomes manifest only where the literary experience of the reader enters the horizon of expectations of his life, forms his interpretations of the world, and thereby has an effect on his social actions."[35] Although Jauss was concerned primarily with the modern audience, we shall be concerned with ancient audiences. An attempt must be made to reconstruct the "horizon of expectations" of the ancient readers, by which we may assess the history of reception.[36] In this vein, social theory is used as a heuristic device throughout this study. Literature has a social function; social models can help to recover it. To use an analogy from functional linguistics: words can be intelligibly interpreted only by what they meant at the time of their use, within the language system and social context of both the speaker and the listener.[37] If literary history is to go beyond mere *formal* description and actually explain textual transformations, we must understand how texts *functioned* in society.

Naturally, care must be exercised in the use of social models. Jauss cautions that "the social dimension of literature and art with respect to their reception is limited to the secondary function of only allowing an already previously known (or ostensibly known) reality to be *once again recognized.*"[38] Jauss's understanding of the social function of literature highlights the proactive as well as the reactive aspect of literature. In other words, literature is not merely socially determined; it is also socially formative. The problem may be illustrated by George Mendenhall and Norman Gottwald's enormously influential sociological studies of early Israel. Ultimately, these studies failed simply because social theory took precedence over textual and archaeological evidence; this failure became increasingly clear as more archaeological data emerged from surveys throughout the land of Israel.[39] This is not an argument intended to minimize the importance of social theory; rather, it is simply intended to emphasize that the historical data should dictate the use of social theory.[40]

This study uses social theory as a heuristic device. Social theories are employed if they seem to offer some useful way of framing particular historical moments. This study is not, however, an exercise in sociological criticism. It is literary history. Social theory is useful because literary history does not arise in a vacuum. People read literature. A pervasive—and sometimes quite justified—critique of sociological studies is simply that they often arise from comparisons that show little regard for cultural or chronological differences. Then again, the success of biblical analysis can often depend on the breadth of knowledge and experience which scholars bring to the text.[41] Social theory brings new perspectives to the text and helps us imagine the contexts in which texts are read.

Finally, society is dynamic, not static. It is not sufficient to speak of the "preexilic" or "postexilic" periods as though they were some kind of static entity. To properly apprehend the reception of texts, we must understand as precisely as possible the society within which they were produced. A variety of different social models can serve as heuristic devices, including state formation, urbanization, rapid social change, cognitive dissonance theory, and colonialism.

One significant problem with source and redaction critical studies is the failure to adequately investigate the sociopolitical context to which sources and redactional layers were attributed. A corollary problem is the use of texts alone to reconstruct social and political backgrounds for sources and redactions—clearly a circular enterprise. We cannot assign compositional dates to texts, redactions, and sources without first having a clear conception of sociopolitical contexts, and naturally these same texts, redactions, and sources should not provide the only evidence for sociopolitical reconstructions. Some attempt to reconstruct the historical moments of ancient Palestine should precede the study of texts, redactions, and sources.

Significance of This Study

The purpose and significance of the present study can be understood by comparing it with recent trends in biblical scholarship. The present study cuts against the grain of two related trends without necessarily denying the validity of either. Canonical criticism, usually associated with Brevard Childs, focuses the meaning of the text in its canonical context as Scripture.[42] It removes the text from its original audience and focuses on the meaning for another later audience—namely, the church. Recent literary approaches to the Bible also move away from historical moorings.[43] These literary approaches have tended to focus on artistic aspects of biblical literature, especially as they are perceived by modern readers. The text is treated as a modern artifact; historical moorings are ignored at best and snubbed at worst. Without its historical moorings, texts are empty vessels, filled by the whimsy, foolish or profound, of modern readers. It seems worthwhile and even incumbent to ask what these biblical texts meant when they were written to the people for whom they were written. More than this, I assume that biblical literature was much less occupied with literary artistry than its modern critics. By abandoning historical criticism, modern critics are left with little else than the literariness of texts. This is not to say that biblical literature employs no literary devices or has no artistic appeal but rather that the meaning of biblical texts is shaped by readers' religious and political motivations at particular historical moments.

The significance of the present study can also be illustrated by setting it against previous studies on 2 Samuel 7 and the Davidic dynasty tradition. Traditional studies like Leonard Rost's classic *Die Überlieferung von der Thronnachfolge Davids*, and the many studies of Timo Veijola have emphasized traditional literary approaches (i.e., source, redaction, and form criticism as well as tradition history) without engaging the social and political contexts of the ancient readers and interpreters of the text.[44] Some newer literary studies have jettisoned any attempt to understand the text in its ancient social and political context.[45] The studies by Antti Laato attempt to combine redactional approaches with rhetorical criticism; despite his analysis of texts from disparate historical periods, he does not actually do literary history.[46] Ultimately, Laato is concerned with the background of Christian messianism for which 2 Samuel 7 plays a central role. The social and historical contexts of messianic exegesis play superficial roles in his analysis. In a similar vein comes the recent dissertation turned monograph by Ken Pomykala, *The Davidic Dynasty Tradition in Early Judaism: Its History and Significance for Messianism*, surveys the "Davidic dynasty" in the literature from 400 BCE to 100 CE by taking an "historical" approach yet not engaging literary history. As a methodological presupposition, Pomykala argues that within the complex of ideas and literature we must "investigate each text . . . in its own integrity."[47] He intends to let each text stand alone. But do texts stand alone? Perhaps they can be made to do so. But are not texts part of—in Pomykala's words—"a complex of ideas"? Do they not form part of a ongoing discourse? This is a fundamental premise of *inner-biblical discourse*. It is fair to assume that the authors and audiences knew texts like 2 Samuel 7, Psalm 132, 1 Kings 8, Isaiah 7, and Amos 9; hence, to judge the reception of the text, we need to set it in the audience's social and political horizons as well as their literary horizons.

An example of the importance of social and political contexts for understanding literary history is an article by Baruch Halpern entitled, "Jerusalem and the Lineages in the Seventh Century BCE: Kinship and the Rise of Individual Moral Liability."[48] In this outstanding article, Halpern wishes to explain the development from collective to individual moral responsibility in biblical literature. Halpern recognizes, however, that the understanding of literary history begins with developments in the social and political contexts; in his words, "The answers to these questions begin far afield."[49] To address his questions about the development of individual morality in literary texts, he must adduce a wealth and variety of archaeological evidence in order to reconstruct changes in Judaean society during the seventh century. For example, he derives one incisive observation from an analysis of pottery; in short, the size of cooking pots become smaller in the seventh century as society moves from larger clan structures toward a nuclear family! This movement toward smaller families heightened individualization. Here, I oversimplify Halpern's detailed argument, but it nevertheless serves to illustrate the importance that archaeology and social anthropology can have for understanding literary history. Halpern's study thus underscores the importance of both social context and diachronic development for studying biblical literature.

The present study is not, however, intended to be primarily a reconstruction of the historical moments and social matrices of ancient readers. To be sure, this is a first step. To understand the reading of a text at any particular historical moment, one must understand the readers' "horizon of expectations," to use Jauss's term. In this respect, the historical moments are critical. Ultimately, however, the present work seeks to re-create the cultural discourse that arises from and is contextualized within the readings of the Promise to David. Along these lines, reconstructions of particular historical moments are not necessarily complete, nor is the analysis exhaustive. Repeatedly, I resisted the temptation to overburden the study with banal controversies over particular historical reconstructions. I defend my reconstructions, but only to a point, because these reconstructions are not the point of the book. Primarily, I am advocating a method for studying the literary history of biblical texts and not particular reconstructions of historical moments. Still, there should be a dynamic and symbiotic relationship between the study of literary history and the study of social history. This study, hopefully, contributes to our understanding of the social history of ancient Israel and early Judaism.

Recent literary approaches have tended to treat the biblical text synchronically. The text has no sources, no redactional history, no editorial revisions—or, at least, such diachronic concerns are irrelevant. A major criticism of traditional diachronic approaches by newer literary critics has been lack of attention to the final form of the text. The last decades have witnessed a growing polarization between synchronic and diachronic approaches to the biblical text.[50] Some mediation between the extremes of synchronic and diachronic approaches may be found in inner-biblical interpretation. On the one hand, inner-biblical interpretation requires a diachronic view; that is, a text is historically related to a previous text or tradition. On the other hand, inner-biblical interpretation employs a careful reading of the text as we have it. The phenomenon of inner-biblical interpretation has attuned scholars to the place of text within a stream of interpretation.

One shortcoming of recent studies in inner-biblical interpretation is its inattention to the role of social and political contexts in shaping interpretation. For example, the growing movement that has applied sociological theory to the study of ancient Israel has yet to contribute in the field of inner-biblical interpretation.[51] This study fills this lacuna in a small way by showing how sociopolitical contexts can inform and enrich the study of inner-biblical discourse. There will be some objections to my particular reconstructions of the sociopolitical contexts of discourse, but ultimately we cannot ignore the implications that sociopolitical contexts had on discourse.

The present study also runs counter to the recent fashion which envisions biblical literature as a fiction of the Persian and Hellenistic era.[52] Those who imagine that biblical literature was invented in the Second Temple period disregard a long literary and linguistic development.[53] Although the canonical form of the Hebrew Bible reflects editorial work of Persian, Hellenistic, and even Roman periods, this canonical process touches primarily the structure and shaping of earlier literary units. It does not demolish these literary units. Biblical literature testifies to a long period of literary and linguistic development that simply cannot be accounted for by those who imagine it as a fiction of the Persian or Hellenistic periods. The present study underscores the long literary history of 2 Samuel 7:1–17, reflecting a variety of sociopolitical contexts in which it was read and rewritten.

By analyzing the reception history of the Promise to David, we witness the historical unfolding of the meaning and influence of the Promise. Each successive epoch reads the tradition in the light and with the baggage of previous discourse. Each successive epoch reads the tradition in its own particular sociopolitical context. Each particular epoch shapes and is shaped by the literary discourse and sociopolitical context. In the end, I hope this reception history of the Promise to David provides insight into the intellectual history of ancient Israel and early Judaism and serves as a paradigm for the study of the Bible's literary history.

2

Forging a Common Ideology: Origins of the Promise

You said, "I have made a covenant with my chosen one, I have sworn to my servant David: 'I will establish your descendants forever, and build your throne for all generations'" —Psalm 89:3–4

The rise of the United Monarchy is one of the curiosities of history. The geography of Palestine lends itself to neither a united nor independent polity. The position of Palestine between the African and Asian continents made it the crossroads of commerce and conflict and usually resulted in its domination by foreign powers—Egypt, Assyria, Babylon, Persia, Rome, and the Arab empires. The local topography subdivides the land into relatively small geographical units. These small geographical entities are more naturally suited to loosely organized, clan-based chiefdoms. These relatively weak, decentralized political systems further encourage Palestine's domination by outsiders. The formation of a large independent state in Palestine thus swims against several currents, and it should hardly be surprising that some scholars wish to dispose of it completely.[1] Only within a unique configuration of historical circumstance and individual personality did a united and independent state emerge under David and Solomon. It lasted scarcely more than a generation, even according to the biblical account. Yet, through the nostalgic literary development of a golden age of David and Solomon, it lived on and grew.

The Promise to David was critical to the emerging monarchy. The Davidic monarchy was beset with the difficulties that naturally accompany all societies in transition. The Promise to David gave divine sanction to the emerging monarchy and a centralization of political power, even while it stopped short of sanctioning a centralization of religious authority. One of the most curious aspects of the Promise to David in 2 Samuel 7:1–17 is the real ambiguity it leaves surrounding the Jerusalem temple. After all, 2 Samuel 7:5 asks David: who are you to build God a temple? It then further explains in verses 6-7 that YHWH had never asked for a temple. Attempts to whitewash this very apparent rejection of a centralized temple reflect the later social contexts of reading. The easiest explanation of this ambiguity is simply that the temple and a centralization of religious authority were points of tension in the sociopolitical situation of an emerging monarchy. The diverse clans and tribes of Palestine needed a common political ideology to knit their new union together, apparently, they did not need a common religious focal point at this time. The Promise to David, both in liturgy and narrative, provided the ideological glue holding together the emerging monarchy.

State Formation and the United Monarchy

A political vacuum in Palestine followed the decline of the Late Bronze Age civilizations in Egypt and Mesopotamia and provides the backdrop for the emergence of a state in Palestine.[2] After the bipolar power structure collapsed, the concomitant political vacuum was filled by new and competing ethnicities in Syria-Palestine during the Iron I Period (ca. 1200–1000 BCE) including the Phoenician city-states, the Aramaean tribes, the Philistine confederacy, and the Israelite tribes. The broad parameters of this background are well known. By the late thirteenth century the Israelites were already present in the hill country as indicated by the Merneptah Stela.[3] About 1000 BCE, archaeological evidence, along with biblical narratives, points to the emergence of a new, united state structure emerging from the hill country. Beyond this skeleton, however, the reconstruction of the sociopolitical background must remain tentative for three reasons: (1) the limitations of current archaeological data, (2) the scarcity of Near Eastern texts, and (3) the nature of the biblical literature.

The archaeological data yield an incomplete, sometimes piecemeal picture. One example of this problem is Solomon's "missing" temple—no archaeological evidence has been unearthed in Jerusalem to corroborate a Solomonic temple. On this basis, some have made the argument that Solomon did not build a temple! Of course, we also do not have evidence for Ezra and Nehemiah's temple, but few would want to conclude that there was no temple in the Persian period. Excavations naturally have unearthed more complete and pristine examples of the latest archaeological strata. In spite of the fact that William Dever's statement of more than a decade ago still holds true—namely, "there has to date been no large-scale clearance of any tenth century site"[4]—it nevertheless can be argued that "Solomon, despite the debate that swirls round his historicity, can be credited with significant, archaeologically detectable achievements."[5] It is easy to fall into the trap of either overstating or understating these achievements.[6]

The scarcity of Near Eastern texts reflects the weakness of the empires in Egypt and Mesopotamia in the late Iron I and early Iron II period; this weakness is paradoxically both the reason that a United Monarchy could emerge in Palestine and the reason that we find little evidence for a United Monarchy in Palestine from Near Eastern sources. A decline in Egypt began in the twelfth century and a two-century gap in historical sources reigns from the account of the Sea Peoples incursions against Rameses III (ca. 1175 BCE) until the campaign of Pharaoh Shishak in

Palestine (ca. 925 BCE). The decline in Assyria follows Tiglath-Pileser I (ca. 1116–1078 BCE); this weakness not only allowed the Davidic monarchy to emerge in Palestine but also facilitated the rise of the Aramaean states in Syria.[7] Quite literally, there are almost no Near Eastern sources concurrent with the early Israelite state, so the absence of sources hardly translates into evidence of absence.

The biblical texts preserve some literature from the emerging United Monarchy. At the same time, the biblical literature comes to us through a long process of transmission. It is a secondary source. This problem is naturally raised by a host of scholars. Shemaryahu Talmon, for example, writes, "The problem presented by the heterogeneity of sources concerning the concept of monarchy is compounded by the difficulty of dating them."[8] This is no reason to dismiss attempts to recover earlier stages in biblical literature. Both the history of interpretation within biblical literature (or inner-biblical discourse) and the history of the Hebrew language give us tools with which we may recover some of the earlier stages of biblical literature.

Still, the reception and transmission of biblical texts by later tradents leave them open to a hermeneutic of suspicion. In recent years, a few studies have called into question the very existence of David, Solomon, and the United Monarchy.[9] They are described as fictions written by Jewish authors in the Persian or Hellenistic periods. These proposals are unconvincing. Such hypotheses make biblical literature one dimensional. They account for no growth of tradition. They leave no room for rewriting of older traditions. They allow for no variation in the Hebrew language. It is simply impossible to explain the exegetical permutations of biblical literature which this study explores within the time frame of the Persian or Hellenistic period. It is likewise impossible to explain the variability within the Hebrew language of biblical texts without recourse to a long period of development and a diverse cultural milieu.[10] Biblical literature evinces both literary and linguistic stratification. This, as we shall see, is critical for understanding the traditions concerning the Promise to David. Meanwhile, the limitations of these three types of evidence—biblical literature, archaeology, and Near Eastern texts—will render social theory all the more important as a heuristic device for reconstructing the sociopolitical background of the Promise.

The biblical tradition points to the late eleventh and early tenth centuries as a period of transition from the charismatic and ad hoc leadership of diverse tribes to a united and centralized government by David and Solomon. Archaeological excavations and surveys continue to undercover evidence for the early formation of a state in Palestine around 1000 BCE. At the same time, the archaeological record also suggests that biblical authors aggrandize what was apparently a relatively small and emerging state.

Archaeological Evidence for the Emergence of a State

Archaeological data pertaining to the emergence of a centralized state in Palestine come from two types of sources: surveys and excavations. Although major excavations have been conducted in Palestine for well over a century, extensive survey data has emerged only in the last couple of decades. These data taken together complement each other and round out the archaeological picture.[11] Both lines of evidence point to a seminal transformation associated with the transition from Iron I to the Iron II Period, usually dated to about 1000 BCE. Recent debates about the precise date of this transition are not of particular importance to the present study because ultimately we are concern with the sociopolitical *process*, not the chronological dating.[12]

Evidence from surveys indicates that a shift in settlement patterns laid the groundwork for the emergence of monarchy. To begin with, Late Bronze Age settlements in Palestine were larger (mean, ca. 3 ha; median, ca. 5 ha) than their Iron I counterparts (mean, ca. 1.7 ha; median, 1.0 ha). Moreover, the total settled area in Late Bronze was 69 ha, whereas in Iron IA it increased to 192 ha, representing a 2% per year increase in population between 1200 and 1150 BCE. This demographic shift precipitates the transition from a pastoral to a more agrarian and urbanized society.[13] As Nadav Na'aman observes, the enormous growth of settlement and population "enabled the emerging states to mobilize many people and send them on military operations and corvée work (2 Sam 20:24; 1 Kgs 4:6; 5:27–28; 9:15; 1:28 [*sic* 11:28]; 12:3–14, 18)."[14]

The demographics and political structures of ancient Israel were shaped by its environment, and particularly the geography.[15] The geography of Palestine was well suited to the small, isolated city-states of the type we see only too clearly in the Amarna Letters during the Late Bronze Age. Samaria and Galilee are divided by the Jezreel Valley—the main crossroads for international trade—whereas Judah is isolated in the southern range. Although travel into the northern hill country around Shechem was relatively easy, the southern hill country was insulated by deep ravines, which made travel and commerce inevitably more difficult. In the words of the classic study by George Adam Smith, "The northern [range] is as fair and open as the southern is secluded and austere, and their fortunes correspond."[16] For these reasons, the great cities of the second millennium—Hazor, Megiddo, Beth-Shan—were located in northern Palestine and on the crossroads of the major international lines of commerce and conflict. Even in the hill country, Shechem far surpassed Jerusalem in size, power, and prosperity. These factors must have influenced the brevity of the United Monarchy. Along these lines Israel Finkelstein observes, "The demographic dispersal of the tenth century may also explain one of the reasons for the division of the United Monarchy—the much larger and wealthier population of the central hill country arose against the dynasty of the poor and underpopulated south."[17] These demographic differences reflect the natural economic advantages that the geography of Palestine offered to the north. As a result, the northern kingdom was more densely populated and urbanized than Judah. It should not be surprising that the more affluent north broke away from the south after the death of the charismatic leaders who created the United Monarchy.

The demographic shift between Iron I and Iron II was accompanied by urbanization. Although there has not been any large-scale excavation of tenth century city which would allow us to speak directly of town planning, there are indications of centralized planning. Well-laid-out cities from the Iron II Period at Beersheba, Mizpah, and Tell Beit Mirsim were constructed following architectural plans going

Table 2.1. City Gates at Gezer, Hazor, and Megiddo

	Gezer	Hazor	Megiddo
Length	19.0	20.3	20.3
Width	16.2	18.0	17.5
Between towers	5.5	6.1	6.5
Entrance width	4.1	4.2	4.2
Wall width	1.6	1.6	1.6
Total casemate width	5.4	5.4	5.5

back to the tenth century.[18] Domestic architecture in the tenth century city at Tirzah suggests social stratification. The important site of Hazor (Stratum X) developed into an exclusively royal enclosure without evidence for domestic dwellings. A parade example of defensive fortifications has been the city gates at Gezer, Megiddo, and Hazor as in table 2.1 and figure 2.1 (note 1 Kgs 9:15–17).[19]

There also emerges a palace architecture based on Syrian models as well as administrative buildings (referred to alternatively as "storehouses," "stables," "barracks," and "marketplace") unique to early Israel.[20]

A system of fortresses was established in the Negev highlands in the tenth century. These fortresses were organized around the trade routes from Eilat (or Ezion-geber) and depended on a centralized state for their development and maintenance.[21] In fact, at no time does such a system of fortresses arise apart from a strong, centralized state. Later in the tenth century, Pharaoh Shishak made an incursion into the Negeb. The account of Shishak's incursion eastward into the Negeb suggests (1) that a trading infrastructure was established by Israel in the early tenth century and (2) that Egypt attempted to recover the trade and mineral resources of the Negev highlands. The other prime examples of the development of the Negev include the late Judaean monarchy and the Byzantine period.[22] All this points to the development of a centralized state that likely would have required a developed administration and the use of forced labor (cf. 1 Kgs 9:15). Although we should not exaggerate the grandeur of the emerging state, there is no question about the signs. It is within this context of an emerging state that the Promise must be assessed.

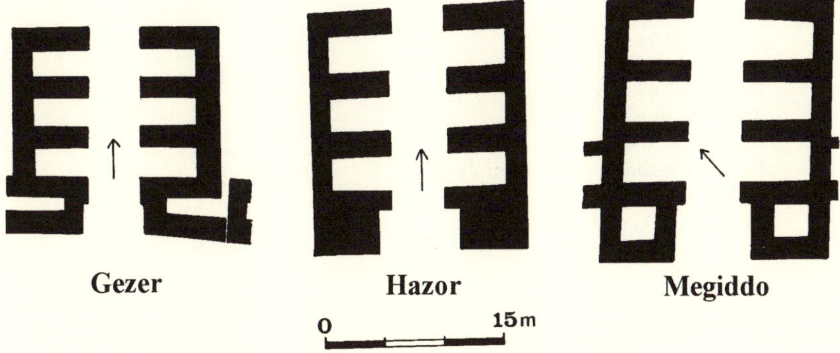

Figure 2.1: The Scale of the City Gates

Stages of State Formation

The process and characteristics of state formation have generated considerable interest among social anthropologists. The emergence of states is usually divided into three stages, which may be summarized as chiefdom, early state, and mature state, although the terms used vary.[23] These models are developed from modern cases, and in ancient societies it is not always easy to distinguish between the stages.[24] Service, for example, formed his model by looking at modern examples and assuming that they were fossilized examples of his stages. The earliest stage, the chiefdom, is characterized by strong familial bonds and a weak central government. Administrative offices remain with those who are closely related to the ruler. Characteristics that mark the transition from chiefdom to the early state include (1) independence, (2) a regular surplus in productivity used for state maintenance, (3) social stratification, (4) citizenship which is determined by territory, and (5) a common ideology on which the legitimacy of the rulers is based.[25] Archaeology provides some evidence for the first three items. The last two items can be elucidated only through literary evidence. The present archaeological evidence also provides little precise information about the stages and people involved in this transition. Again, we must turn to biblical literature. Here it worth considering how biblical literature describes the transition to early state. Much of the information relevant to this description can be culled from more annalistic sources like lists and building reports. Finally, it should be recognized that these stages represent an ideal evolutionary progress that not all states take. For example, after the breakdown of Late Bronze city-states, the infrastructure of these states could be retained and transferred to a later state. In short, the evolutionary model oversimplifies state development. All models tend to oversimplify but still may serve as useful heuristic devices.

John Holladay has summarized some recent anthropological discussions on the characteristics of a "state" and argues that the archaeological evidence points to the emergence of a state in the tenth century.[26] Holladay lists the following socioanthropological characteristics of early states:

Population over 20,000
Urban-based hierarchical settlement pattern
Regional centers
Frontier defenses
Stratified society
Headed by a king or emperor
Standing army
Centralized bureaucracy
Palace distinguished from temple
Economics based on tribute, taxes, and tolls
Redistribution of resources
Generally having a writing system

Holladay argues that archaeology provides evidence for all of these, with the possible exception of a centralized bureaucracy, in the early tenth century in Palestine.

The stages of state formation may also be evaluated from biblical literature. According to the preceding criteria, Saul's reign may be recognized as an early chiefdom. It was characterized by a struggle for independence with the Philistines, which culminated in the death of Saul (1 Sam 31). There is little evidence for social stratification in the Saulide period, and administrative officials are closely related to the ruling family. This is indicated, first of all, by the fact that Saul's uncle Abner was his military commander (1 Sam 14:50; 20:25). David—apparently another military commander of Saul's—is taken into the family by marriage with Saul's daughter (1Sam 18:20; 25:44). The demise of the Saulide dynasty itself is testimony to the fragile legitimacy of the ruling family. The fact that there are three separate accounts of Saul's acclamation as king in the biblical narrative points to the struggle the early monarchy faced in developing a common ideology on which its legitimacy could be based. Narrative accounts have Saul chosen by God via the prophet (1 Sam 9:1–10:16), chosen by lots from the people (10:17–27a), and legitimated through military achievement (10:27b–11:15).[27] Additionally, Saul is characterized as being endowed charismatically by the spirit—something typical of the judges of Israel but not the kings (cf. Judg 3:10; 6:34; 11:29; 13:25; 1 Sam 10:6, 10; 11:6).[28] Also charismatically anointed by the spirit is David (cf. 1 Sam 16:13; 2 Sam 23:2), but not his son Solomon or any other king in the Davidic line. The multiple arguments for Saul's legitimacy in the books of Samuel suggest a struggle to find a basis to support a fledgling monarchy.

Contrast the administration under David. David's military was manned by an independent professional class (cf. 2 Sam 23:8–39).[29] It included foreigners like Uriah the Hittite—an indication that tribal and familial affiliations may have been becoming less important. Yet, David's sons were still the chief officials in the service of the king (1 Chr 18:17), and David's sons were appointed to the priesthood (2 Sam 8:18). A powerful argument for the antiquity of these Davidic administrative lists is the absence of Yahwistic theophoric elements in the personal names. This suggests that the lists date to a period before the exclusive devotion to Yahweh—that is, before the ninth century BCE, when Yahwistic names begin to dominate the Hebrew onomasticon.[30] According to biblical narrative, it is David who first establishes the independence of the united Israelite tribes. The recent decipherment of two ninth century inscriptions that mention the "house of David" substantiates David as the founder of a dynasty and the emerging state.[31] David's tenure according the biblical record, however, was completely occupied with expansionism, and there is little in the biblical account to indicate the establishment of state structures. In this respect, while the reliability of the biblical narratives is subjected to increasing skepticism, they mirror the stages of state formation known from socioanthropological analogy. Likewise, though archaeological evidence cannot pinpoint the establishment of state structures, it also suggests that the process of state formation began in the tenth century.

Only in the period of Solomon are the signs of a more developed state evident in the biblical account. The state itself has moved from the defensive posturing characteristic of the Saulide period, to the expansionist efforts associated with David, to a consolidation of the borders which involved massive building projects.

State maintenance was minimal under Saul. It could be financed by booty during David's expansionism. Hence, it is not surprising that the taxation and corvée systems are attributed precisely to Solomon (2 Chr 11:5–12; 1 Kgs 5:12–18; 9:15–19).[32] The use of forced labor for large-scale building projects indicates that the economy generated regular surpluses that could be diverted into state maintenance. The employment of Phoenician craftsmen and sailors points to developing specialization and professional classes characteristic of a complex economy (cf. 1 Kgs 5:1–12; 9:26–28). King Solomon himself is no longer a military leader like Saul or David; this task is now completely in the hands of professionals (cf. 1 Kgs 3:7), even though military skills were the chief characteristic of Israel's premonarchical leaders. There is also some indication that foreign populations integrated into the citizenry, along with an accommodation of their diverse religious backgrounds (1 Kgs 11:1–8).[33] According to the biblical account, then, the classic characteristics for an early state emerge only in the Solomonic period.[34]

Although the biblical narrative portrays the Israelite state as essentially a creation of David, even the biblical narrative suggests that his son Solomon guides the transition from chiefdom to state. It should not be surprising that David, as the founder of the dynasty, is aggrandized. Indeed, the legitimacy of both the state and its dynastic rulers depended on David—they could not help but aggrandize and even eventually mythologize him. In fact, this aggrandizement was critical to the development of the state itself because it provided the *common ideology* on which subsequent rulers based their legitimacy.

Near Eastern Parallels to State Formation

The people of Israel ask for a king "like all the nations" (1 Sam 8:5, 20). Implicit here is that Israelite kingship was framed in terms common in the Near East. We must imagine that aspects of the formation of the state followed along lines known elsewhere in the Near East. The purpose here is to elucidate the context for the Promise both by comparison with other Near Eastern states and through the application of sociological and anthropological models. This approach is borne out, for example, in Marc Brettler's study, *God Is King: Understanding an Israelite Metaphor*, which applies literary metaphor theory to the study of divine kingship and illustrates it with clear parallels in other ancient Near Eastern cultures. This method can have its pitfalls, though. As Henri Frankfort points out in his classic work, *Kingship and the Gods*, it is the unique elements of ancient Israel—those things which distinguished it from its neighbors—that characterize it. At the same time, much can be gleaned from a simple understanding of the common fabric which Israel shared with its environment.

Peter Machinist probed possible parallels between the rise of the Assyrian state and the Davidic monarchy in an insightful article, "Literature as Politics: The Tukulti-Ninurta Epic and the Bible." He begins by emphasizing that "literature is essentially a political act, created to explain and justify major political and cultural shifts."[35] This point can hardly be underemphasized in the context of recent literary trends, which have lost the historical moorings of the biblical narrative. Biblical literature evolved within, was shaped by, and responded to particular social, political, and cultural moments. The first question we must ask of this ancient literature is what it meant for those *for whom it was written.* To ask this is to ask a socially, politically, and historically conditioned question. Machinist suggests that the best evidence for political literature in the Bible come from "the texts relating to the United Monarchy of David and Solomon."[36] Machinist is also drawn to these texts and this period because of close parallels between the external setting of the early Israelite monarchy and that reconstructed for the Tukulti–Ninurta Epic. Thus, "as for Tukulti-Ninurta so for David and Solomon, literary composition was an important means of expressing and resolving conflict. That importance, indeed, is underscored by the large volume of literary activity inaugurated by the two Israelite kings, which as Biblical tradition seems to attest, have never before been seen in Israel."[37] Machinist's focus was on selected psalms and the major literary epic known as *J*, attributed to the Yahwist, and traditionally dated to the tenth century BCE.[38] Second Samuel 7 receives scant mention, although he thinks the cultural tensions that provide a backdrop for the United Monarchy "would help explain Nathan's eventual refusal, in 2 Sam 7, to permit David to construct the Jerusalem temple."[39] These cultural tensions include (1) northern Israelites who complained of the excessive favoritism of Judah (2 Sam 20:1–2; 1 Kgs 12:1–19), (2) continued adherence to the house of Saul (2 Sam 16:5),[40] (3) traditional tribal institutions, and (4) the excessive taxation and urbanization that accompanied the rise of the state (1 Kgs 5:27 [5:13, ET]; 9:15–19; 1 Sam 8:11–18).

Shemaryahu Talmon compares the formation of a monarchy in Palestine with neighboring states in Moab, Ammon, and Edom.[41] Unfortunately, there is little evidence apart from biblical narratives. One notable exception is the Mesha Stela which provides clear testimony for dynastic leadership in Moab at the beginning of the ninth century BCE ("I am Mesha, son of Kemosh[yat], king of Moab, the Dibonite. My father ruled over Moab thirty years and I ruled after him"). Although evidence for the early formation of states in Transjordan is even sparser than in Cisjordan, it is reasonable to suppose that there were some similarities. The Edomite Chronicle twice preserved in biblical texts (Gen 36:31–39; 1 Chr 1:43–50) suggests an early monarchy in Edom: "These are the kings who reigned in the land of Edom, before any king reigned over the Israelites" (Gen 36:31; cf. 1 Chr 1:43). However, the list names eight unrelated rulers, each ruling from a different city. This suggests more the model of the judges period than a real state in Edom. Archaeological evidence also suggests that the emergence of a state in Edom was late (perhaps seventh century) and brief.[42] Turning to the north, the biblical account mentions a certain Nahash, king of Ammon, in the period of Saul and David (1 Sam 11:1–2; 12:12). Later during David's reign Hanun, son of Nahash, is the king of Ammon indicating a dynastic succession (2 Sam 10:1; 1 Chr 19:1–2).

The Zion tradition is an important territory for comparative study. J. J. M. Roberts, in particular, has argued for placing the origins of the Zion tradition within the United Monarchy.[43] There are five motifs associated with the Zion tradition[44]: (1) Zion is identified with the high peak called Mount Zaphon, (2) the rivers of paradise flow out of Zion to bring fertility and healing to the people, (3) YHWH defeats chaos, (4) Zion is the center of foreign pilgrimage and tribute, and (5) the defeat of the nations who attack Jerusalem. The first three motifs find parallels in Ugaritic and Babylonian mythology. Zaphon is the dwelling place of Baal, according to Ugaritic mythology. It is also apparently here on Mount Zaphon where the assembly of gods meets with El, and from here stream forth "the two rivers, the source of the two seas."[45] As Roberts recognizes, however, this identification must be secondary because sacred mountains are identified with real peaks. In this case, its identification with the temple in Jerusalem meant it was placed on one of the lowest hills in the region, with, as the psalmist says, the mountains surrounding it (cf. Ps 125:1). Given the awkward nature of the transfer, it is not surprising that higher peaks support the Promise to David: "Zaphon and Amana[46] you created; Tabor and Hermon shout for joy at your name" (Ps 89:12 [MT, 13]).

Another comparison might be drawn with the choice of Hammurabi in Babylonian tradition and Marduk's choice of Babylon. Likewise, the choice of David and Jerusalem are often associated. We can wonder, however, whether this comparison is apt. After all, Babylon had a long and prestigious religious tradition before Hammurabi's time. Hence, the argument is something like: just as Marduk choose Babylon, so also he has now chosen Hammurabi. Jerusalem had no similar religious prestige. If anything, it was David's choice of Jerusalem that lent authority and prestige to the city. In the Promise, for instance, the choice of Jerusalem will be far from clear. In fact, the history of the Zion tradition evidences an attempt to manufacture religious prestige for Jerusalem. Hence, in the postexilic period, Mount Moriah suddenly is identified with Mount Zion and the temple (cf. 2 Chr 3:1; Gen 22). The problem of Jerusalem's prestige is finally remedied by later inner-biblical and early Jewish interpretation of Nathan's prophecy (e.g., 1 Kgs 8:15–22; 1 Chr 17:1–14; 3 Kgdms 8:16; Ps 78:68; 132:10–18).[47]

Transition to State Religion

Temple building was an essential element of the emergence of a state. For example, in the Babylonian creation epic, the Enuma Elish, the creation climaxes with the building of the city of Babylon and the temple of Marduk. The founding of capital cities was accompanied by the establishment of a national cult.[48] In the case of ancient Israel, the establishment of a royal shrine and national cult in Jerusalem meant a radical transformation of the religious institutions of premonarchical Israel.

The transition from a pastoralist tribal culture toward an urbanized state presents a classic breeding ground for social unrest and political dissent. Instead of decentralized political, civil, and religious institutions, the state introduced monarchy, the capital city with a centralized administration (e.g., 1 Kgs 9:15–17), and a national cult. Indeed, the political tensions this transition inevitably imposed are reflected in the stories of David and Solomon recounted in the books of Samuel and Kings.[49] Alongside the political tensions were religious tensions that resulted from the transition from a religious system centered on family piety and alliance to the tribe to an official state religion and temple.[50] First Samuel 9 to 1 Kings 2 is usually read as an apology attempting to justify this radical transformation.[51] Certainly, the movement of the ark to Jerusalem was critical to securing the religious legitimacy of the new national temple (2 Sam 5–6). In its literary context, 2 Samuel 7 follows on the heels of the transfer as an attempt to give the Davidic monarchy some divine legitimacy.

Open cult sites are characteristic of the premonarchical Israel. Beginning in the Late Bronze Age and continuing throughout the Iron I Period (i.e., 1300–1000 BCE), small open-air cult sites located on hilltops (hence, the biblical term *bamah*, "high place") are characteristic of the central hill country of Palestine.[52] Special features of these sites in both the biblical narratives and the archaeological record are altars "built in the open outside of a settlement."[53] The best known cult site of this period is Mount Ebal, which has been excavated by Adam Zertal.[54] This site is especially significant because it coexisted with a large temple complex in the Late Bronze-Iron I city-state of Shechem. This suggests a distinction between the religious practices of the Late Bronze city-states and the new agrarian settlements of the early Israelites.[55] It is difficult to identify the god worshiped at these cult sites, but the recovery of a bull at one site in Manasseh suggests that it might have been Baal or Hadad. In fact, the book of Judges actually points to a Baal cult among the Israelites during the Iron I Period (cf. Judg 6:25). Then again, YHWH was also worshipped in the form of a bull, as we may infer from the golden calf incident (Ex 32), as well as from the religious shrines of Jeroboam I (1 Kgs 12:25–31). There is little evidence, however, that YHWH was exclusively worshipped by the early Israelite tribes during the Iron I Period.

The transition to a national cult evidently began in the tenth century and by the late eighth century was quite ingrained in Judaean society. The primary archaeological evidence for this comes from personal names found on seals, seal impressions, and ostraca. Theophoric elements in personal names (i.e., -yahu, -el, -baal) give us a view of the deities worshiped in early Israel. Jeffrey Tigay notes, "Sensitivity to the theophoric element was so great in Israel that in later time some scribes felt compelled to change name that seemed pagan in manuscripts of Samuel."[56] Notably, Yahwistic names begin to appear only in the late tenth century. This is true in both the archaeological record and biblical literature.[57] It is an unexpected fact that none of the patriarchal figures or even the first kings have Yahwistic names. In Judah, the first king with a Yahwistic name was apparently Jehoshaphat, who reigned in the early ninth century. Given that names reflect the parents' religious beliefs, the entrenchment of YHWH could not have begun before the late tenth century BCE. By the eighth century the Judaean onomasticon points to almost exclusively Yahwistic allegiances.

The use of theophoric names in Judah parallels a rise in nationalism in other geographically isolated Palestinian states (e.g., Moab and Edom). Stephen Grosby notes the similar development in Edom. Especially beginning in the eighth century BCE, Grosby observes,

> The names of the kings of Edom contained the divine name "Qaush," for example, Qaushmalaka ("Qaush has become king," from the reign of Tiglath–pileser III, 744–27 B.C.), Qaushgabri ("Qaush is powerful," from the reign of Esarhaddon, 680–69 B.C.). Is this appearance of Qaush as a prefix to the name of these two

> Edomite kings similar to the increasing frequency of appearance of YHWH as a prefix ("Ja," "Jo") to the names of Judaean kings during the same period?[58]

Grosby goes on to point out that the development of monolatry that is suggested by personal names would have led to an increased degree of sociological uniformity, which is required to speak of a nation. A strong Nationalistic fervor could be fostered through both territorially bounded religion and a common legal code. The situation in these geographically isolated states contrasts sharply with more geographically open and economically interdependent states like Phoenicia and Assyria. In other words, while Yahwistic theophoric names testify to aspects of Judaean religious culture, they also reflect economic and social isolation, which were largely reflexes of geography.

Forging a Common Ideology: The Promise to David

The emergent monarchy forged itself through conquest, through development of administrative structures, through building, and through literature.[59] A critical element for the emerging state was the need for *a common ideology on which the legitimacy of the rulers could be based*. Clearly, Nathan's prophecy to David provides such as basis. The collective memory reflected in the narratives about Saul, David, and Solomon is obsessed with justifying the new monarchy as an institution and the rulers as legitimate. This begins with the three different episodes in the Saul's acclamation as king: the tale of the lost asses and prophetic choice (1Sam 9:1–10:16), Saul lost among the baggage and popular choice (10:17–27a), and the victory over the Ammonites and military legitimation (10:27b–11:15). Even if these accounts are read as an integrated literary narrative, they underscore the importance of legitimizing the new monarchy and its ruler.[60] This leads us to our present concern: the Promise to David.

The Promise serves three overt purposes: (1) it legitimizes David (the usurper) over Saul, (2) it sanctions the dynastic succession, and (3) it justifies the monarchy itself as a divine institution. The concept of dynastic monarchy went hand in hand with the foundation of the state in Israel. It was this monarchical concept that would provide the common ideology critical to a stable government. It has been argued that kingship in northern Israel was charismatic in contradistinction to Judah but this was not the case.[61] Although the ideology of kingship in the northern kingdom is not a direct concern of this book, a short digression is worthwhile. Even though there were numerous disruptions in dynastic succession in the north, nevertheless, dynastic succession was the assumed normal principle (e.g., 1 Kgs 11:37–38; 14:7–14; 16:3–12; 2 Kgs 9:9; 10:30–31). The monarchical principle was also entrenched in Samaria, but the monarchy was never dominated by a single family as it was in Judah. It is also important to emphasize that the monarchical principle was something that needed to be defended during the formation of the Israelite state. Unlike the Mesopotamian ideology, which has kingship "lowered from heaven" (e.g., Sumerian King List; cf. Enuma Elish), kingship in Israel had to be justified because it was an abrogation of previous societal structures. Through the person of David Nathan's prophecy justifies the monarchy itself as a legitimate institution.

Although the common ideology that was a pillar of the United Monarchy focused on the *person of David*, it probably was not entrenched in the *time of David*. David rose to power in the wake of a power struggle after the death of Saul. David was crowned king of Judah in Hebron, while Saul's son Eshbaal leads the northern tribes. The bitter struggle lasts seven years before David is finally made king of all Israel (cf. 2 Sam 3:1; 5:1–5). This unorthodox transition must obviously have raised questions as to its legitimacy. For example, Absalom's revolt against David was supported by the house of Saul (2 Sam 16:5–8). The house of Saul is finally totally eliminated by David (2 Sam 21:1–6); and although the genocide of Saul's house is excused by the biblical narrative, the political underpinnings can hardly be gainsaid. In sum, though a common ideology legitimating the house of David is placed in the time of David—there is little evidence such a common ideology was achieved throughout Israel during the time of David. We can wonder, in fact, if the Promise to David was not part of the propaganda of the Solomonic period. Two things point in this direction. First, the Davidic period did not fully achieve many of the other characteristics of the early state, so a common ideology was probably not among the chief concerns of this expansionist period. Second, the Solomonic period was characterized by much more developed state administration, which, in turn, made the production and dissemination of political literature and ideology more effective.

Additionally, we must be careful not to tie the creation of a common ideology too closely with literary production in a society that was primarily oral. For example, it is tempting to place a national epic, the so-called *J* source as articulated by Julius Wellhausen, in this sociopolitical context.[62] However, the dissemination of the emergent monarchy's ideology must have taken a primarily oral form. In this respect, the liturgical literature reflecting on the Promise must be taken seriously. The present literary framework of the Promise, if not its form, is the result of much later editorial activity. As we shall demonstrate (in chapter 4), the explicit citation of the Promise as known from 2 Samuel 7 began only in the seventh century BCE. Thus, while it will be convenient to couch the discussion of the formation of a common ideology of a Davidic Promise in literary terms, it is important to remember that the culture in which it was created and disseminated was largely oral.

2 Samuel 7:1–17: A Promise to David

Second Samuel 7:1–17 is the main source for the Promise to David. This text is commonly assumed to be part of a pre-Deuteronomistic complex of sources that dates to the period of David and Solomon.[63] This premise is critical to the present chapter. Consequently, it is necessary to defend it against possible challenges.

The most significant evidence for the antiquity of the Promise to David is the repeated process of reception and transmission—that is, the process that has been called inner-biblical exegesis. The classic early study of this phenomenon was by Nahum Sarna, who demonstrated that Psalm 89 was an interpretation (and not a recension) of 2 Samuel 7.[64] Sarna analyzed the textual interplay between 2 Samuel 7 and Psalm 89 and demonstrated the chronological priority of 2 Samuel 7.[65] The approach of inner-biblical interpretation illustrated by Nahum Sarna's study was developed in Michael Fishbane's *Biblical Interpretation in Ancient Israel.* It leaves little question about the priority of 2 Samuel 7:1–17, but, more important, it narrows the options for dating the Promise. Sarna, for example, gives cogent arguments for dating Psalm 89 to the late eighth century (though, as I argue in chapter 4, a seventh century date is more likely). Some of the eighth century Isaianic oracles depend on 2 Samuel 7 (see chapter 3). The reuse and adaptation of the Promise in Solomon's prayer (1 Kgs 8:15–22)—the work of a seventh century Josianic redactor—also imply that the Promise predates the Josianic redactor (see chapter 4). The Promise continued to be reworked, rewritten, and recontextualized in the exilic period (see chapter 5), in the early Second Temple period (see chapter 6), and in the late Second Temple period (see chapter 7). Given the subsequent reuses of the Promise that can be fairly certainly dated, we are left no choice but to posit an early date for the Promise that became the fount for subsequent literary discourse. To be sure, the exact date cannot be ascertained. Indeed, the subsequent reuses only point to a pre-eighth century date. Nevertheless, the sociopolitical context of the emerging monarchy is a compelling sociopolitical context for the Promise to David.[66] The sociopolitical background points specifically to the Davidic-Solomonic period, when the creation of a common ideology was critical to the formation of the state.

Survey of Research on 2 Samuel 7:1–17

The literature on 2 Samuel 7 is so immense that a complete survey would encompass an entire monograph,[67] and, needless to say, such a survey is beyond the purview of the present study. Nevertheless, a brief survey highlighting some of the more important figures and studies is in order. Any discussion of the source-critical approach to Nathan's prophecy must begin with Julius Wellhausen, even though Leonard Rost's study is the classic application of a source-critical approach to 2 Samuel 7.

As in Pentateuchal studies, Julius Wellhausen's pervasive influence has left its mark on the study of monarchy in ancient Israel. Wellhausen's approach was couched in a source-critical analysis of 1 Samuel 7-12. He identified two sources: an early, authentic, promonarchical source (1 Sam 9:1-10:16; 11) and a late, corrupted, antimonarchical source (1Sam 7:2–8:22; 10:17–27; 12). This source critical analysis allowed Wellhausen to conclude that the monarchy was "the greatest blessing of Jehovah."[68] Unfortunately, Wellhausen's analysis of ancient Israelite political institutions, just like his analysis of its religious institutions, was shaped by his personal religious and political beliefs. In particular, Wellhausen believed that Bismarck's unification of Germany represented the pinnacle of political evolution; in fact, Wellhausen actually presented this interpretation in a tribute on the occasion of the kaiser's birthday.[69] There persists a bipartite source analysis of the rise of monarchy focusing on antimonarchy and a promonarchy sources. In light of the social forces which were at work during the transition from chiefdom to state,

Wellhausen's analysis cannot be maintained. One of the primary issues in the early formation of the state is the development of a common ideology, which supported the emerging administrative structures against strong and entrenched institutions that were being supplanted.[70] There is little reason to envision an early promonarchy source and a late antimonarchy source; both forces must have accompanied the formation of the state.

Leonard Rost's approach has been a traditional starting point for subsequent redaction analyses. Rost argued that 2 Samuel 7:11b and 16 reflect the oldest version of Nathan's oracle, which he dated to David. The major part of the oracle (vv. 8–11a, 12, 14–15, 17), Rost dated to the late eighth century—the time of Isaiah—and, the promise of a temple in verse 13a was a late Deuteronomic insertion.[71] Rost's redactional analysis has been roundly criticized as rather arbitrary. His study epitomizes the problem with much source and redaction criticism—namely, the lack of objective criteria for distinguishing editorial, redactional, and scribal hands that meddle with the text. The present study would argue that there is no carefully reasoned defense behind Rost's dating of the various redactional layers.

In his classic study, *Überlieferungsgeschichtliche Studien*, Noth argued that a single Deuteronomistic editor composed the complex Deuteronomy–2 Kings (hence, the Deuteronomistic History or "DtrH") by working from sources. These sources were given shape and punctuated by a series of speeches from the leading players in the drama (i.e., Moses, Josh 1:11–15; Joshua, Josh 23; Samuel, 1 Sam 12; Solomon, 1 Kgs 8:14–51) or from the narrator's own reflections (Josh 12; Judg 2:11–23; 2 Kgs 17:7–23). Conspicuously missing from this list is the Promise to David, which Noth considered part of a pre-Deuteronomistic complex of sources. Sigmund Mowinckel also considered Nathan's prophecy to be an early source. Mowinckel considered it a theological explanation of why David did not build the temple dating to the time of Solomon.[72] His approach was followed by Artur Weiser, who classified the text as a royal novel after the Egyptian style and used this classification as a further argument for Solomonic composition.[73] M. Görg has pressed the Egyptian parallels to Nathan's prophecy,[74] but his analysis was dependent on yet another (rather arbitrary) literary critical analysis that saw verses 1–7 (without Nathan mentioned) continued by verses 8b, 9, 11b, 12–16 as the earlier version of the oracle. He then compared it with "The Decree or Blessing of Ptah on Ramesses II and III" and "The Prophecy of Neferti." Even if the Egyptian comparisons were valid, they presume the rather subjective source-critical analysis to be correct. As Antonio Loprieno points out, however, the *Königsnovelle* itself is not a genre limited to Egypt.[75] Consequently, it seems unlikely that there is any direct dependence of the Promise to David on the Egyptian genre. The Egyptian genre certainly provides no reliable tool for either source or redaction criticism.

Recent analysis of the Promise has followed a pan-Deuteronomism.[76] R. A. Carlson, for example, is skeptical about the possibility of recovering any pre-Deuteronomic layer of tradition about David and this includes the Promise.[77] Dennis McCarthy argued in favor adding 2 Samuel 7 to Noth's list of Deuteronomic speeches suggesting that "this passage fills the same function as the key passages picked out by Noth."[78] He advanced three (unconvincing) arguments for understanding 2 Samuel 7:1–17 as a Deuteronomic composition: (1) the term "my servant David," (2) the concept of rest, and (3) the contrast with the judges. Although McCarthy pointed out that only David and Moses are called "my servant" in DtrH, the title is quite broadly applied in the Hebrew Bible (e.g., Abraham, Gen 26:24; Israel, Isa 41:8; Jacob, Isa 44:1; Babylon, Jer 25:9, 27:6; Job, Job 42:8). The concept of rest is mentioned in 2 Samuel 7:1 and 11 is not central to the Promise itself. The period of the judges is central to the issues of state formation but is not integral to the structure of DtrH. For the biblical narrative, the transition to state already has taken place with Saul, and the mention of the judges within the Promise actually might seem somewhat misplaced. There are, of course, other problems that may be related to Noth's idea of a single exilic redactor; namely, the notion of rest unexpectedly disappears with the exile in DtrH. Likewise, the Promise comes to a poorly developed, although not completely unexpected, conclusion in DtrH. These problems are well-known and form some of the primary arguments for a Josianic redaction of DtrH. The most influential argument for a Josianic redactor of DtrH was made by Cross in his *Canaanite Myth and Hebrew Epic* and subsequently developed by Richard Nelson, Steven McKenzie, and Gary Knoppers. Cross stressed the importance of 2 Samuel 7 to the structure of DtrH, but he also allowed for a pre-Deuteronomic source behind the text.[79]

The hand of new literary critics has also reached DtrH and the Promise. Most recently, Lyle Eslinger has criticized the literary dissection of the Promise and attempted a sensitive reading of the text as it stands. His reading certainly sheds light on how the text may be read in its final form—that is, in its Deuteronomic garb.

Table 2.2. Purpose of the Temple

Reference	Speaker	Temple for dwelling	Temple for name
2 Sam 7:2	David	√	
2 Sam 7:5	YHWH	√	
2 Sam 7:13	YHWH	√ (1 Chr 17:12)	√
1 Kgs 3:2	narrator		√
1 Kgs 5:3	Solomon		√
1 Kgs 5:5	YHWH		√
1 Kgs 8:13	Solomon	√	
1 Kgs 8:17	Solomon		√
1 Kgs 8:18	YHWH		√
1 Kgs 8:19	YHWH		√
1 Kgs 8:20	Solomon		√
1 Kgs 8:29	YHWH		√
1 Kgs 8:43	Solomon		√
1 Kgs 9:3	YHWH		√
1 Kgs 9:7	YHWH		√
2 Kgs 21:4	YHWH		√
2 Kgs 21:7	YHWH		√
2 Kgs 23:27	YHWH		√

Yet, the dismissal of literary sources and redactional layers is neither necessary nor convincing. This may be illustrated by Eslinger's treatment of one critical development within DtrH—namely, its "name" theology, which suggests that only YHWH's name dwells in the temple and not the deity himself. Eslinger graphically illustrated the role of the temple in DtrH,[80] although his analysis needs to be enhanced by some text critical observations (see Table 2.2). The meaning of Table 2.2 is quite dependent on the literary assumptions with which one begins. Eslinger argues on the basis of this chart that the temple as the dwelling place for YHWH in 2 Samuel 7:2 is rhetorical. Certainly, the chart provides evidence that a Deuteronomic author viewed the temple as the dwelling place for YHWH's name. A closer look, however, lends further insight. The Promise in 2 Samuel 7:1–17 explicitly and implicitly makes the temple YHWH's actual dwelling place with the notable exception of 2 Samuel 7:13a. It should hardly be surprising, then, that the parallel account to 2 Samuel 7:13 in 1 Chronicles 17:12 omits this crucial phrase, reading simply, "He shall build a house for me (הוא יבנה־לי בית)." One might have a tendency to dismiss this omission as the Chronicler's own tendentious omission, until one realizes that the expression, "a house for the name of YHWH," is actually *more frequent* in Chronicles than Kings! If the Chronicler purposely omitted it, then he missed a chance to use one of his pet expressions (cf. 1 Chr 22:7, 8, 10; 28:3; 29:16; 2 Chr 2:1, 4; 6:7, 8, 9, 10). Because the Chronicler probably used an earlier version of DtrH,[81] the more likely scenario is that the expression "for my name" was added at a later stage in the shaping of DtrH or in the early scribal transmission of the text. Chronicles reads simply, "he shall build a house for me" because the expression "for my name" was not in its source. In other words, the expression "a house for my name" was likely not in the Chronicler's source or in the original version of the Promise. A similar analysis can be applied to the one verse in the Prayer of Solomon (1 Kgs 8:13) that also disrupts the Deuteronomic pattern. The Prayer of Solomon is widely viewed as composed of three separate parts representing different sources or compositional stages.[82] The first of the three prayers (which are dealt with separately in this book in chapters 2, 4, and 5) is probably an early liturgical fragment incorporated into a Deuteronomic framework. Actually, Eslinger is quite right that the literary framework gives these verses a rhetorical quality; however, in making this observation, we should not dismiss the historical process through that we receive the text. This historical process points to earlier stages of these texts which conceived of YHWH physically dwelling in a temple, not unlike other Near Eastern deities.

Literary Analysis of the Promise to David (2 Samuel 7:1-17)

> [1]When the king was seated in his house, and YHWH had given him rest from all his enemies around him, [2]the king said to the prophet Nathan, "See now, I am seated in a house of cedar, but the ark of God sits in a tent." [3]Nathan said to the king, "Go, do all that you have in your heart; for YHWH is with you." [4]But that same night the word of YHWH came to Nathan: [5]"Go and tell my servant David: Thus says YHWH: Shall you really build me a house for my dwelling? [6]Indeed, I have not dwelled in a house since the day I brought up the people of Israel from

> Egypt to this day, but I have been wandering about in a tent and a tabernacle.
> 7Wherever I have wandered among all the people of Israel, did I ever speak a word
> with one of the tribal leaders of Israel, whom I commanded to shepherd my people
> Israel, saying, 'Why have you not built me a house of cedar?'
>
> 8Now therefore thus you shall say to my servant David: Thus says YHWH of
> hosts: I took you from the pasture, from following the sheep to be prince over my
> people Israel; 9and I have been with you wherever you went, and have cut off all
> your enemies from before you; and I will make for you a great name, like the name
> of the great ones of the earth. 10And I will appoint a place for my people Israel and
> will plant them, so that they may live in their own place, and be disturbed no more;
> and evildoers shall afflict them no more, as formerly, 11from the time that I ap-
> pointed judges (שפטים) over my people Israel; and I will give you rest from all your
> enemies. Moreover YHWH declares to you that YHWH will make you a house.
> 12When your days are fulfilled and you lie down with your ancestors, I will raise
> up your offspring after you, who shall come forth from your body, and I will estab-
> lish his kingdom. 13He shall build a house for my name, and I will establish the
> throne of his kingdom forever. 14I will be a father to him, and he shall be a son to
> me. When he commits iniquity, I will punish him with a rod such as mortals use,
> with blows inflicted by human beings. 15But I will not take my steadfast love from
> him, as I took it from Saul, whom I put away from before you. 16Your house and
> your kingdom shall be made sure forever before me; your throne shall be estab-
> lished forever. 17In accordance with all these words and with all this vision,
> Nathan spoke to David.

So basic is perpetuity to the Promise—"your throne shall be established forever"—that it is inconceivable that this text originates after the exile, and so central is the rewriting of this Promise within and outside DtrH that it is difficult to place its origin later than the Davidic and Solomonic period. Indeed, the Promise itself points to the United Monarchy, which lasted less than a century. The division of the kingdom, for example, occasioned another prophecy that nullifies the full import of the Promise and explains how the sins of Solomon resulted in the division of the kingdom (cf. 1 Kgs 11:11–13). Weinfeld points out how the editorial use of the partially or not at all fulfilled—"runs through the whole of Deuteronomic literature."[83] The thesis that the Promise originates with the emergence of the Davidic monarchy is thus well founded.

The present analysis of the Promise as narrated in 2 Samuel 7:1–17 begins with formal observations which lead to redaction criticism. The Promise easily divides into two separate prophecies in verses 4–7 and 8–16. The first prophecy deals with David's offer to build a house for YHWH and YHWH's rejection of that offer. The second is YHWH's promise to build a house for David. The first prophecy is formally marked by the divine messenger formula (v. 4), and the second also begins—somewhat unexpectedly—with a repetition of the divine messenger formula in verse 8: "Now therefore thus you shall say to my servant David: Thus says YHWH of hosts." At the very least, the repetition of the messenger formula sets verses 8–16 apart from verses 4–7 as a separate literary unit. The first unit deals with David's request to build a temple, which is rebuffed by YHWH. The second unit is the promise to build a dynasty for David. The editorial markers, when considered alongside the different themes of these two prophecies, would suggest we are dealing with two separate sources.

The two prophecies are abruptly juxtaposed, yet there is no tension in meaning. Rather, the houses (בית) in the two parts play on each other. YHWH says that David will not build a house for God (i.e., a temple), but promises to build a house for David (i.e., a dynasty).

A critical tension is introduced between the two prophecies in verse 13a. There, the temple is introduced into the second literary unit with a play on the word *house* (בית) from the first literary unit. As we shall see, however, this verse is a later Deuteronomic insertion. It is formally marked by a *Wiederaufnahme*—that is, by the use of a framing repetition regularly employed by authors, editors, redactors, and scribes.[84] The passage may be outlined as follows:

Ancient Prophecy:	12 When your days are fulfilled and you lie down with your ancestors, I will raise up your offspring after you, who shall come forth from your body, and I will establish his kingdom (והכינתי את־ממלכתו).
Insertion:	13 *He shall build a house for my name* (הוא יבנה בית לשמי),
Resumption:	and I will establish the throne of his kingdom forever (וכננתי את־כסא ממלכתו עד־עולם).

In verse 13a, YHWH now promises that David's son will build a temple. Because this particular statement contradicts the earlier rejection, it is not surprising that many have suggested that this verse is a secondary addition.[85] However, verse 13a is not an awkward addition made by a bungling redactor. Rather, it appears to be an exegetical comment which plays on the double meaning of "house" (בית).[86] As Michael Fishbane shows in his studies of ancient exegesis, pronouns—in this case "he" (הוא)—often introduce exegetical comments.[87] A particularly apt, though later, example of the use of הוא as an exegetical marker can be found in 4QFlorilegium (4Q174), which uses the term "he" (הוא) to introduce interpretations of the Promise (see further chapter 7).[88] Citing 2 Samuel 7:10, where God promises, "I shall establish a place (מקום) for my people," the Qumran *pesher* interprets this "place" as an eschatological temple (l. 2): "This is the house (הואה הבית) which He shall build for you in the last days." The pronoun "he" (הוא) introduces the identification of the "place" with "the house." Although the Qumran reading is markedly different from 2 Samuel 7:13a, it nevertheless illustrates (1) the use of "he" (הוא) as an exegetical marker, and (2) how the ambiguity of the term "house" (בית) invites interpretation. In the present case, the use of the pronoun in verse 13a, along with the *Wiederaufnahme*, doubly marks an exegetical comment, which puns on the meaning of "house" (בית) to justify the Solomonic temple.

Note must be made of the careful manner in which the exegetical comment is incorporated into the Promise. The very fact that the exegetical comment (v. 13a) is doubly marked—first by the *Wiederaufnahme*, then by the deitic pronoun—suggests that an editor felt he was dealing with an early and authoritative source. He was not free to rewrite wholesale but carefully preserved the ancient oracle even while inserting a carefully marked exegetical comment.

Who was responsible for this exegetical comment in verse 13a? The telltale sign of a Deuteronomistic historian can be easily identified in the expression "for my name" (לשמי).[89] It will be argued that this addition is to be understood first as reflecting YHWH's exclusive claim to the temple (see chapter 4) and later indicating that only YHWH's name dwelt in the temple but not the deity himself (see chapter 5). This characteristic Deuteronomic expression is the only trace of Deuteronomic editing within the Promise—which adds a third argument for seeing verse 13a as a secondary addition to the original oracle. The Deuteronomist added verse 13a to the ancient prophetic text when it was incorporated into DtrH. When verse 13a is understood as an exegetical comment by a Deuteronomic redactor eager to underscore the legitimacy of the one centralized temple, the tension with the earlier content of the prophecy can be readily understood. Indeed, the exegete's comment probably arises from an ambiguity in the Hebrew in verse 11b: והגיד לך יהוה כי־בית יעשה־לך יהוה. This is usually translated, "YHWH declares to you that He, YHWH, will establish a house for you" (NJPS; cf. NRSV); that is, YHWH will give David a dynasty. Yet, the Hebrew might be construed to mean "YHWH declares to you that he [i.e., David's son] will establish a house for you, O YHWH." In fact, this is how the LXX translators rendered the Hebrew (see discussion in chapter 7).

The only other place where a Deuteronomic author may have been at work is in the notion of "rest" found in the editorial framework in verse 1b: "then YHWH gave rest around about him from all his enemies" (ויהוה הניח־לו מסביב מכל־איביו). Moshe Weinfeld points out that rest was an essential aspect of Deuteronomic theology, although he is uncertain about whether the references to rest within the Promise (vv. 1 and 11) can be explained as Deuteronomic editing.[90] Indeed, it would be rather difficult to explain verse 1b as Deuteronomic editing because Deuteronomic editor is usually credited with Solomon's claim that God only gave rest to Israel only in his days and this is why David was not allowed to build the temple (1 Kgs 5:3–4). The general language from verse 1b is found repeatedly in DtrH; a notable example may be adduced from the centralization law in Deuteronomy: "(YHWH) gave rest to you from all your enemies around about" (והניח לכם מכל־איביכם מסביב; Deut 12:10; cf. Deut 3:20; 25:19; Josh 1:13, 15; 21:44; 23:1; 1 Kgs 5:18). It is also quite unlikely that the reference to rest in verse 11, "And I have given you rest from all your enemies" (והניחתי לך מכל־איביך), can be assigned to Deuteronomic editing. There are no formal markers (contrast v. 13a) indicating that this phrase was a secondary addition. Moreover, it again emphasizes that rest was given in David's days, not in Solomon's time.

The use of "place" (מקום) in the Promise to refer to the land that YHWH was giving Israel runs counter to a central Deuteronomic theological issue. In Deuteronomic theology the idea of a *place* is always associated specifically with the "*place* that YHWH would choose" for his temple (e.g., Deut 12:5; 1 Kgs 8:16; 2 Kgs 21:7).[91] In fact, later recontextualizations of the Promise within DtrH specifically highlight this difference by reinterpreting the meaning of the "place (מקום)" as the temple and thereby further integrating a promise for the temple into the Promise (see further chapter 4). In sum, there is tension between Deuteronomic theology and the Promise that had to be alleviated. This was first of all accomplished by the integration of verse 13a into the Promise itself and finally completed through the recontextualization of the Promise in other narrative contexts within the books of Kings.

These observations hardly exhaust the intertextuality of the Promise. John van Seters, for example, has claimed that the language of verse 10 "sounds as if it were borrowed from the salvation oracles of the prose of Jeremiah."[92] In particular, van Seters points to the "almost exclusive use of *nṭ*^{c}, 'to plant,' referring to the people of Israel as the object of God's planting in Jeremiah (Jer 1:10; 2:21; 18:9; 24:6; 31:28; 32:41; 42:10; 45:4; cf. also Amos 9:15)."[93] However, van Seters assumes that the direction of influence is from Jeremiah to the Promise—hardly a convincing assumption. Moreover, there is no close textual connection between the any of the Jeremiah passages and the Promise. Van Seters notes two further places where the ideology and language of the Promise appear—namely, Amos 9:15 and Exodus 15:17. Despite some argument about the dating of the conclusion in Amos 9 (see further chapter 3), a general consensus, which is well-supported by linguistic considerations, dates the composition of the Song of Moses at least in the early monarchy (if not before). Exodus 15:17 will be explicitly incorporated into the literary horizon of the Promise in the LXX (see chapter 7). The forecast of uprooting in Jeremiah hardly accords well with the promise that Israel shall dwell secure forever (2 Sam 7:10). In this respect, it is difficult to see how the Jeremiah passages could possibly have influenced the Promise. The converse is the only alternative.

One of the most striking aspects of 2 Samuel 7:1–17 is its ambivalent attitude toward the Jerusalem temple. This results from the originally separate status of the two parts of the prophecy and the secondary Deuteronomic addition in verse 13a. It is, first of all, quite surprising that the temple is left in a lurch, so to speak, by the words in verses 5–7: "Thus says YHWH: Shall you really build me a house for my dwelling? Indeed, I have not dwelled in a house since the day I brought up the people of Israel from Egypt to this day. . . . Wherever I have wandered among all the people of Israel, did I ever speak a word . . . saying, 'Why have you not built me a house of cedar?'" The rhetorical nature, "shall you *really*," is suggested by the context. To begin with, the emphatic use of prepositions in verse 5 emphasizes the contrast between YHWH and David. The question begins by attaching an interrogative to the pronoun (האתה); however, because the person is marked by the verb, the pronoun is unnecessary except for rhetorical emphasis. In contrast, the first-person suffix appears twice for YHWH, as if to say, "Can *you* really do this for *me*?" YHWH then points out that he has never before needed a temple. As we shall see in later chapters, the unfailing tendency among later interpreters was to make 2 Samuel 7:1–17 into a promise for the temple and the priesthood—sometimes even at the expense of David and the monarchy. Actually, the question may be posed: how can the temple recover from such damning questions? Certainly these questions run counter to everything we see from a Deuteronomic author for whom the centrality of the Jerusalem temple was a chief concern (e.g., 1 Kgs 8:48; 2 Kgs

21:7; 23:27). The rhetorical questions in verses 5–7 seriously question the need for a temple.

By contrast, verse 13a nevertheless promises that David's son would build a temple. After David passes away, YHWH promises to raise up his son and "he shall build a house for my name." This promise, however, is quite unexpected. It introduces the temple into the second oracle in a rather awkward place, but does not answer the questions posed in verses 5–7. For this reason, as well as those previously stated, verse 13a has been widely understood as a later Deuteronomic insertion into the narrative. Even the Deuteronomic insertion in v.13a does not completely resolve the problems posed by the question in verses 5–7. Source and redaction critics have usually exploited the ambiguity as reflecting tensions between different sources in the narrative.[94] More recently, new literary studies have read these tensions as rhetorical and aesthetic devices.[95] Although David's offer to build a temple is initially accepted by Nathan, later the prophet receives a special word from YHWH that strongly rejects the possibility of David's building a temple for YHWH (vv. 3–4). The rhetorical questions God poses to David in verses 5–7 underscore the categorical nature of YHWH's rejection: "Shall you build me a house to dwell in?" "Did I ever ask any of the judges of Israel . . . 'Why haven't you built me a house of cedar?' " YHWH had never asked for a temple. Nathan's response to David's initial offer highlights this fact: "Go and do all that is in *your* heart ..." (v. 2). YHWH reverses David's offer by promising to build a dynasty for David.

Seen from this perspective, Sigmund Mowinckel's argument that the intention of 2 Samuel 7:1–17 was to explain why David did not build the temple is not plausible.[96] In fact, this problem was not even an issue in 2 Samuel 7:1–17. Later Deuteronomic redactors raise this problem in other contexts. For example, according to an explanation given by Solomon in 1 Kings 5, "My father David was not able to build a house for the name of YHWH his God because of the warfare with which his enemies surrounded him, until YHWH put them under the soles of his feet. But now YHWH my God has given me rest on every side" (1 Kgs 5:3–4 [ET, 5:17–18]); however, the premise of 2 Samuel 7 is that *God had given David rest from his enemies* (v. 1)! The book of Chronicles takes care of this glaring contradiction by (1) eliminating the references to rest within the Promise (cf. 1 Chr 17:1, 10), (2) relocating the rest in Solomon's day (1 Chr 22:9), and (3) changing the explanation so that David is forbidden from building the holy temple because he is a "man of bloodshed" (1 Chr 22:8). From these developments in the tradition, it should be clear, on the one hand, that 2 Samuel 7 predates basic Deuteronomic texts like 1 Kings 5; on the other hand, the Deuteronomistic author has not rewritten the original oracle—that is to say, DtrH evidences a redactional process which preserves earlier layers of the tradition even while reinterpreting them. In contrast, Chronicles rewrites so as to eliminate narrative tensions caused by this redactional process.

The Promise highlights the cultural transformation from a pastoral and nomadic lifestyle to an agrarian and sedentary lifestyle. Robert Polzin, for example, observes a transition from movement to stability in the two prophetic oracles in 2

Samuel 7:1–17.[97] The initial response of God emphasizes movement: "I was moving about in a tent" and "in all the places where I moved about." Likewise, the model of leadership reflects instability; the judges arose sporadically and were commanded to shepherd—that is, pastoral nomads. The transition to monarchy implies a dramatic change: "I took you from the pasture, from following the sheep to be a prince over my people Israel." The model of leadership has changed, and David no longer is a shepherd but rather a prince. Perhaps just as important, Israel has changed from being a collection of *tribes* to *my people Israel.* This change involved a lifestyle change as well: Israel is no longer of collection of tribes pasturing sheep; rather, God gives them a *place*, and they are to be *planted in the land.* The transition to nation is accompanied by the transition of pastoral nomads to an agrarian lifestyle—that is, the same changes attendant in the transition toward monarchy. Likewise, God builds David a *house* which is to be *established* (v. 12), *firm* and *forever* (v. 16). David's house is not like the previous unstable house of Saul because YHWH promises not to take his "steadfast love (חסד) from him," as YHWH had from Saul (v. 15). Although the temple is explicitly rejected, the ideal of stability in the monarchy anticipates an established temple. If the transition from judges to kings marked a transition from movement to stability, should not the same transition be anticipated for the cult? That is certainly what should be inferred from the Promise to David, but it is by no means explicit. In fact, just the opposite is explicit. While a transition from judges to monarchy is highlighted, the transition from tabernacle to temple is explicitly rejected (7:6–7) and then postponed (7:13a).

The stability in the monarchy is also expressed through the use of the adoption formula in verse 14a: "I will be a father to him, and he shall be a son to Me." This adoption formula has its original *Sitz im Leben* in Near Eastern family law, where a father legally adopts a child by declaring, "You are my son" (cf. Code of Hammurabi §§170–71; *ANET*, 173).[98] The use of the adoption formula divinely sanctions the sons of David as legal heirs to the throne of Israel. There could be no more powerful argument for the legitimacy of the sons of David.

How shall we interpret the conflicting visions of the Promise? I would argue that these competing visions reflect the tensions within the early Israelite monarchy. While the vision of a Davidic dynasty had to be stated unequivocally, the status of the royal Jerusalem temple was allowed to remain ambiguous. Indeed, a central shrine struck at the heart of the "religion of the fathers"—that is, at the religious practices characterized by the Iron I local high places in the central hill country.[99] The local, open-air cultic shrines that characterized the early Israelite settlements were located in places like Mount Ebal. Such sites epitomized the tribal origins of the emerging monarchy and contrasted with urbanized Late Bronze Age city–states with their centralized temples (e.g., Shechem). In fact, the two religious practices evidently coexisted in tension during the Iron I Period, as may be implied from the proximity of the early Israelite shrine at Mount Ebal and the Tower Temple in the valley below at Shechem. The centralized temple in Jerusalem no doubt represented another major transition for the emerging state, and the ambiguous status of the temple in the Promise probably reflects this tension. It would remain for later generations of interpreters to revise and reverse this situation.

Early Royal Liturgies

The task of the present study would certainly be less complicated if it had to contend with only one text, 2 Samuel 7:1–17. Although I have focused the attention of the present study on the Promise as presented in 2 Samuel 7:1–17, early liturgical texts have also shaped the cultural discourse. There are a number of liturgical texts or fragments that likely originated in the period of David and Solomon and probably should be located within the cultic *Sitz im Leben* of a royal enthronement ceremony. To be sure, the dating of liturgical texts is often a matter of intense debate. I am quite aware of this conundrum. Nevertheless, to ignore the compositional moment of these liturgical texts would mean depriving this literature of an important moment in its reception and influence. Judging from the later adaptation of these texts, they must have played a critical role in the cultural discourse.

At least three ancient liturgies—Psalm 89:3–18, 1 Kings 8:12–13, and Psalm 132—may originate in the emerging monarchy. Obviously, there is no conclusive method to date these texts. In spite of the difficulty in dating liturgical texts, however, some clues to dating can be arrived at by using linguistic criteria. As Avi Hurvitz has shown, language may serve at the very least to distinguish between postexilic and preexilic psalms.[100] Beyond this, certain linguistic features also serve to distinguish Classical Hebrew from archaic poetry.[101] Archaic poetry shows close similarities with Northwest Semitic literature of the Late Bronze Age, particularly Ugaritic and the Amarna Letters. These affinities are usually ascribed to a common scribal culture, which is reflected by the uniformity of the language of the Amarna Letters in the Late Bronze Age and the uniformity of Canaanite scripts borrowed from the Phoenicians. Judging from the rise of national scripts (paleography) and increased linguistic differentiation, the common Canaanite scribal culture only breaks down in the ninth century as a result of competing nationalisms.[102] Poetry reflecting a strong influence from Canaanite scribal schools points back to the late second and early first millennium—that is, before the rise of Syro-Palestinian nationalism and the breakdown of the common scribal schools.

The *Sitz im Leben* of these enthronement liturgies adds another argument to locating their initial *composition* in the early monarchy—perhaps composed for Solomon's coronation or at the dedication of the temple. Nevertheless, such liturgies were in continual use throughout the history of the monarchy. It is only natural that such liturgies should attract further elaboration over the centuries. In fact, it is to be expected if we wish to believe that such liturgies were actually used. In this respect, the modern reader must look for the historical layering, even though the recovery of the various stages is not as simple as many source and redactional critical studies would lead us to believe. Indeed, the difficulty with recovering the stages of the liturgy lies precisely in its *genre*—namely, *oral* liturgy. These were not primarily *written* texts, although their final form has disguised and deceived many exuberant historical critics. In this respect, it is somewhat of a misnomer even to speak of these liturgies as "compositions" in that this term usually implies a written literary text.

Psalm 89:3–18: An Ancient Liturgy

3 I have made a covenant with my chosen one,
I have sworn to my servant David:
4 "I will establish your descendants forever,
and build your throne for all generations." Selah.
5 The heavens praise your wonders, O YHWH,
your faithfulness in the assembly of the holy ones.
6 For who in the skies can be compared to YHWH?
Who among the heavenly beings is like YHWH?
7 God is feared in the council of the holy ones,
great and awesome above all that are around him.
8 O YHWH God of hosts, who is like you?
Mighty is YH, and your faithfulness surrounds you.
9 You rule the raging of the sea;
when its waves rise, you still them.
10 You crushed Rahab like a carcass;
with your mighty arm you scattered your enemies.
11 The heavens are yours, the earth also is yours;
the world and all that is in it—you have founded them.
12 The north and the south—you created them;
Tabor and Hermon joyously praise your name.
13 You have a mighty arm;
strong is your hand,
high your right hand.
14 Righteousness and justice are the foundation of your throne;
loyalty and faithfulness go before you.
15 Happy are the people who know the festal shout,
who walk, O YHWH, in the light of your countenance;
16 in your name they rejoice all day long, and in your righteousness they exalt.
17 For you are the glory of their strength;
by your favor our horn is exalted.
18 For our shield belongs to YHWH, our king to the Holy One of Israel.

The most important of the early liturgical reflections on the Promise is contained within Psalm 89.[103] Psalm 89 divides into three distinct literary units.[104] Verses 1–18 [MT, 2–19] are a hymn on God's creation that culminates in the election of David. Verses 19–37 [MT, 20–38] are a detailed discursive of the Promise to David. Verses 38–51 [MT, 39–52] are a lament over the demise of David's kingdom. A strong argument can be made for dividing these literary units into three separate parts which originated at different times. The first part will be attributed to the tenth century as part of the literature associated with the foundation of the Davidic dynasty discussed later in this chapter. The second part is placed in the context of the late eighth century; its author interpreted the preservation of Jerusalem and the Judaean monarchy in the light of the Fall of Samaria as the ultimate vindication of the Promise to David (see chapter 3). The final section is assigned to the exilic period because it reflects on the Davidic Promise in the light of the new reality of the exile and the dissonance between the Promise and the exile (see chapter 5). As Marc Brettler observed in his study of 2 Kings 17 (the fall of Samaria), some issues and texts become so central that they attract, and even invite further elaboration.[105] Psalm 89 is one such example.

Dating liturgical texts is notoriously difficult and Psalm 89 is no exception. However, there are cogent reasons for accepting an early date for the opening hymn in Psalm 89. To begin with, the content points to the period of the United Monarchy, particularly in verse 12, where we read, "*The north and the south*—you created them; *Tabor* and *Hermon* joyously praise your name." An early date for the opening hymn (vv. 1–18) was suggested on different grounds by W. F. Albright, who observed "Canaanite archaisms" that pointed to a tenth century date.[106] Albright's linguistic arguments have been strengthened by the recent studies of Yitzhak Avishur and Richard Hess. Avishur actually suggests that Psalm 89:5–14 [MT, 6–15] "has been quoted from an ancient hymn which bears affinities to Ugaritic texts."[107] This hymn has stark affinities to Psalm 74, although Psalm 74 more closely parallels ancient Ugaritic poetry.[108] He points to the motif of God's struggle with the sea juxtaposed to the motif of creation and the comparison of God's greatness to the heavenly beings (בני אלים). Additionally, the hymn uses a number of terms and concepts found in the Canaanite pantheon including *qhl qdwšym* (v. 6), *bny ᶜlym* (v. 7), *swd qdwšym rbh* (v. 8), and *sbyb* (vv. 8, 9). At the same time, Avishur sees a "fundamental and radical adaptation."[109] The Sea is not personified, it is an object. The sea monsters are not mentioned, and in their stead we find Rahab who is not described as a monster and who is, in any case, known to us only through Hebrew literature.[110] The fundamental reworking can be illustrated by comparing similar passages from Psalm 74 and 89:

> You divided Sea by your might (אתה פוררת בעזך ים);
> you broke the heads of the dragons in the waters.
> You crushed the heads of Leviathan;
> you gave him as food for the creatures of the wilderness.
> (Ps 74:12–13 [MT, 13–14])
>
> You rule the raging of the sea (אתה מושל בגאות הים);
> when its waves rise, you still them.
> You crushed Rahab like a carcass;
> you scattered your enemies with your mighty arm.
> (Ps 89:9–10 [MT, 10–11])

The change is perhaps encapsulated by the use of the definite article with "Sea," thereby reducing it to an object over which God has control.

There are also striking parallels between Psalm 89 and the Amarna correspondence. In an article detailing comparisons between the Hebrew Psalms and the Amarna correspondence, Richard Hess argues that the parallels between the Psalms and Amarna correspondence indicate a common source in Canaanite scribal tradition, as well as common purposes behind the composition of both political and religious documents.[111] Some parallels between Psalm 89 and the Jerusalem Amarna Letters include the expression "strong arm of the king" (*zu-ru-uḫ*

LUGAL-*ri* KAL.GA; EA 286:12; 287:27; 288:14; cf. Ps 89:11, 14), the use of the "name" as reflecting the extent of the overlord's power (cf. EA 288:6–7 with 89:13), the motif of the incomparability of the overlord (e.g., EA 288:5–7 with 89:6–7), and numerous parallels in rhetorical style that Psalm 89 shares also with Ugaritic poetry. One prominent rhetorical technique in the Jerusalem Amarna correspondence is the use of threefold repetitions (e.g., EA 289:29–31; 290:8–11, 15–17). This finds a striking parallel in Psalm 89:13 [MT, 14]: "You have a mighty arm; strong is your hand, high your right hand (לך זרוע עם־גבורה תעז ידך תרום ימינך)." Hess makes the case that a professional scribal tradition was located in Jerusalem which may have continued from the Late Bronze Age through the Israelite period.[112] These parallels are suggestive of an early date for the hymn in Psalm 89:3–18. More important, they do point to an early political undercurrent to its religious language.

1 Kings 8:12–13: YHWH's Dwelling Place

The prayer of Solomon in 1 Kings 8 is the longest and most complex text that cites the Promise.[113] The prayer itself is actually three prayers (vv. 12–13, 14–21, 22–61), each introduced by a separate introductory formula and containing a different conception of the location where YHWH dwells.[114] According to the first prayer, YHWH will actually dwell in the Solomonic temple. The second prayer emphasizes that YHWH's name resides in the temple. The third prayer suggests that YHWH actually dwells in heaven and hence the temple is only a place from which to pray to YHWH. It is difficult to conceive of these three conceptions of YHWH's dwelling place deriving from the same hand at the same historical moment. Configured as they are together, they reflect an evolving theology of the temple. The scholarly consensus is that the first prayer is an ancient poem preserved by the later authors.[115] It is to the possibility that this first prayer dates to the Solomonic period that we must turn our attention.

There is a broad consensus that the prayer(s) of Solomon in 1 Kings 8 depends on the Promise from 2 Samuel 7. This is especially true of the second (vv. 14–21) and third (vv. 22–61) prayers. The first prayer is independent, but there are some points that may associate the first prayer with 2 Samuel 7. It bears no indication of Deuteronomic influence, and Weinfeld describes it as an "ancient song" which was "apparently recited by Solomon during the temple inauguration ceremonies."[116] First Kings 8:12–13 reads,

> אז אמר שלמה יהוה אמר לשכן בערפל בנה בניתי בית זבל לך מכון לשבתך עולמים
>
> Then Solomon said, "YHWH has said that he would dwell in thick darkness. I have built you a house of habitation, a place for you to dwell in forever."

The language here alludes to 2 Samuel 7. According to this source, YHWH will dwell (לשבתך) in the temple which Solomon is building. Likewise, David wants to build a place for YHWH to dwell (2 Sam 7:5, לשבתי), and although YHWH rejects David's offer to build a temple it is still clear that YHWH himself dwells in earthly edifices like the tent and tabernacle (vv. 6–7). The relationship between 1 Kings

8:12-13 and 2 Samuel 7:1-17 is only thematic; both assume YHWH's physical dwelling place is in the temple.

Psalm 132:1–18: The Ark Liturgy

1O YHWH, remember in David's favor all the hardships he endured;
2how he swore to YHWH and vowed to the Mighty One of Jacob,
3"I will not enter my house or get into my bed;
4I will not give sleep to my eyes or slumber to my eyelids,
5until I find a place for YHWH,
 a dwelling place for the Mighty One of Jacob."
6We heard of it in Ephrathah; we found it in the fields of Jaar.
7"Let us go to his dwelling place; let us worship at his footstool."
8Rise up, O YHWH, and go to your resting place,
 you and the ark of your might.
9Let your priests be clothed with righteousness,
 and let your faithful shout for joy.
10For your servant David's sake
 do not turn away the face of your anointed one.
11The YHWH swore to David a sure oath
 from which he will not turn back:
 "One of the sons of your body I will set on your throne.
12If your sons keep my covenant and my decrees that I shall teach them,
 their sons also, forevermore, shall sit on your throne."
13For YHWH has chosen Zion; he has desired it for his habitation:
14"This is my resting place forever;
 here I will reside, for I have desired it.
15I will abundantly bless its provisions; I will satisfy its poor with bread.
16Its priests I will clothe with salvation, and its faithful will shout for joy.
17There I will cause a horn to sprout up for David;
 I have prepared a lamp for my anointed one.
18His enemies I will clothe with disgrace, but on him,
 his crown will gleam."

Psalm 132 is difficult to date precisely.[117] Psalm 132 focuses on the movement of the ark into the temple—something difficult to envision coming whole cloth from a postexilic writer. In addition, the Psalm's emphasis on the temple as YHWH's actual, physical dwelling place is typical of preexilic literature. The pervasive influence of Deuteronomic theology, which described the temple as the dwelling place for YHWH's *name*, is conspicuously absent from Psalm 132 and suggests that Psalm 132 is not a Deuteronomic composition. Linguistic evidence also points to a preexilic dating, although it is difficult to be more precise.

Jean-Marie Auwers interprets Psalm 132 as a postexilic composition that begins with a midrashic elaboration on 2 Samuel 6–7 but continues in a manner closer to Jeremiah 33:14–26; she sees the same kind of democratization in Psalm 132 as is seen in Isaiah 55 (see chapter 5).[118] Auwers does not, unfortunately, account for the linguistic evidence. It is clear from 2 Chronicles 6:40–42, that Psalm 132 continued to be sung in temple services and was likely revised at certain points. All in all, the psalm illustrates the innate problem of liturgy—namely, the continual use in the community, which undoubtedly revised and updated it. This reflects the basic orality of liturgy. Then again, the differences between Psalm 132:8–10 and the Chronicler's citation of it suggest that its textual form became fixed before the days of the Chronicler (i.e., before fifth century BCE). More than this we cannot say with certainty. Because the content of the psalm suggests it was first composed for the movement of the ark into the Solomonic temple, I have located the discussion here.

The book of Chronicles cites Psalm 132:8–10 at the conclusion of Solomon's Prayer (2 Chr 6:1–40; cf. 1 Kgs 8:12–53). As such, it intentionally places Psalm 132 within the literary horizon of the Promise.

Psalm 132:8–10	*2 Chronicles 6:41–42*
Advance, O YHWH, to your resting-place, You and Your mighty Ark! Your priests are clothed in triumph; Your loyal ones sing for joy. For the sake of your servant David, do not reject your anointed one.	Advance, O YHWH God, to your rest, You and Your mighty Ark. Your priests, YHWH God, are clothed in triumph; Your loyal ones will rejoice in Your goodness. O YHWH God, do not reject Your anointed one; remember the covenant loyalties to your servant David.

Psalm 132:8–10 (//2 Chr 6:41–42) emphasizes YHWH's actual presence in the temple. In this processional song, the actual presence of YHWH is enjoined to enter his resting place in the temple. Chronicles thereby underscored the importance of the temple by emphasizing YHWH's actual presence in the face of the theology of the name, which implied that only God's name dwelt in the temple. Indeed, name theology would have been one of the main arguments against the rebuilding of the Jerusalem temple.

The relationship between Psalm 132 and 2 Samuel 7:1–7 is primarily thematic. There are two explicit references to YHWH's oath to David (vv. 2, 11) but no explicit intertextual connections. The psalm does develop motifs known from 2 Samuel 7:1–17, like David's enduring line (cf. 2 Sam 7:14–16 with Ps 132:10–12b), and David's desire to build the temple (2 Sam 7:2–4 with Ps 132:2–5). Psalm 132 certainly puts more emphasis on the temple (vv. 2–5, 6–7, 13–14). The priesthood is also drawn into the liturgy (vv. 9, 16). These could be the result of later liturgical development, or they may just reflect the psalm's *Sitz im Leben* in the temple cult. Psalm 132 also picks up on the "lamp of David" theme (v. 17), so well known from the books of Kings (1 Kgs 11:36; 15:4; 2 Kgs 8:19). Again, it is difficult to know at what historical moment it might have been introduced into the psalm. Overall, however, the use of the Promise is allusive. Whatever additions, elaborations, or revisions might have been made reflect a primarily oral setting, not a textual one.

A particularly important idea in Psalm 132 is the theme of the temple as the deity's resting place. Moshe Weinfeld argues, for example, that this concept finds "its fullest expression in Psalm 132: 'This is my resting-place for always; here I shall dwell, for I have desired it . . . . There shall I make David's standard sprout forth. I have prepared a lamp for my anointed.' The idea of a Davidic house here joins together with the idea of the chosen house, and the circle is closed."[119] The idea of the temple as the deity's resting place is explicitly absent from DtrH and, in particular, from 2 Samuel 7. In fact, it is clear in both that it is the people who find a "resting place" in the land. Thus, the narrator prefaces the Promise by stating, "Now when the king was settled in his house, and YHWH had given him rest from all his enemies around him" (2 Sam 7:1), and in the midst of the Promise, YHWH grants rest to David and the people, "I will give you rest from all your enemies" (v. 11). The people's rest contrasts with YHWH's situation: "I have not lived in a house since the day I brought up the people of Israel from Egypt to this day, but I have been moving about in a tent and a tabernacle" (v. 6). The books of Chronicles remedy YHWH's homelessness but at the cost of a resting place for YHWH's people. On the one hand, Chronicles removes the references to the people finding a resting place (cf. 1 Chr 17:1, 10); on the other hand, it introduces the term "house of rest" (בית־מנוחה) for the temple (cf. 1 Chr 28:2).[120] This theological concept in Psalm 132 undoubtedly is what drew the Chronicler's attention, yet it is difficult to say when it was first introduced.

The Promise as Early Political Literature

My discussion of the Promise to David as early political literature is sure to be challenged. It certainly cuts across the current of recent fashion that dates biblical literature quite late. For this reason, it was with some hesitancy that I adopted the current position. In the end, however, I see little escape from this conclusion. First of all, we must account for the layers of literary tradition. Since 2 Samuel 7:1–17 is reinterpreted within DtrH and by later biblical texts, there are certain constraints to dating. Second, some sense must be made of the ambivalence about building the temple in 2 Samuel 7:5-7. This ambivalence is tied precisely to the tribal and pastoral origins of the Israelites in verses 6-11. There seems to be little point in locating such ambivalence in a much later historical period—for example, the Hezekian or Josianic periods—when the Jerusalem temple was a long established *fait accompli.* Although one could plausibly connect such ambivalence with the exilic and early postexilic periods (when, by the way, such ambivalence would open the door to fundamental reassessments of the temple), such late dating does not account for the intertextuality. The easiest way to understand the Promise to David is as an early political text that reflected the needs and problems of an emerging monarchy.

It remains for us to reflect on how the Promise functioned as political literature justifying the United Monarchy under David and Solomon. The Promise was crucial for creating a *common ideology* on which the legitimacy of the Davidic ruling line was based. It is a given that a common ideology was essential to the formation and development of the Davidic monarchy. Once we realize this, it becomes clear that the common ideology represented by the Promise serves David's successors and not David himself. Mettinger, for example, identifies two points where "there must have been a strong need for legitimation": (1) the Solomonic succession and (2) the Jerusalemite claim to sovereignty over the whole nation.[121] Judging from the biblical narrative and from social anthropology, the latter must have been the greater problem. Indeed, the Promise only indirectly addresses the former problem of particular succession (in v. 13). Rather, the latter problem—tied up as it was with the transition from chiefdom to state—was a particular focus of the Promise to David. Hence, the language that God choose David "to shepherd" Israel. Nathan's oracle dwells on the previous status of Israel and of YHWH. They were wanderers. They lived in tents. They were ruled by clan chiefs (שׁפטים). But this is no longer the case. Now YHWH has given them a place (v. 10) and a kingdom. Moreover, the promise is eternal to David's house—as compared with the temporary authority granted Saul (v. 15).

The rise of a unified state ran counter to Israel's diverse ethnic origins and to the land. In the words of George Adam Smith, "Palestine, formed and surrounded as it is, is a land of tribes."[122] The introduction of the monarchy marginalized and disrupted tribal social structures. The Promise attempted to legitimate the new monarchy, even while it placated the old tribal structure of ancient Israel.

Biblical traditions attest a deep conflict with the fledgling monarchy. This is explicit in Samuel's speech in 1 Samuel 8. Although a king is allowed, it is with the observation that Israel rejected YHWH from being king over them (v. 7). In a similar vein, Gideon is offered hereditary kingship after he leads Israel to victory over the Midianites but rejects the offer, saying, "I will not rule over you, and my son will not rule over you; YHWH will rule over you" (Judg 8:23). The Bible deals with the ideology of the monarchy primarily indirectly through the observation of the narrator or prophetic reaction to narrative events. DtrH does provide a programmatic ideology of monarchy with the "Law of the King" (Deut 17:14–20). This is then taken up explicitly within the historical narrative including Gideon's speech (Judg 8:22–23), Jotham's parable (Judg 9:7–20), Samuel's speech (1 Sam 8:4–22), and the Promise (2 Sam 7:1–17). Issues of kingship are woven implicitly into the fabric of the narrative.[123]

Twice in the biblical narratives we hear the cry of rebellion against the house of David. The first time is situated early in the formation of the state during David's time. Second Samuel 20:1 reads, "Now a scoundrel named Sheba son of Bichri, a Benjaminite, happened to be there. He sounded the trumpet and cried out, 'We have no portion (חלק) with David, no inheritance (נחלה) with the son of Jesse! Everyone to his tent (לאהליו), O Israel!'" The very terms used here—"tents (אהל)," "portion (חלק)" and "inheritance (נחלה)"—reflect a tribal society.[124] The next narrative occurrence appears after the state is well established, but the words are the same. During the days of David's grandson, Rehoboam, we read the similar cry in 1 Kings 12:16: "When all Israel saw that the king [Rehoboam] would not listen to them, the people answered the king, 'What portion (חלק) do we have with David? We have no inheritance (נחלה) with the son of Jesse. To your tents (לאהליך), O Israel! *Look now to your own house, O David.*' So Israel went away to their tents

(לאהליו)." The two accounts are echoes of one another and nicely reflect the tribal origins of the United Monarchy, which contributed to the fragile unity. The latter episode concludes with the added statement, "Look now to your own house, O David" (עתה ראה ביתך דוד). This is a direct rejection of the Promise that granted David an eternal house-dynasty (בית).

Along these lines, Hayim Tadmor points out that the traditional institutions of the Israelite tribes persist even after the rise of the state.[125] The primary traditional institutions were the elders, the people, and the army. In the premonarchical period the elders were the people's source of authority in everyday matters. They "sat in the gate" to render civil judgments and were empowered in times of crisis to select leaders (e.g., Judg 11:8). On occasion, however, the "people" as a whole selected their leader or elected a king. Biblical literature uses several terms to refer to the "people." The most important of these is "assembly (עדה)," which is an ancient technical term.[126] Other common terms include "congregation (קהל)," "Israel (ישׂראל)," "all Israel (כל ישׂראל)," "the people of Israel (עם ישׂראל)," or simply "the people (העם)." Tadmor has shown that the term "the men of Israel" (איש ישׂראל), is a technical term referring to the army of Israel (with "men of Judah" איש יהודה referring to the army of Judah).[127] Not surprisingly, the army frequently steps in to support an unorthodox change of power (e.g., 1 Kgs 16:16).

The transition to monarchy threatened the traditional institutions, particularly the elders. It should not be surprising, then, that the traditional powers—the elders, the army, and the people—abandoned David and backed Absalom's rebellion (cf. 2 Sam 16:15; 17:3–4). We can only surmise that the young upstart promised to restore privileges and power lost in the transition to monarchy. In fact, even after the death of Absalom, the elders were reluctant to bring David back and had to be cajoled into reinstating their former monarch: "King David sent this message to the priests Zadok and Abiathar, 'Say to the elders of Judah, "Why should you be the last to bring the king back to his house? The talk of all Israel has come to the king" ' " (2 Sam 19:11 [MT, 12]).

The rebellions against David were also shaped by a geopolitical tension between north and south. David's transfer of the capital from Hebron to Jerusalem is often attributed to David's political genius. The fact of the matter is, however, that this move alienated his main power base in the south. It comes as no surprise, then, that Absalom's rebellion is represented as being centered in Hebron (cf. 2 Sam 15:7–12), and David's support against Absalom comes from Transjordan! To reestablish his power base, David evidently gave special privileges to Judah that may have included exemption from or reduction of both taxes and corvée. In the second rebellion against David by Sheba, then, we see a quite different relationship. David's attempt to curry favor in Judah is already clear during David's military escort back to Jerusalem after Absalom's revolt: "Then all the army of Israel (איש ישׂראל) came to the king, and said to him, 'Why have our kindred, the army of Judah (איש יהודה), stolen you away, and brought the king and his household over the Jordan, and all David's men with him?' " (2 Sam 19:41 [MT, 42]). The Judaeans then claim that David is their relative (vv. 42–43 [MT, 43–44]). The tables had now turned, and the slogan of the new opposition would be that "we have no portion in

David, every man to his own tent, O Israel!" Eventually, this rift would divide the kingdom in half.

There was also a religious element to the rift. This is first of all suggested by the archaeological evidence, which contrasts the centralized, urban religious praxis reflected in the Late Bronze Age with the hilltop religion of the Iron I Period. The movement toward more centralized control was still an issue in the Josianic period when the historian can still complain that "they made high places on every hill and under every tree" (cf. Deut 12:2; 1 Kgs 14:23; 2 Kgs 16:4; 17:10). This aspect comes into focus by virtue Jeroboam's establishment of alternative shrines in Bethel and Dan (cf. 1 Kgs 12:25–31). Jeroboam allegedly follows in a religious tradition associated with Aaron and the golden calf (cf. Exod 32:8 and 1 Kgs 12:28)—a tradition that must have been regarded in a positive light in spite of its decidedly negative treatment at the hands of a Josianic historian. Tadmor surmises, "The utterly negative view of the Deuteronomist, who characterizes Jeroboam as the archetype of all the royal offenders of the Northern Kingdom, reflects, after all, a historical truth, once we regard it as a mirror-image of reality."[128]

The social tensions that arose from the emergence of the United Monarchy provide the most plausible explanation for the enigma of the Promise; namely, why did God reject David's plan to build the temple? The fact that this incident is the topic of inner-biblical discourse both within DtrH and in the books of Chronicles demonstrates the antiquity of the problem. As Victor Hurowitz points out, there are several possible methods for deciding to build or not to build a temple.[129] These can be summarized as follows:

1. A god may initiate a building project and select the builder.
2. A king will decide to build a temple and will see if his plan meets with divine approval before the project begins.
3. A king will decide to build a temple, but the god will reject the decision.

The Nathan narrative falls into this last case with a twist: the deity appoints an alternate temple builder. Why? Another possibility presents itself. A king may begin a project without divine approval and then receive a message of disapproval. This actually may be inferred in David's case in that David receives the approval from Nathan, but then the dream comes by night and reverses the initial approval.

The temple building was a symbol of political power and a means of administrative centralization. The opposition to temple building then should be viewed as opposition to royal power and administrative centralization. In other words, the opposition to David's temple building was a product of the social tension inherent in the emergence of the monarchy. The delay of temple building allowed the emerging dynasty to consolidate its power. David may have even made the preparations to build a temple (e.g., 1 Chr 22–28), but encountered political opposition. Temple building was a prerogative, even a duty, of kingship throughout the Near East. As a result, the divine rejection of David's building project cries out for explanation. Later authors eagerly answered this enigma. The explanation for David's rejection provided by the Deuteronomistic Historian—namely, that he was occupied with wars (1 Kgs 5:3 [MT, 5:17])—is not completely convincing. The real opposition to temple building—this symbol of royal power—was internal. The pun on the "house" in the Promise then might be extended to the opposition cry, "What portion do we have in the house [i.e., both the kingdom and the temple] of David?" It cannot be viewed as fortuitous that the usurper Jeroboam sets up both a rival kingdom and rival temples. It is not a mere literary flourish, but rather the pun on "house" encapsulates the expected social tensions during the transition to monarchy.

Literature is an important means for expressing and resolving conflict. The Promise highlights aspects of the conflict engendered by the formation of the Israelite state. As such, the Promise addresses the former situation of the tribes. It raises the problem of a centralized temple. While foreshadowing the eventual construction of a royal shrine in Jerusalem, it also acknowledges the multiplicity of sacred sites characteristic of pastoral nomads. Implicitly, however, the Promise moves away from the former customs of the tribes. By giving the people—not the tribes—a land in which they shall no longer wander, the Promise moves toward a central shrine. The reason that YHWH never had a central shrine and never needed one is eliminated by the promises of a land and the monarchy that would rule it. The assurance of an eternal dynasty to David's family, however, is the foremost concern of the Promise. The paradox of the central shrine in the Promise undoubtedly responds to the particular sociopolitical setting from which it arises. It allays the fear of the growing power of the new monarchical institution by postponing the construction of one central symbol and tool for the administration of the emerging state.

3

Kingdoms in Crisis: Vindicating the Promise

Hear this, you rulers of the house of Jacob and chiefs of the house of Israel, who abhor justice and pervert all equity, who build Zion with blood and Jerusalem with wrong!
–Micah 3:9

Archaeological excavations and surveys have made it clear that Jerusalem underwent a rapid urbanization, which began in the late eighth century. These demographic changes catapulted Jerusalem from a small isolated city into a major urban center. Jerusalem's rapid growth was tied to two influxes of refugees. First, in the late eighth century, a large number of refugees fled south in the wake of Assyrian campaigns against the northern kingdom of Israel. These refugees were largely responsible for at least a fourfold increase in the size of the walled city of Jerusalem in the late eighth century BCE. A second wave of refugees into the Jerusalem environs in the early seventh century BCE, following the campaign of Sennacherib against Judah, further expanded the size of Jerusalem itself, as well as the density of agricultural settlements in its immediate vicinity. Accompanying these rapid demographic changes was political centralization. In the words of Johannes Pedersen, "When the northern kingdom collapsed, Jerusalem became the pivot round which everything turned."[1] This insight begs for further elaboration.

The focus of the present chapter, then, is the reception and transmission of the Promise to David within this unique sociopolitical context. From the anthropological and sociological perspectives, rapid and profound demographic changes had profound implications for Judaean society and ultimately for the composition of biblical texts during the late monarchy. The wholesale shift in the demographic picture of Judah in the late eighth through seventh century forms the background in which to assess the composition of early prophetic works—particularly Isaiah of Jerusalem and Amos—as well as the early history writing. On the one hand, they will reflect the vindication of the Davidic dynasty implied by the survival of Jerusalem after the fall of Samaria. On the other hand, the rapidly changing social context would shape a growing tension between urban and rural culture, between the new ways and the good old days.

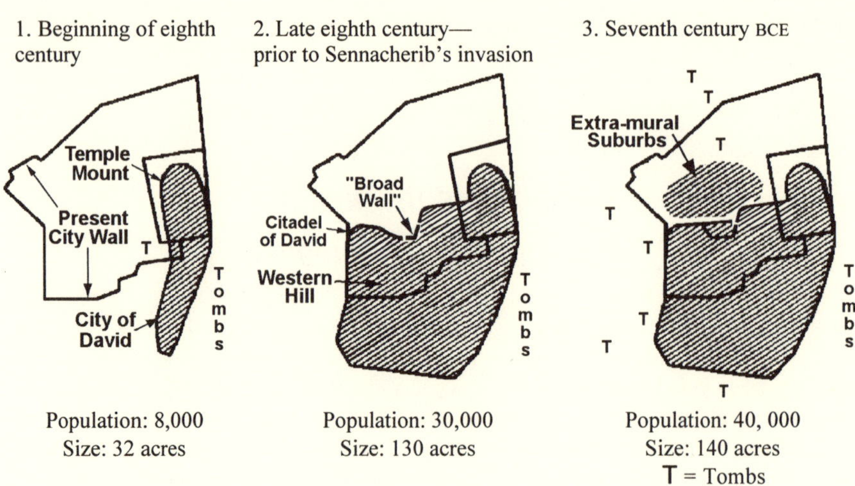

Figure 3.1. Growth of Jerusalem

Jerusalem in the Late Eighth Century BCE

Up until the last twenty years, there was considerable debate about the size and extent of Jerusalem during the period of the monarchy.[2] The early explorers such as F. J. Bliss and A. C. Dickie had argued in the nineteenth century that the wall must enclosed the entire western hill. There were skeptics of this maximalist interpretation, particularly Kathleen Kenyon, who argued, "The excavations of our 1961–67 expedition did not provide any firm evidence of expansion onto the western ridge during the period of the monarchy." At the same time, Kenyon reluctantly admitted, "There was plenty of Iron Age II pottery, but this was either associated with quarrying or with dumped deposits."[3] Kenyon's explanation became implausible following Avigad's excavations in Jerusalem's Jewish quarter, which uncovered a city wall more that seven meters wide, hence dubbed "the broad wall."[4] The wall dates to the late eighth century and is attributed to Hezekiah's preparations for an expected Assyrian onslaught.[5] Excavations in the citadel of David (the northwestern corner of the western hill) and in the Protestant Cemetery (the so-called Gate of the Essenes) now fill out the line of the wall at the edges of western hill; further excavations in the extra-mural suburbs of Jerusalem indicate that the city spread to the north (of the broad wall) during the late eighth century and especially in the seventh century BCE.[6] The growth of the city is illustrated in Figure 3.1. The only remaining question is how to account for this expansion.

The classic explanation for Jerusalem's growth was articulated by Magen Broshi shortly after Avigad's excavations: "The main reasons behind this expansion was the immigration of Israelites who came to Judah from the Northern Kingdom after the fall of Samaria in 721 B.C., and the influx of dispossessed refugees from the territories that Sennacherib took from Judah and gave to the Philistine cities."[7]

With the aid of recent archaeological evidence, we can further refine this explanation and draw out some its implications. To begin with, the expansion needs to be separated into two distinct phases: (1) the immigration of Israelites to Judah after 721 BCE, and (2) the influx of dispossessed Judaeans after 701 BCE.

Through most of the eighth century, the western hill was largely unpopulated.[8] A necropolis was in use on the eastern slope of the western hill until the eighth century but did not continue into the seventh century; that is, when the western hill was enclosed by Hezekiah's fortifications this necropolis was abandoned. This provides one reliable chronological point for the growth of the city because tombs (noted by "T" in Figure 3.1) were not ordinarily placed within city limits.[9] The tombs to the north and west of the western hill date primarily to the seventh century, again suggesting that extensive settlement began only in the late eighth century. Also consistent with a western hill largely founded by refugees is the assessment that the northern and western necropolises were "mainly for the lower classes"—that is, with a population consistent with political refugees.[10] This provides the framework for Jerusalem's expansion.

One problem that Jerusalem's rapid growth must have presented to the city is water. In fact, Dan Bahat cites this problem as a limiting factor for the size of Jerusalem.[11] While this is quite true, it should not be surprising that the water problem was addressed specifically in the late eighth century. Bahat himself points out that the upper pool of Bethesda "provided an additional [water] supply for the growing city" and appears "to belong to the later centuries of the First Temple Period."[12] Josephus mentions the "Pool of the Towers" (*War* v, 468; known today as "Hezekiah's Pool") on the northwest side of the western hill, which he associates with the "First Wall" (built by Hezekiah); this pool dates at least as far back as the Roman Period, but it has never been adequately investigated and could also originate in the late Iron II Period.[13] Three independent biblical accounts also mention Hezekiah's water projects. The book of Isaiah records that Hezekiah "collected the waters of the lower pool" (22:10) and "made a reservoir between the two walls for the water of the old pool" (22:11). According to the Deuteronomistic Historian, Hezekiah "made the pool and the conduit and brought water into the city" (2 Kgs 20:20), and the Chronicler writes, "This same Hezekiah closed the upper outlet of the waters of Gihon and directed them down to the west side of the City of David" (2 Chr 32:30; cf. 32:2–4). These biblical citations evidently refer to "Hezekiah's tunnel," which was most likely built prior to Sennacherib's invasion and whose purpose must have been to bring the main water supply closer to the western hill.[14] In sum, the very fact that so many water projects are attributed specifically to Hezekiah in the late eighth century suggests rapid growth in the population of Jerusalem that made these projects necessary.

Water projects testify to the ongoing urbanization and centralization of Jerusalem. In Wittfogel's classic study, *Oriental Despotism*, he relates the organization of society to the economics of regimes in Mesopotamia.[15] His basic thesis was that centralization of state control arose through the maintenance of water rights and canal systems. In Jerusalem, the problem of water supply probably also encouraged centralization of state control, even though a number of other forces were at work.

Ultimately, Wittfogel concluded that this centralization leads to despotic rule—an overgeneralization that has been rightly criticized. Yet, there certainly would be a tendency for centralization of state control to provoke harsh reactions from the countryside. Along these lines, we should probably understand some of the negative portrait of Manasseh in biblical literature as resulting from the social dynamics of centralization and urbanization.

There is also evidence that Hezekiah attempted to integrate northern refugees into his kingdom. First of all, Hezekiah names his son Manasseh, a name well known as one of the leading tribes of the northern kingdom. This must be viewed as an attempt to build bridges to the northern refugees. He also arranges a marriage between his son and a family from Jotbah in Galilee (cf. 2 Kgs 21:19), which can only have been an attempt by Hezekiah to control influx of northern refugees into his capital.[16] The prophet Isaiah enigmatically names his son "a-remnant-shall-return" (Isa 7:3), a veiled reference to the remnant of the northern kingdom destroyed by the Assyrians. Later, the prophet refers to Galilee and Samaria "as a land of deep darkness" ravaged by war and claims that the governance of the Davidic family will be their salvation (Isa 9:1–7 [MT, 8:23–9:6]). Another tradition—namely, that Manasseh followed in the sins of King Ahab of Israel—suggests that the northern émigrés left their mark on religious practice in Jerusalem (2 Kgs 21:3; cf. Mic 3:9–10).[17] Archaeological support for Hezekiah's attempt to integrate the north into his kingdom might also be inferred from *lmlk* seals found at northern sites.[18] These *lmlk* seals were developed by Hezekiah's administration and are precisely dated to the late eighth century. They reflect increasingly sophisticated governmental control by Jerusalem, and even their limited presence in the north might suggest that Hezekiah's administration attempted to incorporate the north. Second Chronicles 30 also highlights an integration of northern Israel into the Passover celebration: "Hezekiah sent word to all Israel and Judah, and wrote letters also to Ephraim and Manasseh, that they should come to the house of YHWH at Jerusalem, to keep the Passover to YHWH the God of Israel" (2 Chr 30:1).[19]

A second phase of expansion follows Sennacherib's invasion in 701 BCE. Sennacherib's invasion devastated the Judaean Shephelah. According to the calculations of Israel Finkelstein, "About 85 percent of the settlements of the Shephelah in the eighth century had not been reoccupied in the last phase of the Iron II. The total built-up area decreased by about 70 percent." [20] Yehuda Dagan, who has comprehensively surveyed the Shephelah, indicates that the decrease was primarily in small agricultural settlements and not in the larger cities and towns.[21]

Corresponding to the devastation of the Judaean foothills, we see an *increase* in smaller settlements around Jerusalem established in the late eighth or seventh century. New agricultural villages and farmsteads were founded at Er Ras, Beit Ṣafafa, Malḥa, En Yael, and Mevasseret Yerushalayim, forming an agricultural and industrial hinterland for Jerusalem.[22] Additionally, Gibeon (7 km north) emerges as an industrial center in the late monarchy.[23] The royal administrative center at Ramat Rahel (3 km south of Jerusalem) was established in the late eighth century and flourished in the seventh century[24]; apparently, the site served as a secondary capital and administrative center, alleviating crowding in Jerusalem. The City of

David itself was expanded by Manasseh: "he built an outer wall for the City of David west of Gihon, in the valley, reaching the entrance at the Fish Gate; he carried it around Ophel, and raised it to a very great height" (2 Chr 33:14).[25] Much of this growth may be accounted for as the aftermath of Sennacherib's campaign, wherein he claims to have "laid siege to 46 of [Hezekiah's] strong cities, walled forts and to the countless small villages in their vicinity" (*ANET*, 288; cf. 2 Kgs 18:13). Thus, Jerusalem's growing hinterland corresponds to (1) the demographic shift from the Shephelah to the hill country, (2) the need for agricultural production to supply Jerusalem and Hezekiah's administration, and (3) the need to replace the devastated agricultural infrastructure of the Shephelah.[26]

In sum, beginning in the late eighth century, Jerusalem underwent a process of rapid urbanization. Israel Finkelstein describes it as follows: "In the later days of Hezekiah and in the reign of Manasseh, Judah went through a painful transformation from a relatively large state with a varied economic system to a small community, in fact not much more than a city-state, with a large capital and a small but densely settled countryside."[27] The centrality of Jerusalem became the de facto result of at least a fourfold increase in its population. Jerusalem, which had represented about 6% of Judah's total population in the middle eighth century, suddenly became about 29% in scarcely two generations.[28] Even if some settlement on the western hill began before the collapse of Samaria, still, the rapid growth of Jerusalem cannot be explained as anything other than abnormal. Jerusalem was a sleepy little city isolated in the mountains of Judah. There was no reason to expect its transformation into a large urban center, given its historical geography. Prior to these tumultuous events, Judah had a relatively rural population with a small urban capital. Archaeological finds suggest now that the advent of the Assyrian empire in Palestine wiped out many of these smaller settlements while the larger cities were preserved. Hence, there is a general trend toward urbanization that is nowhere more dramatic than in Jerusalem.

Social Anthropology of Jerusalem's Urbanization

Social anthropology can help us understand the impact of such urbanization on Judaean society. Social anthropologists define *urbanization* as the transformation of a random rural form of settlement into a system with an urban center functioning as a central place.[29] Although population and size are the primary considerations in defining urban centers, five other factors should also be considered: (1) the settlement has to form a topographical unit, enclosed by a town wall, (2) the settlement has to be densely occupied, (3) the architecture has to reflect social differentiation and administration, (4) there should be signs of specialization, economic accumulation, and distribution, and (5) it has to function as a central place.[30] Given the limits of Jerusalem's archaeology, it is difficult to address all these criteria exhaustively; however, ample evidence points to Jerusalem's emergence as an urban center in the late eighth century.

The urbanization of Jerusalem is part of a larger trend that characterizes the neo-Assyrian period.[31] This trend can be easily explained from a sociological perspective. Gideon Sjoberg observes:

> The concentration of population into a relatively small space makes possible certain kinds of protection that are usually unavailable to ruralities. People scattered about the countryside or living in small villages, lacking as they do the economic resources and technical skills to build fortifications like the wall that have surrounded most preindustrial centers, have been more exposed to invading armies and especially to local marauders. Nor can the village population take full advantage of the society's military power, which is most effectively employed within limited areas—as say, around cities.[32]

The rise of Assyria in the eighth century began a succession of world empires that devastated smaller states. The ferocity of the Assyrian empire pressured rural populations toward the cities, where they could find protection. By the end of the eighth century, Assyrian monarchs are usually involved with siege warfare as opposed to open-field battles; this indicates their relative superiority.[33] Baruch Halpern uses the term *hedgehog* defense to characterize the movement from open field warfare to a pattern of fortified cities and towns.[34] This type of defense was ideal for the smaller Judaean state. Yet, it required centralization of power to build fortifications, which translated into an abandonment of the countryside and its political disenfranchisement.

It is impossible to explain Jerusalem's rapid growth in purely natural terms. Indeed, perhaps the strongest evidence for a minimalist approach to Jerusalem's size has been simply that its geographical location and natural resources do not lend themselves to a major urban and commercial center. Yet, the archaeological support for Jerusalem's growth is now incontrovertible. It was not Jerusalem's viability as an economic center led to its transformation into a large urban city. Sjoberg points out, "Nowhere do cities, even commercial ones, flourish without the direct or indirect support of a well-established state system."[35] Sjoberg adds, "Unquestionably, the factor of political power, much more than commerce, is the key to the rise and spread of urban centers."[36] Indeed, the choice of Jerusalem as the capital of the United Monarchy rested not on commercial but rather on political foundations; its emergence into a major urban center in the late eighth century also relied on political factors. These factors begin with Assyria. It was the rise of Assyria that brought waves of refugees into the Jerusalem environs. The Assyrian threat also necessitated enhanced fortifications and administrative centralization.

Urbanization is invariably accompanied by social differentiation and its associated social critique. The social critique of the northern kingdom, which we see particularly in the prophets Amos and Hosea, is a critique of an urban elite. Sociological studies on preindustrial cities indicate that the elite have an urban social location, even though they may be rural landowners.[37] This is hardly surprising because demographic studies of ancient Palestine indicate that the north was much more densely settled with a much greater urban population. From the perspective of historical geography, the north was also much more open to contacts—both political and commercial. These commercial and political contacts are played out, for example, in the Elijah-Elisha narratives. Although Judah had been a relatively poor, sparsely populated state (especially compared with Samaria), this situation began to change in the late eighth century. Nels Anderson writes, "The rural village within the influence sphere of a city, however firmly resolved it may be to maintain its social and cultural isolation, can neither keep all of its people in nor the unwanted influences out."[38] As Judah was transformed into a more urbanized state, it could no longer remain culturally and religiously isolated.

The social influences in Jerusalem were twofold. First, there were the numerous northern émigrés. These people came from a more urban and cosmopolitan culture.[39] In fact, Israel Finkelstein suggests, "The demographic dispersal of the tenth century may also explain one of the reasons for the division of the United Monarchy—the much larger and wealthier population of the central hill country arose against the dynasty of the poor and underpopulated south."[40] In the late eighth century, these wealthier, more cosmopolitan northerners were thrust back on Judaean society. The acceptance of these new settlers—particularly in Jerusalem as opposed to the rural communities—was probably eased by the lineal ties with the northern dynasty of Ahab through Athaliah (cf. 2 Kgs 8:26–27).

Second, Assyrian domination meant contact with Assyrian culture and religion. However we view this imposition, the Assyrian administration resulted in cultural contact, and at least to some degree, cultural influences were unavoidable.[41] D. Hillers observes, "In numerous less developed societies, after a period of contact with a technically superior civilization in which the natives freely accept the goods and customs of the foreign society, there is a sudden reversal and utter rejection of foreign cultural elements."[42] In the late eighth through seventh centuries, Jerusalem and Judah had contact with two foreign cultures: Samaria and Assyria. It is hard not to view the Josianic reforms as a reaction against these foreign cultural influences.

The rapid growth and change in Jerusalem during the late eighth through early seventh centuries naturally attracted social, political, and religious interpreters, which may be conveniently separated into two groups according to their social location: urban and rural. Although this oversimplifies the situation, it provides a logical starting place. Jerusalem's growth translated into increasing power and prestige for the urban and ruling elite. The increased population in pre-industrial cities, which in Jerusalem's case was greatly dependent on northern refugees, translated into power. The building projects (e.g., "broad wall," Hezekiah's tunnel) and centralized administrative system (e.g., *lmlk* jars) are the earmarks of this power. By contrast, Jerusalem's increasing domination meant a marked decrease in the independence of rural villages, smaller towns, and other cities throughout Judah.

Ironically, the dissatisfaction with the increasing centralization and urbanization of Judah in the beginning of the late eighth century was associated with the then defunct northern kingdom. Undoubtedly, Broshi was correct in envisioning a large influx of northerners into the small Judahite kingdom after the collapse of Samaria. For example, the prophet Micah was from a smaller town in the Judaean foothills, Moresheth-Gath. His critique of Judah in the late eighth century assumes a major influence from the northern kingdom: “Harness the steeds to the chariots, inhabitants of Lachish; it was the beginning of sin to daughter Zion, for in you were found *the transgressions of Israel* (Mic 1:13).” The “transgressions of Israel” refer to the northern kingdom. And, when Micah envisions the ultimate destruction of Jerusalem, it is clear that the demise is directly associated with the influence of the north in Judah:

> Hear this, you *heads of the house of Jacob and chiefs of the house of Israel*, who abhor justice and pervert all equity, who build Zion with blood and Jerusalem with wrong! Its rulers give judgment for a bribe, its priests teach for a price, its prophets give oracles for money; yet they lean on YHWH and say, “Surely YHWH is with us! No harm shall come on us.” Therefore because of you Zion shall be plowed as a field; Jerusalem shall become a heap of ruins, and the mountain of the temple a wooded height. (Mic 3:9–12)

The “heads” and “chiefs” are related to the house of “Jacob” and “Israel”—that is, the north. These are the ones who build Jerusalem. In the context of the enormous growth in Jerusalem’s size at this time, the use of the verb “to build (√בנה)” should be understood as having a concrete referent. The new inhabitants of Jerusalem—apparently, many of them from the north—are accused of perverting social values. Notably absent here is anything reminiscent of the later Deuteronomic religious critique. There is no hint of Deuteronomic language or its typical invectives. Rather, the critique compares with the prophetic critiques in Amos and Hosea—a hint that these books also received their final form from Judahite editors around 700 BCE. All respond to the social differentiation that became a growing part of Jerusalem’s landscape beginning in the late eighth century.

Biblical Texts in the Context of Rapid Social Change

The tumultuous events of the late eighth century had a profound impact on ideology and the literature that arose in that context. More to the point, the sociopolitical climate *generated* literature that reflected on the rapid political and social changes. This literary production was related to the prophets Isaiah, Micah, Amos, and Hosea, as well as a pre-Deuteronomic historical work. It is not coincidental that Proverbs 25:1 relates that “the men of Hezekiah copied the proverbs of Solomon.” Although there may be cause to cast a skeptical eye at the attribution of the proverbs to Solomon, there is little reason to question the editorial work of the “men of Hezekiah.” Additionally, there must have been poetic and hymnic compositions, although these are for the most part lost or irretrievable. I shall suggest, however, that Psalm 78:67–72 and Psalm 2 were composed in the late eighth century.

The Hezekian period provided a unique challenge to scribes in the Judaean royal court. On the one hand, the fall of Samaria proved to be the vindication of the Promise to David. On the other hand, these writers needed to reintegrate the remnants of the north in order to strengthen the remaining Judaean monarchy.

Proto-DtrH: A Hezekian Historical Composition

There has been a recent trend to identify an earlier pre-Deuteronomic layer to the Deuteronomistic History (= DtrH), and, in particular, to the books of Kings.[43] There is some justification for this opinion, as I shall articulate. In general, early sources were critical to Martin Noth's original hypothesis of a Deuteronomistic History; however, Noth did not view these sources as an independent composition providing structure for his single Deuteronomistic historian. That is, Noth saw *sources* where some more recent studies have seen *redactions*. This raises the question: what distinguishes a complex of sources from a redactional layer? To have a redactional layer rather than just a complex of sources, there must be identifiable themes, motifs, and structure, which may be truncated, eclipsed, or reinterpreted by a later redactor.

Most of the arguments for a proto–DtrH redaction of Kings have been based on formal characteristics like accession and succession formulae, judgment formulae, the David theme, or the attitude toward the high places (במות).[44] What makes this new evidence compelling, however, is the sociopolitical context that must have prompted this early composition. With the fall of Samaria, there was an influx of refugees into Jerusalem. Concomitantly, the invasion of Sennacherib resulted in both a general depopulation of the rural regions and a further expansion of Jerusalem. It is difficult not to see that the first "conclusion" of the book of 1 Kings is with the fall of Samaria (1 Kgs 17). This text has certainly been thoroughly reworked, but it marks the end of the northern kingdom. Although later writers adopt an almost entirely negative attitude toward the north, at the same time there are remnants that suggest a positive, almost nostalgic view of the northern kingdom. These include the Elijah-Elisha narratives which are rather mixed in their attitude toward the northern kingdom varying from unabashedly negative (e.g., 1 Kgs 18, 21) to rather supportive (e.g., 1 Kgs 22, 2 Kgs 6–7, 13:14–21). Additionally, the northern kings are generally praised for their military strength whereas the southern kings rarely are (cf. 1 Kgs 16:5, 27; 22:45; 2 Kgs 10:34; 13:8, 12; 14:28). These might be explained by parataxis—that is, by a composition built up of earlier sources (not editions) of varied length.[45] Yet, the question becomes: how were these earlier sources transmitted? Were they fragmentary or joined into a composition? The use of a standard formula to praise the northern kings necessarily stems from a continuous pre-Josianic composition rather than from parataxis. The analyses of Weippert, Provan, Halpern and Vanderhooft, and others only serve to underscore this point. There must have been a preexilic historical composition written during the period of Hezekiah that reflected on the fall of Samaria and the survival of Jerusalem. This historical work served as a source for later authors, though it has been so completely rewritten by Josianic and exilic authors that it is no longer entirely recoverable.

Yet, distinct formulaic and thematic traces point to this earlier edition. In addition to the formulaic elements referred to previously, it should also be noted that the books of Kings preserve two similar assessments of the division of the kingdom that must have originated within the Hezekian period. The first summarizes the narrative of the division, in which Rehoboam foolishly follows his young counselors: "So Israel has been in rebellion against the house of David (בית דוד) until this day" (1 Kgs 12:19). It is noteworthy that there is no prophetic justification in this summary (contrast 1 Kgs 11:9–13); that is, it does not follow the strict style and dogma of the Deuteronomic redactors, which emphasize the role of the prophets in framing events (e.g., 1 Kgs 13:1–2; 2 Kgs 23:16–18). Moreover, the transgression implied by the verb "to transgress, rebel (√פשע)" is against the *house of David*. The highly edited narrative about the fall of Samaria in 2 Kings 17 also preserves a fragment from this perspective—though it has often been mistranslated. In 2 Kings 17:20–21a, we read,

> וימאס יהוה בכל־זרע ישׂראל ויענם ויתנם ביד־שׁסים עד אשׁר השׁליכם מפניו
> כי־קרע ישׂראל מעל בית דוד וימליכו את־ירבעם בן־נבט
>
> YHWH rejected all the seed of Israel; he punished them and gave them into the hand of plunderers until he had banished them from his presence *because Israel had torn away from the house of David*. Then they made Jeroboam, son of Nebat, king.

Here the exile of the northern kingdom results from Israel breaking away from Judah. Although the Hebrew syntax is clear, commentators sometimes miss the point and interpret the action as passive. For example, the NRSV translates as a clause dependent on the following statement, "When he had torn Israel from the house of David, they made Jeroboam son of Nebat king." This translation violates rules of Hebrew grammar. The verb "to tear" (√קרע) is active, not passive; the noun "Israel" is the subject and not the object.[46] The main reason for translating this clause as a passive would seem to be preconceived notions about how the exile of Samaria was interpreted in ancient Judah. It is clear that Jerusalem interpreted the fall of Samaria as a vindication of the Davidic dynasty, especially in immediate aftermath. This perspective was fundamentally political. These two passages (1 Kgs 12:19; 2 Kgs 17:20–21a) reflect the perspective of a longer Hezekian historical work that vindicated the Davidic line as the legitimate heirs to a united kingdom. Both parts of the kingdom were presented because Hezekiah reunited the divided kingdom. The early division of the kingdom after Saul was critical because David reunited the kingdom and Hezekiah followed in his steps. Hezekiah reestablished the Davidic kingdom. Here I agree with Ian Provan and others who argue that Hezekiah is presented in Kings as the "new David." [47] But this is more than a literary viewpoint, it reflected government propaganda conditioned by the sociopolitical situation in the late eighth century.

This view must have far-reaching ramifications for the Josianic author of the DtrH. The Josianic themes are focused around religious rather than political issues. Whereas Hezekiah tries to *integrate* the north, Josiah only *castigates*. Whereas Josiah's centralization is unabashedly religious, Hezekiah's centralization was secular and precipitated by the growth in physical size and political importance of Jerusalem. Positing a major Hezekian historical composition answers some lingering questions about DtrH. How relevant was an extinct northern kingdom a century later? How about two centuries later? The books of Chronicles illustrate of the likely role of the north in much later literature—it is almost completely omitted.

The fate of northern kingdom must have weighed most heavily in the life and literature of Judah in the years immediately following Samaria's destruction and exile. It surely did not centuries later.

Isaiah ben Amoz

The well-known messianic prophecies in Isaiah 7–11 were intended initially to address the sociopolitical situation of the late eighth century. These chapters are part of the larger literary unit, chapters 5–12, which focus on the punishment of the northern kingdom by Assyria and the associated restoration of the Davidic empire.[48] Although it is clear that these chapters presuppose the Promise to David, they do not explicitly cite it. I will argue here and in chapter 4 that the allusive use of the Promise in these chapters reflects the history of prophecy itself—namely, the orality of the early prophets. This allusive use, which is typical of an oral culture, gives way to the explicit citation of the prophetic text as ancient Israel becomes a more textual culture.

The dating of these Isaianic oracles is critical. There is a some consensus that the so-called *Denkschrift* or Isaianic Memoir (Isa 6:1–9:7 [MT, 9:6]) dates to the eighth century prophet.[49] Its literary envelope (Isa 5:1–30; 9:7–12:6), on the other hand, has been the subject of more debate. It is difficult to empathize with those few scholars who wish to dissect these chapters on few or no redactional grounds.[50] Usually these analyses are based on a critic's feeling about what could or could not be written in the particular historical context. Yet, as this study shows, all the so-called messianic prophecies in Isaiah 7–11 are entirely appropriate to the sociopolitical context of the late eighth century. A more serious proposal comes from Marvin Sweeney, who argues that "several portions of the text, including 7:1–9, ch. 10, and 11:1–12:6, appear to have been composed during the reign of King Josiah (639–609), in order to support his program of religious reform and national restoration for Israel, while the balance was composed by Isaiah at various periods during the late eighth century."[51] Sweeney offers four substantive arguments: (1) the imagery of a new shoot growing out of an old stem (11:1) supposedly relates to the near destruction of the Davidic dynasty in 640, when Amon was assassinated; (2) the cessation of enmity between Ephraim and Judah points to Josiah's ambitions to rebuild the Davidic empire; (3) the use of exodus imagery corresponds to Josiah's Passover celebration (cf. 11:12 with 2 Kgs 23:21–23; 2 Chr 35:1–19), and (4) the reference to a small child's leadership (11:6–9) presupposes the young Josiah's installation. These arguments, however, are not compelling. In the first, it is a matter of interpretation as to what is intended by the expression often translated as "A shoot shall come out from the stump of Jesse" (NRSV; MT, ויצא חטר מגזע ישי). However, the semantic range of the term "stump" (גזע) is far broader; it also means "trunk," which hardly implies an end to the Davidic dynasty.[52] On the contrary, the root imagery probably alludes to the division of the kingdom into north and south and its restoration as is suggested by Isaiah 7:17 (cf. Amos 9:11 and see discussion later in this chapter). The second argument again points more to Hezekiah than to Josiah. While Hezekiah openly courts the remnant of the northern kingdom, Josiah's reforms are predicated on their open hostility toward northern religious traditions (i.e., Jeroboam) that have corrupted the south. As for the exodus imagery, because Hezekiah also celebrated a Passover that explicitly incorporated the northern exiles (cf. 2 Chr 30), the use of the exodus imagery actually fits the Hezekian period as well as the Josianic period. Sweeney's strongest argument is the inference he draws from "a little child shall lead them (ונער קטן נהג בם)" (Isa 11:6). The poetic nature of this vision, however, will not bear the weight alone, especially when the poetry continues with images of children of various ages: "The nursing child shall play over the hole of the asp, and the weaned child shall put its hand on the adder's den (ושעשע יונק על־חר פתן ועל מאורת צפעוני גמול ידו הדה)" (11:8).

The Immanuel Prophecy in Isaiah 7 is set within the context of the Syro–Ephraimite war—the war that precipitated the Assyrian incursions against Damascus and Israel in 734–732 BCE. The alliance between Rezin and Pekah against Judah threatened to overthrow the Davidic dynasty, and "when the house of David (בית דוד) heard that Aram allied itself with Ephraim," they were afraid and turned to the prophet Isaiah (Isa 7:2–3). The narrative's choice of the expression "house of David" (also in v. 13) here quite intentionally recalls the promise of an eternal house to David's sons (2 Sam 7:11–16). The prophet's words conclude by highlighting the rebellion of the northern kingdom from Judah: "YHWH will bring on you and on your people and on your ancestral house such days as have not come *since the day that Ephraim departed from Judah*—the king of Assyria" (Isa 7:17). In other words, couched within the context of a threat to the house of David, the prophet identifies the disaster of Ephraim as beginning with its rebellion against Judah in the days of Rehoboam.

The well-known prophecy in Isaiah 9:1–7 [MT, 8:23–9:6] begins with the "gloom that is in Galilee" (9:1)—no doubt a reflection of recent Assyrian conquests of Galilee. The reversal of this utter defeat—that is, the light that "has shined on them" (9:2)—is found with the chosen son who sits on the throne of David (vv. 6-7). Indeed, such a description presumes the Promise to David, though it makes no explicit reference to it. Isaiah 11 describes the Davidide root of Jesse: "A shoot shall come out from the stump of Jesse, and a branch shall grow out of his roots" (v. 1). This is another allusion to David's promised heir, who ultimately "will assemble the outcasts of Israel, and gather the dispersed of Judah" (v. 12).

These prophecies evidence strong thematic associations with the Promise but not the explicit textual citation of 2 Samuel 7:1-17. On the one hand, these prophecies resonate with the recent destruction of the north, which vindicated the Davidic monarchy—a monarchy which itself had been threatened by the now dismantled northern kingdom. On the other hand, these prophecies envision the ingathering of the northern remnant by the promised Davidic line, thereby restoring the glory of Israel's golden age. The lack of explicit citation of 2 Samuel 7:1-17 must be viewed as a reflex of the basic orality of the prophetic word and Judaean society in the late eighth century. The movement toward textuality is marked by the Josianic reforms, where a book becomes the blueprint for the religious reformation. To be sure, societies exist on a continuum between orality and textuality. In the late 8th century, the rise of Assyria set into motion a series of events that would reshape Judean society.

Amos and "the Fallen Hut of David"

> [11]On that day I will raise up the fallen booth of David (אקים את־סכת דויד הנפלת), and repair its breaches, and raise up its ruins, and rebuild it (ובניתיה) as in the days of old; [12]in order that they may possess the remnant of Edom and all the nations who are called by my name, says YHWH who does this. [13]The time is surely coming, says YHWH, when the one who plows shall overtake the one who reaps, and the treader of grapes the one who sows the seed; the mountains shall drip sweet wine, and all the hills shall flow with it. [14]I will restore the fortunes of my people Israel, and they shall rebuild the ruined cities and inhabit them; they shall plant vineyards and drink their wine, and they shall make gardens and eat their fruit. [15]I will plant them on their land (ונטעתים על־אדמתם), and they shall never again be plucked up out of the land that I have given them, says YHWH your God. (Amos 9:11–15)

The concluding verses of Amos draw on the Promise to David. It shall be argued here that these verses were added when the book of Amos received its final form in the Hezekian period. Admittedly, the composition of Amos has been a matter of considerable debate. The most recent commentaries by David Noel Freedman and Shalom Paul, for example, argue that the book essentially dates to the days of the prophet, with little subsequent editing.[53] To arrive at this conclusion, one must dance around rather unequivocal references pointing to the late eighth century. Certainly, the clearest of these is the reference to the disappearance of Philistine Gath referred to in Amos 6:2. Gath was known to have been destroyed by Sargon's invasion in 712 BCE.[54] The reference to the ruined cities of "my people Israel" (9:14) must then be taken very literally as reflecting the Assyrian destruction of the northern kingdom; indeed, this should be the a priori assumption because the expression "my people Israel" refers explicitly to the northern kingdom elsewhere in Amos (cf. 7:8, 15; 8:2) and well as frequently in the Hebrew Bible (e.g., 1 Kgs 14:7; 16:2; Jer 7:12).

Undoubtedly, Amos was preserved in the south because (1) the prophet was understood to have correctly foreseen the exile of Samaria and (2) this was interpreted as further legitimizing the Davidic dynasty. The prophecies in Amos repeatedly point to the collapse of the north: "Fallen, never to rise again, is the virgin Israel" (5:2). And there is a certain finality to this destruction: "The end has come on my people Israel; never again will I pass by them" (8:2). As Ronald Clements points out, "In the broad context of the events of the eighth century B.C. it must appear that the terrifying fulfillment of this threat occurred with the collapse of the Northern Kingdom of Israel under pressure from Assyria . . . ."[55] Yet, Amos never singles out Assyria as the rod of God's anger; the prophet shows no awareness of the agent of this destruction. This is strong evidence that the core of Amos's prophecies predate the destruction and that the literary preservation of Amos in the south was precisely because he was understood as correctly foretelling the collapse of the north.

A mainstay of arguments for postexilic editing of Amos is chapter 9, verse 11: "On that day I will raise up the booth of David (סכת דויד) that is fallen, and repair its breaches, and raise up its ruins, and rebuild it as in the days of old." This verse has been widely analyzed as part of a postexilic addition to the book that included at least 9:11–15 or perhaps 9:7–15.[56] The arguments may be summarized as follows: (1) the expectation of the restoration of the Davidic kingdom, (2) the promise of restoration contradicts the threat of destruction throughout the book, (3) the promise of restoration without ethical demands contradicts Amos's message elsewhere, (4) the historical background presupposes exile, and (5) the language is late biblical Hebrew. Given the sociopolitical background described here, the first four arguments may be disregarded. The last linguistic argument has never been properly developed and does not bear up to scrutiny. The critical plank in this argument is the *plene* spelling of the name David, admittedly a late tendency; however, as James Barr has shown, spelling is not a reliable means of dating because it often reflects scribal transmission more than authorship.[57] There is then no reason to see this passage as a very late addition when we now have a more plausible context in the late eighth century.

The conclusion of Amos draws from two sources: Amos 5:26–27 and 2 Samuel 7. The enigmatic prophecy in Amos 5:26–27 is preserved in the MT as follows: "You shall take up Sakkuth your king (את סכות מלככם), and Kaiwan your star-god, your images, which you made for yourselves; therefore I will take you into exile (והגליתי אתכם) beyond Damascus, says YHWH, whose name is the God of hosts." This text has generated endless debates over its meaning. This debate need not concern us here. What is relevant is not what it meant to the prophet Amos but rather how it was interpreted by the redactor of Amos 9:11.[58] In this enigmatic prophecy, the redactor sees a correctly predicted exile of the northern kingdom. More than this, the redactor apparently asks two questions: (1) "Who is your legitimate king (מלככם)?" and (2) "What is the *Sikkuth* (סכות)?" The answers are unequivocal. The legitimate king must be David. The fallen "hut" of David (סכת דויד הנופלת) is the division of the kingdom which now will be mended (√גדר to repair, √בנה to build, √קום to rise up). The verbs in 5:26 and 9:11 "to lift up" (√נשׂא) and "to rise up" (√קום) should be understood as intentionally parallel. The kingdom will be restored "like the days of old" (כימי עולם)—that is, the golden age of David and Solomon.

Kenneth Pomykala would like to see Amos 9:11–15 as a postexilic addition, with the "booth of David" referring to Jerusalem rather than the Davidic dynasty. Although he acknowledges that the phrase "I will build it (ובניתיה) as in the days of old" harkens back to the Promise in 2 Samuel 7:11–16, he nevertheless argues that there are problems with seeing "the booth of David (סֻכַּת דויד)" as referring to the Davidic dynasty. He notes that it "is never used in the Hebrew Bible for a kingdom or dynasty, but is used in Isa 1:8 for Jerusalem ('And the daughter of Zion is left like a booth [סכה] in a cucumber field')."[59] However, Amos 9:11 (סֻכַּת דויד) explicitly interprets the enigmatic expression from Amos 5:26 literally rendered as "Sikkuth of your king (סכות מלככם)." The royal aspirations of the Davidic dynasty are in play here, as indicated by the following verse: "in order that they may possess the remnant of Edom and all the nations" (Amos 9:12). Pomykala should have at least noticed that the two verses, 5:26 and 9:11, are cited together in the Qumran texts. Pomykala thinks that the expression "as in the days of old" itself indicates a postexilic dating, though it seems more likely that it refers to the perceived golden age in the days of David and Solomon. Pomykala's arguments, which appear so weak, actually demonstrate how difficult it is to make an objective case for the late dating of Amos 9:11. Most of all, however, they assume that Amos 9:11 is inappropriate to a preexilic context—and this assumption is hardly warranted.

The concluding verses, though written as prophetic, refer to the aspirations of Hezekiah's reign. The prophecy begins, "On that day I will raise up the fallen booth of David" (9:11); the reason for preserving Amos's prophetic vision is simply because "that day" was understood as Hezekiah's own time. The reference to being "plucked up out of the land" (v. 15) points to an exile—but Israel's exile, not Judah's. This is clear because "Israel" throughout the book of Amos refers exclusively to the northern kingdom. When the book of Amos concludes that God "will restore the fortunes of my people Israel and they shall rebuild the ruined cities" (vv. 13–14), it means to suggest that through Hezekiah the northern kingdom would be reintegrated and thereby restored. Placed in this context, the "fallen booth" must be a metaphor for the division of David's kingdom. It is this model kingdom which Hezekiah wanted to resurrect "as in the days of old."

Hosea and "David Their King"

The critique of northern kingship in the Book of Hosea probably received its final shape in the aftermath of Samaria's fall and Jerusalem's survival. The superscription to Hosea describes the prophet's activity as continuing into the Hezekian period, and the book actually foresees the miraculous deliverance of Jerusalem: "But I will have pity on the house of Judah, and I will save them by YHWH their God; I will not save them by bow, or by sword, or by war, or by horses, or by horsemen" (Hos 1:7). R. E. Clements—for reasons that are quite unclear—ascribes this verse to a late seventh century editor. It seems more likely, however, that the verse was part of an editorial framework given the book when it was brought down from the north in the aftermath of the destruction of Samaria. The late seventh century was characterized by fierce polemic against Jeroboam's religious practices and, as such, hardly makes an appropriate context for the integration of northern prophetic traditions. If there was to be an integration of northern literary traditions in Jerusalem, it certainly makes more sense to see them in the immediate aftermath of the fall of Samaria with its concomitant influx of refugees to the south, than to place them a century later in the context of religious reforms aimed at eradicating northern cultural influences!

Many commentators have pointed out the largely negative portrait of monarchy in the book of Hosea. Perhaps the most quoted example is Hosea 8:4: "They made kings, but not through me; they set up princes, but without my knowledge." Ultimately however, the meaning of this critique within the book as a whole must be read through the lens of Hosea 3:4–5: "For the Israelites shall live (יֵשְׁבוּ) many days without king or prince, without sacrifice or pillar, without ephod or teraphim. Afterward (אַחַר) the Israelites shall return (יָשֻׁבוּ) and seek YHWH their God, and David their king; they shall come in awe to YHWH and to his goodness in the latter days." The temporal relationship between verses 4 and 5 is marked by the preposition, "afterward" (אחר). For a period, the northern kingdom did not have a king, but then they were drawn into the fold under the Davidic dynasty. It is natural to assume that this refers to the period following the fall of Samaria until the time of the author. The author argues that David is "*their* king" (מלכם), implying that the former northern kingdom and its kings were illegitimate. The idea that the Israelites would be incorporated *again* into the kingdom fits into the context we know in the late eighth century and early seventh century, but it is difficult to place within any later exilic or postexilic context. Such northern prophetic texts would have been given a Jerusalemite redaction soon after they arrived in the south—that is, if they were to be preserved at all. It should be clear that such a reading of the prophet Hosea follows along with the interpretation given the fall of Samaria in 2 Kings 21:20-21a, as well as Isaiah 7:17. It would also dovetail nicely with the proposed Hezekian reading of the prophet Amos as advocating the restoration of the United Monarchy under Davidic leadership. These readings now begin to have a cumulative weight.

Psalm 78:67–72: God Rejects Shiloh but Chooses Jerusalem

> 67He rejected the tent of Joseph,
> he did not choose the tribe of Ephraim;
> 68but he chose the tribe of Judah,
> Mount Zion, which he loves.
> 69He built his sanctuary like the high heavens,
> like the earth, which he has founded forever.
> 70He chose his servant David,
> and took him from the sheepfolds;
> 71from tending the nursing ewes he brought him
> to shepherd his people Jacob,
> and Israel, his inheritance.
> 72With upright heart he tended them,
> and guided them with skillful hand.

Psalms are notoriously difficult to date, and Psalm 78 is no exception. Opinions on the date of its composition have ranged as early as the tenth century and as late as postexilic period. Gunkel, for example, thought the mixture of genres in the psalm was the conclusive evidence for a postexilic date.[60] Gunkel's use of genre as a criterion for dating, however, is a dubious methodology. In spite of Gunkel's opinion, there seems to be some consensus that the psalm dates to the preexilic period. The most objective criterion for dating psalms is language.[61] Linguistic dating gives only a relative dating, distinguishing between ABH (= Archaic Biblical Hebrew, i.e., before the eighth century), SBH (= Standard Biblical Hebrew, i.e., eighth-sixth centuries BCE), and LBH (= Late Biblical Hebrew, i.e., postexilic Hebrew). In this case, linguistic criteria would also point to the preexilic period. If anything, linguistic evidence points to an early (ABH) rather than a late date (LBH). Robertson, for example, thinks that the archaic features in Psalm 78 point to a date "between 930 and 721,"[62] though such a specific date reflects also Robertson's particular interpretation of the psalm's polemic against the northern kingdom. Archaic elements can probably be accounted for, as we shall see later, by the psalm's dependence on earlier archaic Hebrew poetry. It is difficult to arrive at a precise preexilic date by linguistic criteria. In the final analysis then, we are forced into the more subjective process of correlating content with sociopolitical context—that is, if we are interested in literary history at all. The careful reconstruction of sociopolitical history provided in the first half of this chapter thus forms the basis for my dating of Psalm 78. For reasons enumerated later, it would be difficult to envision sociopolitical context outside the late eighth century, when the content of Psalm 78 would make any sense.

Indeed, an argument for placing Psalm 78 within the context of the Hezekian reforms was already made by Richard Clifford.[63] Clifford sees, for instance, the reference to "the day of battle" (v. 9), along with other military allusions in Psalm 78 (e.g., "bowmen," vv. 11, 57), as pointing to the devastation of Samaria. Clifford also contrasts the rejection of Shiloh in Psalm 78 with the two references in Jeremiah where Shiloh becomes a warning to Judah of its impeding doom (Jer 7:1–15; 26:1–24). Nevertheless, Clifford wants to see the term "Israel," as well as the destruction of Shiloh, as referring all the tribes—north and south—a viewpoint that is difficult to understand. As Williamson showed, the term "Israel" does not come to be used generally for all Israel until the postexilic period.[64] For example, one cannot have the parallelism of Jacob and Israel in verses 5, 21, and 71 refer to the northern and southern tribes on the one hand and yet the term "Israel" in verses 58–61 limited to the northern tribes:

> For they provoked him to anger with their high places;
> they moved him to jealousy with their idols.
> When God heard, he was full of wrath,
> and he utterly rejected *Israel.*
> He abandoned his dwelling at Shiloh,
> the tent where he dwelt among mortals,
> and delivered his power to captivity,
> his glory to the hand of the foe.

In this argument, Clifford specifically counters those—for example, the influential writings of Bernhard Duhm—who see Psalm 78 as targeting the corruption of only the northern tribes.[65] Inasmuch as the wilderness and premonarchic traditions refer to all the tribes, Clifford is correct. Yet, although I sympathize with Clifford's intentions, the fact remains that no explicit unfaithfulness or punishment is ascribed specifically to Judah. By contrast, the northern tribes are explicitly singled out in the end: "He rejected the tent of Joseph, he did not choose the tribe of Ephraim" (v. 67).

Although the rejection of the northern tribes would seem to point to the Assyrian exile, there is no explicit historical reference that extends beyond the Philistine destruction of the shrine at Shiloh. Why? On this basis, we *might* be tempted to contextualize Psalm 78 within tenth century literature supporting the claims of the newly emergent United Monarchy under David and Solomon. A linguistic basis for such an early date is certainly lacking. More than this, however, the psalm itself purports to explain “lessons from antiquity” (חידות מני־קדם, verse 2). Here, Clifford correctly sees the teachings of “our forefathers” (אבותינו, verses 3, 5, 8) as a key theme of the prologue, which sets up the didactic purpose of Psalm 78. Thus, the story told in Psalm 78 is one passed on from generation to generation and from father to son (vv. 5–6): “He established a decree in Jacob, appointed a law in Israel, charging our ancestors to teach to their children so that the next generation might know them—children yet to be born—and in turn they will grow up and recount them to their children.” The appeal here is to the forefathers, to a golden age of remote antiquity. Psalm 78 cannot be contextualized in the period of David and Solomon because it reflects back on that golden age.

An appeal to remote antiquity colors the language in Psalm 78. The psalmist is particularly influenced by the archaic Song of the Sea (Ex 15:1–17) in its long description of the victory at the Red Sea (Ps 78:44–55). In fact, the archaic aspects of the poetry in Psalm 78 can probably best be explained by its reliance on archaic Hebrew epic poems. While the reliance on the Promise can best be described as thematic, the use of Exodus 15 is quite explicit. Of particular interest is the use of Exodus 15:17,

> תבאמו ותטעמו בהר נחלתך מכון לשבתך פעלת יהוה מקדש אדני כוננו ידיך
> You *brought* (√בוא) them in and planted (√נטע) them on the *mountain* of your own possession, the place, O YHWH, that you made *your dwelling*, the *sanctuary*, O YHWH, that *your hands* have established.

The closest parallel is found in Psalm 78:54–55: “And he *brought* them (√בוא) to his holy realm, to the *mountain* that *his right hand* had acquired. He drove out nations before them; he allotted them a territory of *inheritance* and caused the tribes of Israel *to dwell* in their tents.” Further touchpoints can also be found. For example, the expression in Exodus 15:16b, “the people whom you acquired” (עם־זו קנית), probably influenced the phraseology of Psalm 78:54b, “the mountain that his right hand acquired” (הר־זה קנתה ימינו). Further dependence on Exodus 15:17 can be seen in the concluding verses of Psalm 78, particularly verse 69, which refers to “his sanctuary” (מקדשו). We may also highlight echoes of the Promise. The notion of planting (√נטע) Israel in the land is closely paralleled in 2 Samuel 7:10.

Exodus 15:17 would become closely associated with the Promise in the later readings reflected by the Septuagint and Qumran literature (see chapter 7). Its close association with the Promise is already evident here, although we must suspect that both together formed important elements of the emergent monarchy’s common ideology.

The focal point of David’s leadership, ironically, is not Judah but rather Israel. The concluding section (vv. 67–72) of Psalm 78 begins with the rejection of the northern shrine and leadership in verse 67: “He rejected the tent [or shrine (אהל)] of Joseph, he did not choose the tribe [or rod (שבט)] of Ephraim.” Translations of this verse hide the double meaning of the Hebrew terms *ʾōhel* (אהל), which might be taken as either “tent” or “shrine” and *šēḇeṭ* (שבט), which might be either “tribe” or “rod.” The latter term might also be translated “scepter,” reflecting its use as a symbol of leadership (e.g., Gen 49:10).[66] The implication is that God rejected both the religious shrine and secular leadership within the northern tribes in favor of Zion and David. This rejection, however, did not mean the rejection of the people. Instead, David is portrayed as shepherding his people Jacob and Israel, his inheritance (v. 71). Although there is a natural inclination to make the reference to Jacob and Israel here as reference to the southern tribe of Judah, this is not the plain sense. The entire psalm has been directed specifically toward the northern tribes, and the claim here seems to be that David is the chosen leader of the northern tribes. More than this, David is the one who had led the northern tribes with skill and integrity (v. 72): "With upright heart he tended them, and guided them with skillful hand." What possible context can be envisioned for such a portrait of Davidic leadership as the golden age for the northern tribes? By the exilic period, the northern tribes were irrelevant. In the Josianic reformation, the north was the scapegoat for a violent religious reform. In the period of Hezekiah, however, both literary and archaeological evidence suggest a reintegration of northern Palestine into the kingdom of Hezekiah. The appeal to a golden age under David then explains the tragic fate of the northern tribes at the hands of Assyria, while offering hope for their restoration under the Davidic dynasty.

Psalm 78:67–72 presumes the Promise but does not explicitly cite the Promise. This, as we have seen, is a developing pattern in the texts cited here. In fact, I would even argue that explicit textual citation would preclude an eighth century date because it would assume a textual model—a model that does not emerge until the seventh century during the Josianic reforms.

Psalm 2: An Enthronement Liturgy for the Sons of David

Psalm 2 is a royal psalm. From all internal evidence, its apparent *Sitz im Leben* was either a royal coronation or perhaps a hypothetical yearly celebration of the king's accession. The overwhelming consensus of scholarship places this psalm in the preexilic period. Indeed, it is difficult to imagine why such a psalm would have been written if there were no monarch or king. Where to place the psalm within the monarchical period of Judah is much more difficult to determine. Earlier scholars tended to attribute the psalm to either David or Solomon;[67] more recent scholars are more uncertain as to the exact date.[68] Because the psalm shows no indications of Deuteronomistic influence, however, the Hezekian period is the most plausible context. Indeed, the psalm's opening charge—namely, "Why do the nations conspire, and the peoples plot in vain? The kings of the earth set themselves, and the rulers take counsel together, against YHWH and his anointed" (vv. 1–2)—could fit nicely into the aftermath of the Syro-Ephraimite crisis, the fall of the northern kingdom, and the rise of the Assyrian empire. Indeed, in this context the psalm's otherwise enigmatic use of the Aramaic word for "son" (בר), can make sense. The psalm uses the Aramaic deliberately and rhetorically in the context of an Aramaean-Samarian attempt to dethrone the legitimate rulers, the sons of David. Admittedly, this evidence is merely suggestive and illustrates the unavoidable subjectivity in dating liturgical literature. Nevertheless, there is no other suitable context outside the extremes of the Davidic-Solomonic period or the Hasmonean period—that is, either too early or too late.

Psalm 2's use of the Promise is more thematic than textual. Again, the allusive nature of Psalm 2's dependence on the Promise might be attributed to the basic orality of Judaean culture. The closest textual association between Psalm 2 and the Promise is its use of the adoption formula known from 2 Samuel 7:14a: "I will be a father to him, and he shall be a son to me." In Psalm 2:7, we read,

> Let me tell of the decree: YHWH said to me,
> "You are my son; today I have begotten you.

Naturally, the adoption formula emphasizes the particular choice of David and his sons over against any other claimants. The following verses (vv. 8–9) of the psalm,

> I will make the nations your domain;
> your estate, the limits of the earth,
> You can smash them with an iron mace,
> shatter them like potter's ware,

point to territorial aspirations of the Davidides, according to my proposal, Hezekiah. In sum, Psalm 2's representation of the royal motif draws on the Promise to David and would fit nicely into the social, political and literary context of the late eighth century. More than this we cannot say.

Vindication and Revitalization of the Davidic Dynasty

Archaeological evidence in concert with Near Eastern and biblical literature now combine to sharpen the picture of the late eighth century in Jerusalem and its environs. The rise of the Assyrian empire precipitated a movement toward urbanization throughout the periphery of the empire. Fortified cities offered the only hope for those wishing to withstand the Assyrian onslaught. The northern kingdom of Israel stood right in the path of Assyrian imperial plans. It fell in two stages (733 and 721 BCE). An influx of refugees added to the growing population in Jerusalem, as well as elsewhere in southern Palestine. The relatively isolated position of Judah, however, meant that it was not a direct target of Assyrian expansionism.

Following the fall of the northern kingdom, Hezekiah made preparations to reestablish Judaean independence. The growth and urbanization of Jerusalem had already contributed to a centralization of power in Jerusalem. Under Hezekiah, further centralization took place, as reflected by a system of administration that used the royal *lmlk* jars. Public works were carried out, particularly in Jerusalem (water projects, fortifications), but undoubtedly also throughout the major urban centers in Judah. An attempt at rebuilding the kingdom of Judah in the idealized image of the Davidic Kingdom is reflected by both the archaeological and literary evidence. The appearance of the *lmlk* jars in the north already suggests projection of Judah's presence northward. The naming of the crown prince after one of the prominent tribes of the fallen north, Manasseh, undoubtedly reflected an attempt to curry favor. For these reasons (and others), we must take seriously the Chronicler's account of Hezekiah's Passover, which intentionally sought to include the remnants of the northern population. Indeed, the Passover was quite possibly chosen explicitly by Hezekiah because it was a powerful symbol of liberation from oppression—in this case, Assyria. Hezekiah also extended his reach westward, reincorporating the Philistine plain into the Judaean kingdom. Indeed, the account in 2 Kings—namely, that Hezekiah "overran the Philistines as far as Gaza and its territory"—is echoed by Sennacherib's annals (cf. *ANET*, 287–88).

The demise of Samaria and rise of Jerusalem vindicated the Promise. The fall of Samaria was interpreted as resulting from its rebellion against the legitimate Davidic dynasty. This is clear in a few places within Kings (e.g., 1 Kgs 12:19; 2 Kgs 17:20–21a) and probably formed a leitmotif for a Hezekian historical work. There are structural elements that point to the existence of such a work, but the Deuteronomic composition has, for the most part, incorporated it almost seamlessly into its narrative. The words of northern prophets like Hosea and Amos were read by Hezekian editors as correctly foreseeing the final demise of Samaria and thereby vindicating Jerusalem and the Davidic dynasty. The editing of these northern prophets in the Judaean court did more than vindicate the Judaean state—it also mediated an integration of the remnants of the north into the Judaean state. The Promise to David was the blueprint for this new United Monarchy. While the prophet Isaiah's words recalled the "gloom of those in anguish" (Isa 9:1 [MT, 8:23]), they also pointed to the Davidic scion who would restore the kingdom: "There shall be no end to the increase of his authority and the peace; on the throne of David and his kingdom, he shall establish it and sustain it with justice and with righteousness from now and forevermore" (Isa 9:7 [MT, 9:6]). The hope of the northern refugees and remnant was in the kingdom of David's sons. Nevertheless, it was undoubtedly crucial for Judah to integrate the northern remnant to strengthen its position against Assyria. Hezekiah's expansionism, however, would bring him into fatal conflict with Assyria.

4

Josianic Reforms: A New Place for the Promise

New religious movements are important indicators of stressful changes in culture and society. They are also interesting attempts to come to terms with rapid social change by imposing new interpretations on it and by experimenting with practical responses.

—James Beckford

The rising tide of the Assyrian empire transformed the Near East as a whole and along with it, the tiny Judaean state. A series of cultural revolutions followed in Assyria's wake. These began with urbanization. The social structure of Judah shifted away from the countryside toward cities. The Assyrian empire would integrate Judah for the first time into a world economy, with all the attendant exposure to foreign cultures. It is hardly surprising within this social upheaval and cultural invasion that the seventh century in Judah was marked by a proliferation of religious movements that culminated in a conservative backlash—namely, the Josianic religious reforms. The task of the present chapter, then, is to describe the social fabric of the late seventh century, as revealed by archaeological and literary sources to properly assess the Josianic Reformation in general and then the reception and transmission of the Promise to David in particular.

In the turmoil of the seventh century, the Promise would be redirected toward the Jerusalem temple. The city itself had already become the political center. The authority of the chosen city and its temple was now employed to enforce a more traditional cultural uniformity. The temple and the city that God had chosen were for YHWH's name alone. The Promise was read anew in this moment as emphasizing Solomon's role as the chosen temple builder. Jerusalem and its temple were read into the Promise as the place YHWH had chosen for himself.

The Sociopolitical Context of the Late Judaean Monarchy

The Assyrian campaigns in Syria-Palestine during the late eighth century precipitated momentous economic, political, religious, and cultural changes in Judah. These began with the Assyrian campaigns in Galilee and Samaria, which brought an end to the northern kingdom of Israel and, more important, brought a wave of refugees into Judah. A campaign by Sargon in 712 BCE reached into the foothills west of Jerusalem to destroy the Judaean cities of Gath and Azekah. A permanent Assyrian administrative and economic center was set up at Ekron at that time.[1] After Sargon's death, Hezekiah's attempt to regain Judaean autonomy brought devastating consequences. In his annals, Sennacherib claims that he "laid siege to 46 of his strong cities, walled forts and to the countless small villages in their vicinity" and to have "exiled 200,150 people" (cf. *ANET* 288). Although there is a natural tendency to believe Sennacherib was embellishing, archaeological surveys reveal that the population of the Judaean foothills decreased by 70%—substantially confirming Sennacherib's claims. Whatever continuity in settlement remained was concentrated in larger towns, while smaller villages largely disappeared. When the armies of Sennacherib left, some residents returned—*but primarily to the larger cities and towns.* Undoubtedly, this was partially because the larger walled cities offered more security than the smaller towns and villages, but this marked a sharp break in the culture of the Judaean countryside. Amihai Mazar describes the countryside as follows:

> An Israelite countryside town was thus a combination of an agricultural village and a fortified town with governmental, military, commercial, and industrial function; there was not clear differentiation between "town" and "village," and agriculture dictated the character of life in the towns. In the vicinity of the towns, there were isolated farms and groups of buildings known in the Bible as the "daughters" of the towns or *Hatzerim* (farmsteads).[2]

Premonarchical Israel was a village culture. Although the monarchy introduced a centralized system into Palestine, it did so unevenly. The north was the center of the urbanization, whereas the south remained—to a great extent—a village culture. After Sennacherib's invasion, this picture shifted. Larger cities became the focus of more settlement, and smaller villages and farmsteads disappeared. The village was an intermediate political unit that was disenfranchised by the centralization and urbanization of Judaean society.[3] Although the countryside population was still composed mainly of farmers, their locus became the larger cities. It seems that the farming of the countryside came to be supervised by the government. This trend would have been first of all fostered by the Assyrian administration. There is evidence of direct Assyrian administration of the country at Megiddo, Tel Jemmeh, and Samaria, as well as the organization of a large industrial production center for the Judaean Shephelah at Ekron.[4] When Judaean control of the Shephelah and coastal plain was reestablished in the late seventh century BCE, this institutional infrastructure was apparently taken over. An ostracon found at Meṣad Ḥashavyahu, for example, suggests a structured administration of agricultural workers.[5] The royal *lmlk* storage jars suggest government involvement in agricultural production.[6]

The profound change in Judaean society during seventh century BCE can be illustrated by a comparison of the ceramic repertoire in the Judaean city of Lachish. Orna Zimhoni describes an almost surprising uniformity among the pottery of the late eighth century at Lachish, especially as compared with the variety of influences represented by the late seventh century. She writes, "The ceramic uniformity of

Lachish Level III [i.e., destroyed by Sennacherib in 701 BCE], and its orientation towards the Shephelah–hill country, are replaced in Level II [i.e., destroyed by Nebuchadnezzar in 588 BCE] by a more diverse, coastal plain–oriented assemblage."[7] A similar picture is also reflected at the sites of Timnah (Tel Batash) and Ekron (Tel Miqne). Zimhoni concludes that the pottery reflects the changing sociopolitical situation of Lachish in the eighth–seventh centuries:

> The Lachish ceramic assemblage reflects the environment of *Pax Assyriaca*, an open political and economic system under the aegis of the Assyrian Empire, conditions which continued to prevail later under Egyptian occupation. The diverse character of the ceramic assemblage complements the historical picture and can be understood in view of the political changes that took place during that period.[8]

In other words, the ceramic assemblage until the period of Hezekiah reflects a highly insulated economy with few significant foreign cultural influences. By contrast, the period of Josiah, or the late monarchy in general, is marked by an open economy and a wide variety of cultural influences. Implicit in these differences is a monumental shift in Judaean society away from the isolated, rural nation that characterized its first few centuries into a more urbanized, cosmopolitan state. As Max Weber pointed out, urbanization does not occur at all in cities or districts without commercial links to the outside world.[9] The ceramics in Lachish III (eighth century) evidence little commercial contact with the outside world. We must surmise that there was minimal urbanization in Judah prior to the late eighth century. Urbanization began in the capital, Jerusalem, in the late eighth century and spread to the countryside in the seventh century. The ceramic repertoire at Lachish thus reflects the profound change in Judaean society and culture. It only remains to reflect on its implications for Judaean politics, religion, and society in the late seventh century.

The Rise of Literacy and Social Formation

Accompanying the urbanization in the late eighth century was an increase in literacy. It is no coincidence that the book of Proverbs attributes literary activity to the period of Hezekiah (Prov 25:1). It was during this time that Israel *began* to make the transition to a literate culture. Controlled archaeological excavations, along with illicit digging, have recovered a remarkable variety of epigraphic evidence concentrated in the late monarchy, including letters, receipts, royal stamps, seals and their bullae, legal documents, and graffiti.[10] To be sure, the evidence suggests mundane literacy—that is, the ability to write one's name, to read and write receipts, and to read and perhaps compose simple letters. This is the kind of literacy that would naturally accompany an increasing bureaucracy. Essentially, what we see is significant movement on a continuum from orality toward literacy. This movement is evidenced in both the archaeological record and biblical literature, and increased literacy shaped the reading and use of written texts in the late monarchy.

The evidence for growing literacy is compelling. The first thing that impresses the observer is the volume and variety of epigraphic remains. Perhaps the best illustration is the considerable mass of seals and seal impressions (i.e., bullae) found in and around Judah from the late eighth and especially the seventh century. The bullae point to a great quantity of papyrus and parchment documents that did not survive the vicissitudes of climate and military conflict. More important, the seals and bullae reflect the entire scope of Judaean society including the lower classes. Avigad's observations about one large collection are reflective of the whole corpus of seventh century seals and bullae:

> Many of the seal-owners, possibly even the majority, seem to have been private citizens rather than officials, and some of them may even have been of the lower classes, of such limited means that them apparently prepared their own seals in order to be able to seal a document. This may be indicated by the careless execution and clumsy forms of many of the inscriptions."[11]

At the bare minimum, this reflects widespread signature literacy in Judah during the late seventh century. The uniqueness of the situation in Judah is indicated by quick comparison with surrounding states in Aram, Phoenicia, Ammon, and Moab. It is telling that Aramaean, Ammonite, Moabite, and Phoenician seals are commonly anepigraphic, iconographic seals, whereas the late Judaean seals have a marked preference for using only personal names.[12] From another perspective, the widespread evidence for seals is further evidence for urbanization and an increasingly complex economy that prompted the rise of literacy.

In the seventh century, writing became accessible to the poorer classes. This access of literacy to those outside the closed scribal schools is poignantly illustrated in "the letter of a literate soldier" (Lachish 3).[13] In this text, a superior officer had suggested that a junior officer might need to employ the services of a professional scribe—a suggestion that offended the junior officer, who protested that he had never needed the services of a scribe. The tone of the letter is most instructive because it indicates that literacy was the *expected* norm by both the senior and junior officer. Another ostracon from Meṣad Ḥashavyahu records the complaint of an agricultural worker against a supervisor that his garment was taken (in pledge) and not returned.[14] The location of this ostracon in a remote agricultural outpost and the poor style suggest that it might have been written by the worker himself; its compositional style certainly does not indicate an accomplished scribe. The frequent attribution of this ostracon to a scribe, despite its poor style, results from the dubious assumption that the worker *could not have written it*. Other telling evidence for literacy is graffiti which also suggests the ability to write among non-professional classes. Such evidence can be found in the graffiti from the burial caves at Khirbet el-Qôm where graffiti written by a stonecutter reflects a crude ability compose a simple blessing. Signature literacy is indicated by a recently published ostracon containing a list of seventeen different signatures of individuals apparently signing for a receipt or payment.[15] Particularly striking is the poor handwriting from several individuals, which indicates a widespread yet quite basic ability to read and write. From this evidence, we may deduce that literacy had spread well beyond the narrow confines of scribal schools. Reading and writing were accessible to all classes.

This rise in literacy must have profoundly shaped the development of Judaean culture in the seventh century. In Jack Goody's classic work, *The Domestication of the Savage Mind*, he points out:

> Culture, after all, is a series of communicative acts, and differences in the mode of communication are often as important as difference in the mode of production, for they involve developments in the storing, analysis, and creation of human knowledge, as well as the relationships between the individuals involved. The specific proposition is that writing, and more especially alphabetic literacy, made it possible to scrutinise discourse in a different kind of way by giving oral communication a semi-permanent form; this scrutiny favoured the increase in scope of critical activity, and hence of rationality, scepticism, and logic.[16]

The rise in literacy in the late monarchy corresponds to seminal changes in the character of Judaean religious practice, particularly the emergence of *authoritative written texts*. Goody argues that "literacy encouraged, at the very same time, criticism and commentary on the one hand and *the orthodoxy of the book* on the other."[17] Goody's observation should quickly call to mind particular events of the Josianic period, particularly the finding of the "book of the covenant," which became the basis of the Josianic reforms described in 2 Kings 22–23. The spread of literacy in Israel introduced a new mode of communication—the written word—with all the attendant authority that the written word conveys. Given evidence for the rise of literacy in the late monarchy, the prominence of a *written* scroll—usually understood as some form of the book of Deuteronomy—in the Josianic reforms should hardly be considered surprising. Written authority became the basis of religious critique.

The book of Deuteronomy evinces throughout its reliance on a textual model that presupposes a literate culture. This is implicit in the exegetical techniques of Deuteronomy that include *Wiederaufnahme*, deitic particles, and Seidel's Law; that is, it uses editorial and redactional techniques that presume a textual model.[18] Not only does the book claim to describe orthodoxy, but also it interprets previous traditions by using a textual hermeneutic. As Goody pointed out, the rise of alphabetic literacy brought an increase in critical activity. In Deuteronomic terms, for example, Deuteronomy 13's insistence on comparing the word of the prophet with the fulfillment reflects the critical model of a literate culture. In fact, this further suggests that the paradigm shift from an oral to a written word of God began already in the late Judaean monarchy, even if it does not culminate until much later.

The textual model that arises from a literate culture transformed ancient Israelite prophecy. This transition is clear already in the postexilic prophets, among whom arises the phenomenon of scribal prophecy.[19] Yet, the phenomenon of intertextuality is an explicitly literary phenomenon, which presumes a literate culture. Such intertextuality is evident in the Josianic historian's work (as discussed later). In contrast, an intertextual model does not work well for the use of the Promise in the oracles of Isaiah of Jerusalem (see previous chapter). Steven Geller articulates the difference nicely:

> Simply put, Isaiah never quoted scripture, and Job never cited a verse to prove his case. But King Josiah, instigator of the great Deuteronomic reform of 621 BCE, is specifically said to have based it not on a direct divine command, but rather on the Book of the Law (probably a form of Deuteronomy) that the priests said they found in the temple.[20]

Only with the rise of literacy in the seventh century does explicit textual citation arise.

"The People of the Land" ('Am Ha'aretz) *: A Rural Judaean Politic*

King Josiah accedes to the throne after a court conspiracy at only eight years of age. He apparently owed his position and perhaps even his life to the "people of the land (עם הארץ)," or *'Am Ha'aretz*, who put to death his father's assassins and crowned him king. At the very least, the early years of his kingship must have been shaped by the *'Am Ha'aretz*, who had rescued and supported his kingship. Thus, to understand the *'Am Ha'aretz* is to understand at least some of Josiah's reign. Unfortunately, the precise identity of the *'Am Ha'aretz* has been somewhat of a *crux interpretum* in biblical studies.

Usually translated innocuously as "the people of the land," the term *'Am Ha'aretz* occurs fifty-two times in biblical literature. It appears twenty-two times in the books of Kings and Chronicles but does not appear in Joshua–2 Samuel. *'Am Ha'aretz* also appears frequently in Jeremiah (seven times) and Ezekiel (nine times) but not in Isaiah (no occurrences).[21] In all these instances, it refers to a specifically Judaean group. All cases where it refers to non-Judaean groups are clustered in the Pentateuch (nine times); in these cases it should not be understood as a technical term.[22]

The apparent inconsistency of usage has led to widely divergent interpretations. Sociologist Max Weber saw the *'Am Ha'aretz* as elite social class (*Landadel*), and his interpretation has been followed, with some nuance, by S. Daiches and Robert Gordis.[23] Mayer Sulzberger and Elias Auerbach defined *'Am Ha'aretz* as a "national council."[24] Martin Noth suggested that they were "die Gesamtheit der judäischen Vollbürger," and Roland de Vaux wrote similarly that they stood "for the whole body of citizens."[25] A. Menes and K. Galling independently arrived at the description of the *'Am Ha'aretz* as a proletariat opposed to the elite class.[26] Hanoch Reviv equates the *'Am Ha'aretz* with the "elders of Judah"—that is, with the old traditional tribal leadership.[27] This variety drove E. W. Nicholson to despair, and he concluded that there was no fixed meaning to the term.[28]

There is no reason to despair, however. First of all, not all references to the *'Am Ha'aretz* are created equal. In the Pentateuch, *'Am Ha'aretz* is a general reference meaning "people who live in the land" and does not seem to be a technical term (cf. Gen 23:7, 12, 13; 42:6; Exod 5:5; Lev 4:27; 20:2, 4; Num 14:9). A cluster of references to the *'Am Ha'aretz* in later political contexts would suggest that the term *'Am Ha'aretz* represents a particular group beginning in the late monarchy. Therefore, the context of discussion for the term *'Am Ha'aretz* should be narrowed to the books of Kings, where we might expect a consistent meaning for the term.

A few texts illustrate a special technical meaning for the term *'Am Ha'aretz* in Kings. Perhaps the most important text is the coup d'état against Athaliah involving the *'Am Ha'aretz* described in 2 Kings 11. Because the term occurs four times in this context alone, it is worthwhile to cite an extended passage from 2 Kings 11:13–20:

> [13]When Athaliah heard the noise of the guard and the people, she went into the house of YHWH to the people; [14]when she looked, there was the king standing by the pillar, according to custom, with the captains and the trumpeters beside the king, and all the *'Am Ha'aretz* rejoicing and blowing trumpets. Athaliah tore her clothes and cried, "Treason! Treason!" [15]Then the priest Jehoiada commanded the captains who were set over the army, "Bring her out between the ranks, and kill with the sword anyone who follows her." For the priest said, "Let her not be killed in the temple of YHWH." [16]So they cleared a pathway for her, and she entered the royal palace through the horses' entrance, and there she was put to death. [17]Jehoiada made a covenant between YHWH, the king, and the people, that they should be YHWH's people; also between the king and the people. [18]Then all the *'Am Ha'aretz* went to the house of Baal, and tore it down; his altars and his images they broke in pieces, and they killed Mattan, the priest of Baal, before the altars. The priest posted guards over the house of YHWH. [19]He took the captains, the Karites, the guards, and all the *'Am Ha'aretz*; then they brought the king down from the temple of YHWH, marching through the guards' gate to the palace. He took his seat on the royal throne. [20]*So all the 'Am Ha'aretz rejoiced, but the city was quiet after they had put Athaliah to death with the sword in the palace.*

The *'Am Ha'aretz* first restore the rightful Davidic heir, then they immediately take action against the foreign cults associated with Athaliah (v. 18). This last action certainly dovetails nicely with the events following Josiah's installation. Also critical for understanding the precise identity of the *'Am Ha'aretz* is verse 20 where two different reactions to the coup d'état are juxtaposed: the *'Am Ha'aretz* rejoice, but the *city* is quiet. This contrast suggests that the city supported Athaliah while the countryside—that is, the *'Am Ha'aretz*—opposed Athaliah.[29] The city supported the foreign princess, who undoubtedly brought new religious traditions and a more cosmopolitan perspective to the Judaean capital. Who were Athaliah's supporters? How did she successfully seize the throne from the Davidides? The *city* supported her. This scenario implies a clear opposition between the city and the countryside, between the urbanites and the *'Am Ha'aretz*. This contrast can also be illustrated by 2 Kings 25:19; there, we read about a Babylonian commander rounding up "sixty men of the *'Am Ha'aretz* who were found in the city." Evidently, not all people in the city could be classified as *'Am Ha'aretz*; moreover, one has the impression that it was somewhat unusual to find the *'Am Ha'aretz* in the city.

The only question remaining is whether the *'Am Ha'aretz* can be considered a well-organized political group. Perhaps the references in Dtr^1 (= Josianic edition of DtrH) can support this, but the picture changes when we look at the whole of the books of Kings. For example, in Nebuchadnezzar's first campaign against Judah (ca. 597 BCE), he exiles principally the urban and social elite and leaves the *'Am*

Ha'aretz, undoubtedly because they were necessary to cultivate the land: "He carried away all Jerusalem, all the officials, all the warriors, ten thousand captives, all the artisans and the smiths; no one remained, except the poorest people of the land (זולת דלת עם־הארץ)" (2 Kgs 24:14).[30] After the final exile, the Babylonians "left some of the poorest of the land (מדלת הארץ) to be vinedressers and tillers of the soil" (2 Kgs 25:12). To see the *'Am Ha'aretz* as a well-organized political group, these last few references would need to be set aside. Then again, these last two references do derive from an exilic redactor's hand, and the meaning of *'Am Ha'aretz* changed over time. The postexilic writings of Ezra-Nehemiah regularly use the plural, *'Amê Ha'aratzôt* (עמי הארצות), referring to the nations, and the singular still refers to those not considered Jews by Ezra's party (cf. Ezra 4:4). In rabbinic literature, the *'Am Ha'aretz* are the uneducated and not particularly observant people living in the land (*Ab* 2:6; 3:11).

Still, it is clear that the *'Am Ha'aretz* play a pivotal role in the politics of the seventh century until the fall of Jerusalem. Along these lines, Shemaryahu Talmon points out, "The *'Am Ha'aretz* intervenes to counteract an imminent threat to the continuity of the Davidic dynasty, a threat which was brought about by regicides from among the royal courtiers who hatched their plots in the metropolis. This recurring constellation indeed may disclose an underlying tension between the *'Am Ha'aretz* and the city, or the acropolis of Jerusalem."[31] The relevance of the *'Am Ha'aretz* to the Davidic dynasty is emphasized by Talmon in his parting words:

> Viewed in historical retrospect, the *'Am Ha'aretz* served as an important means for the implementation of an ideology inspired by the Davidic dynasty which took the form of a prophecy from the mouth of Nathan 2 Sam 7:16: ונאמן ביתך וממלכתך עד־עולם—'And your house and your kingdom shall be made sure for ever'.[32]

Talmon's analysis is close to the mark. It is impossible, however, to reconcile the variety of references to the *'Am Ha'aretz* with the proposition that they were an organized political group. Rather, *'Am Ha'aretz* refers to "the people of the countryside" outside Jerusalem. Along these lines it is noteworthy that outside the book of Kings the term *'Am Ha'aretz* often emphasizes the indigenous population as opposed to foreigners. For example, in Exodus, Pharaoh complains that the Hebrews "are more numerous than the *'Am Ha'aretz*" (5:4). In Numbers, the Israelites are told, "Do not fear the *'Am Ha'aretz*" (14:9)—that is, the native population of Canaan. This emphasis on an indigenous population would be especially appropriate in the context of a foreign queen like Athaliah or in the seventh century, when Judah was overrun—at least from the perspective of the natives—by foreign refugees and inundated by foreign cultural influences.

As has been already pointed out, we first meet the *'Am Ha'aretz* in the book of Kings in their opposition to a foreign queen, Athaliah, and restoration of the indigenous ruler. This scenario should help us understand another attempted coup d'état against Amon, son of Manasseh, in 640 BCE: "The servants of Amon conspired against him, and killed the king in his house. But the *'Am Ha'aretz* killed all those who had conspired against King Amon, and the *'Am Ha'aretz* made his son

Josiah king in place of him (2 Kgs 21:23–24)." The particulars of this assassination are not described. Who were the servants of Amon? What was the reason for the attempted *coup d'état*? These questions are difficult to answer for certain; however, the assassins were likely related in some way with the royal house. The queen mother provides some insight into the Judaean royal house: "Amon's mother's name was Meshullemeth daughter of Haruz of Jotbah" (2 Kgs 21:19). It cannot be fortuitous that Manasseh's wife came from Jotbah *in Galilee*—the north—and that the queen mother in Amon's time was not explicitly a Yahwist by name.[33] The use of non-Yahwistic names for the kings, Manasseh and Amon, as well as for the queen mother, differs from the onomastic evidence from this period which points almost exclusively to Yahwistic theophoric elements.[34] It also breaks a chain of Yahwistic names for Judaean kings and queen-mothers. How is it that Manasseh comes to be married to a northerner a generation after the fall of the northern kingdom, and what does this tell us about the royal Judaean house? This marriage must reflect political aspects of Judah that began in the late eighth century as the southern kingdom struggled into integrate elements of the once larger and stronger northern kingdom. After the attempted coup d'état, the *'Am Ha'aretz* moved in and crowned the new leader, Josiah whose family came from Bozkath, a remote village in the Judaean countryside. The *'Am Ha'aretz* thus moved to support a young new king whose family ties are to the Judaean countryside, as opposed to the previous two generations, with their ties to the northern kingdom. Small wonder that this new king will move to eradicate all traces of the religion of Jeroboam and Ahab from Judah! It is natural to assume that their role is intimately related to Judaean society during this period—a context now illuminated by archaeological studies.

Rapid Social Change and New Religious Movements

New religious movements proliferate in times of rapid social change.[35] The seventh century was just such a time. James Beckford points out that "religious movements are inextricably woven into the social fabric, although the actual manner of their interweaving varies greatly across movements, time, and place."[36] A description of the changing tapestry of Judaean society thus sets the scene for events in Judah during the seventh century, as well as for the reading of the Promise to David.

As has been pointed out, the rise of Assyria precipitated Judah's rapid and dramatic social upheavals. Assyrian campaigns in the north resulted in a large influx of refugees. Sennacherib's campaign wreaked massive destruction while depopulating the Judaean countryside. The demographics of Judah were completely transformed. Larger cities continued, but smaller villages disappeared from the Judaean foothills. The population of Jerusalem and its environs mushroomed. New settlements appeared in the Judaean wilderness and Negeb. Power increasingly shifted from the countryside to Jerusalem. A world empire replaced regional rivals. The Assyrian empire set up regional administrative centers and a global economy. This was a time ripe for proliferation of new religious movements as people searched for meaning in the face of the social turmoil.

In this context the biblical depiction of the reign of King Manasseh in Judah should hardly seem surprising. According to 2 Kings 21:2–9,

[2]He acted wickedly in YHWH's eyes following the abominable practices of the nations that YHWH drove out before the people of Israel. [3]He rebuilt the high places that his father Hezekiah had destroyed. He erected altars for Baal. He made a sacred pole, as King Ahab of Israel had done. He worshipped all the host of heaven, and served them. [4]Now he also built altars in the house of YHWH, of which YHWH had said, "In Jerusalem I will put my name." [5]He built altars for all the host of heaven in the two courts of the house of YHWH. [6]He made his son pass through fire. He practiced soothsaying and augury, and dealt with mediums and with wizards. He did much evil in the sight of YHWH, provoking him to anger. [7]The carved image of Asherah that he had made he set in the house of which YHWH said to David and to his son Solomon, "In this house, and in Jerusalem, which I have chosen out of all the tribes of Israel, I will put my name forever; [8]I will not cause the feet of Israel to wander any more out of the land that I gave to their ancestors, if only they will be careful to do according to all that I have commanded them, and according to all the law that my servant Moses commanded them." [9]But they did not listen; Manasseh misled them into doing more evil than the nations that YHWH destroyed before the people of Israel.

What is remarkable about the condemnation of Manasseh is not the severity of condemnation—that is to be expected of the author—rather, it is the variety of religious practices attributed to Manasseh. Some have read these accusations quite literally and accuse Manasseh of introducing rampant idolatry into Judaean religion at this time.[37] Others have recognized that ideology shapes the number and severity of the charges against Manasseh.[38] From a literary point of view, Manasseh was critical to both the Josianic and exilic redactors. For a Josianic author, Manasseh sets up Josiah's reforms, especially in that Hezekiah was pictured as a relatively good king who even introduced some religious reforms himself (cf. 2 Kgs 18:3–5). For the exilic redactor, Manasseh becomes the scoundrel ultimately responsible for the exile (e.g., 2 Kgs 24:3–4). As a result, we need to be cautious about reading the description of Manasseh's religious apostasy too literally. The account was fashioned by authors who had little interest in accurately assessing the causes of the religious movements of the period. Rather, they characterize the period first from the perspective of religious reformers (i.e., Dtr^1) and then as theologians seeking to explain the exile (i.e., Dtr^2 = the exilic edition of DtrH).

So what was the reality? From a sociological perspective, we must expect that the period of Manasseh was characterized by new religious movements, even if we cannot be certain what role the king himself played in the advancement of these religious movements. The influx of foreign culture and social reorganization invited new religious movements. Gosta Ahlström argued that the charges against Manasseh reflect only a return to traditional religious practices.[39] It is true that new religious movements usually present themselves as more original or authentic reflections of older religious movements. As James Beckford notes, new religious movements are "rooted in older and broader religious traditions."[40] This hardly means that the religious practices under Manasseh represented a return to tradition. Precisely the contrary. New religious movements represent themselves under the guise of older religious traditions precisely because they are new and therefore in need of the authority which tradition affords.

The biblical traditions need not be completely discarded, however. They reflect a late seventh century author's knowledge of the variety of religious practices in Judah. Even if we do not hold Manasseh personally responsible for all these practices, this is valuable information. The biblical traditions concerning Manasseh and Josiah embody the spirit of the age. They set the context from which we may assess the reading of the Promise to David. In the Book of Chronicles reflect a different period and not surprisingly Manasseh's religious practices will receive a different, more sympathetic reception. At the end of his reign Manasseh is portrayed as returning to true Yahwism, although "the people still sacrificed at the high places, but only to YHWH their God" (2 Chr 33:17). Still, both Kings and Chronicles describe numerous unorthodox religious practices (orthodoxy being defined by the Deuteronomists) in the Josianic period: (1) the high places that his father, Hezekiah, had destroyed, (2) altars for Baal, (3) a sacred pole (or *Asherah*) according to Phoenician practice (i.e., like Ahab), (4) worship of the host of heaven, (5) possibly child sacrifice associated with the cult of Molech (i.e., "He made his son pass through fire"), and (6) magic and witchcraft (i.e., soothsaying, augury, mediums, and wizards). The fertile soil of social upheavals cultivates such new religious movements during the reign of Manasseh. James Beckford writes,

> *New religious movements are important indicators of stressful changes in culture and society*. They are also interesting attempts to come to terms with rapid social change by imposing new interpretations on it and by experimenting with practical responses. They therefore amount to social and cultural laboratories where experiments in ideas, feeling and social relations are carried out. They are a normal aspect of social life and *a critical guide to societal problems and prospects* [emphasis added].[41]

In other words, as much as social turmoil leads us to expect and even look for new religious movements, biblical descriptions of new religious movements in the time of Manasseh and Josiah presuppose stressful changes in culture and society. It is in this context that we assess the Josianic Reformers' reading of the Promise to David.

Josianic Reformers Recontextualize the Promise (Dtr^1)

The Josianic reformers read of Judah's history through a Deuteronomic lens. This has been a widely held opinion of many recent studies of DtrH. The study of DtrH takes its point of departure from the seminal work of Martin Noth.[42] Noth proposed that a single exilic author composed the entire DtrH (Deuteronomy-2 Kings) by using earlier written sources. Noth's departure from source critical approaches has found a wide following, though it has seldom been accepted whole cloth. Variations on Noth's hypothesis have followed four lines. Some have adhered to the theory of a single exilic edition, albeit with additions, but without further editions. Continental scholars of the Smend-Göttingen school have isolated an exilic history (which they call DtrG) and two further redactional hands (prophetic [= DtrP] and nomistic [= DtrN]), although they differ on whether to characterize this process as editions or scribal additions. A third school follows the dual redaction theory, especially as articulated by Frank Moore Cross. Cross argued that the original edition of the DtrH (= Dtr[1]) was written in the preexilic period to support the reforms of Josiah and was later updated by an exilic editor (= Dtr[2]), who was concerned to explain the Babylonian exile. A fourth school essentially adheres to the dual redaction theory but finds an earlier redactional stage indicated by structure elements of the books of Kings (e.g., accession formulae, death-burial notices, religious evaluations). The first redactional stage of the triple redaction theory is placed in the Hezekian period.

Cross's hypothesis has had a wide appeal. This may be explained by the fact that Cross's dual redaction theory, on the one hand, accounts for the unevenness of the DtrH, and on the other hand, it provides a simple, coherent theological and historical basis for the differentiation of the two layers in the DtrH. Although the triple redaction theory has had growing popularity among a variety of continental and American scholars, it has yet to move beyond the structural indications delineating the early redactional stage of DtrH. There may be a coherent theological and historical basis for this earlier edition (e.g., the need to account for the fall of Samaria), but it is unclear that we shall be able to separate it from the later redactional layers. The Smend-Göttingen school has yet to attract much of a following outside Germany. A weakness of this approach, which proposes multiple exilic editions or redactions, is simply that DtrP and DtrN lack a powerful theological or historical basis. Indeed, the very methodology of isolating different editorial, redactional, or scribal hands simply on the basis of thematic issues—that is, prophecy or law is highly questionable. Are prophecy and law so opposed that they require different editors? What were the historical situations that allowed the DtrH to go through so many redactional or editorial hands in such a short period of time? Although there is no consensus concerning the composition of Kings, nevertheless, the dual redaction theory, which posits Josianic and exilic editions of DtrH, holds a privileged place in this discussion. This assessment may be justified by the longevity of the theory, which was first proposed in the nineteenth century, and the variety of its adherents, which include both Continental and American scholars.

2 Samuel 7:13a: "He Shall Build a House For My Name"

Although Nathan's prophecies derive from early sources, the framework in which we meet them in 2 Samuel 7 comes from a Josianic historian (Dtr[1]). As I already pointed out in chapter 2, 2 Samuel 7:13a, "He shall build a house for my name," is an insertion placed within the Promise via the redactional technique of *Wiederaufnahme* (i.e., repetitive resumption) and using the deitic pronoun "he" (הוא) to introduce a Deuteronomic author's exegetical comment. It is worth outlining the insertion again here:

Ancient Prophecy:	[12]When your days are fulfilled and you lie down with your ancestors, I will raise up your offspring after you, who shall come forth from your body, and I will establish his kingdom (והכינתי את־ממלכתו).

Deuteronomic Insertion:	13*He shall build a house for my name* (הוא יבנה ית לשמי),
Resumption:	and I will establish the throne of his kingdom forever (וכננתי את־כסא ממלכתו עד־עולם).

The insertion reflects the particular interests of the Josianic historian in the temple, as well as his peculiar Deuteronomic jargon and theology, reflected by the expression "a house for my name." There is no other incontrovertible evidence of a Deuteronomic redactor's hand in 2 Samuel 7:1–17. It seems unlikely that the joining of the two parts of 2 Samuel 7:1–17—namely, the request to build a temple in verses 1–7 and the promise of a kingdom and a land in verses 8–16—were the work of the Josianic redactor (see the arguments in chapter 2). Perhaps one of the strongest arguments for the pre-Deuteronomic nature of the Promise is simply that the prophecy is not explicitly tied with a fulfillment, as would be expected if it were of Deuteronomic origin. Instead, it is the subsequent Deuteronomic citations of the Promise (see later in this chapter) that address the typical Deuteronomic prophecy-fulfillment framework.

The Deuteronomistic History uses a variety of phrases to express its "name theology."[43] These include "the place that YHWH shall choose to put his name (המקום אשר יבחר לשכן שמו שם)" (Deut 12:11; 14:23; 16:2, 6, 11; 26:2; also cf. Jer 7:12; Neh 1:9; Ezr 6:12), "to put his name there (לשום שמו שם)" (Deut 12:5, 21; 14:24; cf. 1 Kgs 9:3; 11:36; 14:21; 2 Kgs 21:4, 7), "so that his name shall be there (להיות שמו שם)" (cf. 1 Kgs 8:16, 29; 2 Kgs 23:27), "to build a house for his name (בנה בית לשם יהוה)" (cf. 2 Sam 7:13; 1 Kgs 3:2; 5:17, 18, 19; 8:17, 18, 19, 20, 44, 48), and "to dedicate a house for the name of YHWH (הקדיש בית לשם יהוה)" (cf. 1 Kgs 9:7).[44] The expression "the house/city which is called by my name" (הבית/העיר אשר נקרא שמי עליו)" (1 Kgs 8:43; Jer 7:10, 11, 14, 30; 25:29; 32:34; 34:15) appears in exilic or postexilic literature and is influenced by Deuteronomy. As Weinfeld observes, however, this expression "to attach a name to X (קרא שם על־X)" appears in earlier literature (e.g., 2 Sam 6:2; 12:28; Isa 4:1; Ps 49:12) and cannot be considered exclusively Deuteronomic. Rather, it is the use of this language particularly about Jerusalem and the temple that indicates Deuteronomic influence.

The significance of the Deuteronomic terminology "a house for YHWH's name" lies in the exclusivity of worship and not its abstraction. Gerhard von Rad's classic *Studies in Deuteronomy* popularized the idea that the Deuteronomic "name theology" reflected an abstract theological concept that was intended to subvert the prevalent Priestly conception, which depicted the temple as the deity's actual dwelling place.[45] It is important to contextualize von Rad's argument by one of his beginning premises: namely, Deuteronomy comes together in the exilic period. The force of this premise for shaping von Rad's argument is explicit in the very first sentence of his thesis: "Deuteronomy makes its appearance at a definite point in the history of Israel's faith."[46] Even though von Rad accepted the arguments of W. M. L. de Wette that the book discovered in the temple was at least the kernel of the book of Deuteronomy, he was also working under Noth's premise of a Deuteronomic historical work composed in the exilic period. This meant for von Rad that Deuteronomy and, more important, DtrH crystallized after the destruction of the temple during the Babylonian exile. It is only natural with such a premise to understand Deuteronomic name theology as an abstraction that was after all necessitated by the destruction of the temple. A better way to address the destruction of the temple, however, would be to eliminate the need for it entirely (e.g., Isa 66:1–2; see chapter 5). Even if it came to be understood as an abstraction—especially by Protestant theologians—it is unlikely to have been *invented* as one.

Deuteronomic name terminology, like the structure of the book of Deuteronomy itself, can be traced to Near Eastern antecedents. For example, the Amarna letters (ca. 1400 BCE) reflect this concept: "As the king has placed his name (*šarri šakan šumsu*) in Jerusalem forever, he cannot abandon it—the land of Jerusalem" (EA 287:60–63).[47] The language of putting a name in a place is also typical of royal inscriptions and particularly of erecting a stele, where the king is said to place his name.[48] Everywhere the king places his name, he claims exclusive ownership. Even in biblical literature, the attaching of a name to a place claims ownership; for example, we read in Deuteronomy 3:14, "Jair the Manassite took the whole region of Argob as far as the border of the Geshurites and the Maacathites, and he *named* them—that is, Bashan—after himself, Havvoth-jair, as it is to this day." Likewise, when David conquers Jerusalem, he renames it "the city of David" (2 Sam 5:9). The concept of the name in both Near Eastern and biblical literature indicates that to put one's name somewhere meant to claim exclusive ownership. Indeed, this was the thrust of the Josianic reforms: the exclusive worship of YHWH in a temple that YHWH shared with no other gods. There is no implication that YHWH's name was an abstraction of the deity. Rather, the abstraction of YHWH's name was most likely a later exilic reflection; originally, the claim that YHWH "put his name" in Jerusalem and in the temple expressed YHWH's exclusive claims.[49] In this respect, name theology was simply another expression of the religious centralization of the Josianic reforms.

Citations of the Promise within Dtr[1]

The first citation of the Promise to David within Dtr[1] itself comes in Solomon's discourse with Hiram of Tyre about his plan to build a temple. In 1 Kings 5:16–19 [ET, 5:2–5] we read,

> Solomon sent word to Hiram, saying, "You know that my father David could not build a house for the name of YHWH his God because of the warfare with which his enemies surrounded him, until YHWH put them under the soles of his feet. But now YHWH my God has given me rest on every side; there is neither adversary nor misfortune. So I intend to build a house for the name of YHWH my God, as YHWH said to my father David, 'Your son, whom I will set on your throne in your place, shall build the house for my name.' "

There are a few typically Deuteronomic phrases in this passage. The expression "the house for my name" is characteristically Deuteronomic; in this case it will also point back precisely to the Promise (see later). Likewise, the expression "to give rest" is typically Deuteronomic (cf. Deut 3:20; 12:10; 25:19) and also contradicts the narrative introduction to the Promise where David has supposedly been given rest from all his enemies (cf. 2 Sam 7:1). This tension, which, by the way, the books of Chronicles would correct (cf. 1 Chr 17:1), strongly supports a pre-Deuteronomic origin for the narrative framework of the Promise, minimally 2 Samuel 7:1–16.

Solomon's words not only add to but also contradict 2 Samuel 7:1–17. The Promise explains that David cannot build a temple for YHWH because YHWH never required or requested a permanent temple (2 Sam 7:6–7). Certainly there is no hint of any inadequacy on David's part. More than this, according to 2 Samuel 7, verses 1 and 11, God had already given David rest from his enemies. This rest is what occasions David to contemplate building a temple for YHWH! It is a curious statement attributed to Solomon—namely, that David could not build a temple because he was too preoccupied with wars. In the end, though, Solomon justifies himself as the builder of the temple by paraphrasing 2 Samuel 7:13. The citation follows the exegetical technique known as Seidel's Law with the lemma chiastically citing the two parts of 2 Samuel 7:13:

2 Samuel 7:13	*1 Kings 5:19*
הוא יבנה־בית לשמי וכננתי את־כסא ממלכתו עד־עולם	בנך אשר אתן תחתיך על־כסאך הוא־יבנה הבית לשמי
he shall build a house for my name; and I shall establish the throne of his kingdom forever.	your son who I shall put in your place on your throne, he shall build the house for my name.

In repeating the lemma, 1 Kings 5:19 slips in a definite article—that is, "he shall build *the* house for my name." The apparent implication is that there is only one house for YHWH's name. In a similar vein, the reversal in the order highlights the building of the Solomonic temple. In 2 Samuel 7:13 we have two separate and independent statements, whereas in 1 Kings 5:19 the phrase "he shall build" now explicitly modifies "your son": "your son, he shall build the house for my name." This deft maneuver underscores the special interests of the Josianic readers in "the house for YHWH's name."

The next citation of the Promise to David appears in the Prayer of Solomon in 1 Kings 8. As was pointed out in chapter 2, the Prayer of Solomon is actually three prayers (vv. 12–13, 14–21, 22–61), each introduced by a separate introductory formula and containing a different conception of the location where YHWH dwells.[50] The first prayer, which implies that YHWH actually could dwell in the Solomonic temple, is a pre-Deuteronomic source that dates to the Solomonic period. I shall argue in the next chapter that the third prayer, which locates God in heaven and not in a human temple, dates to the exilic period. Our attention presently turns to the second prayer (vv. 14–21), which can be attributed to Dtr^1.[51]

The second prayer is clearly marked off from the first by the introductory formula that begins verse 14, "The king turned around and blessed all the assembly of Israel, while all the assembly of Israel was standing, and he said." The blessing which follows is widely considered a Deuteronomic composition:

> 15He said, "Blessed be YHWH, the God of Israel, who with his hand has fulfilled
> what he promised with his mouth to my father David, saying, 16'Since the day that
> I brought my people Israel out of Egypt, I had not chosen a city from any of the
> tribes of Israel in which to build a house, that my name might be there; but I chose
> David to be over my people Israel.' 17My father David had it in mind to build a
> house for the name of YHWH, the God of Israel. 18But YHWH said to my father
> David, 'You did well to consider building a house for my name; 19nevertheless
> you shall not build the house, but your son who shall be born to you shall build the
> house for my name.' 20Now YHWH has upheld the promise that he made; for I
> have risen in the place of my father David; I sit on the throne of Israel, as YHWH
> promised, and have built the house for the name of YHWH, the God of Israel.
> 21There I have provided a place for the ark, in which is the covenant of YHWH
> that he made with our ancestors when he brought them out of the land of Egypt."

The speech reverses the apparent meaning of 2 Samuel 7:1–17. It quotes 2 Samuel 7:1–17 using an explicit citation formula and then paraphrases and rewrites the entire Nathan narrative. So convincing are this citation and the paraphrase that Jon Levenson assesses verses 15–21 as follows: "1 Kgs 8:15–21 does not dwell on 2 Sam 7:8–16 so much as it recreates it, or most of it, without deviation or innovation."[52] Simple comparison, however, reveals a quite seminal transformation. The argument in this second address of Solomon may be summarized as follows. While it is true that God had not chosen a city (2 Sam 7:6–7), he did chose David to build a dynasty; and, while it is true that David was not allowed to build the temple, he did do well to desire building the temple. Yet, God choose David's son to build the temple. Nowhere is it explicit that God choose the city, Jerusalem; however, it is implicit in the repeated assertion that God's name would reside in the Jerusalem temple. The choice of the house of David becomes the means by which Solomon justifies building the temple for YHWH's name. In this respect, the temple rather than the Davidic dynasty is what is promised, according to this recontextualization of the Promise. Thus, while Levenson is correct in saying that the author of this second address had the Promise in mind, he rewrites the text and refashions its meaning. Now the temple is the focus of the Promise. It is the place God chose for himself.

The creative reworking of 2 Samuel 7:1–16 can be further illuminated by a careful comparison of some of the language employed in Solomon's speech. Often the correspondences are quite close, though not exact. Beginning in verse 16, we read, "from the day which I *brought out my people* Israel from Egypt" (מן־היום אשר הוצאתי את־עמי את־ישראל ממצרים), as compared with 2 Samuel 7:6, "from the day which I *brought up the sons of* Israel from Egypt" (למיום אשר העלתי בני ישראל ממצרים). These differences are small, but significant. For example, a study of the verbs "to bring out (הוציא)" and "to bring up (העלה)" by Wijngaards shows that the "to bring up (העלה)" formula is gradually superseded by "to bring out (הוציא)" probably because of theological preference by the Deuteronomists.[53] In other words, the use of the two different formulas suggests two different hands. Second Samuel 7:6 is earlier and 1 Kings 8:16 is a later reuse.

The phrase "I had not chosen a city but I had chosen David" (לא־בחרתי בעיר ... ואבחר בדוד) is absent from the Promise in 2 Samuel 7:1–17. This addition employs clear Deuteronomic phraseology with the verb "to chose" (√בחר, 1 Kgs 8:16), thereby betraying the ideological bent of its author. The language in Solomon's Prayer at this point more exactly parallels the law of centralization in Deuteronomy (cf. Deut 12:5, "the place which YHWH your God shall choose (המקום אשר־יבחר יהוה אלהיכם) from all your tribes to set his name there."[54] The influence of the centralization law here shows where the real interests of Dtr^{1} lie, even here in Solomon's Prayer. Perhaps more telling of Dtr^{1}'s creative reworking of the Promise is the repeated locution that the temple is only "for YHWH's name" (vv. 16, 17, 19, 20).[55] The Promise styles the proposed temple as "a house of cedar (בית ארזים)," which contrasts with the mobile shrine in which YHWH had dwelled (cf. 2 Samuel 7:2, 6–7). It is clear in the Promise that the temple was a place for YHWH to dwell—it was just a question of moving YHWH from a tent into a permanent shrine. This contrasts sharply with the notion in Solomon's second prayer that the temple was only a place for YHWH's name—a concept absent from the Promise except for the Deuteronomic insertion in 2 Samuel 7:13a. In any case, the frequent use of "a house for my name" in Solomon's second prayer is typical Deuteronomic language and certainly reworks the basic conceptual framework of the Promise.

Verse 19, "Only *you are not the one* that shall build *the* temple" (רק אתה לא תבנה הבית), clears up ambiguities in 2 Samuel 7:5, "*Shall you* build *a* temple for me to dwell in?" (הַאַתָּה תבנה־לי בית לשבתי). The meaning of this rhetorical question in the Promise itself is clarified by the following verses, which point out that YHWH had not asked for a temple and had been doing just fine in tents and tabernacles. The problem was with the temple itself, not with the person who wanted to build it. This idea is certainly subverted by Solomon's second prayer, which suggests that the problem is simply that David was not the person chosen to build the temple. As I shall detail in later chapters, this interpretative tradition is picked up in Chronicles and continues throughout the Second Temple period. Notably, verse 19 is the only place in verses 15–21 where the temple is not explicitly called "a house for YHWH's name." This may reflect the influence of 2 Samuel 7:5. Nevertheless, the addition of the definite article is critical because it emphasizes that we are speaking of "the" temple (הבית)—not just "a" temple (בית) as 2 Samuel 7:5 suggests. This addition is again in keeping with what we might expect of a Deuteronomic author for whom the centrality and exclusivity of Solomon's temple were paramount. It should not be surprising that this interpretative trajectory continues in the book of Chronicles (see chapter 6).

The continuation of verse 19 mentions the promised son of David, "your son who shall come forth from your loins" (בנך היצא מחלציך). This could be seen as a paraphrase of 2 Samuel 7:12, "your seed after you who shall come forth from your inner parts" (את־זרעך אחריך אשר יצא ממעיך). It seems more likely, however, that an allusion is being made to the patriarchal promise known from Genesis 35:11, "and kings shall go forth from your loins" (ומלכים מחלציך יצאו). It is only in Genesis that we find a parallel for the usual expression of children going forth from the loins (חלצים). The possible allusion to this version of a promise in Solomon's second prayer is strengthened in the context by verse 21, which refers to "the covenant of YHWH which was made with our forefathers."

In contrast to the third prayer which is usually dated to the exilic period, there is no conditional element to the Davidic promise in Solomon's second prayer. The focus is on the fact that David was chosen to be ruler over all Israel and to bring forth a dynasty that would begin with Solomon; then, Solomon emphasizes that he was chosen to build the temple.

Excursus: 4QKgs for 1 Kings 8:16

A small Qumran fragment (4Q54) from 1 Kings 8:16–17 has been published by J. Trebolle-Barrera. This fragment is quite important as it shows a substantial addition to the MT reading. [56]Trebolle-Barrera compares this fragment with other textual versions, especially noting the similarity with the Chronicles tradition. The reconstructed fragment is placed here in parallel columns with 1 Kings (MT), 2 Chronicles 6:5–6, and 3 Kingdoms (LXX):

1 Kings	*4QKgs*	*2 Chr 6*	*3 Kgdms*
מִן־הַיּוֹם אֲשֶׁר הוֹצֵאתִי		מִן־הַיּוֹם אֲשֶׁר הוֹצֵאתִי	ἀφ' ἧς ἡμέρας ἐξήγαγον
אֶת־עַמִּי אֶת־יִשְׂרָאֵל		אֶת־עַמִּי	τὸν λαόν μου τὸν Ισραηλ
מִמִּצְרַיִם		מֵאֶרֶץ מִצְרַיִם	ἐξ Αἰγύπτου
לֹא־בָחַרְתִּי בְעִיר		לֹא־בָחַרְתִּי בְעִיר	οὐκ ἐξελεξάμην ἐν πόλει
מִכֹּל שִׁבְטֵי יִשְׂרָאֵל		מִכֹּל שִׁבְטֵי יִשְׂרָאֵל	ἐν ἑνὶ σκήπτρῳ Ισραηλ
לִבְנוֹת בַּיִת		לִבְנוֹת בַּיִת	τοῦ οἰκοδομῆσαι οἶκον
לִהְיוֹת שְׁמִי שָׁם	להיות שמי שם	לִהְיוֹת שְׁמִי שָׁם	τοῦ εἶναι τὸ ὄνομά μου ἐκεῖ
	ולא־בחרתי באיש	וְלֹא־בָחַרְתִּי בְאִישׁ	
	להיות נגיד	לִהְיוֹת נָגִיד	
	על עמי ישראל	עַל־עַמִּי יִשְׂרָאֵל	
	ואבחר בירושלם	וָאֶבְחַר בִּירוּשָׁלַם	καὶ ἐξελεξάμην ἐν Ιερουσαλημ
	להיות שמי שם	לִהְיוֹת שְׁמִי שָׁם	εἶναι τὸ ὄνομά μου ἐκεῖ
וָאֶבְחַר בְּדָוִד לִהְיוֹת	ואבחר בדוד להיות	וָאֶבְחַר בְּדָוִיד לִהְיוֹת	καὶ ἐξελεξάμην τὸν Δαυιδ τοῦ εἶναι ἐπὶ
עַל־עַמִּי יִשְׂרָאֵל	על עמי על ישראל	עַל־עַמִּי יִשְׂרָאֵל	τὸν λαόν μου τὸν Ισραηλ

> 1 Kings 8:16 MT: From the day I brought My people Israel out of Egypt, I have not chosen a city from among all the tribes of Israel to build a House in order that My name might dwell there; but I have chosen David to rule My people Israel.
> 4QKgs: [From the day I brought My people out of the land of Egypt, I have not chosen a city from among all the tribes of Israel to build a House] in order that My name might dwell there; *nor did I choose anyone to*[*be the leader of*]*my* [*people*]*Israel. 6 But then I chose Jerusalem for My name to abide there*, and I chose David [to rule My people I]srael. {Outlining above and bracketing in translation indicates reconstructed text.}
> 2 Chronicles 6:5: From the day I brought My people out of the land of Egypt, I have not chosen a city from among all the tribes of Israel to build a House in order that My name might dwell there; *nor did I choose anyone to be the leader of my people Israel. 6 But then I chose Jerusalem for My name to abide there*, and I chose David to rule My people Israel.

> 3 Kingdoms 8:16: From the day I brought My people Israel out of Egypt, I have not chosen a city from one tribe of Israel to build a House in order that My name might dwell there. *But then I chose Jerusalem for My name to abide there*, and I chose David to rule My people Israel.

According to Trebolle-Barrera, the substantial addition in 4QKgs here may be explained by homoioteleuton; consequently, he would restore the urtext on the basis of Chronicles and 4QKgs. This restoration, however, must be regarded with suspicion when we realize that the addition in the 4QKgs fragment happens to fall at one of the most theologically critical points in the prayer of Solomon. It should arouse further suspicion because 4QKgs also represents a substantive departure from the LXX. How are we to account for the fact that MT ≠ LXX ≠ 4QKgs? Adding other versions into the picture hardly clarifies things; for example, the Greek Lucianic version follows the MT, not 4QKgs.[57] The only evidence that supports 4QKgs is Chronicles, and this should hardly be comforting to the text critic. Although in many cases Chronicles provides helpful evidence for textual emendation, it is also clear that (1) the author of Chronicles used an earlier *redaction* of Kings, not simply a better *text* than the MT[58] and (2) the author of Chronicles often rewrites his source at theologically sensitive points in the story.[59] Thus, Chronicles may provide valuable evidence for textual criticism, but it is not simply another textual witness. In the present case, 1 Kings 8:16 is exactly the type of text we should have expected the Chronicler to rewrite because it touches on particularly important themes in his work: the house of David, Jerusalem, and the temple. Indeed, 1 Kings 8 itself already evidences a highly edited text, with a long history of inner-textual interpretation before it reaches the form we know in the Masoretic tradition. In sum, there is no compelling reason to believe that 4QKgs represents the urtext, if we can speak of such a thing.[60]

The next question is how the addition in 4QKgs materially affects the literary reading of Solomon's Prayer here. This has been answered by Gary Knoppers, who accepts without question the 4QKgs reading. Knoppers suggests that "the Deuteronomist actually champions the novelty of the deity's choice of ruler and city."[61] Yes, but this hardly acknowledges the fundamental rewriting of the Promise! Knoppers argues, "The MT as it stands contains a *non sequitur*. YHWH responds to his previous history of never electing a city by electing David."[62] Yet, the non sequitur basically follows the narrative line of 2 Samuel 7:5–16. In the Promise to David, there is no hint that the city of Jerusalem was *chosen*. The language of a *chosen* city derives from Deuteronomy 12. Indeed, the point was that no location was chosen to house the tabernacle permanently (2 Sam 7:6). Yet, since the longer version in 4QKgs depends on Deuteronomy 12, one plausible explanation of the manuscript might associate it with the Josianic redaction of Kings. This, however, is hardly conclusive. It is just as likely that 4QKgs represents a later postexilic elaboration. The exact mechanics of the omission in the MT, partial omission in LXX, and preservation in Chronicles remains a mystery. Perhaps it did arise from purely mechanical errors in the MT and LXX. More likely, these changes were at least subconsciously theologically motivated; that is, a mechanical error may have been subconsciously conditioned by theological beliefs—"Freudian" slips. In this particular case, textual criticism reveals as much or more about the hermeneutic processes as it does about textual history.

Allusion to the Promise in Dtr¹: The Lamp of David

The Deuteronomistic Historian (Dtr¹) alludes to the Promise particularly in references to the perseverance of the dynasty, or "the Lamp of David."[63] The Promise to David is circumvented by the prophecy of Abijah, which in turn will allow one tribe remaining as "a lamp" for David (1 Kgs 11:34–36).

> 34Nevertheless I will not take the whole kingdom away from him but will make him ruler all the days of his life, for the sake of my servant David whom I chose and who did keep my commandments and my statutes; 35but I will take the kingdom away from his son and give it to you—that is, the ten tribes. 36Yet to his son I will give one tribe, so that my servant David may always have a *lamp* (ניר) before me in Jerusalem, the city where I have chosen to put my name.

The promise of a "lamp" (ניר) for David must depend on the Promise to David. It is characterized by the premise that *God chose both David and Jerusalem*. This interpretation then forms a *leitmotif* in DtrH (cf. 1 Kgs 14:21; 15:4; 2 Kgs 8:19; 19:34; 20:6; 21:7). The lamp for David is contextualized by the division of the kingdom. It should not be surprising then that the *leitmotif* appears in the accession formula of the first king of the *divided* kingdom, Rehoboam: "Now Rehoboam son of Solomon reigned in Judah. Rehoboam was forty-one years old when he began to reign, and he reigned seventeen years in Jerusalem, the city that YHWH had chosen out of all the tribes of Israel, to put his name there (1 Kgs 14:21)." This is the only place where Jerusalem is modified appositionally within the accession formula as the place God chose to put his name. That God chose (√בחר) Jerusalem picks up the concluding words of Abijah's promise (v. 36) and the second address of Solomon's Prayer (1 Kgs 8:16–21). The leitmotif continues through DtrH until Josiah's reign, but continues no further—for obvious reasons. It assumes the continued existence of the Davidic kingdom. As such, this theme would pose a significant problem for the Jewish people in the exile. Apparently, God had snuffed out the lamp from David and Jerusalem. Prophecy had failed. In light of this, we must consider this reading of the Promise—namely, that God had chosen both David and Jerusalem—as preexilic. The fact that the motif continues up to the reign of Josiah suggests that it formed part of the Josianic redactor's reading of the Promise. The continued existence of Judah after the fall of Samaria and the invasion of Sennacherib undoubtedly gave impetus to this motif. This is even suggested by the repetition of the motif within the account of Hezekiah's reign. First, in the face of Sennacherib's onslaught, we initially read, "For I will defend this city to save it, for my own sake and for the sake of my servant David" (2 Kgs 19:34). Then, after the narrative recounts Sennacherib's withdrawal the prophet Isaiah promises somewhat anachronistically: "I will deliver you and this city out of the hand of the king of Assyria; I will defend this city for my own sake and for my servant David's sake" (2 Kgs 20:6; cf. Isa 38:6).[64] It is difficult to know exactly the source of the lamp metaphor, but it updates the Davidic Promise so that it is relevant only to the tribe of Judah and Jerusalem. This marks a sharp break with the attempt to integrate the north by an appeal to the Promise to David after the fall of Samaria. Now, the Promise is only for the tribe of Judah and Jerusalem.

Allusion to the Promise in Dtr^{1}: The "Sure House"

In three places, DtrH uses the expression "a sure house" alluding to the Promise. This expression recalls 2 Samuel 7:16: "Your house and your kingdom *will be sure* forever before me" (ונאמן ביתך וממלכתך עד־עולם ‹לפני›).[65] The most direct allusion is 1 Samuel 25:28, when Abigail attempts to allay David's anger against her foolish husband, "Please forgive the trespass of your servant; for YHWH will certainly make my lord a sure house (בית נאמן), because my lord is fighting the battles of YHWH; and evil shall not be found in you so long as you live." Abigail thus foreshadows Nathan's prophecy, albeit without the forecast of perpetuity.

The promised perpetuity of the Davidic dynasty is revised by the prophet Ahijah the Shilohite in 1 Kings 11:29–40. There, the prophet promises Jeroboam: "If you will listen to all that I command you, walk in my ways, and do what is right in my sight by keeping my statutes and my commandments, as David my servant did, I will be with you, and I will build you a sure house (בית נאמן), as I built for David, and I will give Israel to you" (1 Kgs 11:38). The Promise is applied conditionally to Jeroboam's dynasty and the northern kingdom. Although there have been attempts to isolate a pre-Deuteronomic prophetic source here,[66] there is clear Deuteronomic language in Ahijah's prophecy.[67] As I pointed out previously, the promise of a "lamp" also appears to be a leitmotif in Dtr^{1}. Without objective criteria, by which I mean obvious editorial or redactional markers, it is impossible to subdivide Ahijah's prophecy into sources. Undoubtedly, Jeroboam needed to support his newly established kingdom, and Ahijah's prophecy probably does originate in some early northern tradition supporting the foundation of the northern kingdom. In its present guise, however, such a tradition is not recoverable. In its canonical form, the Ahijah prophecy focuses on Jeroboam—a figure critical to the Josianic historian's rendering of history (e.g., 1 Kgs 13:2). Jeroboam's failure is the counterpoint to the Josianic reforms. The demise of his kingdom is set in sharp relief by the enduring house of David.[68]

The most intriguing use of the expression "a sure house" occurs in an oracle against Eli's priestly family. In 1 Samuel 2:35, we read, "I will raise up for myself a faithful priest (והקימתי לי כהן נאמן), who shall do according to what is in my heart and in my mind. I will build him a sure house (ובניתי לו בית נאמן), and he shall go in and out before my anointed one (משיחי) all the days." Here, a dynastic-like Promise is unexpectedly applied to the priesthood. From a narrative viewpoint, this allusion (also 1 Sam 25:28) precedes the actual Promise to David. The question then becomes, What is its relationship to the Promise? It is difficult to find any objective criteria for assigning a date. Tryggve Mettinger would date it to the Solomonic period and associate its composition with an early rivalry among the priesthood.[69] Timo Veijola states, "Die Ankündigung des beständigen Priesterhauses 1Sam 2:35 gehört zu den Jugendgeschichten Samuels 1Sam 1–3." [70] But how can such a position be substantiated? While Kyle McCarter argues that the Eli narrative "functioned in the pre-Deuteronomic prophetic history," he also notes that the consequence of this prophecy—namely, that Eli's family would need to beg for food from the priestly portions—was fulfilled in the Josianic reforms (cf. 1 Sam 2:36 with 2 Kgs 23:9). McCarter concludes, "This passage is replete with the devices and clichés of the Josianic historian."[71] In other words, in its present form 1 Samuel 2:35 derives from Dtr[1], whatever its origin.

Psalm 89:19–37 [MT, 20–38]: Citation and Revision

> 19Then you spoke in a vision to your faithful one, and said:
> "I have set the crown on one who is mighty,
> I have exalted one chosen from the people.
> 20I have found my servant David;
> with my holy oil I have anointed him;
> 21my hand shall always remain with him;
> my arm also shall strengthen him.
> 22The enemy shall not outwit him,
> the wicked shall not humble him.
> 23I will crush his foes before him
> and strike down those who hate him.
> 24My faithfulness and steadfast love shall be with him;
> and in my name his horn shall be exalted.
> 25I will set his hand on the sea
> and his right hand on the rivers.
> 26He shall cry to me, 'You are my Father, my God,
> and the Rock of my salvation!'
> 27I will make him the firstborn,
> the highest of the kings of the earth.
> 28Forever I will keep my steadfast love for him,
> and my covenant with him will stand firm.
> 29I will establish his line forever,
> and his throne as long as the heavens endure.
> 30If his children forsake my law
> and do not walk according to my ordinances,
> 31if they violate my statutes
> and do not keep my commandments,
> 32then I will punish their transgression with the rod
> and their iniquity with scourges;
> 33but I will not remove from him my steadfast love,
> or be false to my faithfulness.
> 34I will not violate my covenant,
> or alter the word that went forth from my lips.
> 35Once and for all I have sworn by my holiness;
> I will not lie to David.
> 36His line shall continue forever,
> and his throne endure before me like the sun.
> 37It shall be established forever like the moon,
> an enduring witness in the skies." Selah.

Psalm 89, particularly in its second (vv. 19–37 [MT 20–38]) part, represents the most sustained reflection on the Promise to David. I proposed (in chapter 2) that the three parts of the psalm reflect three separate stages in the development of the psalm. I argued that the first section (i.e., the initial hymn, vv. 3–18) should be contextualized within the early monarchy. The second part is marked off from the previous hymn by the term "then" (אז) in verse 19. It is further marked off from the subsequent section by the enigmatic term *Selah* and the disjunctive expression, "But now you" (ואתה), which begins the third part in verse 38. Presently, I argue that the second part should be placed within the turbulent years of the Josianic reforms.

The key that unlocks the dating of this second part is the partial conditionalization of the Promise in verses 30–37. The poet writes, "If his children forsake my law . . . then I will punish their transgression"; however, still YHWH maintains his promise, "I will not remove from him my steadfast love; . . . His line shall continue forever and his throne endure before me like the sun." On the one hand, the poet acknowledges that the *sons* of David may be reprimanded, yet on the other hand the *dynasty* shall endure forever. It is important to note that both *lineage* and *throne* endure. The throne is the symbol of the sitting monarch; in other words, there is still a Davidic kingdom in the author's worldview. Whereas there can be a continuation of the *lineage* of David without a sitting king or actual kingdom, the symbol of the throne points to the continuing Davidic kingdom. This would not be natural to an exilic or postexilic author. Why, then, the image of punishment? Three possible referents spring immediately to mind. First, there is the division of the Davidic kingdom under Rehoboam. Two more events are closer chronologically to the readers: the invasion of Sennacherib and its attendant destruction, although this destruction did not touch the Davidic monarch himself, and, more pointedly, the assassination of Amon and his replacement by the eight-year-old boy Josiah must have sent shock waves through the kingdom. The assassination of the monarch throws the succession into question. The explanation for Amon's assassination would certainly be summarized by the Josianic reformers as resulting from that—in the words of Psalm 89—"his children forsook YHWH's law, did not obey His ordinances, violated His statutes, and did not obey His commandments" (vv. 30–31). The depiction of a monarch disobeying the Law on the one hand and yet the insistence nevertheless on the endurance of the Davidic line and throne can be contextualized only in the period of Josiah.

The conditionalization in Psalm 89:30–37 introduces the concept of fidelity to Deuteronomic law into the Promise. A new emphasis can be seen by comparing Psalm 89 with 2 Samuel 7:14–15:

2 Samuel 7	*Psalm 89*
14when he commits iniquity (בהעותו), I will punish him with a rod such as mortals use, with blows inflicted by human beings.	30If his children forsake my law (תורתי) and do not walk according to my ordinances (משפטי), 31if they violate my statutes (חקתי) and do not keep my commandments (מצותי), 32then I will punish their transgression with the rod and their iniquity with scourges;

[15]But I will not take my steadfast love from him, as I took it from Saul, whom I put away from before you.	[33]but I will not remove from him my steadfast love, or be false to my faithfulness. [34]I will not violate my covenant, or alter the word that went forth from my lips. [35]Once and for all I have sworn by my holiness; I will not lie to David. [36]His dynasty (זרעו) shall continue forever, and his throne endure before me like the sun. 37 It shall be established forever like the moon, an enduring witness in the skies.

Psalm 89:30–32 replaces the ambiguous "commit iniquity" with the specific offenses which warrant punishment. Verses 33–37 are concerned with the fate of David's sons in contrast to 2 Samuel 7:15, which is particularly concerned with the fate of Saul. The particular litany of law, ordinances, statues, and commandments is typical Deuteronomic language, which itself suggests an affinity to the Josianic reforms (e.g., Deut 5:31: 6:1; 7:11; 1 Kgs 8:58; 2 Kgs 17:37).[72] The *prophetic* Promise to David comes under the strictures of false prophecy (Deut 18:18–22), hence God "will not violate his covenant, or alter his word" concerning the Davidic throne. Such Deuteronomic strictures about the prophetic word underscore the literary character of the Promise, which must be fulfilled according to the letter of the written word. The emphasis on the perpetuity of the Promise to David's sons, in spite of punishment for violation of the Deuteronomic law, points to a period when the Davidic monarch might be perceived as punished, yet there was a continuing issue of succession. All this fits nicely into the days of Josiah. After all, Josiah comes to the throne after the assassination of King Amon. The unorthodox succession must have raised questions: Why was the Davidic monarch assassinated? Who is the rightful successor? These are the kind of questions Psalm 89:30–37 answers. Psalm 89:30–37 assumes the existence of the monarchy, even while making clear that the monarch is obliged to follow the Deuteronomic law.

Psalm 89:25–26 makes a slight but important revision of the adoption formula from 2 Samuel 7:14. The comparison can be facilitated by placing them side-by-side:

2 Samuel 7:14a	*Psalm 89:25–26*
"I will be a father to him,	He shall cry to me, 'You are my father, my God, and the rock of my salvation!'
and he shall be a son to me."	I will make him the firstborn, the highest of the kings of the earth.

Psalm 89 actually seems to develop out of the *Sitz im Leben* of a royal coronation or perhaps an annual festival celebration of the coronation (cp. Psalm 2). The first part, verse 25, emphasizes the role of God as deliverer. This may have been intended to dismiss any possibility that the king could be understood as the actual son of God (and therefore, perhaps, divine). The second verse emphasizes the king's relationship to all the kings of the earth. In this context, the change from "son" to "firstborn" reflects an attempt to single out the Davidide king from all the neighboring nations. Perhaps we may summarize the reading as one legitimate king, one legitimate temple.

Religion and Interpretation

The rise of the Assyrian empire transformed the landscape of the Near East. For Judah, it would lead to a rapid urbanization and centralization of power in Jerusalem. These factors altered the social structure and political fabric of the isolated little kingdom centered in Jerusalem. Power shifted from the periphery to the center. At the same time, refugees, political contacts with Assyria, and a broadening network of commerce together brought a deluge of foreign cultural influences. Religious movements proliferated in the early seventh century. The Josianic religious reforms represent a backlash against both the proliferation of religious movements in Judah and the breakdown of traditional political and social structure in Judah.

The temple became a focal point of the Josianic reforms. It, first of all, became a symbol of the new orthodoxy. Centralization, which may be attributed to essentially political and social factors beginning in the early eighth century, became a religious tool, enforcing the new orthodoxy. Centralization itself, however, was a social and political fact that began in the late eighth century. The Assyrian empire conditioned the rapid urbanization of Jerusalem and a centralization of political power. The Assyrians strictly circumscribed the borders of Judah. As a result, the promised "place" from 2 Samuel 7:10, "I will appoint a *place* (מקום) for my people Israel and will plant them," could hardly be understood by the Deuteronomists as anything other than Jerusalem. Indeed, it was only Jerusalem that YHWH had delivered from Sennacherib.

Two themes are reflected in Josianic reception and transmission of the Promise during the late seventh century. First, there is a concern to include the temple "for YHWH's name" as part of the Promise. Deuteronomic name theology is usually understood as opposing the patently anthropomorphic priestly viewpoint which derived from early sacral conceptions (e.g., 1 Sam 4:4; 2 Sam 6:2; Ps 80:2).[73] Von Rad, for example, argued that the Deuteronomic terminology was intended to combat the popular belief that YHWH actually dwelled in the temple.[74] Actually, the idea of a name being associated with a place is attested already in the Jerusalem Amarna Letters (e.g., EA 287:60–61; 288:5–7). The language apparently derives from Akkadian royal inscriptions in which the king establishes his name in a particular locale. As such, it maintains the king's dominion and exclusive claim over the place. The abstraction of the name was a later development within the Deuteronomistic literature. The idea of the temple as a place for YHWH's name within the context of the Josianic religious reforms undoubtedly intended to affirm YHWH's exclusive right against other deities. We read, for example, in 2 Kings 21:7: "The carved image of Asherah that [Manasseh] had made he set in the house of which YHWH said to David and to his son Solomon, 'In this house, and in Jerusalem, which I have chosen out of all the tribes of Israel, I will put my name forever.' " The sin of Manasseh is herein depicted as abrogating YHWH's exclusive claim to Jerusalem and the temple. Deuteronomic name theology in the Josianic reforms then was aimed specifically at YHWH's exclusive presence in the temple and not initially intended as an abstraction of YHWH's presence in the temple.

The second theme reflected in Josianic articulation of the Promise is a concern for the king's obedience to Deuteronomic law. In a new twist, the Promise is no longer conditionalized by generic "iniquity" but more specifically by the Deuteronomic teachings. This specific condition should hardly be surprising because Deuteronomy requires the king to write for himself a copy of the law and study it all the days of his life (Deut 17:18–20; cf. Josh 1:8). What was the "iniquity" referred to by the Promise (2 Sam 7:15)? For the Deuteronomists, it could be only transgression of their laws. With this condition, Josiah's supporters could also explain the fate of certain kings who did not follow Deuteronomic law; particularly, the assassination of Manasseh's son Amon and his replacement with the juvenile Josiah must have raised questions about legitimate succession. As a result, the Josianic reading nevertheless dwells on the perpetuity of the Promise to *one of David's sons*. The Promise continues for David and his sons.

The limitation of royal power in Deuteronomic literature is a somewhat unexpected development. At the same time, if my reconstruction of the sociopolitical context of the Josianic reforms is correct, this limitation should not be entirely unexpected. After all, the Josianic reforms arise as a reaction to the centralization of political power that accompanied the demographic and social changes in Judaean society. The seventh century saw a centralization of power in the cities in general and Jerusalem in particular. The clan structure of the early monarchical period broke down with the movement toward urbanization and with the influx of foreigners (both settlers and merchants) into Judah. The marginalization of the more traditional structures of Judaean society eventually resulted in a backlash, which we call the Josianic reforms. It begins with the "people of the land" stepping in, just as they had in the days of Queen Athaliah, to install a new child king, and this new juvenile monarch ostensibly reorganizes the power structure of Judah. Deuteronomic ideology justifies and shapes this social and political backlash. Although the Josianic reforms in fact radically changed Judaean religion, this is certainly not the way they conceived of their reforms. They were restoring old-time religion. They were turning back the clock, restoring the old order.

The seminal changes in Judaean society actually began a century earlier with the rise of Assyrian domination. The centralization of the cult was, in fact, made possible by the demographic and political centralization of the late eighth and seventh centuries. The Josianic reformers were actually trying to return to the good old days. Such a return was, of course, impossible. The centralization of the cult was an attempt to regulate Judaean religious life and bring it back to its Yahwistic roots by eradicating the foreign cultural and political influences of the last century. Ironically, the centralization of the cult became the most radical change of all.

5

"By the Waters of Babylon": The Promise Fails

How lonely sits the city that once was full of people! –Lamentations 1:1

The Babylonian exile is a watershed in the history of the Jewish people. The Davidic kingdom had come to an end. The Jerusalem temple was in ruins; the people, exiled. Although many remained in the land, life could not continue as normal. The social institutions of monarchy and temple that had dominated Judaean life for four centuries had vanished. A new imperial world order replaced them. Key religious, commercial, and administrative leaders were either killed, exiled, or fled to Egypt. Life could not continue as it had before. The Babylonian exile precipitated a crisis that affected the sense of meaning and order.[1] Not the least of the crisis was the failure of the Promise to David as it had come to be read. The Promise was a focal point for the institutional structure of Judah by the late monarchy, and consequently the need to make sense of the Promise during this crisis was acute. In the present chapter, we begin with observations about the sociopolitical context of the Babylonian exile before moving on to a specific analysis of the Promise.

The disappearance of the social structures of ancient Israel forced a radical and mysterious rereading of the Promise. How could the Promise be read in the absence of the Davidic monarchy and the Jerusalem temple? To begin with, the Promise could not fail because it was YHWH's Promise. If it failed, so did the credibility of Israel's God. Out of this quandary was born the concept of the inscrutability of the divine Word. God's words, his prophetic Promise to David, were beyond simple human comprehension. YHWH's Promise was still being fulfilled, though mysteriously, through the agent of Cyrus and through YHWH's people.

Exile and Crisis

The extent of the Babylonian exile and its importance to the history of the Jewish people have recently reemerged. A question arises, first of all, from archaeological evidence highlighting continuity between the Iron IIIa (701–586 BCE) and Iron IIIb (586–539 BCE) periods—that is, between the late Judaean monarchy and the Babylonian periods.[2] To be sure, the evidence for continuity should not be surprising. Even biblical literature suggests as much. Both Kings and Jeremiah testify that there was a remnant left in the land from the "poorest people of the land":

> But some of the poorest in the land were left by the chief of the guards, to be vinedressers and field hands (2 Kgs 25:12).

> This is the number of those whom Nebuchadrezzar exiled in the seventh year: 3,023 Judaeans. In the eighteenth year of Nebuchadrezzar, 832 persons were exiled from Jerusalem. And in the twenty-third year of Nebuchadrezzar, Nebuzaradan, the chief of the guards, exiled 745 Judaeans. The total amounted to 4,600 persons (Jer 52:28–30).

Peasant farmers were left to cultivate the land. They had to be substantial in number in order to properly perform this essential task. These people came to be identified with the "people of the land" (עם הארץ; cf. 2 Kgs 24:4; 25:3; Hag 2:4; Zech 7:5; Ezra 4:4). The Babylonians were not interested in having the land lay fallow; they needed the agricultural production for their infrastructure—particularly for their ambition to control Egypt. And, if we look at the numbers of exiles suggested by Jeremiah, this could hardly have amounted to more than 10% of the population. To be sure, a large number of Judaeans were killed in the Babylonian campaigns, and perhaps even greater numbers fled the country to Egypt and elsewhere. Archaeological surveys do indicate a precipitous depopulation in the Babylonian period,[3] although by no means was the land empty.

The recent study by Hans Barstad exemplifies the current trend to minimize the Babylonian exile. Barstad examines what he has termed "the myth of the empty land"[4] and emphasizes the biblical, archaeological, and comparative evidence for continuity in Palestine during the Babylonian period (ca. 586–538 BCE). Barstad presumes that "this society must have consisted not only of peasants. . . , but also of artisans, traders, village and town elders, scribes, priests and prophets."[5] His approach moderates C. C. Torrey's arguments positing that the exile and return were fictions of the Persian period. Barstad, however, overstates the continuity. To begin with, he never reflects on the *type* of continuity. He also relies on questionable assumptions; for example, he writes, "With the majority of people still left in the country, obviously all the basic organizations continued much in the same way."[6] Despite the definite continuity in the material culture after 586 BCE, the cessation of the Davidic dynasty and temple after four centuries alone justifies the traditional model. By analogy, there was continuity in the material culture of post-World War II Germany and Japan, but who would argue that life quickly returned to normal? In another place, Barstad admonishes that we need to consider the perspective of the Babylonians. To continue the analogy, however, how much time must be devote to the perspective of the Germans as opposed to the Polish during World War II? In any case, the present study focuses on the literary history of the Promise and consequently needs to focus on the perspective of the Judaeans. In Judah, there was mass exodus by flight, mass destruction of cities, towns, and villages; and a significant exile of the most important and skilled individuals in Judaean society. Amihai Mazar summarizes the situation:

> Most of the Judaean towns and fortresses excavated in the Shephelah, the Negev, and the Judaean Desert were destroyed during the Babylonian invasion. . . . All the fortresses and towns of the northern Negev, and the fortress at Kadesh-Barnea, were devastated, perhaps by the Edomites who invaded the region following the Babylonian conquests in the heart of Judah.[7]

Life does not go on as normal in the face of this kind of mass destruction and political upheaval. Although Barstad is certainly correct that the myth of an empty land served the ideology of Ezra by giving the returnees a privileged place in the revitalized community, the Babylonian invasion was nevertheless a significant disjunction.

Second, this "myth of the empty land" also raises the question of *whose* "horizon of expectations" we are reconstructing. Who are the readers of the texts? Who shaped the intellectual and cultural history of postexilic Judaism? To understand the literary history of the Promise we must focus particularly on the community that read and used the literature. Although such a procedure will not give a full picture of the Babylonian period, this is not the present objective. The extant literature in which Promise to David was received and transmitted is limited to the postexilic returnees. To be sure, the fact that these returnees actually may have been a minority—considerable as they might have been—is itself important for understanding their use of the Promise to David. *A priori* it would suggest that their use of the Promise is partly intended to justify their own ideology against the "people of the land."

The book of Ezra pits the returnees against the "people of the land," who oppose the reconstruction of the temple: "Thereon the people of the land undermined the resolve of the people of Judah, and made them afraid to build" (4:4). From this, it is apparent that the people who remained in the land were opposed to the rebuilding of the temple. This opposition is undoubtedly reflected in the book of Haggai, which highlights an apathy toward rebuilding the temple in the early Persian period. The apology for the rebuilt temple in the books of Chronicles, then, should be largely set against this backdrop.

The Psychology of Exile and Mass Destruction

The crisis that ensued following the Babylonian exile should occasion some reflection on the psychology of exile. One illuminating study of the Babylonian exile is Daniel Smith's *The Religion of the Landless: The Social Context of the Babylonian Exile*. Smith takes a comparative anthropological approach to the exile. He argues that the most accurate basis from which to understand the exile is that of a minority community in "conditions of forced removal and settlement under imperial control and power."[8] Four case studies inform Smith's analysis: (1) Japanese-American internment during World War II, (2) South African movement of black Africans to Bantustans, (3) slave societies in the pre-Civil War United States, and (4) the 1950s movement of the population of the Bikini Islands by the United States n order to conduct atomic tests. Smith identifies four sociopsychological behaviors that recur in conditions of forced mass displacement:

1. Structural adaptation of leadership and authority patterns, as well as in the basic social units, as a conscious strategy of survival and resistance
2. Division in leadership between new leaders and old leaders, and between those advocating a strong, often violent, strategy of resistance and those advising social resistance
3. The creation or elaboration of patterns of ritual practice that emphasize resistance against foreign elements, often expressed in terms of purity and pollution
4. The creation of folk literature or folklore patterns, especially the "hero" story as a paradigm for the group

Smith understands these behaviors as mechanisms for survival employed by social groups to maintain their identity, social structure, and religious life during crisis. Applying these to ancient Israel, Smith suggests that social structural adaptation among the exiles led to large, fictitiously named "fathers' houses (בית אבות)" intended to preserve identity and facilitate self-management, while they coped with the economic and political demands of the exile. The prophetic leaders Jeremiah and Hananiah are viewed as reflecting the dichotomy between social resistance and violent physical resistance. Rituals of survival in the Priestly Code are interpreted as measures to ensure social "boundary maintenance," along the lines of Mary Douglas's work on purity and social threat.[9] Finally, the stories of Daniel and Joseph, as well as Isaiah's Suffering Servant, are seen as Diaspora "hero" stories depicting a hero rising to prominence in non-Jewish eyes. Most important, although there are various possible mechanisms for survival, they all inevitably lead toward a solidarity of the community and the creation of a "community of crisis." This community of crisis becomes critical for understanding not only the Babylonian exile but also the period of the return. The difficulties between those returning to Zion and those who remained in the land undoubtedly lie in the strong sense of community that necessarily developed in the Babylonian exile.

There are some problems with Smith's application of social anthropology to biblical texts. As Norman Gottwald notes, "The limits of Smith's project have their premise in his choice of a structural-functional paradigm rather than a historical-material paradigm."[10] There will be real questions, for example, about how much Japanese internment during World War II can really serve as a paradigm to explain the Babylonian exile. There are also questionable analyses of biblical texts, which can be illustrated by one example. On the one hand, Smith claims in his subtitle that he will be writing about "The Social Context of the Babylonian Exile." Yet, on the other hand, the examples he takes to illustrate the creation of a hero literature—namely, Daniel and Joseph—were probably not composed during the Babylonian Exile. Although the Daniel tales are set in the context of the Babylonian exile, the consensus of scholarship places their final composition in the second century BCE. Likewise, although it is difficult to precisely date the Joseph narratives (Genesis 37, 39–48), they seem to derive from the period of the late Judaean monarchy. In Smith's defense, both the respective historical contexts for the Daniel and Joseph stories fit many of the characteristics of social groups fighting to maintain their identity, social structure, and religious life. Moreover, Smith's comparative approach is intended to bring new perspectives to the text and is not forced wholesale onto the data.

The Babylonian exiles were a minority community in a foreign context, which naturally threatened their identity. One means for survival in this context is self-chosen isolation. A typical Diaspora maintains identity through sacred categories including language, myths, and Scriptures.[11] The ultimate survival of the exiled minority depends on the formation of a closely knit community with clearly marked social boundaries.

Although there is sparse evidence for life among the Babylonian exiles, one important source comes from the Murashu documents discovered in 1893 at Nippur. They contain the business records of a Jewish family, known as the "Murashu" family. The documents initially stirred up interest because of the presence of Jewish names among the onomasticon of some 2,500 names.

The onomasticon and the artistic traditions preserved in the Murashu documents provide clues to beliefs and customs, as well as to social pressures. In a comprehensive glyptic study of the Murashu documents, Linda Bregstein notes that Jews in particular avoided using representations of Babylonian religious themes: "It is striking that none of the Jews used a seal with a Babylonian worship scene, a religious ritual that they perhaps deemed inappropriate for the personal emblem of a non-Babylonian. Also, the Jews did not care for scenes featuring typically Babylonian fantastic winged animals or composite monsters, although these creatures did appear in their contest scenes."[12] Bregstein's study nicely dovetails with the evidence from onomastic studies of the Murashu archive. It certainly lends more credence to an early study by Samuel Daiches that concluded, "The Babylonian Jews were firm in their belief in God and were greatly attached to their land and brethren."[13]

The increasing importance of the Sabbath in the Diaspora is reflected in sudden preference for the name Sabtai.[14] The Sabbath no doubt functioned on the one hand to mark a social boundary and on the other hand to create a new sense of meaning and order to replace the institutions of monarchy and temple. Jews in Nippur especially favored ambiguous names.[15] Hence, in the Murashu documents many fathers named their sons Jacob, which is a traditional Jewish name, but whose popularity is undoubtedly related to the similar sounding but unrelated Akkadian verb *qabû* used in personal names of the Neo-Babylonian period. Similarly, the increased preference for the divine element *'el*, which sounded similar to Akkadian *ilu*, in personal names was probably intentionally ambiguous.

The Murashu family probably typifies one aspect of the exilic community—namely, the formation of social groups. As already mentioned, the formation of groups with distinct social boundaries was necessary for the survival of the exiles' group identity,—that is, their Jewish identity. Distinct onomastic and iconographic traditions are evidence—albeit scant evidence—of social boundaries of the exiled Jewish community. The prophets Jeremiah and Ezekiel both mentioned leadership by the "elders" among the exilic community (Jer 29:1; Ezek 8:1; 20:3).[16] Daniel Smith points out the diminishing role for the elders and emphasizes the growing importance of the *Bêt Abôt* (i.e., בית אבות "house of the Fathers") as an organizational division and form of self-government among the exiles. The *Bêt Abôt* appear only after the Babylonian exile. This is indicated by the fact that the group is almost completely absent in DtrH yet appear frequently in the books of Chronicles, Ezra, and Nehemiah.[17] Smith also observes that in postexilic literature: "The elders, while always present, appear to have become less involved."[18] The new organization, the *Bêt Abôt,* was a fictive kin group, and the familial terms of the groups were imposed to assure the survival of the bands of exiles who settled together.[19] The Persians actually encouraged the preservation of such ethnicities as a means of organizing collectives for the purposes of taxation and administration.[20]

The Murashu archives identify one locus of Jewish exiles in the region of Nippur. Their settlement here was part of Babylonian economic policies, which called for the resettlement of workers for building projects. Robert Adams notes that "available documentary evidence suggest that large masses of people were involuntarily transferred as part of intensive neo-Babylonian efforts to rehabilitate the central region of a domain that previously had suffered severely."[21] In the case of the Nippur region, this involved a large canal project on the Kabur River. The prophet Ezekiel was among a group of Judaean exiles who were settled on the Kabur River and probably worked on the major canal projects.[22] There is little doubt that the Judaean exiles were forced to labor on these government projects, and biblical references to forced labor and the oppression of captivity must reflect at least in part the exiles' experience in government construction projects (e.g., Ezek 34:27; Isa 47:6). Psalm 137 actually hints at the work of the Judaean exiles on such a canal project: "*By the rivers of Babylon* (על נהרות בבל)—there we settled down and also we wept when we remembered Zion. . . . For there our captors (שובינו) asked us for songs, and our taskmasters (ותוללינו) asked for mirth, saying, 'Sing us one of the songs of Zion!' " (vv. 1, 3). The locus of the exiles' torment is "by the rivers of Babylon." This suggests the exiles were settled along rivers, but not necessarily in Babylon. The Babylonians are their "captors" (שבה) and "taskmasters" (תולל). The latter term is a hapax legomenon whose etymology has been the subject of some discussion; however, it is clear that it refers to enslavement.[23] The exiles were an oppressed and dominated minority, struggling to maintain their identity "by the rivers of Babylon."

The rise of the synagogue is often placed in the exilic period.[24] The evidence for this, however, quite meager. The reasoning is that the destruction of the temple created a void that had to be filled. The synagogue filled this void. While the reasoning seems sound enough, there is little evidence to lend support. The socioreligious transition from temple to synagogue must already have begun with the Josianic reforms, which wiped out local sanctuaries and would have necessitated the rise of an institution like the synagogue in their place. In this regard, Jon Levenson points to 1 Kings 8, Solomon's Prayer, as critical for understanding the early history of the synagogue. The emphasis there (see discussion later) on praying toward Jerusalem and the temple certainly foreshadows one of the main roles of the synagogue as a place for prayer. There is, nevertheless, no evidence for the synagogue as an *institution*. It is likely that this developed only later.

The Supposed Inviolability of Zion

The notion of the inviolability of Zion probably contributed to the ultimate destruction of Jerusalem. According to the prophet Jeremiah, the people of Jerusalem had a firmly held conviction that the temple and the city that God had chosen would be saved: "When I spoke to you persistently, you did not listen, and when I called you, you did not answer, therefore I will do to the house that is called by my name, *in which you trust,* and to the place that I gave to you and to your ancestors, just what I did to Shiloh" (Jer 7:13–14). Already the explicit confidence in the inviolability of Zion appears in the book of the prophet Micah, the younger contemporary of Isaiah, accusing the people of Jerusalem of saying, "Surely YHWH is with us! No harm shall come on us" (3:11), but Micah predicts that "Zion shall be plowed as a field; Jerusalem shall become a heap of ruins, and the mountain of the house a wooded height" (v. 12).

The origins of Zion theology are often placed in the period of David and Solomon,[25] and the tradition of the inviolability of Zion is often explicitly connected with Zion theology. However, there is no reason that the two must have arisen together. Even if we accept the comparative arguments that ancient Canaanite mythic elements were part and parcel of Zion theology, the tradition of Zion's inviolability was not part of the Canaanite background of the Zion tradition.

It seems more likely that the tradition of Zion's inviolability should be related to the unexpected survival of Jerusalem in the days of Sennacherib. Whatever the facts of that episode, the people of Jerusalem perceived it as a miraculous deliverance. A form of this tradition even trickled down to the Greek historian Herodotus (II, 141). At the very least, the tradition of a miraculous deliverance of Jerusalem must have contributed to a growing sense of Zion's inviolability in the last days of Jerusalem. One theme of the Josianic historian—namely, the "lamp for the sake of David and Jerusalem" (1 Kgs 11:36; 15:4; 2 Kgs 8:19)—was part and parcel of this inviolability tradition.

Ultimately, the origins of the Zion theory are irrelevant to the present study. What is important is that the theology of Zion's inviolability reached its zenith in the late Judaean monarchy. For example, in the Josianic historian's rendition of the Prayer of Solomon, we read, "Now YHWH has upheld the promise that he made; for I have risen in the place of my father David; I sit on the throne of Israel, as YHWH promised, *and have built the house for the name of YHWH, the God of Israel*" (1 Kgs 8:20). The fulfillment of the Promise to David included the building of the Jerusalem temple (see further chapter 4). And both David and Jerusalem are spared from the fate of Samaria, according to the Josianic historian by the Promise: "for the sake of David" and "Jerusalem where I put my name" (e.g., 1 Kgs 11:13; 15:4; 2 Kgs 19:34; 21:4). The prophet Jeremiah in particular must contend with those who rely on this promised temple. The prophet warns those who trust in the promised temple, "Go now to my place that was in Shiloh, where I made my name dwell at first, and see what I did to it for the wickedness of my people Israel" (Jer

7:12). It would seem that the belief in Zion's inviolability, both in the Promise to David and the temple, were quite entrenched in seventh-century Judaean society, which made the destruction of the temple and exile all the more catastrophic.

When Prophecy Fails

The impact of the Babylonian conquest on the psyche of the Judaeans cannot be understated. The Promise had failed. Robert Carroll writes, "The destruction of Jerusalem in 587 must have deeply disappointed those who believed that the city was inviolable because it was YHWH's residence. Disintegration of cult, community and city must have created serious dissonance for any Judaeans who expected YHWH to intervene on their behalf to defend his people."[26] Carroll goes on to point out that prophecy itself as a social movement was threatened by the catastrophe (cf. Lam 2:14; Ps 74:9). Indeed, the end of prophecy has been linked to the demise of the monarchy, not only by scholars but also by the rabbis.[27] Prophecy ended because it failed. But did prophecy fail? And if it did, how is it that it survived? These questions set within the context of the Babylonian exile provide fertile ground for applying the social psychological theory of cognitive dissonance.

In the 1950s, the theory of cognitive dissonance was first articulated by Leon Festinger, a professor of psychology.[28] The theory grew out of social psychological work in the principles of consistency, balance, and congruity. The heart of the theory is observation of human behavior when two cognitions are in conflict—that is, dissonance. In the present case, the eternal Promise to David's sons and the end of the monarchy. According to Festinger, people invariably try to avoid, reduce, or resolve dissonance. This theory produced a flood of studies and has become a watershed for the study of social psychology: "No theory in social psychology has stimulated more research than the theory of cognitive dissonance."[29] Cognitive dissonance theory had its heyday in the 1960s and early 70s, but fell into disuse until recently. Elliot Aronson points out that cognitive dissonance theory is still basic to social psychology and is currently enjoying a resurgence, though under a variety of new names.[30]

Cognitive dissonance conditions a number of responses: (1) avoidance, (2) rationalization, and (3) social support. Whatever has produced or may produce dissonance must be avoided. Avoidance, however, is not always simple. In the case of ancient Judah, the Babylonian exile created a dissonance between the Promise and reality. The social support group is paradoxically both the main cause of cognitive dissonance and the major vehicle for alleviating dissonance. Festinger points out that, ironically, disconfirmation can result in deepened conviction. This scenario is dependent on a number of conditions: (1) a belief must be held with deep conviction and must have some relevance to how the believer behaves; (2) the believer must be committed to the belief in a way that is difficult to undo, and the more difficult to undo, the greater the commitment to the belief; (3) the belief must be sufficiently specific that it may be unequivocally refuted; (4) the refutation of the belief must be recognized by the believer; and (5) the individual believer must have social support. All these conditions are met by the Promise in the aftermath of the temple's destruction and the end of the monarchy.

The first attempt to apply dissonance theory to biblical texts was Robert Carroll's *When Prophecy Failed.* Carroll suggested that the "concern with consistency (consonance) between expectation and experience, and the avoidance or reduction of inconsistency, makes the theory eminently suitable for the analysis of predictive prophecy in terms of responses to problems of realized expectations."[31] Carroll applies this approach to Isaiah 40–66. Following the traditional division of the book of Isaiah, he sees in Second Isaiah (40–55) an anonymous prophet who "greeted the rise of Cyrus to power as the occasion of YHWH's salvation of community and city."[32] Second Isaiah's "oracles were an attempt to resolve the dissonance caused by the continued failure of the positive aspects of prophecy by identifying the release of the Babylonian captives with the expected salvation."[33] Ironically, Carroll sees a gap between the proclamation of Second Isaiah and the reality, which created only greater dissonance. Third Isaiah (56–66) then tries to reduce some of the dissonance. According to Carroll, Third Isaiah issues from Second Isaiah's followers, who "accepted the truth of their master's vision" and therefore "had to show how that expectation was true but had not yet materialized."[34]

While Carroll's analysis is insightful, it is difficult to agree with his premise that the expectations of Second Isaiah had not materialized. On the contrary, by focusing so sharply on the figure of Cyrus as the agent of God's salvation, the words of Second Isaiah ring all too true. The problem is then not unrealized expectations but rather how to rationalize the new expectations. Second Isaiah substitutes Cyrus and the people as a whole for the expected Davidic leader, the expected anointed one. This is accomplished through clever allusion to the "Branch" prophecy from Isaiah 11 in the Cyrus oracles on the one hand and the Suffering Servant theme on the other.[35] Then, the Promise is thus democratized and the Servant becomes all Israel. The Deuteronomist, on the other hand, will conditionalize the Promise. The exile thus becomes the expected result when one fails to keep the conditions of the Promise.

Reading a Promise in Crisis

Exilic literature had to come to grips with the destruction of the temple and the forced deportation of much of the population. The crisis itself precipitated the collection and editing of traditions that were in danger of being lost. As a result, the exilic period represents a particularly rich period for biblical literature, including the rewriting of DtrH, the editing of many prophetic books—particularly Isaiah and Jeremiah—and the composition of many psalms and the editing of the parts of the Psalter.

The Exilic Deuteronomic Readers (Dtr^2)

I have already dealt with the first two parts of Solomon's prayer at the dedication of the temple in 1 Kings 8. I have argued that these first two parts are preexilic (see chapters 1 and 3). The third part of Solomon's prayer, verses 22–53, has its locus in the exilic experience. Solomon's third prayer suggests that YHWH actually dwells in heaven and hence the temple is only a place from which to pray to YHWH. This seminal development in religious thought is couched in the exilic experience—namely, when the people are no longer in the land of their ancestors.

Exilic Prayer: 1 Kings 8:22–53

> [22]Then Solomon stood before the altar of YHWH in the presence of the whole assembly of Israel, and spread out his hands toward heaven. [23]And said, "O YHWH, God of Israel, there is no God like you in heaven above or on earth beneath, keeping covenant and steadfast love for your servants who walk before you with all their heart, [24]the covenant that you kept for your servant my father David as you declared to him; you promised with your mouth and have this day fulfilled with your hand. [25]Therefore, O YHWH, God of Israel, keep for your servant my father David that which you promised him, saying, 'There shall never fail you a successor before me to sit on the throne of Israel, if only your children look to their way, to walk before me as you have walked before me.' [26]Therefore, O God of Israel, let your word be confirmed, which you promised to your servant my father David.
>
> [27]"But will God indeed dwell on the earth? Even heaven and the highest heaven cannot contain you, much less this house that I have built! [28]Regard your servant's prayer and his plea, O YHWH my God, heeding the cry and the prayer that your servant prays to you today; [29]that your eyes may be open night and day toward this house, the place of which you said, 'My name shall be there,' that you may heed the prayer that your servant prays toward this place. [30]Hear the plea of your servant and of your people Israel when they pray toward this place; O hear in heaven your dwelling place; heed and forgive. [31]"If someone sins against a neighbor and is given an oath to swear, and comes and swears before your altar in this house, [32]then hear in heaven, and act, and judge your servants, condemning the guilty by bringing their conduct on their own head, and vindicating the righteous by rewarding them according to their righteousness. [33]"When your people Israel, having sinned against you, are defeated before an enemy but turn again to you, confess your name, pray and plead with you in this house, [34]then hear in heaven, forgive the sin of your people Israel, and bring them again to the land that you gave to their ancestors. [35]"When heaven is shut up and there is no rain because they have sinned against you, and then they pray toward this place, confess your name, and turn from their sin, because you punish them, [36]then hear in heaven, and forgive the sin of your servants, your people Israel, when you teach them the good way in which they should walk; and grant rain on your land, which you have given to your people as an inheritance. [37]"If there is famine in the land, if there is plague, blight, mildew, locust, or caterpillar; if their enemy besieges them in any of their cities; whatever plague, whatever sickness there is; [38]whatever prayer, whatever plea there is from any individual or from all your people Israel, all knowing the afflictions of their own hearts so that they stretch out their hands toward this house; [39]then hear in heaven your dwelling place, forgive, act, and render to all whose hearts you know—according to all their ways, for only you know what is in every human heart—[40]so that they may fear you all the days that they live in the land that you gave to our ancestors. [41]"Likewise when a foreigner, who is not of your people Israel, comes from a distant land because of your name— [42]for they shall hear of your great name, your mighty hand, and your outstretched arm—when a

> foreigner comes and prays toward this house, [43]then hear in heaven your dwelling place, and do according to all that the foreigner calls to you, so that all the peoples of the earth may know your name and fear you, as do your people Israel, and so that they may know that your name has been invoked on this house that I have built. [44]"If your people go out to battle against their enemy, by whatever way you shall send them, and they pray to YHWH toward the city that you have chosen and the house that I have built for your name, [45]then hear in heaven their prayer and their plea, and maintain their cause. [46]"If they sin against you—for there is no one who does not sin—and you are angry with them and give them to an enemy, so that they are carried away captive to the land of the enemy, far off or near; [47]yet if they come to their senses in the land to which they have been taken captive, and repent, and plead with you in the land of their captors, saying, 'We have sinned, and have done wrong; we have acted wickedly'; [48]if they repent with all their heart and soul in the land of their enemies, who took them captive, and pray to you toward their land, which you gave to their ancestors, the city that you have chosen, and the house that I have built for your name; [49]then hear in heaven your dwelling place their prayer and their plea, maintain their cause [50]and forgive your people who have sinned against you, and all their transgressions that they have committed against you; and grant them compassion in the sight of their captors, so that they may have compassion on them [51](for they are your people and heritage, which you brought out of Egypt, from the midst of the iron–smelter). [52]Let your eyes be open to the plea of your servant, and to the plea of your people Israel, listening to them whenever they call to you. [53]For you have separated them from among all the peoples of the earth, to be your heritage, just as you promised through Moses, your servant, when you brought our ancestors out of Egypt, O YHWH GOD." [54]When Solomon finished offering to YHWH all this prayer and supplication, he rose from where he had been kneeling, in front of the altar of YHWH, his hands spread out toward heaven.

There is no evidence for the composite nature of Solomon's third address and ample evidence for its literary unity.[36] For example, some critics point to the fact that Solomon is standing at the beginning of the speech (v. 22) and kneeling at the end (v. 54) as evidence of multiple authorship. Levenson rejects this as "the hypercritical eye of the literary critic." [37] Instead, the dependence of 1 Kings 8:23–53 on the collections of Pentateuchal covenant curses in Leviticus 26:14–45 and especially Deuteronomy 28:15–68 suggests a literary unity to Solomon's third prayer.[38] An exilic stamp is put on this speech in verses 44–53, which "strives to awaken in its audience the hope for restoration, secured through experience. This unambiguous hope of return makes sense only within a community already in exile."[39]

In this third speech, the temple becomes a place for prayer because God dwells in the heavens. This new idea is flagged by "place" (מקום). In 2 Samuel 7:11, the "place" is the *land* where God will give the people rest from their wanderings. The term "place" appears once in the second speech (v. 21): "I shall set a place for the ark." This might suggest that God's physical presence was in the temple (cf. Ps 132). In the third speech, the term "place" appears four times in verses 29–30. The temple is the place toward which one prays, and it is the place from which YHWH hears prayers from the place of YHWH's dwelling in the heavens.

An apparent citation of the Promise appears in verse 25. The similarities are apparent in the following parallel:

2 Samuel 7:14b–16	*1 Kings 8:25*
When he commits iniquity, I will punish him with a rod such as mortals use, with blows inflicted by human beings.	Therefore, O LORD, God of Israel, keep for your servant my father David that which you promised him, saying,
But I will not take my steadfast love from him, as I took it from Saul, whom I put away from before you.	"Your line on the throne of Israel shall never end,
Your house and your kingdom shall be made sure forever before me; your throne shall be established forever.	if only your children look to their way, to walk before me as you have walked before me.'

Upon closer examination, however, the citation is illusionary, and this complete conditionalizing of the Promise is completely unknown except in later Deuteronomic and post-Deuteronomic texts. Second Samuel 7:14b–15a may be a source for such conditionalizing: "When he commits iniquity, I will punish him with a rod such as mortals use, with blows inflicted by human beings, but I will not remove my covenant loyalty from him (וחסדי לא־יסור ממנו)." There is not a hint here, however, that the Davidic heir might ever be cut off. On the contrary, YHWH goes on to assure that his throne will be established forever (v. 16). Nevertheless, similar circumscription of the Promise may be found in 1 Kings 2:4, 9:5–7; and Jeremiah 33:17. These passages foreshadow an end of the Davidic dynasty, the destruction of Jerusalem, and the Babylonian exile. It is difficult to imagine them being grafted onto the Promise to David in the preexilic period, particularly in the late monarchy when the tradition of Jerusalem's inviolability was firmly entrenched. The Jeremiah passage gives a clue to the redactional history because Jeremiah 33:14–26 appears only in the Masoretic Text—not in the shorter LXX.[40] Recent text-critical studies on the book of Jeremiah have shown that the shorter LXX version represents an earlier text tradition.[41]

Through a link between the Promise to David and the Mosaic covenant, the author of the third prayer conditionalizes the Davidic Promise and refocuses toward the whole people. In verses 23–24, the Promise and the Mosaic covenant are juxtaposed. The expression in verse 23,

> שמר הברית והחסד לעבדיך ההלכים לפניך בכל־לבם, "keeping covenant and steadfast love for your servants who walk before you with all their heart,"

may be compared with Deuteronomy 7:9,

> שמר הברית והחסד לאהביו ולשמרי מצותו לאלף דור, "keeping covenant and steadfast love with those who love him and keep his commandments, to a thousand generations."

Solomon's prayer at this point is referring to the Mosaic covenant known particularly from Deuteronomy. The required obedience (√שמר) applied to the Davidic covenant by juxtaposition. Verse 24 begins as a dependent clause, "[the covenant] that you kept for your servant my father David" (אשר שמרת לעבדך דוד). The antecedent—the covenant—must be supplied, but the connection between the Davidic covenant and the Mosaic is facilitated by the repetition of the root √שמר and the term "servant" (עבד) from the previous verse. At this point, the prayer goes on to elaborate on the conditional nature of the Davidic covenant. But the tension between the one servant, David and his sons (vv. 24–25), and the many servants of the Mosaic covenant (v. 23) is already present. When the prayer later speaks of *the people* (rather than just Solomon) praying toward the place where YHWH put his name, this transition has already been paved by the juxtaposition of the Mosaic and Davidic covenants. These two covenants correspond to the two houses which—at least according to this author—YHWH has promised to build. Although the promise for the dynasty was circumscribed to David's descendants, the promised temple was for all the people. After the Promise had been extended to the temple, the Promise could also be seen as a promise to the people of Israel (who pray toward the temple) and not just the royal line.

2 Kings 21:7–8: "The House Which I Chose"

As part of the critique of the reign of Manasseh and his religious apostasy, the narrator appeals to the Promise to David *and Solomon.*

> 7 Manasseh set the carved image of Asherah which he made in the house concerning which YHWH said to David and to his son Solomon, "In this house, and in Jerusalem, which I have chosen out of all the tribes of Israel, I will put my name forever; 8 I will not cause the feet of Israel to wander any more out of the land that I gave to their ancestors, if only they will be careful to do according to all that I have commanded them, and according to all the law that my servant Moses commanded them."

2 Kings 21:7–8 allegedly quotes from the Promise to David *and Solomon*. What follows are allusions to texts known already from 2 Samuel 7 (the Promise to David) and 1 Kings 8 (the Prayer of Solomon). The statement in verse 8, "I will not allow the feet of Israel to wander (להניד) any more out of the land," recalls the Promise in 2 Samuel 7:10, "I will establish a home for My people Israel and will plant them firm, so that they shall dwell secure and shall tremble (ירגז) no more." The shift in the verbal idea here, from "to tremble (להניד)" to "to wander (לרגז)," along with the emphasis on the conditional nature of the Promise in 2 Kings 21:8, reflects an exilic context. The statement in verse 7 that YHWH chose Jerusalem and its temple to put his name is not in 2 Samuel 7:1–17, however, and must be sought in Solomon's Prayer. The idea that Jerusalem and the temple are the chosen place for God's name is particularly prominent in the third sections of Solomon's Prayer (see previous discussion). The Prayer of Solomon, in fact, is explicitly incorporated into the Promise by the narrator's reference to "that which YHWH said to David and to his son Solomon." However, the inclusion of Solomon is implicitly

also an interpretation of the statement in 2 Samuel 7:12, "I will raise up your offspring after you, one of your own issue, and I will establish his kingship." Rather than reading this as promising a dynasty, as preexilic readers had, 2 Kings 21:7 reads the Promise as referring to Solomon alone. Such a reading begins to alleviate some of the dissonance between the Promise of an eternal kingdom for the sons of David and the plight of the exiles. The Promise was to David and his son Solomon. The Promise now has even more to do with the Temple *for YHWH's name* than the kingdom. Such maneuvering could not have been completely satisfying, but at least it closes some of the distance between the Promise and reality.

Psalm 89:38–51: "Lamenting the Promise"

38But now you have spurned and rejected him;
you are full of wrath against your anointed.
39You have renounced the covenant with your servant;
you have defiled his crown in the dust.
40You have broken through all his walls;
you have laid his strongholds in ruins.
41All who pass by plunder him;
he has become the scorn of his neighbors.
42You have exalted the right hand of his foes;
you have made all his enemies rejoice.
43Moreover, you have turned back the edge of his sword,
and you have not supported him in battle.
44You have removed the scepter from his hand,
and hurled his throne to the ground.
45You have cut short the days of his youth;
you have covered him with shame. Selah.
46How long, O YHWH? Will you hide yourself forever?
How long will your wrath burn like fire?
47Remember how short my time is—
for what vanity you have created all mortals!
48Who can live and never see death?
Who can escape the power of Sheol? Selah.
49Lord, where is your steadfast love of old,
which by your faithfulness you swore to David?
50Remember, O Lord, how your servant is taunted;
how I bear in my bosom the insults of the peoples,
51with which your enemies taunt, O YHWH,
with which they taunted the footsteps of your anointed.

Psalm 89 divides into three distinct literary units. The first two have been dealt with in earlier chapters. The last unit, verses 38–51 [MT 39–52], is a communal lament over the demise of David's kingdom, which the present study assigns to the exilic period.[42] Verse 52 is a hymnic conclusion to the Korahite psalms (Psalms 84–89).[43] In the first chapter, I already addressed some of the reasons why this last unit of Psalm 89 should most likely be placed in the exilic period. At this point, it is worthwhile to rehearse and elaborate on these points.

Although Psalm 89 at no point explicitly describes the Babylonian exile, it is certainly implicit in much of its language. For example, the questions in Psalm 89:46, "How long, O YHWH? Will you hide yourself forever? How long will your wrath burn like fire?" (עד־מה יהוה תסתר לנצח תבער כמו־אש חמתך), point to a catastrophic event. Its language is also remarkably similar to Psalm 79:5, a psalm which does explicitly refer to the exile: "How long, O YHWH? Will you be angry forever? Will your jealousy burn like fire?" (עד־מה יהוה תאנף לנצח תבער כמו־אש קנאתך). The number of historical contexts in such statements can be situated is limited, and the Exile is the most obvious. A classic study in inner-biblical exegesis by Nahum Sarna argued that Psalm 89 as a whole should be contextualized in the period immediately following the Syro-Ephraimite war, that is, the late eighth century.[44] Although Sarna's arguments have merit, there are some troubling aspects to his early dating, especially in the third part (vv. 38–51 [MT 39–52]). I have already articulated reasons that the first two sections belong in the tenth and seventh centuries, respectively. In the final part, the Psalm speaks of God's rejection of his anointed in language reminiscent of exilic psalms: "But now you spurned and rejected him (ואתה זנחת ותמאס); you are full of wrath against your anointed. You have renounced the covenant with your servant; you have defiled his crown in the dust" (vv. 38–39). Or what can be meant by the charge, "You have removed the scepter from his hand, and hurled his throne to the ground" (v. 44)? Is this not the removal of the Davidic monarch? How many contexts does this actually apply to? Although Kraus claims there is no hint of the Exile, what should be inferred from the statements in verses 40–41, "You have broken through all his walls; you have laid his strongholds in ruins. All who pass by plunder him; he has become the scorn of his neighbors," and verses 50–51, "Remember, O Lord, how your servant is taunted; how I bear in my bosom the insults of the peoples, with which your enemies taunt"? These at least hint at the exile. It should also be remembered that the exile itself was not complete. Only in later Persian literature does the myth of a complete exile arise. The exile itself may have been no more than a tenth of the population. The destruction of the city, the temple, and its institutions (especially the Davidic monarchy) were the seminal features of 586 BCE. These are exactly the issues addressed in Psalm 89:38–51. Finally, the shift in the genre, alongside the change in tenor in the third part of the psalm, cries out for explanation. It seems that the traditional explanation—namely, that at least the final part of the psalm was composed in the exilic period—is the most plausible solution.

An early dating for the whole of Psalm 89 has been critical to the myth-ritual school. One advocate of the myth-ritual school, Artur Weiser, argues:

> Most commentators seek to identify the catastrophe, which gave rise to this lament, which exposed the country to destruction and looting and deprived the king of his autonomy, with the downfall of Judah in 587 BC; they therefore regard the psalm as belonging to the exilic or postexilic period. Since, however, the psalm does not exhibit any concrete feature pointing to that event, such as, for instance, the capture of the king and the deportation of the people, it is presumably a question of an earlier defeat.[45]

Such attempts to minimize the completely negative outlook of this last part of Psalm 89 and have not been accepted because they depend on an a priori acceptance of the myth-ritual model. To his credit, Aubrey Johnson tries to account for the third part (vv. 38–51), where the king is "cut off and rejected," by drawing an analogy with the ritual humiliation of the king in the Babylonian *akitu* Festival.[46] Because the hymn leaves the king with his enemies taunting and mocking him (v. 51), this is still an unsatisfactory explanation of the misery of the king, the people, and the land. In sum, commentators are quite correct in seeing this last section as emanating from the exilic period.

The references to the Promise in the final section of Psalm 89 are rather limited, especially when compared with the detailed discourse with 2 Samuel 7:1–17 that pervades the second unit (see chapter 3). In the last stanza, the poet seems concerned first of all with his own plight, which is naturally linked to the plight of the Davidic dynasty. The purpose of the last stanza, however, is somewhat deceptive. It begins with nine verses questioning whether God intends to reject the Davidic covenant forever (vv. 38–46 [MT, 39–47]) but then turns to the poet's real concern in verses 47–48 (MT, 48–49). There the poet implores God, "Remember me (זכר־אני)! What is my lifespan?—For what vanity you have created all mortals! Who can live and never see death? Who can escape the power of Sheol?" The psalm then ends by alternating between appeals to the Promise made to David (vv. 49, 51 [MT, 50, 52]) and the poet's own personal appeals (vv. 47–48, 50 [MT, 48–49, 51]). If author himself actually comes from the line of David, then there is no tension between the personal appeal and the appeal to the Promise. Is such an interpretation really warranted? The personal appeal of the poet is to consider his lifespan, the fact that he is mortal like all mankind (כל בני־אדם). Rather than suppose the poet must have been of Davidic lineage, it seems preferable to see a democratization of the Promise not unlike what we witnessed in Solomon's Prayer (1 Kgs 8:22–53) and Isaiah 55. This process is actually facilitated by the Psalm's use of the term "covenant" (ברית). The opening hymn refers unambiguously to the Davidic covenant: "I have made a covenant with my chosen one (כרתי ברית לבחירי), I have sworn to my servant David (נשבעתי לדוד עבדי)" (v. 3 [MT, 4]). In the second stanza, YHWH's voice assures us that he will be faithful to his covenant with David (vv. 33–36 [MT, 34–37]). Now, the final stanza refers to the "covenant of your servant (ברית עבדיך)" (v. 39 [MT, 40]). Although throughout the psalmist refers to the Davidic covenant, the use of the term "covenant" (ברית) cannot help but recall the better known Mosaic covenant between YHWH and his people. The possibility of broadening the Promise arises in the poem itself:

> Happy are the people (אשרי העם) who know the festal shout,
> who walk, O LORD, in the light of your countenance;
> they exult in your name all day long,
> and extol your righteousness.
> For you are the glory of their strength;
> by your favor our horn is exalted.
> For our shield belongs to YHWH,
> our king to the Holy One of Israel. (vv. 15–18 [MT, 16–19])

There really is no reason, then, to pursue an interpretation of Psalm 89, and particularly its last stanza, as emanating from a poet of royal lineage. Rather, in its final form, the psalm reflects the application of the Davidic Promise to the Jewish people. They, too, were the chosen of YHWH (v. 3 [MT, 4] בחיר; cf. Ps 105:43; 106:5; Isa 43:20; 45:4; 65:22; 1 Chr 16:13). The questioning of the covenant between YHWH and his people Israel was quite common during the exile,[47] and the only new twist here is the implicit linkage between the Sinaitic and Davidic covenants. It is this linkage that enabled the poet to associate the fate of the Davidic dynasty with that of all Israel.

"Second" Isaiah

The present study understands the final shape of book of Isaiah as arising in the late sixth century—after the rise of Cyrus. This is not the place to become mired down in the debate about the compositional history of the book of Isaiah that has ensued ever since Bernard Duhm's classic study. A few words, however, are necessary to place the present study within the context of the current debate. Duhm's thesis that the book of Isaiah actually is made up of three separate parts may be roughly summarized as follows: Isaiah ben Amoz dating to the eighth century (chapters 1–39), the anonymous prophet called Deutero-Isaiah active during the Babylonian exile (chapters 40–55), and another anonymous prophet called Trito-Isaiah (chapters 56–66) living in the postexilic period. Although there has been a broad consensus that the book of Isaiah is composed of three discrete compositions, recent trends have challenged this thesis on a number of fronts. The most important challenges come from (1) those scholars who see only two Isaiahs[48] and (2) those who argue that the redactional stages cannot be neatly separated.[49] Marvin Sweeney summarizes an emerging consensus when he writes, "Although chs. 1–39 clearly portray an eighth-century historical setting much earlier than that of chs. 40–55 or 56–66, there is no evidence that chs. 1–39 ever constituted a distinct prophetic book separate from their present literary context of the book of Isaiah."[50] The present study follows a compositional model similar to that of Menachem Haran and most recently advocated by Benjamin Sommer in *A Prophet Reads Scripture: Allusion in Isaiah 40–66*. I find only two major redactional stages: the oracles of Isaiah of Jerusalem contained within chapters 1–35 and an early postexilic editing of those chapters, along with the supplement contained in chapters 36–66 (ca. 525 BCE?). Some change in perspective between 40–55 and 56–66 is posited by the movement of Second Isaiah from Babylon to Jerusalem. Then again, Menachem Haran and Benjamin Sommer point to the unique style and rhetoric that inextricably tie 40–55 and 56–66 together. Along these lines, H. G. M. Williamson's recent monograph, *The Book Called Isaiah*, has drawn attention to the hand of Second Isaiah in shaping the oracles of Isaiah of Jerusalem. As Christopher Seitz points out, "Separation of Second Isaiah from their Isaianic context has led to an overemphasis on exilic provenance, and the historical circumstances associated with deportation, with a consequent underemphasizing of the significance of Zion."[51] Second Isaiah must be understood as a reading of the oracles of Isaiah ben Amoz and, in our particular case, a reading of the Zion tradition with attention to the Promise to David.

Isaiah 55:3–11: Democratizing the Promise

> 3 Incline your ear, and come to me; listen, so that you may live. I will make with
> you an everlasting covenant, assured covenant loyalties for David. 4 See, I made
> him a witness to the peoples, a leader and commander for the peoples. 5 See, you
> shall call nations that you do not know, and nations that do not know you shall run
> to you, because of YHWH your God, the Holy One of Israel, for he has glorified
> you. 6 Seek YHWH while he may be found, call on him while he is near; 7 let the
> wicked forsake their way, and the unrighteous their thoughts; let them return to
> YHWH, that he may have mercy on them, and to our God, for he will abundantly
> pardon. 8 For my thoughts are not your thoughts, nor are your ways my ways, says
> YHWH. 9 For as the heavens are higher than the earth, so are my ways higher than
> your ways and my thoughts than your thoughts. 10 For as the rain and the snow
> come down from heaven, and do not return there until they have watered the earth,
> making it bring forth and sprout, giving seed to the sower and bread to the eater,
> 11 so shall my word be that goes out from my mouth; it shall not return to me
> empty, but it shall accomplish that which I purpose, and succeed in the thing for
> which I sent it.

In an attempt to rationalize the failure of the Promise, Isaiah 55:3–11 extends the everlasting covenant with David to all Israel. Discussions of this chapter have focused on one of its most interesting and enigmatic verses—Isaiah 55:3: "Incline your [pl.] ear, and come to me; listen, so that you [pl.] may live. I will make with you an everlasting covenant (ואכרתה לכם ברית עולם), assured covenant loyalties to David (חסדי דוד הנאמנים)." The difficult expression, *ḥasᵉdê Dawid* (חסדי דוד), has been a centerpiece of scholarly discussion.[52] The enigmatic term *ḥesed* is here translated as "covenant loyalties" to highlight its juxtaposition with the term *berît*, "covenant"; however, there is an extensive literature on this term whose exact meaning has been the subject of some debate.[53] There is some consensus among scholars that Isaiah 55:3b alludes back to the Promise to David in 2 Samuel 7. Specifically, the "assured covenant loyalties to David" recalls 2 Samuel 7:15–16, where God promises, on the one hand, that he will not withdraw his *ḥesed* from David (וחסדי לא־יסור ממנו) and, on the other hand, that David's dynasty and kingdom will be *made sure* (cf. ונאמן with הנאמנים, both *Niphal* verbs from √אמנ). Although a covenant is perhaps implicit in the Promise, the term never actually appears in 2 Samuel 7. To find the Promise described by the term "covenant (ברית)," we must turn to the poem in 2 Samuel 23 known as the "last words of David." According to this poem, David claims that YHWH "has made with me an everlasting covenant (כי ברית עולם שם לי)" (v. 5). Likewise, the opening hymn of Psalm 89 mentions the covenant God made with David (89:3 [MT, 4], כרתי ברית לבחירי נשבעתי לדוד עבדי). The association of "covenant (ברית)" and "loyalty (חסד)" is also known from a royal liturgy, Psalm 21. Thus, early liturgical texts indicate that the Promise was from early days conceptualized in covenantal terms. Isaiah 55:3 thus follows in the tradition of liturgical sources that associate the idea of covenant (ברית) and loyalty (חסד).

A democratization of the Davidic Promise in Isaiah 55:3 is accomplished by its juxtaposition beside a covenant made with all Israel. This democratization, however, must be regarded as most curious because the Promise to David had apparently come to naught in the exilic or early postexilic period when Isaiah 55 was supposedly composed. What could possibly be the value in extending a failed promise to all Israel? Sense can be made of this democratization only if Isaiah 55:3 is placed in the broader context of chapter 55.

Isaiah 55 is often read as two discrete prophetic oracles (vv. 3–5 and 6–11); however, when read from the perspective of dissonance theory, the two parts come together nicely. The first oracle raises the specter of the apparently disproven Promise. In what respect was it legitimate to speak of "an everlasting covenant" or "the assured covenant loyalties to David"? The "midrash on the word" in verses 10–11 then redresses a very concrete referent, YHWH's everlasting Promise to David. The oracle begins by recalling the conditional nature of YHWH. Just as is emphasized in Dtr^2, the Promise to David is conditional on David's sons' attitude toward YHWH: "let the wicked forsake their way, . . . let them return to YHWH" (v. 7). Implicit in the command to seek God is need for both mercy and pardon "he may have mercy on them, . . . for he will abundantly pardon" (v. 7). In other words, it addresses the condition of the Babylonian exiles. Moreover, it provides hope for restoration. To reduce the dissonance between the promised everlasting covenant and the destruction of both dynasty and kingdom, the poet appeals to the inscrutable nature of YHWH: "my thoughts are not your thoughts" (v. 8). At the same time, there is the ambiguous promise that God will fulfill his promise (דבר); just as the rain mysteriously brings forth from the ground (v. 10), so also God's promise (דבר)—that is, the promise that is now not only assured to David but also extended to Israel—"shall not return to me empty, but it shall accomplish that which I purpose, and succeed in the thing for which I sent it" (v. 11). By underscoring the inscrutability of the prophetic word, Isaiah 55 alleviates the *apparent* dissonance between the Promise and the destruction of the Judaean state. Even more remarkably, this inscrutability also facilitates the application of the Promise to all Israel. Ultimately, then, the Promise may be fulfilled through Cyrus and his decree to return and rebuild (cf. Isa 45:1–4; Ezr 1:1–4). The fate of the Davidic dynasty had been the fate of all Israel. Conversely, the mysterious purpose of the Promise is fulfilled through the restoration of the people![54]

Isaiah 66:1: Who Needs a Temple?

Isaiah 66:1 participates in a discourse generated by 2 Samuel 7. Employing a rhetorical question, the poet writes, "Thus says YHWH: 'Heaven is my throne and the earth is my footstool; what is the house that you would build for me (בית אשר תבנו־לי אי־זה), and what is my resting place?' " This statement echoes God's words in 2 Samuel 7:5: "Thus says YHWH: 'Are you the one to build a house for Me to dwell in (האתה תבנה־לי בית לשבתי)?' " The language is quite similar, especially תבנה־לי בית in Samuel and בית אשר תבנו־לי in Isaiah. Isaiah evidently interprets the question "Are you the one to build" in 2 Samuel to mean "What kind of the house could you build since I dwell in heaven?" A similar concept underlies an allusion in Isaiah 63:15. There we read, "Look down from heaven; see from your holy and glorious habitation (וראה מזבל קדשך ותפארתך)" (v. 15a). The use of the term "habitation (זבול)" here may allude to the poetic fragment preserved in the first prayer of Solomon; in 1 Kings 8:13, Solomon addresses God: "I have built you a house of habitation

(בית זבול), a place for you to dwell in forever" (cf. 2 Chr 6:2). Quite unlike the poetic fragment that opens Solomon's prayer, the habitation of God, according to Isaiah 63 and 66, is in heaven. The locus of God's dwelling has shifted in Isaiah 63 and 66. Now God dwells in heaven, not in the Solomonic temple. The impetus for God's literary exodus from the Temple was undoubtedly the Babylonian destruction of the Temple. For at least a few generations during the Babylonian period, God was again a vagabond—much as he was reputed to be in 2 Samuel 7:6: "From the day that I brought the people of Israel out of Egypt to this day I have not dwelt in a house, but have moved about in tent and tabernacle." During the Babylonian period, God is returned to this once familiar state. It should hardly be considered coincidental that Isaiah 66:1 relies directly on 2 Samuel 7:5 in transforming the role of the temple. Later texts, including 1 Chronicles 17:4, the Greek translations of 2 Samuel 7, and a Qumran *pesher* on 2 Samuel 7 (4Q174), will also continue in this discourse.

The launching point for Isaiah 66:1's question is the meaning of the "place (מקום)" in DtrH. In 2 Samuel 7:10, God promises, "I will establish a place (מקום) for My people Israel and will plant them firm, so that they shall dwell secure." It is clear that the "place" intended here is the land of Israel. In the Prayer of Solomon, however, this "place" is interpreted initially as the temple (1 Kgs 8:21) and then the temple is understood as "a place for prayer" (1 Kgs 8:29–30; see previous discussion). The third part of Solomon's prayer even asks a question echoing Isaiah 66:1: "But will God really dwell on earth? Even the heavens to their uttermost reaches cannot contain You, how much less this House that I have built!" (1 Kgs 8:27). The understanding of the temple as a place for prayer also appears in the latter chapters of Isaiah, where we find the designation of the temple as a "house of prayer" (Isa 56:7). Such an understanding of the temple opens it to the whole community, not just priests (note the context in Isa 56:3–8). In other words, the temple is now community property. It is also democratized. No doubt this democratization was facilitated by the destruction of the temple, just as the understanding of the temple as the place toward which one prays was also facilitated by its destruction.

Rationalizing the Promise

The Babylonian destruction and exile marked the end of the Promise as well as its rebirth. The crisis brought on by the end of the Davidic monarchy and the destruction of the Jerusalem temple necessitated a creative, innovative reading of the Promise to David. No longer could it be understood to give divine sanction to a simple reading of the Promise to David—that is, to continuous line of David's sons sitting on the throne in Jerusalem. No longer could it be read as ensuring the safety of Jerusalem and its temple. The sharp dissonance between the Promise and the exile forced a radical rereading of the Promise.

The end of the monarchy ironically forced the democratization of Israel. Monarchy is an autocratic form of government. The end of the monarchy brought with it a dramatic restructuring of the political and social institutions of ancient Israel. Apparently, a traditional form of social organization led by the elders gave way to a new fictive kin group known as the *Bêt Abôt*. It is hardly surprising that the exile engendered new forms of leadership. The Promise to David receives a radical new understanding as applying to all Israel. This is accomplished in part by associating the Promise with the covenant of Sinai. The *eternal* Promise to David becomes a *conditional* covenant with David. Emphasizing the Promise to David as a covenant introduces all the attendant conditions of the covenant. Additionally, because the Sinai covenant was for all Israel, so all the Davidic covenant is for all Israel. Such a reading could be managed only by appealing to the mysterious and inexplicable nature of God's words (in Isa 55).

The end of the temple ironically brought with it a universal ization of YHWH. If YHWH was to survive, he could no longer be a local deity or a national god. There was no longer a locale, nor was there a nation. If YHWH was to survive, he had to be resurrected as an universal god whose dominion was the entire earth. The exilic Deuteronomic historian would emphasize that Jerusalem and the temple were only the place toward which one would pray. Along similar lines, the latter chapters of Isaiah describe the temple as a "house of prayer" and mock the idea that YHWH could dwell in an earthly temple. The entire earth was now YHWH's dominion. While such a revolutionary universalization was perhaps necessary, it fundamentally undermined the Jerusalem temple—a development that would pave the road for Second Temple period Jewish sectarianism.

Two touchpoints again come to the fore in the discourse about the Promise during the Babylonian period. First is the question posed in 2 Samuel 7:5: "Shall you build a house for my dwelling place (הַאַתָּה תִּבְנֶה־לִּי בַיִת לְשִׁבְתִּי)?" Already for DtrH, this text had been a focal point for explaining why David was not allowed to build a temple. For a people living partially in exile, without a national shrine, and entirely under foreign domination, it justifies the rationalization that the God of Israel did not need a temple at all because the entire earth (where his people were now scattered) was his domain. The second is the meaning of the "place (מקום)." The Promise to David allotted "a place for his people" where they were "planted" and not to be disturbed (2 Sam 7:10). The Deuteronomistic reading of this place localized it in Jerusalem and its temple through the centralization law (Deut 12; 2 Kgs 22:16–20). To the exilic readers, however, this place becomes as amorphous as the God whose dwelling was the entire earth.

6

In Persia's Shadow: Restoring the Promise

Thus says King Cyrus of Persia: YHWH, the God of heaven, has given me all the kingdoms of the earth, and he has charged me to build him a house at Jerusalem, which is in Judah. Whoever is among you of all his people, may YHWH his God be with him! Let him go up! —2 Chronicles 36:22–23; Ezra 1:2–4

The edict of Cyrus ushered in a new era in the religion, literature, and history of the Jewish people. The Jewish exiles were allowed to return to their ancestral homeland. They were allowed to rebuild their temple. On the extreme periphery of the Persian empire, the returnees joined those who had remained in the land and attempted to restore the Jewish people and their heritage. In the early period of Persian rule, Yehud was an obscure province in a remote part of the empire, but the rise of the Greeks, along with revolts in Egypt, cast a spotlight on Yehud. A second wave of Jewish returnees, which included Ezra and Nehemiah, coincided with this closer Persian oversight of Yehud. These events form the backdrop for rewriting the story of the Jewish people, with the Promise to David as a central theme.

The attempt to restore the temple met with apathy. Some found in the Promise to David real questions about the importance of the temple to the God who dwells in heaven. The exile had evoked visions of an ideal heavenly temple. There was also some feeling about the inferiority of the rebuilt temple, which must have contributed to questions about its adequacy and relevance. At the same time, the return rekindled aspirations for the restoration of the Davidic monarchy. Under the long Persian domination, these aspirations dimmed, though they would not die. The power and influence of the temple and priesthood grew. Their authority was read into the Promise to David.

The Colonial Empire and the Satrapy of Yehud

The administrative structures of the Assyrian empire were transferred successively to the Babylonian and then Persian empires. Yehud (as Judah is known in the Persian period) formed a small but independent province of the Babylonian and Persian empires.[1]

The Persian administration of the "Satrapy beyond the River" divides in two periods separated by the Egyptian revolt in 460 BCE. This revolt became a catalyst for the Persian military buildup throughout the eastern Mediterranean. It also sounded an alarm, calling for closer attention to the administration of the region. Up until the Egyptian revolt Yehud was geographically isolated, impoverished and largely forgotten. Athens's support of the Egyptian revolt signaled a period of increasing tension with the Greeks. Although the "peace of Callius" represented a temporary hiatus in the military confrontations between Athens and Persia, it hardly removed the specter of the Greeks from the eastern extent of the Persian empire. As such, the Egyptian revolt represented a serious threat to the Persian control of the eastern Mediterranean. It called for extraordinary actions by the Persians to secure the eastern Mediterranean. The missions of Ezra and Nehemiah should be understood, at least in part, as a result of imperial concerns in the context of the Egyptian revolt and its aftermath.[2] The age of Ezra and Nehemiah begins a new era of Persian interest in Palestine.

The new Achaemenid attention to Yehud apparently resulted in some administrative restructuring. Yehud was ruled by a succession of governors in the Persian period. The early governors claimed Davidic lineage. This is obviously the case with Zerubbabel and Sheshbazzar (cf. 1 Chr 3:10–23). Striking archaeological evidence also speaks to the continuing importance of the Davidic line in the early Persian period. The Shelomith seal bears the inscription, "belonging to Shelomith, maidservant of Elnathan the governor."[3] Shelomith was, according to 1 Chronicles 3:19, the daughter of Zerubbabel. Elnathan apparently married the daughter of Zerubbabel, Shelomith, to attach himself into the Davidic line and thereby legitimize his rule. In this respect, the transition to Nehemiah's leadership marks a sharp break with the tradition of Davidic governors, which is suggested both by literary and archaeological sources. In the second phase of the Persian period, Jewish leadership become distanced from the Davidic dynasty as Ezra and Nehemiah redefined the symbols and structure of the Jewish leadership.

Demography and Settlement Patterns

The Babylonian period began with the widespread destruction evidenced in archaeological excavations throughout Judah. Cities, towns, and villages were destroyed. People were killed, went into exile, or fled. An increase in the population of the Persian province of Yehud begins only in the latter part of the Persian period. Archaeologically (as well as administratively), the Persian period can be separated into two phases: (1) Persian I, ca. 539–460 BCE, and (2) Persian II, ca. 460–332 BCE. Although the Babylonian period or Iron IIC, ca. 586–539 BCE, by most accounts was characterized by substantial continuity in material culture, in the sixth century the pottery forms show a marked decline in quality.[4] The resurgence in the population and economy of Yehud would coincide with a marked military buildup in the region beginning in the Persian II period—that is, the midfifth century BCE.

Table 6.1: Number of Regional Settlements in Palestine

Region	Iron II	Persian
Benjamin and hill country of Ephraim	51	15
Judah	27	34
Judaean desert	27	2
Ephraim and Manasseh	119	81

Chart follows M. Kochavi (ed.), *Judaea, Samaria, and the Golan: Archaeological Survey 1967–1968* (Jerusalem: The Survey of Israel, 1972) [Hebrew]; summarized by K. Hoglund, "The Achaemenid Context," in *Second Temple Studies. 1. Persian Period* (ed. P. Davies; JSOTSS, 151; Sheffield: JSOT, 1991), p. 58.

A process of ruralization began with the Babylonian conquest and continued into the early Persian rule. This can be readily seen in the archaeological surveys (Table 6.1). In general, there is a sharp drop in the number of settlements from the Iron II into the early Persian period. Although the region of Judah represents an apparent exception, showing a superficial increase, these are quite small unwalled villages, and the overall population still reflects a decline.[5] Overall, this reflects the situation through the country: 65% of the Persian settlements had no occupation in Iron II. In other words, there is significant discontinuity in the settlement pattern and in the demographic distribution, which must have been precipitated by the Babylonian exile. The fact that 65% of the settlements were new indicates a substantial transition and cautions against overstating the continuity from the Iron Age into the Babylonian and Persian periods. Certainly, there were aspects of continuity, especially at large sites, but there was also a major disjunction.[6] Kenneth Hoglund points out that most of the new Persian settlements "appear to have been founded by the end of the sixth century BCE, that is, *in the course of the return from Babylon of the first groups of exiles*" [emphasis added].[7]

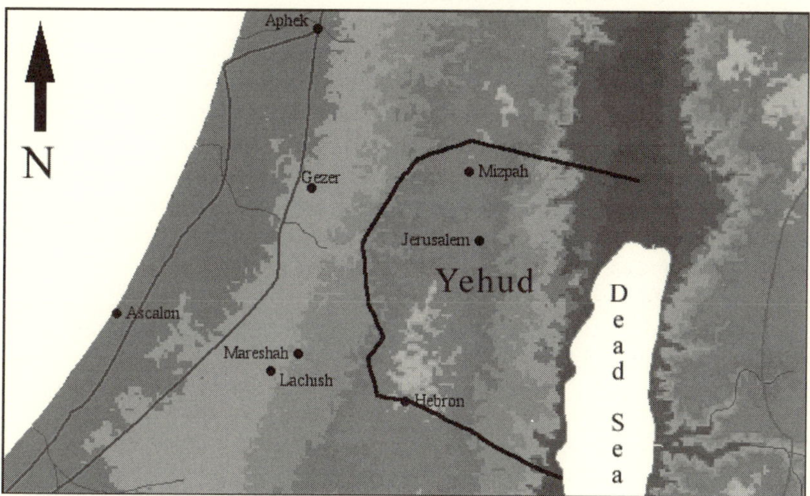

Figure 6.1. Borders of Persian Yehud (after Carter, 1994)

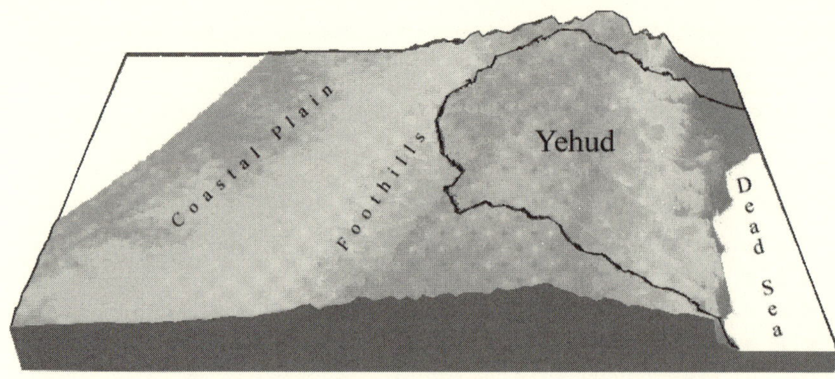

Figure 6.2. 3-D View of Persian Yehud

A ruralization of Yehud was apparently the deliberate policy of the Achaemenid empire. As Kenneth Hoglund notes, the land belonged to the empire, and the imperial center reorganized the rural countryside "in order to fuel the bureaucracy necessary for the administration of the imperial program."[8] As such, the struggle between the "returnees" and the "remainees" was probably not over land rights, as is often suggested.[9] The settlement patterns imply that the "returnees" were not competing over land but rather resettling the sparsely populated countryside.

The Economy of Persian Yehud

The geographical situation of Yehud naturally made it one of the poorer satrapies of the Persian empire. Archaeological surveys and excavations confirm this observation.[10] Yehud remained an independent province,[11] but its boundaries were circumscribed so as to afford little opportunity for commerce (see figures 6.1 and 6.2). International commerce along the great trunk route (or Via Maris) and maritime trade were beyond the bounds of Yehud. Even the more fertile alluvial valleys in the Judaean foothills (near sites like Lachish, Mareshah, Azekah, and Gezer) were outside the control of Yehud. The province of Yehud was isolated in the remote hill country. Even in the hill country, the fertile agricultural vineyards of Hebron were south of Yehud's control. Its boundaries left Yehud with limited economic potential and cast its economy into a precarious situation.

By the midfifth century, in the days of Ezra and Nehemiah,[12] Yehud was further impoverished by the increasing taxes of the Persian administration, as is illustrated in Nehemiah 5:1–5:

> Now there was a great outcry of the people and of their wives against their Jewish kin. For there were those who said, "With our sons and our daughters, we are many; we must get grain, so that we may eat and stay alive." There were also those who said, "We are having to pledge our fields, our vineyards, and our houses in order to get grain during the famine." And there were those who said, "*We are having to borrow money on our fields and vineyards to pay the king's tax.* Now

> our flesh is the same as that of our kindred; our children are the same as their children; and yet we are forcing our sons and daughters to be slaves, and some of our daughters have been ravished; we are powerless, and our fields and vineyards now belong to others."

As a result of these dire circumstances, Nehemiah forced the wealthy to restore property seized for back payment and to stop taking interest on loans (vv. 6–12).

Integration of Palestine into the network of international commerce began already in the seventh century BCE under the Assyrian administration. In the Persian period, there was extensive trade with the entire Mediterranean world. Even though Yehud was geographically isolated, it was still a part of the Persian empire. Commercial activity can be documented in both archaeological and literary sources, though to be fair this activity is best known in the Persian II period after the Egyptian revolts around 460 BCE. In Nehemiah, for example, we read, "*Tyrians who lived in the city* brought in fish and all kinds of merchandise and sold them on the Sabbath to the people of Judah, and in Jerusalem" (Neh 13:16). Another evidence of international trade is coins, which were first used in Palestine in the sixth century; however, very few coins are found from this early period. It is only in the Persian II period—the late fifth century—that coins become common in Palestine reflecting the increasing importance of the region.[13] In the archaeological record, we have evidence of imported pottery, mostly Greek, all over Yehud. In Yehud, we see a development of ceramics specifically as containers for transport.[14] Concomitantly, there was both the establishment and development of ports in Palestine, as well as commercial ties with Phoenicia (e.g., Neh 13:16), to facilitate trade in the Mediterranean. As Hoglund points out, the encouragement of commercialization and international trade provided the imperial coffers with taxes without requiring substantive imperial investment. Additionally, this interdependency fostered the attitude that economic prosperity depended on loyalty to the empire.

Persian economic development of Palestine focused on the Mediterranean ports and the trade routes. New ports (i.e., not in use in Iron IIb) were established all along the coast at sites like Tel Michal, Apollonia Arsuf, Dor, Atlit, Shiqmona, and Tel Abu-Hawam. Other places like Ashkelon, Jaffa, Tel Kudadi, and Acco continued to be used and developed.[15] A military buildup in Yehud, as evidenced by the fortresses throughout Palestine built in a distinctively Persian style,[16] also focused on the trade routes. Hoglund points out that these fortresses are situated along roadways throughout the Levant and obviously intended to control major trade routes. The appearance of these fortresses in the fifth century suggests that they were, at least in part, a response to the threat from Greece over control of the eastern Mediterranean. Hoglund then places the mission of Nehemiah in 445 BCE in the context of this militarization.[17] The refortification of Jerusalem is thus part of a larger Persian program dependent on imperial supplies and a military leadership (e.g., Neh 2:8; 7:2).

The tiny, impoverished, and isolated Yehud was insignificant in the Persian empire, especially prior to the Egyptian revolt in the midfifth century. Although one might think that the Persian administration kept a sharp eye on Yehud from the accounts in Ezra and Nehemiah, these undoubtedly reflect the idiosyncratic perspective of the biblical writers living in Jerusalem. Once the Persian interests in Palestine are to be understood in the context of commercialization and exploitation, Yehud recedes into the background until after the Egyptian revolts in 460 BCE. Its borders placed it at the margins of an economic and military buildup of the "Satrapy beyond the River." It was only the problems in Egypt and the specter of Greece that directed Persian attention toward Yehud.

The ethnic exclusivity of the returnees was first necessitated by the Babylonian exile and later encouraged by the Persian administration. For the Babylonian exiles, the development of a closed social group was a necessary mechanism of survival. The Persians, however, purposely encouraged ethnic distinction as a means of distinguishing specific enclaves. Hoglund suggests that these enclaves or collectives were then "administered, taxed and regulated as a corporate unit."[18] The collective nature of the returnees is reflected in both language and culture. The expression "the assembly of the exile" (קהל הגלה) reflects a community that returned to its homeland and rebuilt its national shrine. The vehement opposition to intermarriage by Ezra and Nehemiah indicates the exclusivity of the group. Marriage had social and economic implications. It brought outsiders into the group, and likewise property had be shared with these outsiders. Hence, it should not be surprising that intermarriage was punished by divestiture and exclusion from the "assembly of the exile." Hoglund posits that the imperial administration may even have insisted on ethnic exclusivity as a reflection of security concerns in the region.

In the postexilic literature, "Israel" is defined as those who go to Babylon and return.[19] On the ground, the exile was not complete. The land was not empty when Cyrus issued his proclamation that allowed the Jews to return to their homeland. Many had remained in the land, and the material culture essentially continued many aspects of the late monarchy (or Iron IIb Period). Archaeologically speaking, the Babylonian-Persian period continues the material culture of the monarchy. The destruction of Jerusalem is, as Gabriel Barkay points out, "of historical rather than archaeological significance."[20] Then again, there should be no doubt that the Babylonian conquest and exile brought a significant cultural disjunction. Independent monarchical government ended. Temple religion ceased in Judah. There were mass flights to Egypt. Scores of cities, towns, and villages were destroyed. The most affluent and skilled individuals were exiled to Babylon.

Literature of the Restoration Program

Accompanying the return of the exiles to the land was the formation of literature reflecting their issues and interests. Although the concern of the present study is particularly in the Promise, it seems likely that the formation of the Pentateuch and the final compilation of much of the prophetic corpus should be situated in this context.[21] The most important text for the present study is Chronicles, which rewrites the Deuteronomistic History and recasts the Promise to David. The importance of the Promise in Chronicles stands in sharp contrast to Ezra-Nehemiah, where the Promise is essentially absent. The reception history of the

Promise, especially in the books of Chronicles, must necessarily begin with the problematic issue of dating. This is especially critical since I have argued that the social context of Yehud dramatically changes in the midfifth century.

EXCURSUS: The Dating of Chronicles

There is widespread agreement in recent literature that the Chronicler wrote under the shadow of Persian administration, but little agreement as to exactly when during the Persian period.[22] Other than general considerations that relate the purpose and themes of Chronicles to the sociopolitical context, there is little objective evidence by which to assign a date. Yet, the importance of dating may be illustrated by Kenneth Pomykala's study on the Davidic dynasty tradition, which assigns Chronicles a date in the late Persian period. Once this date is assumed, Pomykala can repeatedly query, "Where was this lamp [for David] in the intervening 150–225 years between the fall of the Davidic dynasty and the Chronicler [*sic*] own time?"[23] Likewise, Sara Japhet dates Chronicles to the late fourth century and hence is forced to the amazing conclusion that "the concept of a covenant with David has no importance or theological significance in the book of Chronicles."[24] The pervasiveness of the Promise to David in Chronicles and its careful reworking, however, refute such an opinion. To be sure, *the books of Chronicles were produced in priestly circles*. There is no question on this point. But *it is just this point that makes the references to and recontextualizations of the Promise all the more remarkable*. Williamson is right in characterizing the Chronicler as royalist (see further later),[25] even though the priestly circles that produced this rewritten history made sure to place the Davidic monarchy in proper balance with priesthood and temple.

Main arguments for the late Persian date (i.e., midfourth century) include the presence of Persian loanwords (e.g., בירה, 1 Chr 29:1, 19; פרבר, 1 Chr 26:18; גנזך, 1 Chr 28:11; אדרכן, 1 Chr 29:7), the relationship with other canonical books, and the genealogy of the Davidic line. These are considered individually before we make a case for an earlier date.

The extent of the influence of the Persian language in Chronicles actually points to its composition in the early Persian period. First of all, the introduction of loanwords into the language scarcely needs to have taken more than a generation, especially when the words are technical words. More to the point, Sara Japhet points out, "Contrary to Ezra-Nehemiah, no trace of the Persian administrative system is evidenced in Chronicles."[26] Japhet inexplicably argues that this is evidence for a very late fourth-century date; however, there is little reason to think that this language would have just disappeared at the very end of the Persian period. It seems more logical to assume that the impact of the Persian language and administrative system was not as extensively felt in Chronicles because its composition *preceded* Ezra-Nehemiah, which was probably compiled in the late fifth century.[27] The early Persian period was marked by a certain distance between Yehud and the Persian heartland, which must have resulted in less extensive influence. The strong Persian presence of the later periods would have resulted in more direct Persian influence, as is suggested by Ezra-Nehemiah, and the continuing use of the Persian loanwords even in Mishnaic Hebrew.[28]

The relationship of Chronicles with other canonical works hardly gives reason for a specific date. Obviously, Chronicles is later than DtrH, which it draws on extensively as a source. Yet, there is wide agreement that DtrH was completed by the midsixth century, which hardly poses a problem for the early dating of Chronicles. Chronicles shares genealogical lists with Ezra–Nehemiah that might imply that Chronicles is later than Ezra-Nehemiah, if one supposes that Chronicles relied on Ezra-Nehemiah for the lists. This cannot be proven. It is just as likely that Chronicles had an independent source or that Ezra-Nehemiah borrows from Chronicles. There is also an apparent citation of Zechariah 4:10 in 2 Chronicles 16:9, which, it might be argued, implies that the book of Zechariah was canonical to the author of Chronicles. The citation is not exact, however, and the verse itself is the type of poetic concept that was not necessarily original to the prophet Zechariah: "For the eyes of YHWH range throughout the entire earth, to strengthen those whose heart is true to him." In any case, there is no reason to think that the book of Zechariah had to be canonical to cite such a verse, Could not the author of Chronicles cite a prophetic contemporary? Likewise, there is no reason to assume that the Pentateuch had to have been in its final form for Chronicles to cite it.

A more serious problem for an early Persian dating is the genealogy of the house of David, which carries on for seven generations after Zerubbabel (1 Chr 3:19–24). Assuming twenty years per generation, this list must have been composed no earlier than about 400 BCE. Obviously, this list must be dispensed with by anyone arguing for an earlier date for the composition of Chronicles. This has been achieved either by arguing that the genealogies (1 Chr 1–9) are a secondary insertion or by arguing that all or part of David's line is secondary (1 Chr 3).[29] A priori such arguments should give rise to suspicion of special pleading and circular argumentation; namely, the genealogy cannot be originally part of the book because Chronicles is early. This being acknowledged, it still seems that the genealogy cannot bear the weight of dating the book. There are irregularities in the final section of the genealogy, which details the continuing Davidic line, that raise suspicions about its composition.[30] Japhet notes that the Babylonian names in the list suggest that "it would be in Babylon, then, that this line was preserved and transmitted for generations."[31] How and why is it, then, that it was procured by a Jew, presumably a priest, in Yehud for use in the opening genealogies? It seems rather counterintuitive to argue that an author, on the one hand, continued the Davidic genealogy through the fourth century, while, on the other hand, he ended his narrative in the sixth century. Something has to give.

There are two ways to arrive at an earlier dating for Chronicles. Either we must ascribe an extension of the Davidic genealogy (3:19–24) to a later scribal hand or the whole opening genealogies (chapters 1–9) can be seen as a later addition. Frank Moore Cross argued that there were three editions of the Chronistic history: Chr_1 (1 Chr 10-2 Chr 34 + the *Vorlage* of 1 Esdr 1:1-5:65) was composed in support of Zerubbabel shortly after 520 BCE; Chr_2 was written after Ezra's mission in 458 BCE (1 Chr 1-9 + 1 Chr 10-2 Chr 34 + the *Vorlage* of 1 Esdr 1:1-5:65); and, Chr_3

(1 Chr 1–9 + 2 Chr 36:23 + Hebrew Ezra-Nehemiah) was edited about 400 BCE.[32] This scheme actually anticipates the separate composition of Chronicles and Ezra-Nehemiah so forcefully argued for by Japhet and Williamson. Cross's scheme also accounts for (although Cross does not mention this) the incongruity between the genealogy of David, which extends around 400 BCE, and the narrative, which ends in 539 BCE. Other incongruities between the genealogies and the narratives should be recognized. The genealogies disproportionately detail the Levitical and Priestly lines (6:1–81; 9:10–34) as opposed to the Davidic line (3:1–24). Certainly, the genealogies also reflect an extensive interest in the tribe of Judah, but this obviously reflects the fact that the entire book essentially concerns the tribe of Judah. The relative proportions and details in the genealogies suggest an author with intimate concerns with Levitical and Priestly power. The narrative—which focuses so heavily on the Davidides—hardly would have prepared the reader for such disproportionate interests. As an analogy, we may compare the concluding hymn in the Wisdom of Sirach (chapter 51). To be sure, David is not omitted and receives due mention, but vastly disproportionate attention is given to the priests, reflecting the importance of the priesthood over against the Davidides in Hellenistic Judaism (see chapter 7). Viewed from another perspective, the Davidides receive scarcely more attention than the Saulides, whose genealogy is actually recounted twice (8:29–40; 9:35–44)! One problem of the opening genealogies is how to account for the almost exact repetition of this Saulide genealogy. The only plausible explanation is that the second genealogy (9:35–44) serves as a bridge to the narrative account of Saul's death (chapter 10). This must imply, however, that the genealogies as a whole existed as a separate document. This certainly supports Cross's approach that they were added to the work in a later redactional stage.

A very late dating of Chronicles would mean that we have a work emphasizing the enduring promise to David and the legitimacy of the rebuilt temple and its re-established cultic service that was written over two centuries after the fact! Is this credible? Did the late Persian administration or the apparently peaceful transition to Hellenistic rule warrant the composition of a work emphasizing the house of David alongside the temple? And why did this work end with the sixth century? Could we, for example, imagine Josephus ending his *Antiquities* with the Hasmoneans instead of the Great War with Rome? Once the cogent argument was made by Japhet and Williamson that Ezra-Nehemiah must be separated from Chronicles, we are left with a book that ends in the sixth century. What reason would there be for rewriting DtrH in the late Persian or Hellenistic period, when the priestly leadership and the authority of the rebuilt Temple were well-established facts?

The leadership of the Jewish community increasingly became entrenched in priestly circles during the Second Temple period. Although in the late sixth century there is dual leadership between priest and king, as evidenced by the book of Zechariah, already in the period of Ezra and Nehemiah we see the priesthood taking the reigns of leadership, and by the third century all indications are that the priesthood had taken complete control. Given this, when is it reasonable to suppose that the royalist program of Chronicles was penned, especially given the virtual consensus that the book derives from priestly circles? Would priests who wielded the reigns of power in the fourth century support the royalist propaganda of Chronicles (even if it was balanced with the priesthood)? Unlikely. Rather, Chronicles speaks to the hot issues of the early Persian period (539–460 BCE)—namely, questions about the promised "house of David" and the authority of the Second Temple.

The attachment of the books of Chronicles to Ezra-Nehemiah (via the repetition in 2 Chr 36:22–23 and Ezr 1:1–4) gives the story of the Jewish people a new twist. I would suggest that the genealogies were added at this stage of the editing of Chronicles.[33] Repetition seems to be a crucial feature of this editorial stage. There is repetition of the end of Chronicles and the beginning of Ezra, repetition of the Saulide genealogy, and repetition of some of the list of returned exiles in both Ezra 2:1–70 and Nehemiah 7:6–73. The first two instances are clear editorial bridges. In this late Persian (ca. 400 BCE) editorial stage, the opening chapters of Ezra 1–6 would serve as the transition away from the monarchical aspirations of the early Persian period toward a new life under foreign domination. Royalists aspirations that went unchecked in the early Persian period were checked by the renewed Persian military presence in the region following the Egyptian revolts.

The Chronicler's Reading of the Promise

Much attention has focused on the Chronicler's interest in the legitimacy of the Davidic dynasty.[34] For example, David Noel Freedman argued that the Chronicler's purpose was "to establish and defend the legitimate claims of the house of David."[35] Simon de Vries suggested that the Chronicler "concerns himself so much with David's authority because there was no clear consensus in postexilic Israel about a continuing role for David's successors."[36] While significant attention has been given to the authority and legitimacy of the sons of David in postexilic Israel, surprisingly little attention has focused on the continuing legitimacy of the Jerusalem temple. Yet, by extending the Promise to the temple, the Chronicler tries to sanction the rebuilding of the Second Temple. If there were such questions about a continuing role for the sons of David, it is surprising that the Promise to David could be used as the vehicle to support the legitimacy of a rebuilt Jerusalem temple.

The justification of the Jerusalem temple's authority as the sole legitimate center for worship finds its textual support in the Chronicler's use of the Promise to David.[37] Although the Promise to David clearly supported the dynastic claims of the sons of David, it also expressed a deep ambivalence toward the temple. It is not surprising, then, that the books of Chronicles' main vehicle for justifying and legitimating the temple is a reinterpretation of the Promise to David. The Chronicler reinterprets the Promise to David both by revising 2 Samuel 7 (in 1 Chr 17) and by recontextualizing the Promise in the narratives concerning the construction of the temple. We see the recontextualization in the speeches of David (1 Chr 22 and 23), in narratives concerning Solomon's construction of the temple and his own palace (2 Chr 1–2), and at the completion of the temple (2 Chr 6:41–42).

The reinterpretation of the Promise to David in Chronicles can best be seen by detailed comparison with its apparent source in 2 Samuel 7 (compare the italicized differences):

2 Samuel 7:1–16

1 Now when the king was settled in his house,
and *YHWH had given him rest from all his*
enemies around him,
2 the king said to the prophet Nathan, "See
now, I am living in a house of cedar, but the
ark of God stays in a tent."

3 Nathan said to the king, "Go, do all that you
have in mind; for YHWH is with you."
4 But that same night
the word of YHWH came to Nathan:
5 'Go and tell my servant David: Thus says
YHWH: *Are you the one* to build me *a*
house to live in?
6 I have not lived in a house since the
day I brought up the people of Israel from
Egypt to this day, but I have been moving
about in a tent and in a tabernacle.
7 Wherever I have moved about among all the
people of Israel, did I ever speak a word with
any of the tribal leaders of Israel, whom I
commanded to shepherd my people Israel,
saying, "Why have you not built me a house
of cedar?"
8 Now therefore thus you shall say to my
servant David: Thus says YHWH of hosts: I
took you from the pasture, from following
the sheep to be prince over my people
Israel; 9 and I have been with you wherever
you went, and have cut off all your enemies
before you; and I will make for you a great
name, like the name of the great ones of the
earth.
10 And I will appoint a place for my people
Israel and will plant them, so that they may
live in their own place, and be disturbed no
more; and evildoers shall *afflict them*
no more, as formerly,
11 from the time that I appointed judges
over my people Israel; and I will
give you *rest* from all your enemies.
Moreover *YHWH* declares to you that YHWH
will *make* you a house.
12 When your days are fulfilled and you lie
down with your ancestors, I will raise up your
offspring after you, *who shall come forth*

1 Chr 17:1–14

1 Now when David settled in his house,

David said to the prophet Nathan,
"I am living in a house of cedar, but the
ark of the covenant of YHWH is under cur-
tains."
2 Nathan said to David, "Do all that you
have in mind, for God is with you."
3 But that same night
the word of YHWH came to Nathan:
4 'Go and tell my servant David: Thus says
YHWH: *You are not the one* to build me *the*
house to live in.
5 For I have not lived in a house since the
day I brought out Israel
to this very day, but I have lived
in a tent and a tabernacle.
6 Wherever I have moved about among all
Israel, did I ever speak a word with
any of the judges of Israel, whom I
commanded to shepherd my people,
saying, "Why have you not built me a house
of cedar?"
7 Now therefore thus you shall say to my
servant David: Thus says YHWH of hosts: I
took you from the pasture, from following
the sheep to be prince over my people
Israel; 8 and I have been with you wherever
you went, and have cut off all your enemies
before you; and I will make for you a
name, like the name of the great ones of the
earth.
9 And I will appoint a place for my people
Israel and will plant them, so that they may
live in their own place, and be disturbed no
more; and evildoers shall *wear them down*
no more, as formerly,
10 from the time that I appointed judges over
my people Israel; and I will
subdue all your enemies.
Moreover *I* declare to you that YHWH
will *build* you a house.
11 When your days are fulfilled to go to be
with your ancestors, I will raise up your
offspring after you, *one*

from your body, and I will establish his kingdom. [13]He shall build a house for my name, and I will establish the throne of his kingdom forever.	*of your own sons*, and I will establish his kingdom. [12]He shall build a house for me, and I will establish his throne forever.
[14]I will be a father to him, and he shall be a son to me.	[13]I will be a father to him, and he shall be a son to me.
When he sins, I will punish him with a rod such as mortals use, with blows inflicted by human beings.	
[15]But I will not take my steadfast love from him, as I took it from *Saul*, whom I put away before you.	I will not take my steadfast love from him, as I took it from him who was before you,
[16]*Your* house and *your* kingdom shall be made sure forever before me; *your* throne shall be established forever.	[14]but I will confirm him in *my* house and in *my* kingdom forever, and *his* throne shall be established forever.

A series of changes between 2 Samuel 7 and 1 Chronicles 17 illustrate the Chronicler's purposes in reinterpreting the Promise to David. These changes are well known but cannot be accounted for by appeal to a different *Vorlage*.[38] The Chronicler has often been falsely accused of tendentious rewriting; however, text-critical approaches should not obfuscate the Chronicler's theological creativity.[39] These changes represent the Chronicler's theological interests, which are later developed in non-synoptic recontextualizations of the Promise to David.[40] They mandate the building of the First Temple and the rebuilding of the Second Temple.

In three places, differences concern the Chronicler's ideology of rest. The most obvious change is a simple comparison between 2 Samuel 7:1, 11 and 1 Chronicles 17:1, 10. Chronicles first omits reference to rest from 2 Samuel 7:1 and then changes the second reference from "rest from enemies" (וַהֲנִיחֹתִי) into military subjugation of enemies (וְהִכְנַעְתִּי). The Chronicler's concerns are theological in that it is only YHWH's presence in the temple that brings rest; the Deuteronomist associates rest with the land.[41] As a result, the Chronicler throughout his work will transplant the promised rest from the time of David into the time of Solomon—that is, into the period when the temple was built. For example, in 1 Chronicles 22:8 YHWH promises David, 'I will give (Solomon) rest from all his enemies' (contrast 2 Samuel 7:1, 11). The reason for the switch becomes quite clear in 1 Chronicles 28:2 when David calls the temple a "house of rest" (בית מנוחה). The movement of rest from David to Solomon and from land to temple is finally underscored by the words quoted from Psalm 132 at the temple's dedication: "Advance O LORD God, *to your resting place*, You and the ark of your might" (2 Chr 6:41; cf. Ps 132:8).[42] According to the Chronicler, YHWH himself, along with his ark, come to rest in the temple.[43] Thus, the Chronicler takes out the references to rest in 2 Samuel 7, and recontextualizes and resignifies them in his later references to the Promise to David.

The different perspectives on rest underlying these changes can further help explain the minor variation between 2 Samuel 7:6 and 1 Chronicles 17:5. In Samuel, God says, "I have not lived in a house since the day I brought up the people of Israel from Egypt to this day, but *I have been moving about in a tent and in a tabernacle* (ואהיה מתהלך באהל ובמשכן)." In Chronicles we read, "For I have not lived in a house since the day I brought out Israel to this very day, *but I have lived in a tent and a tabernacle* (ואהיה מאהל אל־אהל וממשכן)." How should we explain the differences here? Lyle Eslinger suggests that God's speech in 2 Samuel 7 "combines the language of the book of Deuteronomy about the place that Yhwh would choose to place his name and the language of verse 6 about his own itinerant past. . . . The party to be anchored to a 'place' [v. 10] is Israel; the place to be 'established' (*śm*) is that for Israel, not a temple for God (as per Deuteronomy)."[44]

The Chronicler's interpretation of the rhetorical question, "Shall you build a house for me to dwell in?" (האתה תבנה־לי בית לשבתי, 2 Sam 7:5), begins to remove the ambiguity about the temple in the Promise. The Chronicler interprets "shall you" (האתה) as a simple exclusion of David as temple builder: "Your are not the one who shall build the house for me to dwell in" (לא אתה תבנה־לי הבית לשבת, 1 Chr 17:4). The Chronicler begins here to redirect attention on Solomon as the chosen temple builder.[45] Hugh Williamson points out that this change "fits in with [the Chronicler's] whole outlook which does not oppose temple building as such, but finds David himself to be unsuitable."[46] In another small change, the addition of the definite article, "the house" (הבית), as opposed to the indefinite "a house" (בית) in Samuel, the Chronicler most likely reflects an emphasis on the exclusivity of Jerusalem's claim. The addition of the definite article also changes the nuance of the statement, which now seems to assume that a house should be built—even if David was not the chosen temple builder.[47] It is important to recognize that these exegetical maneuvers do not just reflect the Chronicler's own creative exegesis. Rather, the Chronicler plows a path already broken by the Deuteronomistic Historian in his recontextualization of the Promise in Solomon's Prayer (see chapter 4).

In the concluding verse of the oracle, the Chronicler's changes point to a theocratic kingdom. There, the Chronicler clarifies any ambiguity about a continuing role for the temple with slight and deft changes in the pronominal suffixes. Second Samuel 7:16 suggests an enduring Davidic dynasty: "And *your* house and *your* kingdom will be firm forever ‹‹before me››. *Your* throne shall be established forever."[48] Chronicles changes pronominal suffixes from "your" (ך-) to "my" (י-), thereby shifting the focus from David's dynasty and kingdom to God's temple and kingdom: "And I shall appoint him in *my* house and in *my* kingdom forever. And *his* throne shall be established forever."[49] Commentators have not adequately explained the change from "your house and your kingdom" in Samuel to "my house and my kingdom" in Chronicles. For example, Curtis and Madsen insist, "*My house* must be taken parallel to *my kingdom*, thus referring to the people of Israel."[50] However, the Chronicler elsewhere employs similar parallelisms for the temple and palace: "a house for the name of YHWH and a house for his kingdom" (בית לשם יהוה ובית למלכותו, 2 Chr 1:18) and "a house for YHWH and a house for his kingdom" (בית יהוה ובית למלכותו, 2 Chr 2:11). In these cases, the parallelism of temple (בית) and kingdom (מלכות) relies on the Chronicler's interpretation of the Promise to David; therefore, Curtis and Madsen's interpretation must be rejected. In sum, the Chronicler's reading of the Promise to David assumes that God promises David that Solomon will build the "temple" (בית) and that God will give David a "kingdom" (מלכות). This essentially reverses the pun on the word "house" (בית) in the earlier version of the Promise and thereby explicitly sanctions the building of the temple. An eternal promise to the Davidic dynasty is now paired with a promise for an eternal temple, as it says, "I shall establish him in my *temple* (ביתי) forever."

Chronicles also recalls the Promise to David at several junctures during the course of temple building. The first question the Chronicler addresses in these passages is, Why did God choose Solomon? Why did YHWH tell David, "You are not the one to build the temple?" In 1 Chronicles 22:7–8, David explains, "My son, I wanted to build a house for the name of YHWH my God, but the word of YHWH came to me, saying, 'You have shed much blood and fought great battles; you shall not build a House for my name for you have shed much blood before me on the earth.' " David's speech supports the change in 1 Chronicles 17:14 by justifying the prohibition: David's many battles debarred him from the task of temple building (cf. 1 Chr 18–20). In David's next speech in 1 Chronicles 28, the Chronicler again emphasizes that God "chose" (בחר) Solomon to build the temple.[51] But why does the Chronicler emphasize that God chose Solomon? Because God's chosen temple builder is therefore a legitimate temple builder and his temple is a legitimate temple.

The narratives describing Solomon's construction of the temple echo Chronicles' version of the Promise to David. In 2 Chronicles 1:18, we are told that Solomon resolved to build "a house for the name of YHWH and a house for his kingdom." In 2 Chronicles 2:11, Hiram praises Solomon who has the wisdom to build "a house for YHWH and a house for his kingdom." In contrast, 2 Samuel 7:16 promises that God will establish the house of David and the kingdom of David. The Chronicler's pairing of the house of God and the house of the kingdom—that is, the temple and the palace—relies on his own revision of the Promise to David (1 Chr 17:14). Thus, the Chronicler connects the building of both the Solomonic temple and the Solomonic palace with God's promise to the house of David in the Promise to David. The speeches of Solomon and Hiram rely on the Chronicler's reinterpretation of the Promise, which assumes that God mandated the building of the temple along with establishing the Davidic dynasty.

Chronicles justifies the building of the temple by David's claim to direct personal revelation. In 1 Chronicles 22:8 and 28:3, David implies that the Promise came directly from YHWH: "the word of YHWH came to me" and "and God said to me." The import of David's claims are underscored in 1 Chronicles 28:12, which says that God gave David the plan of the temple "by the spirit" (ברוח); the term רוח elsewhere denotes the spirit that inspires prophecy (cf. 1 Chr 12:19; 2 Chr 15:1).[52] David again makes a prophetic claim for the temple in verse 19: "all this, the plan of all the works, which YHWH has caused me to understand by his hand on me, I give you [Solomon] in writing." David received the plan for the temple "by the hand of YHWH on him"—an expression that also has prophetic implications. As Simon de Vries points out, the Chronicler patterns the presentation of David as a cult founder after Moses.[53] Just as Moses founded the tabernacle, David founded the temple, which replaced the tabernacle.[54] YHWH not only commanded the building of the temple, but he also divinely revealed the site, the pattern, and the organization of the temple to David. According to the Chronicler, David is prophetically inspired and patterns his founding of the cult after Moses because the Chronicler believed that the Jerusalem temple and cult were as legitimate as their Mosaic counterparts.

In Chronicles, the Promise becomes conditional on the building of the temple. Accordingly, building the temple is tantamount to seeking God and fulfilling the commandments of God. In 1 Chronicles 22:19, David enjoins all Israel, saying, "Set your minds and hearts on worshipping YHWH your God, and build the sanctuary of YHWH your God." David's speech associates seeking YHWH with building the temple. Seeking YHWH and building the temple are one and the same. In David's prayer in 1 Chronicles 29:19, he implores God to give Solomon "a whole heart to observe your commandments, your admonitions, your laws, and to fulfill them all, and to build this temple for which I have made provision." The building of the temple becomes part of the list of commandments. If the Promise is conditional on the observance of the commandments, then the Promise was conditional on building the temple.

This new condition of the Promise—namely, building the temple—was perhaps influential in Zerubbabel's role in the reconstruction of the Second Temple. The early postexilic book of Haggai suggests that Zerubbabel's quest for leadership was associated with building the temple. Just as Solomon was a chosen temple builder, Haggai also applies the term "chosen" (בחר) to Zerubbabel. In Haggai 2:23, God declares, "I will take you, O my servant Zerubbabel, son of Shealtiel, and make you a signet, for I have *chosen* you." Haggai actually commissions Zerubbabel for leadership just as he begins to build the temple. In fact, in Haggai 2:4 the prophet enjoins Zerubbabel with the injunction, "Be strong, do it." This recalls Solomon's commissioning before the assembly to build the temple in 1 Chronicles 28:10: "See now that YHWH has chosen you to build a house for his sanctuary, *be strong and do it*" (emphasis added; also verse 20).[55] So it is no coincidence that Zerubbabel begins to build the temple on the same day Solomon started to build the First Temple, on the second day of the second month (cf. Ezr 3:8 and 2 Chr 3:2).[56] In a real sense, the emphasis on the temple in Chronicles laid a foundation for a rebuilt Second Temple.

The covenantal nature of the Promise to David becomes prominent in Chronicles. Allusions to the Davidic covenant (ברית) are sprinkled throughout the Chronicler's account of the history of Judah. H. G. M. Williamson notes three passages in particular (2 Chr 13:5; 21:7; 23:3) that "are illustrative of the three major situations through which the dynasty would pass whilst remaining intact."[57] These passages indicate that God (1) "gave the kingship over Israel forever to David and his sons by a covenant of salt (ברית מלח)" (2 Chr 13:5), (2) "would not destroy the house of David because of the covenant (ברית) that he had made with David" (21:7; contrast 2 Kgs 8:19), and (3) "promised that the sons of David would reign" (23:3). Additionally, the Chronicler reflects on the Promise when he cites Psalm 132:10 at the conclusion of Solomon's prayer: "Remember your covenant loyalty to David (לחסדי דויד), your servant" (2 Chr 6:42).[58] The most powerful illustration of the increasing importance of the covenantal idea is in 2 Chronicles 7:18, "then I will establish your royal throne, just as I made covenant with your father David (כרתי לדויד) saying, 'You shall never lack a successor to rule over Israel.' " The expression "I made a covenant with David" in Chronicles replaces the expression "I promised concerning David" (דברתי על־דוד) in 1 Kings 9:5 and thereby emphasizes the special covenant with David. Indeed, the emphasis on the covenantal nature of the Promise to David can be seen only as *strengthening* the Promise while at the same time highlighting its conditional nature.

There has been some debate about the relationship between the Davidic and Sinaitic covenants in the books of Chronicles. Much of this discussion has been an offshoot of the debate over the relationship between the books of Ezra-Nehemiah and Chronicles. Williamson observed that Ezra-Nehemiah is largely silent about the Promise to David in marked contrast to Chronicles.[59] This becomes one of the pillars pointing to separate authorship of the two books. Williamson concludes that the Chronicler's treatment of the Davidic covenant results "in a shift away from the emphasis of the Deuteronomistic historian on Exodus and Sinai." Recently, Brian has objected to Williamson's analysis: "It would perhaps be more accurate to describe the Chronicler's outlook as *subsuming* Sinaitic (and patriarchal) traditions into the Davidic covenant, rather than neglecting them."[60] As we have seen in the previous chapters, however, an integration of the Sinaitic and Davidic covenants is already part and parcel of the interpretative tradition that the Chronicler inherited. It underlies a conditionalizing of the Promise, as well as its extension from the Davidides to all Israel. In this respect, the Sinaitic had already been subsumed into the Davidic covenant, or vice versa, centuries earlier.

Zechariah 6:12-13: An Allusion to the Promise

> Thus said YHWH of Hosts: "Behold, a man called the Branch shall branch out from the place where he is, and he shall build the Temple of the LORD. It is he that shall build the temple of YHWH; he shall bear royal honor, and shall sit and rule on his throne. There shall be a priest by his throne, with peaceful understanding between the two of them.

This verse makes an allusion to the Promise. To begin with the repeated statement that "he shall build the temple of YHWH (היכל יהוה)" clearly echoes 2 Samuel 7:13a, "he is the one who shall build a house for my name (הוא יבנה־בית לשמי)." Although these are not exact parallels, the emphatic statement of the subject cannot fail to recall the Promise. Yet, while the subject of 2 Samuel 7:13a is David's son Solomon, the subject of Zechariah is David's distant grandson, Zerubbabel. The alternation between "a house for my name (בית לשמי)" and "the temple of YHWH (היכל יהוה)" is also quite intriguing. It reflects the tendency of Late Biblical Hebrew to substitute "temple" (היכל) for "house" (בית). It also removes an element of literary playfulness in the Promise's use of the term "house" (בית). The use of the term "throne" (כסא) in continuation of Zechariah 6:13 supports a directly textual influence from the Promise which continues in 2 Samuel 7:13b, "and I will establish the *throne* of his kingdom" (וכננתי את־כסא ממלכתו). The introduction of a priest alongside the king here is anticipated in the Chronicler's rendering of the Promise (cf. 1 Chr 17:14). The king's role as temple builder becomes implicit in the Promise here as well as in the book of Chronicles, Haggai, and Ezra 1–6.

It is noteworthy that the interpretation in Zechariah 6:12–13 explicitly cites the Deuteronomic expansion of the Promise, 2 Samuel 7:13a. As pointed out earlier, this verse is a secondary addition to the Promise by a Josianic editor. The development of this particular verse highlights the importance of the literary history of 2 Samuel 7:1–17. By focusing on 2 Samuel 7:13a, the author of Zechariah 6:12-13 clearly follows in an interpretative tradition. The interpretative trajectory precipitates from the Deuteronomistic school, continues through the books of Chronicles, and is taken up in Zechariah.

MT Jeremiah 33:14–22: Davidic Dynasty and Levitical Priesthood

In the MT of Jeremiah 33:14–22, we find the development of Jeremiah 23:5–6 with a broad institutional reading of the Promise. To begin with, it should be recalled that the Jeremiah 33 is missing from the shorter LXX text. This shorter text is now reflected in the Qumran manuscripts, 4QJer^b and 4QJer^d. This has convinced a consensus of scholars that it was missing from the Hebrew *Vorlage* of the Old Greek translation.[61] The MT addition clearly relies on Jeremiah 23:5–6, as can easily be seen in the following comparison (correspondences in italics):

MT Jeremiah 23:5–6	MT Jeremiah 33:14–22
Behold, the days are coming, says YHWH, when	14 *Behold,* the days are coming, says YHWH, when I will fulfill the good promise (והקמתי את־הדבר הטוב) I made to *the house of Israel and the house of Judah.*
I will raise up *for David a righteous Branch,* and he shall reign as king and deal wisely, *and shall execute justice and righteousness in the land.*	15 In those days and at that time I will cause to spring up *for David a righteous Branch*; and *he shall execute justice and righteousness in the land.*
6 *In his days Judah will be saved and Israel will live in safety. And this is the name by which he will be called: "YHWH is our righteousness."*	16 *In those days Judah will be saved and Jerusalem will live in safety. And this is the name by which it will be called: "YHWH is our righteousness."*
	17 For thus says YHWH, "David shall never lack a man to sit on the throne of the house of Israel, 18 and the levitical priests shall never lack a man in my presence to offer burnt offerings, to make grain offerings, and to make sacrifices for all time."
	19 The word of YHWH came to Jeremiah:
	20 Thus says YHWH: If any of you could break my covenant with the day and my covenant with the night, so that day and night would not come at their appointed time,

21 only then could my covenant with my servant David be broken, so that he would not have a son to reign on his throne, and my covenant with my ministers the Levites.
22 Just as the host of heaven cannot be numbered and the sands of the sea cannot be measured, so I will increase the offspring of my servant David, and the Levites who minister to me.

Although it is obvious in this comparison that Jeremiah 33:15–18 is an elaboration of 23:5–6,[62] this still leaves open the precise dating of 33:14–22 (as well as the whole longer MT version). Dates ranging from the early Persian period (Volz) to the Maccabean period (Duhm) have been offered for the longer MT. There is little basis for the late date.[63] McKane makes the helpful point that verse 26 specifically limits the rule of the Davidic ruler to "the offspring of Abraham (זרע אברהם)" and not world domination. This limitation probably reflects the limited aspirations of the postexilic community. It may even point to the limited authority of Davidic figures like Zerubbabel within the Persian empire.[64] The introduction of the priesthood into this oracle points to the increasing power and position of the temple and its ministers over against the royal family in the postexilic period. This change is consonant with Chronicles and Zechariah in its introduction of the priesthood as part of the Promise.

The most intriguing shift from Jeremiah 23 to 33 points to the importance of the city of Jerusalem over against the Davidic dynasty. This shift is witnessed in two important changes.[65] First, the expression "Judah will be saved *and Israel* will live in safety" (23:6) becomes "Judah will be saved *and Jerusalem* will live in safety" (33:16). The second shift plays off this change as the antecedent for the suffix in the expression "and this is the name by which *he* will be called" changes from David (אשר־יקראו; i.e., masculine) to Jerusalem (אשר־יקרא־לה; i.e., feminine).

Jeremiah 33:14–18 introduces, for the first time, the priesthood into the reading of the Promise. The Josianic reading had already emphasized the importance of the temple, but not its personnel. Such a reading, however, introduced a certain imbalance in the Promise. According to the Josianic reading, God promised an eternal kingdom to the sons of David, as well as an eternal temple, without mentioning who was to preside over this temple. The divine commission of the priests is actually mediated by Aaron, according to 1 Chronicles 24:19, "These had as their appointed duty in their service to enter the house of YHWH according to the procedure established for them by their ancestor Aaron, as YHWH God of Israel had commanded him." Such a divine commission, however, was otherwise unknown. Moreover, there is a strong tradition that made David responsible for the organization of the priests: "David organized the priests according to the appointed duties in their service" (1 Chr 24:3; also see 2 Chr 8:14). Perhaps introducing the priestly commission into the Promise to David both added prestige to the priestly office and, ironically, diminished the priestly office's dependence on the authority of David himself.

2 Chronicles 6:41–42: YHWH's Physical Presence in the Temple

Second Chronicles 6:41–42 (adapted from Ps 132:8–10) appears at the conclusion of Solomon's Prayer (2 Chr 6:1–40; cf. 1 Kgs 8:12–53) as part of the prayer itself and enjoins YHWH to enter his newly built temple. In this processional song, the actual presence of YHWH is enjoined to enter his resting place in the temple. Both the citation of Psalm 132 and the Chronicler's contextualization of it as the conclusion to Solomon's Prayer place 2 Chronicles 6:41–42 within the literary horizon of the Promise.

Psalm 132:8–10	*2 Chronicles 6:41–42*
8 קומה יהוה למנוחתך	41 ועתה קומה יהוה אלהים לנוחך
אתה וארון עזך	אתה וארון עזך
9 כהניך ילבשו־צדק	כהניך יהוה אלהים ילבשו תשועה
וחסידיך ירננו	וחסידיך ישמחו בטוב
10 בעבור דוד עבדך	42 יהוה אלהים אל־תשב פני משיחיך
אל־תשב פני משיחך	זכרה לחסדי דויד עבדך
Advance, O YHWH,	Advance, O YHWH God,
to your resting-place,	to your rest,
You and Your mighty Ark!	You and Your mighty Ark.
Your priests are clothed in triumph;	Your priests, YHWH God, are clothed in triumph;
Your loyal ones sing for joy.	Your loyal ones will rejoice in Your goodness.
For the sake of your servant David,	YHWH God, do not reject Your anointed one;
do not reject your anointed one.	remember the covenant loyalties to your servant David.

What new twist does it give to the reading of the Promise in Solomon's Prayer? Second Chronicles 6:41–42 emphasizes YHWH's actual physical movement with the ark and YHWH's actual resting place in the temple. The theology of the temple as a "house of rest (בית־מנוחה)" for YHWH appears repeatedly in Chronicles (e.g., 1 Chr 22:8–10; 28:3), and here it becomes evident that Psalm 132 was a touchpoint for this theological innovation. The citation of Psalm 132:41–42 seems intended to counter the abstraction of the temple as YHWH's dwelling place that one encounters in Solomon's Prayer—especially in the exilic reading of the Promise.

Moshe Weinfeld argues that the idea of the temple as the deity's resting place finds "its fullest expression in Psalm 132: 'This is my resting-place for always; here I shall dwell, for I have desired it . . . . There shall I make David's standard sprout forth. I have prepared a lamp for my anointed.' The idea of a Davidic house here joins together with the idea of the chosen house, and the circle is closed."[66] This idea of the temple as the deity's resting place is explicitly absent from DtrH and, in particular, from 2 Samuel 7. In the midst of the Promise, YHWH grants rest to David and the people, "I will give you rest from all your enemies" (v. 11); the people's rest contrasts with YHWH's situation: "I have not lived in a house since the day I brought up the people of Israel from Egypt to this day, but I have been moving about in a tent and a tabernacle" (v. 6). Chronicles remedies YHWH's homelessness but at the cost of a resting place for YHWH's people. On the one hand, Chronicles removes the references to the people finding a resting place (cf. 1

Chr 17:1, 10); on the other hand, it introduces the term "house of rest" (בית־מנוחה) for the temple (1 Chr 28:2; also note 1 Chr 22:8–10).[67]

The Chronicler's citation of Psalm 132 adds an imperative: "Remember the covenant loyalties to your servant David (זכרה לחסדי דויד)." This injunction apparently derives from the Chronicler's reading of the expression "For the sake of your servant David (בעבור דוד עבדך)" in Psalm 132. The expression recalls the common Dtr[1] expression, "for the sake of David (למען דוד)" (cf. 1 Kgs 11:12, 13, 32, 34, 39; 15:4; 2 Kgs 8:19; 19:34). The exact wording in Hebrew is different, however, and indicates that there is no purely textual relationship. Rather, they reflect a common cultural discourse. Indeed, the expression "covenant loyalties to David (חסדי דויד)" is known from Isaiah 55:3, where it occurs in the context of a covenant (ברית) with David. Its context here, at the end of an extended reflection on the Promise to David written in the early postexilic period, may be fairly understood as a call to restore the Davidic monarchy.

Politics of the Return

The exile had forced a radical reading of the Promise, a reading that undermined the very foundations of the Jerusalem temple. The Promise was for all Israel. Only God's name dwelt in the temple because the whole earth was his dominion (e.g., Isa 66:1-2). These readings democratized exilic society and universalized YHWH, but at what cost? When, in 539 BCE, Cyrus encouraged the Jews to return to Jerusalem and rebuild their temple there, there was evidentally considerable ambivalence. Did the Jewish people still need a temple? Was there any reason to physically return to Palestine? Was God not the God of the whole earth?

Although the Chronicler, as well as the prophets Haggai and Zechariah, felt that the Jerusalem temple needed to be rebuilt, this opinion was by no means unanimous. Second Temple period literature provides hints of a diversity of attitudes toward the Jerusalem temple.[68] To begin with, the laxness toward rebuilding the temple in the book of Haggai suggests that many people were less than enthusiastic about rebuilding the temple. This is confirmed by the report of the people's reaction to the rebuilding of the temple in Ezra 3:12–13, which indicates that there were feelings that the Second Temple was inferior to the first (also note Tob 14:5). Texts like Isaiah 66:1–2 confirm that some may have believed that the temple should not have been built because "God dwells in heaven, how can a temple be built for Him on earth?" Certainly the priestly vision of an eschatological temple in Ezekiel 40–48 was not supportive of the efforts to rebuild the temple. Not surprisingly, Ezekiel 40–48 would later play an important textual role in the Qumran covenanters' rejection of the Jerusalem temple and its priesthood, on the one hand, and for their vision of a heavenly eschatological temple on the other hand.[69] Second Temple literature that looks for a heavenly temple or a temple not built by human hands implicitly rejects the Second Temple.[70] Another later text, Second Maccabees (ca. 100 BCE), still feels the need to emphasize the continuity between the first and second temples, apparently because there were many who doubted the legitimacy of the Second Temple (cf. 2 Macc 1:18–19).[71] These are just hints, but taken together they indicate that there was some question as to the exact role of the temple in the early postexilic Jewish community, and these doubts lingered throughout the Second Temple period.

Obviously, it was in the interests of the priestly circles that authored and edited the books of Haggai, Zechariah, and Ezra-Nehemiah to strongly support the rebuilding of the temple. In spite of these interests, it is clear that there were objections and apathy toward rebuilding the temple. It is within this context, then, that the books of Chronicles, especially in their reception and transmission of the Promise to David, serve as an apologetic for the rebuilt temple.[72]

There are two phases to the Persian period. In the early Persian period, Yehud was depopulated and rural. It lay outside the interests of the colonial empire. In such a context, hopes for the restoration of the Judaean kingdom with a Davidic king and a rebuilt Solomonic temple might quietly flourish. Yehud was an insignificant backwater of the rising tide of the Persian empire. This picture changed radically with the Egyptian revolts in the mid-fifth century. Suddenly, the Satrapy Beyond the River was a focal point of Persian attention as it faced its western menace. It is hardly a coincidence that Persian administrators like Ezra and Nehemiah appear precisely at this time. Nor is it surprising that the books of Ezra and Nehemiah stifle any hints of the restoration of the Davidic kingdom. The later Persian period in Palestine was marked by the building of a military infrastructure that certainly would not have tolerated even a hint of nationalistic aspirations so closely tied to the Davidic Promise. It is perhaps in this context that the Davidic Promise, frustrated by this world, turns apocalyptically to the world to come. But it could do so only on the margins of Jewish society.

7

Second Temple Judaisms Read the Promise

Just as a covenant was established with David son of Jesse of the tribe of Judah, that the king's heritage passes only from son to son, so the heritage of Aaron is for his descendants alone.
—Sirach 45:25

The exile scattered the Jewish people throughout the ancient world, and although a significant number returned and resettled in Palestine, the Diasporas remained the majority.[1] One constant of Jewish identity both inside and outside Palestine was the Jerusalem temple. In this last chapter, we examine Jewish reception and transmission of the Promise to David within the Hellenistic and Roman world.

The practical elimination of any real hope to reestablish the Davidic monarchy translated into increasing power for the priesthood during the Second Temple period.[2] By third century, the focus of the Promise to David had completely shifted from the monarchy to the temple, as we may see, for example, in the book of Tobit:

> When I was in my own country, in the land of Israel, while I was still a young man, the whole tribe of my ancestor Naphtali deserted the house of David and Jerusalem. This city had been chosen from among all the tribes of Israel, where all the tribes of Israel should offer sacrifice and where the temple, the dwelling of God, had been consecrated and established for all generations forever." (1:4)

His reflection on his plight begins with an oblique reference to "the house of David and Jerusalem." The language that follows—that is, "the city chosen"—transfers focus from the chosen scion to the city and its temple. Yet, the temple had become the focus of Jewish life and identity in both Palestine and the Diasporas. To be sure, the shift in power toward the priesthood had its beginnings in the Babylonian exile, which necessitated an establishment of new forms of leadership. The transfer of power to the priesthood reaches, its apex with the Hasmonean priest–kings in the second century BCE. The books of Maccabees which describe the first few decades of Hasmonean rule, witness the complete vanishing of the Davidide dynasty. Jonathon Goldstein observes, "The books [of Maccabees] contain no hint of the expected coming of a wonderful king descended from David or of a figure called the 'Son of Man.' This surprising fact demands explanation."[3] The explanation is not difficult to find. The books of Maccabees were written to support the Hasmonean dynasty as the legitimate priests and rulers of the restored "Davidic" kingdom. Goldstein characterizes the author of 1 Maccabees as a "Hasmonean propagandist" who justifies their authority in secular and sacral matters by their achievements. While this assessment is certainly correct, it also underscores that there must have been lingering questions about the legitimacy of the Hasmoneans as both kings and priests. Literature critical of the Hasmonean dynasty like the Psalms of Solomon reflects—not surprisingly—a strong support of Davidic messianism. The Qumran sect also grew up in opposition to the Hasmoneans, and it is not surprising that they also highlight Davidic messianism, although they are also concerned with the legitimate priests. The Alexandrian Jewish community, by contrast, was uninterested in Jewish nationalism of any kind.

Alexandrian Diaspora: Acculturation and Identity

One of the more energetic parts of the Jewish Diaspora was in the Hellenized Egyptian city of Alexandria. Alexandria was one of the great cultural centers of the ancient world, with its famed library and architecture. Such was its fame that Pseudo-Aristeas wrote that Alexandria "surpasses all cities in size and prosperity" (*Ep. Arist.* 109; cf. Philo, *Legat.*, 308). Its position on confluence of the Nile and the Mediterranean naturally made it a cosmopolitan city and it was accorded great prestige in the Greek and Roman world. The following section looks at the social situation of Jews living in Alexandria and reflects on how this shaped their understanding of the Promise to David.

Egypt was a traditional place of refuge for Jews. More to the point, Egypt was a convenient place of refuge for those living in Palestine. The immigration of Jews into Egypt began already with the Assyrian campaigns against Israel and then with the Babylonian campaigns against Judah and the exiles. Some of these Jews evidently served in the Egyptian military, as is suggested by the Jewish garrison at Elephantine. The conquest of Egypt by Alexander the Great in 332 BCE ushered in a new age in the history of Egypt and for the Jewish Diaspora there. Alexander himself brought new immigrants and Hellenistic culture, but the major influx of immigrants began under the aegis of Ptolemy I Soter in 305 BCE. At this time, the city of Alexandria was founded and quickly grew and acquired international fame. Ptolemaic control of Syria-Palestine from 301 to 198 BCE made migration quite easy. The *Letter of Aristeas* (ll. 12–27) claims that Ptolemy I (305–282 BCE) moved as many as 100,000 Jews from Palestine for slaves and military. Ptolemy II Philadephus (282–246 BCE) allegedly issued a decree freeing Jewish slaves. In addition to forced conscription and slavery, there was also probably an influx of Jews who came to Egypt for economic reasons. Certainly, the establishment of the large and prosperous bureaucratic center in Alexandria both attracted and demanded economic migrants. As John Barclay observes, "The new city of Alexandria and the huge financial bureaucracy of Egypt afforded much greater opportunities for social advancement than the backwater conditions of Judaea."[4] In turn, Egyptian Jews looked to the power of Egyptian—and not to a Davidic messiah—to save their people from Seleucid tyranny. This is especially clear, as John Collins points out, in Sibylline Oracles 3. Foreign kings like Cyrus—a perspective already incipient in Second Isaiah—deliver the Jewish people.[5] The dynastic aspect of the Promise to David became irrelevant at best as Alexandrian Jewry looked to Egypt rather than David for salvation.

Alexandrian Jewry was shaped by two foci held in tension: (1) acculturation into the Alexandrian community through participation in Hellenism and (2) maintenance of Jewish identity through adherence to ancestral traditions.[6] To what extent was this politically possible under Roman law, which restricted Jewish participation in Hellenism? Gregory Sterling cites anecdotal evidences that illustrate the tension. In a papyrus document, a Jew named Helenus identifies himself simply as "Alexandrian"; this was crossed out by an official, who wrote above it: "a Jew from Alexandria." The former, asserts Sterling, "states the aspiration, the latter the reality." The aspiration, however, dominated the community's self-identity. Sterling concludes, "While it is a commonplace to point to Jewish observance of Torah requirements as a central component of Jewish identity, I would like to suggest that in Alexandria the right to participate in Hellenism was intellectually just as important and historically of greater consequence."[7] Philo of Alexandria highlights a sense of distinction that epitomizes the Jewish tradition when he observes that Numbers 23:9, "Behold, a people who will dwell alone, and will not be reckoned among the nations," refers not to territorial separation but rather to the particularity of their customs and their adherence to ancestral traditions (cf. *Mos.* 1.278).[8]

The preservation of the identity of Alexandrian Jewry was facilitated by concentrating settlement in the delta quarter of the city. Although eventually Jews had spread over the entire city, the concentration of settlement encouraged a social conservatism. Josephus suggests that the Jews were granted a quarter "that they might observe a purer way of life, mixing less with people of other races" (*Bell.* 2.488). Barclay notes that in practical terms this meant that Jews would more likely intermarry, keep kosher, practice the Sabbath and festivals, and avoid contact with pagan religious practices.[9] In this respect, we must sharply distinguish the acculturation of the Jewish community from its assimilation. On the one hand, assimilation involves social integration and would have meant abandonment of key Jewish social distinctives like Sabbath observance and intermarriage. Acculturation, on the other hand, pertains to language and education; the Alexandrian Jewish community could develop facility with Greek, awareness of Greek values and literary traditions, and even scholarly expertise (e.g., Philo), while still maintaining its social distinctiveness. John Barclay uses two scales by which to measure assimilation and acculturation (see Figure 7.1).[10] The Alexandrian Jewish community moved much further up the scale of acculturation than it did the scale of assimilation. It is important to point out that acculturation could be used either to submerge Jewish culture uniqueness on one extreme or to employ a well-educated antagonism toward Greco-Roman culture at the other extreme (as with the case of Hellenized Hasmonean literature).[11]

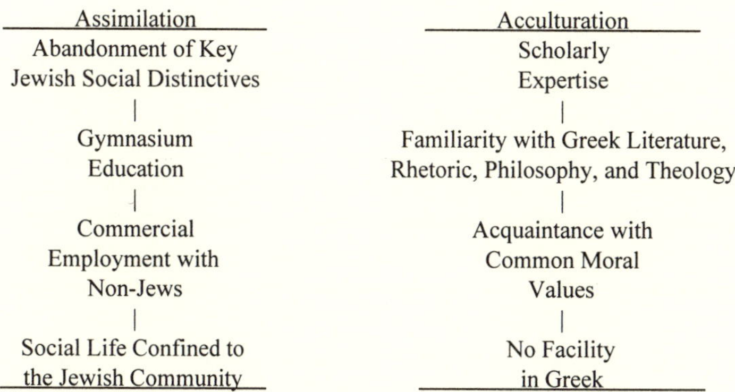

Figure 7.1. Assimilation or Acculturation

The translation of the Bible into Greek typified the Hellenistic acculturation of Alexandrian Jewry.[12] Although *The Letter of Aristeas* suggests that the project began with a suggestion from Demetrius of Phalerum, the librarian of Ptolemy Philadelphus, the project also arose from the needs of the Alexandrian community. It is difficult to know how long and how much Alexandrian Jewry remained bilingual (Hebrew, Greek) after the translation of the Torah into Greek. Yet, its translation into Greek removed one of the ethnic and cultural ties with ancient Israel in favor of acculturation. Eventually, the Alexandrian Jews came to understand their Septuagint as inspired (e.g., *The Letter of Aristeas*) and a point of ethnic pride (cf. Philo, *Mos.* 2.41–43). Barclay points out, however, that it also "gave religious sanction for the use of the Greek language."[13]

The politicization of the priestly office and its eventual merger with the royal office became a critical point of discussion among the Jews in the Egyptian diaspora as well as in Palestine in the second and first centuries BCE. One example of this perspective in the Egyptian diaspora comes from the Septuagint. For example, Johan Lust points out that the Greek translation of Ezekiel 21:30–32 reacts "against the unification of the royal and the priestly functions. It condemns the high priests who prefer the royal powers over the priestly ones and announces the coming of a new high priest who will be worthy of the priestly turban."[14] Although Lust does not try to correlate this translation with the sociopolitical context of the second century, the LXX obviously polemicizes against the increasing politicization of the priestly office, which climaxed in the Hasmonean priest-kings. Lust points out that the LXX of Ezekiel 28:11–19 actually may identify the wicked "Prince of Tyre" with the high priest-king in Jerusalem by using terms like "crown (στέφανος)" and "seal (ἀποσφράγισμα)."[15] There is no need to necessarily place the translation of the Former Prophets, and Ezekiel in particular, in a such narrow time frame. Nevertheless, it is certainly relevant to set the translation in its wider sociopolitical context.

The political struggles within the priesthood culminated in the second century after Onias IV was thwarted in his bid for the high-priesthood and fled to Egypt. In Egypt, Onias was received by Ptolemy Philometor and allowed to establish a rival temple in Leontopolis (cf. Josephus, *Ant.* 13.62–73; *Bell.* 7.421–436). John Barclay notes, however, that although the Oniad temple lasted more than two centuries and was not destroyed until after the Jewish War in 73 CE, still, "extant Jewish literature from Alexandria is silent about this temple, recognizing only the Jerusalem temple as the locale of sacrifice and the object of pilgrimage" (p. 36). In this context, a pro-Jerusalem temple bias of the Alexandrian translation of the Bible (see later) should be seen as explicit support of the Jerusalem temple and priesthood over against the claims of Leontopolis and the Oniad family.

The Alexandrian Greek Translation of the Promise to David

The so-called Septuagint, or LXX, has come down to us in a considerable variety of versions. For the purposes of the present study, we are interested particularly in the LXX^{B}, that version of the LXX which was translated (for the most part) and circulated in Alexandria.[16] This version has its origins in the 3rd century BCE. According to the tradition preserved by Aristobulus (ca. 170 BCE), a translation of the Five Books of Moses was commissioned by Ptolemy II Philadephus (285–246 BCE).[17] A generation later the "Letter of Aristeas" was written glorifying the Jews and their traditions; this tradition then continued to be embellished by later Jewish and Christian writers.[18]

One of the features of the LXX,[19] as I. L. Seeligmann observes, is "the creative power of the theology of the translators."[20] Bickerman writes that, for the translators of the Septuagint, "the Scripture was not a monument of the dead past but a way of their own life."[21] This is hardly a surprising statement. Translation is foremost an act of interpretation. To translate is to interpret and ultimately to betray the text. In spite of this, relatively little attention has been paid to the theological *tendenz* of the Septuagint. Study of the LXX has focused on textual criticism. This is all the more the case with the books of Samuel and, to a lesser extent, Kings. The books of Samuel, which together with the books of Kings comprise the LXX's four books of the Kingdoms, have reached us in a considerable state of textual disarray. It was already recognized by S. R. Driver, who emphasized in his classic work, *Notes on the Hebrew Text of Samuel*, that the Greek versions could be of considerable assistance in that well-known desideratum of text-criticism: the reconstruction of the urtext. Sidney Jellicoe summarized the focus of scholarship: "The Hebrew text of these books [Samuel-Kings] has reached us in a state of considerable disorder, and the main value of the LXX has not unnaturally been measured in terms of an aid to restoration."[22] Not surprisingly, the creative power of the LXX has often been lost in the search for an urtext.

In the following discussion, I quite consciously chose to refer to the "Alexandrian translators" rather than to more abstract and detached terms like the "Greek version" or "Septuagint." These terms remove the human and social elements behind the process of translation. Translation is done by people in places—a point that cannot be lost in the present discussion. My use of the term "Alexandrian translators" then is a rhetorical device intended to emphasize the human context. My use of the plural (i.e., "translators") can be justified if we view the translation as the product of a community rather than an individual. For instance, David

Gooding's study on 3 Kingdoms reflects on the social setting of the Greek translations:

> Now if we look around for some real-life situation from which 3 Reigns in its present form could have emanated, we shall obviously have to look further than a scriptorium where faithful scribes copied out as accurately as they could the Greek manuscript which lay before them. Similarly we shall have to go further than an individual scholar's study, or even "a cell or two", where in a comparatively short while a straightforward translation of the Hebrew *Vorlage* was made. To account for the present state of the text seems to require something more like a rabbinic school, a Beth hamidrash, where varying Hebrew text-traditions and the comparative merits of alternative Greek renderings could be discussed.[23]

There lies behind the Greek translation both an intimate knowledge of the theological discourse and a complex intertextual interplay that derive from the Alexandrian community rather than from any individual.

The Septuagint translation provides two particular opportunities to examine the Alexandrian community's reception of the Promise to David in the translation of the Promise itself (2 Kgdms 7:1–17) and the Prayer of Solomon (3 Kgdms 8:12–53). In these places, the Septuagint focuses its attention on the temple at the expense of the Davidic dynasty. To be sure, a pro-temple bias is evident more broadly in the Alexandrian in the altering and expanding of narratives concerning the temple throughout the Septuagint, but these are beyond the scope of the present study.[24]

J. Coppens has argued that the Septuagint evinces signs of a developing transcendent and supernatural messianism,[25] and Coppens is not alone in this assessment.[26] This argument does not directly bear on the present discussion because the texts Coppens cites do not directly interpret the Promise. Nevertheless, the issue does bear indirectly on the present chapter, and it is worthwhile to point out some problems in Coppens's argument. For example, it is unclear how the translation of "young woman (עלמה)" as "virgin (παρθένος)" in Isaiah 7:14 really makes the passage more "messianic,"[27] unless we fall into the trap of defining messianism according to its Christian incarnation. Certainly, this verse became a focal point in early Christian theology and a focus of later debate, but it hardly seems to indicate developing messianism. Johan Lust rightly criticizes that Coppens overlooks "those texts in which messianic connotation has been weakened or given a different nuance by the LXX."[28] Although Coppens suggests that Isaiah 9:5–6 evidences this developing messianism, Lust is certainly correct in countering that the change in names for the child was so that "God comes to the fore as the saviour whereas the royal child's role is reduced to that of a messenger."[29] To be sure, the very translation of the Bible into Greek would eventually facilitate its use by the early Christian community to justify a developing messianism—but that is another subject. In sum, there is scarcely any evidence suggesting that the Septuagint itself evidences a developing messianism—quite the contrary. This is certainly borne out by the Alexandrian translators' handling of the Promise to David.

The Promise to Build in 2 Kingdoms 7:1–17

Three variants in 2 Kingdoms 7:1–17 (i.e., 2 Sam 7:1–17) discussed here will illustrate the importance of the Jerusalem temple over against the Davidic dynasty for the Alexandrian translators. Appeals to textual criticism and particularly comparisons with the books of Chronicles have tended to minimize these variants. The following discussion shows, however, that while the ideology of 2 Kingdoms accords with the Books of Chronicles, the text of 2 Kingdoms 7 shows only minimal agreement with 1 Chronicles 17. The translators' biases can best be viewed through direct comparisons between the Masoretic and LXX versions of 2 Samuel//2 Kingdoms 7:1–17. These comparisons demonstrate that an ideologically motivated interpretation rather than a different Hebrew *Vorlage* accounts for the variations between the MT and the LXX.

The most unimpeded window into the bias is perhaps in 2 Samuel and 2 Kingdoms 7:11b. There, the Alexandrian translators effect the transfer of the Promise from the Davidic dynasty over to the (Jerusalem) temple:

MT– 2 Samuel 7:11b	*LXX – 2 Kingdoms 7:11b*
והגיד לך יהוה כי־בית יעשה־לך יהוה	καὶ ἀπαγγελεῖ σοι κύριος ὅτι οἶκον οἰκοδομήσεις αὐτῷ
And YHWH promises you that YHWH would make a house for you.	And the Lord promises you that you shall build a house for him.

In the MT, YHWH promises that YHWH shall make a house for David, that is, YHWH will give David a dynasty. This reading is contextually supported in the MT by the next verse (v. 12), which states that God will raise up David's seed after him. It is therefore clear that the MT refers to a dynasty with the term "house" (בית).[30] In contrast, the Greek translation promises that David shall build a temple for the Lord.[31] The LXX omits the subject (יהוה) of the MT,[32] changes the person of the verb from third to second, and changes the prepositional suffix from second to third. These changes can be retroverted into Hebrew as follows: "and you [David] shall build a temple for him (ובית תבנה לו)." Whereas in Samuel "house" (בית) means "dynasty," in the LXX "house" (οἶκος) means "temple." Thus, instead of God "building" the Davidic dynasty as in Samuel, the Alexandrian translator has David building a temple for God. Because David did not actually build the temple, this change ultimately points to Solomon, who built the temple David had wanted to build.[33] Kyle McCarter notes that the LXX is "a reading which curiously anticipates one line of modern interpretation of Nathan's Oracle."[34] More to the point, though, the Alexandrian translators follow a line of reading already begun in the books of Kings, which is further developed in the books of Chronicles, and which has permutations in other Second Temple period literature. No appeal to textual criticism adequately explains the radical transformation. *This quite explicit exegetical move should prepare us for more subtle and creative translations.*

In the canonical form of the Promise to David, there is a clear objection to David's desire to build a temple for YHWH. It begins in 2 Samuel 7:5 with the question "Shall you build a house for me?" and goes on to emphasize that

(1) YHWH had never dwelled in a house but only in a tent and a tabernacle (v. 6) and that (2) YHWH had never requested a house to be built for himself (v. 7). Nevertheless, YHWH acquiesces to David's request but states that his son shall build the temple (v. 13a).[35] As a whole, though, 2 Samuel 7 focuses on YHWH's promise to establish a Davidic dynasty so that David's throne "shall be established forever" (v. 16). The Alexandrian translators alter the entire tenor of the Promise. The first variant comes in YHWH's initial response to David's request to build the temple. The minor change can be observed:

MT 2 Samuel 7:5	*LXX 2 Kingdoms 7:5*
Shall you (האתה) build a house for me for my dwelling?	It is not you (οὐ σὺ) who shall build for me a house for my dwelling.

The Hebrew text may be interpreted in various ways. Is YHWH questioning the whole enterprise of building a temple? Does YHWH just question whether David should be the person to build it? The immediate context (vv. 6–7) suggests that YHWH questions the whole enterprise of temple building because YHWH has no need of a permanent building. Nevertheless, the Alexandrian translators take full advantage of the ambiguity. The translators place emphasis on the adequacy of David as temple-builder by translating the rhetorical "shall you (האתה)" as a direct statement, "It is not you (οὐ συ) who shall build for me a house for my dwelling."

The Alexandrian reception and transmission participate here in a well-established discourse. The Peshitta, for example, renders the rhetorical question as a statement, *ʾth lʾ*, "you shall not build." It reverses the word order so that the focus is not directly on the person of David; David shall not build the temple, but Solomon will. Chronicles have a reading that is also similar to the LXX and may have even influenced the Alexandrian translators' rendering in 1 Chronicles 17:4: "It is not you who shall build the house for me to dwell in" (לא אתה תבנה לי הבית לשבת). Chronicles also adds the definite article to the word "house" (הבית), which makes its connection to the temple more emphatic (see chapter 6). There is no reason to suspect that the LXX and Chronicles reflect a *Vorlage* other than the MT because there is no trigger for a scribal error from האתה to לא אתה. Rather, this change is a theologically motivated interpretation; namely, the books of Chronicles develop a doctrine of the inadequacy of David as temple builder. According to Chronicles, David could not build the temple because he was a man of war and bloodshed (e.g., 1 Chr 28:3; note that this reading was anticipated by 1 Kgs 5:17). In adding their own nuance, then, the Alexandrian translators follow well-established precedents.

In verse 16 of the Promise, the Alexandrian translators introduce ambiguity into the text so that it may be understood to promise an eternal temple. The following parallel will facilitate a comparison:

MT 2 Samuel 7:16	*LXX 2 Kingdoms 7:16*
ונאמן ביתך	καὶ πιστωθήσεται ὁ οἶκος αὐτοῦ
וממלכתך עד־עולם	καὶ ἡ βασιλεία αὐτοῦ ἕως αἰῶνος
‹‹לפני›› כסאך	ἐνώπιον ἐμοῦ καὶ ὁ θρόνος αὐτοῦ
יהיה נכון עד־עולם	ἔσται ἀνωρθωμένος εἰς τὸν αἰῶνα

And your house [i.e., David] and
your kingdom shall be sure forever
before <<me>>, your throne
shall be established forever.

And his house [i.e., Solomon] and
his kingdom shall be sure forever
before me, and his throne
shall be established forever.

The Alexandrian translators follow closely the word order of Samuel but change its suffixes.[36] In one case, the translators were probably working with a superior text; namely, the reading, ἐνώπιον ἐμου, undoubtedly derives from a *Vorlage* that read, «לפני» "before me." The textual error in the MT is an obvious case of dittography, which was undoubtedly conditioned by the use of the second-person suffix (ך-) elsewhere in the verse.[37] This exception only strengthens the case for the exegetical creativity of the LXX because it highlights the correct use of textual criticism. We can both explain the mechanism which created the scribal error (i.e., dittography) and the context which might have conditioned the error (i.e., the other suffixes in the verse). On the other hand, when we come to the LXX's reading of the third masculine singular (ו–) for the second masculine singular (ך–) in this verse, however, there are neither scribal mechanisms nor contextual factors that condition the change. Yet, the seemingly minor change in person effects a fundamental change in the final verse of the oracle. It is no longer a promise for David but now is a promise for Solomon.

What does "his house" refer to in 2 Kingdoms 7:16? On the surface, the phrase "his house" appears ambiguous in the LXX because the three promised items in verse 16—his house, his kingdom, and his throne—are mentioned earlier in verses 11–13. However, "his house" should be understood as a reference to the temple because the Alexandrian translators undo the literary play on house (בית can be either "temple" and "dynasty") by its translation in verse 11, "you (David) shall build a house for him (the Lord)." As a result, "house" is only a reference to the temple. In this case, since Solomon built the temple, it is "his temple," which he built for the Lord.

In sum, the Alexandrian translators of 2 Samuel 7 reflect a pro-temple bias by making the promise of a temple central. Perhaps underlying their translation is the interpretation of the "place" (מקום) that the Lord would establish for Israel in verse 10 as the temple. Second Temple Jewish texts use the term "place" (מקום) as a synonym for both God and the temple ("the place of God"). An interesting example may be brought from Qumran literature where the "place" in 2 Samuel 7:10 is the trigger for 4QFlorilegium *pesher* on the Promise and the eschatological temple (see later).[38] Whereas, in the MT this "place" is the land of rest which David has forged with God's help (cf. verses 1, 11), the LXX may have been influenced by the pervasive use of the term "place" (מקום) for the temple in the Second Temple period. Whether the "revisionism" in the LXX here is intentional or subconscious is difficult to ascertain, but the result is that the underlying negative attitude towards the temple in the MT of 2 Samuel 7 is undone in the Septuagint.

Translating Solomon's Prayer: 3 Kingdoms 8

The Alexandrian translators make the authority of the Jerusalem temple as explicit as possible. This is first apparent in the translation of 2 Samuel 7 and continues in three variations in 3 Kingdoms 8, Solomon's Prayer: (1) the addition in 3 Kingdoms 8:16 (cf. 1 Kgs 8:16), (2) the translation of "house (בית)" as "place (τόπος)" in 3 Kingdoms 8:42 (cf. 1 Kgs 8:42), and (3) the addition in 3Kgdms 8:53α.

A small Qumran fragment (4Q54) from 1 Kings 8:16–17 has already been discussed in an excursus in chapter 4 (see further discussion there). This fragment is quite important and warrants some review in the present context. It may be transcribed as follows:

ל[היות נגיד על עמ]י	to] be a leader over [my] people
]להיות על עמי על[	]to be over my people, over[
י[שראל ויאמר]	I]srael, and he said,[

Trebolle-Barrera compares this fragment with other textual versions, especially noting the similarity with the Chronicles tradition. The variant can be better understood by a simple comparison.

> 1 Kings 8:16 MT: From the day I brought My people Israel out of Egypt, I have not chosen a city from among all the tribes of Israel to build a House in order that My name might dwell there; but I have chosen David to rule My people Israel.
> 2 Chronicles 6:5: From the day I brought My people out of the land of Egypt, I have not chosen a city from among all the tribes of Israel to build a House in order that My name might dwell there; *nor did I choose anyone to be the leader of my people Israel. 6 But then I chose Jerusalem for My name to abide there*, and I chose David to rule My people Israel.
> 3 Kingdoms 8:16: From the day I brought My people Israel out of Egypt, I have not chosen a city from one tribe of Israel to build a House in order that My name might dwell there. *But then I chose Jerusalem for My name to abide there*, and I chose David to rule My people Israel.
> 4QKgs: [From the day I brought My people out of the land of Egypt, I have not chosen a city from among all the tribes of Israel to build a House] in order that My name might dwell there; *nor did I choose anyone to*[*be the leader of*]*my* [*people*] *Israel. But then I chose Jerusalem for My name to abide there*, and I chose David [to rule My people I]srael.

This comparison was discussed in detail in chapter four, but the arguments will be briefly revisited here. It is hardly coincidence that these variations fall at a theologically critical point in the Prayer of Solomon. How should we to account for the fact that MT ≠ LXX ≠ 4QKgs? Adding other versions into the picture hardly clarifies things; for example, the Greek Lucianic version follows the MT, not 4QKgs. 4QKgs is supported by Chronicles, but this should give not comfort to a text critic because the author of Chronicles used an earlier *redaction* of Kings, not simply a better *text* than the MT and rewrites his source at theologically sensitive points in the story. Thus, Chronicles is not simply another textual witness. In the present case, 1 Kings 8:16 is exactly the type of text which we should have expected the Chronicler to rewrite since it touches on particularly important themes in his work: the house of David, Jerusalem, and the temple.

How does the addition in 4QKgs affect the reading of Solomon's Prayer? In the Promise, there is no hint that the city of Jerusalem was *chosen.* The language of a *chosen* city derives from Deuteronomy 12. Indeed, the point was that no location was chosen to house the tabernacle permanently (2 Sam 7:6). How can we explain this variation? LXX's omission highlights the Jerusalem temple at the expense of the Davidic dynasty. This downplaying of the monarchy in the LXX may also be found in the critical narrative where Israel requests a king; there, to the statement in 1 Samuel 8:18, "The day will come when you cry out because of the king whom you yourselves have chosen; and YHWH will not answer you on that day," the LXX adds, "because you will have chosen a king for yourselves (ὅτι ὑμεῖς ἐξελέξασθε ἑαυτοῖς βασιλέα)." This addition is missing in 4QSam^{a}.[39] It is difficult to explain the addition as a simple scribal error. The addition should most likely be understood as an Alexandrian reading that attributed the exile—the ultimate example of God's silence—to the request for a king.

The idea of Jerusalem as the chosen city returns us to the long-standing discourse on the meaning of the "place (מקום)" in the Promise to David (2 Sam 7:10). Deuteronomy 12 interprets the "place" as the location where God will choose to put his name. Along these lines, the translation of the term "house" (בית) as "place" (τόπος) in 3 Kingdoms 8:42 is quite telling. It suggests that the translators were aware of the discourse on the meaning of 2 Samuel 7:10: "I will establish a place (מקום) for My people Israel." Quite clearly the Alexandrian translators wished to read the "place" as Jerusalem and its temple. The reading of the "place" as land would have had clear nationalistic import, which went against the grain of the Alexandrian Jewish community.[40]

The emphasis on the Jerusalem temple is most explicit in an appendix to Solomon's speech at the dedication of the temple, which includes an entire passage, 3 Kingdoms 8:53, that is not found in the MT:

> 8·53 ὅτι σὺ διέστειλας αὐτοὺς σαυτῷ εἰς κληρονομίαν ἐκ πάντων τῶν λαῶν τῆς γῆς καθὼς ἐλάλησας ἐν χειρὶ δούλου σου Μωυσῆ ἐν τῷ ἐξαγαγεῖν σε τοὺς πατέρας ἡμῶν ἐκ γῆς Αἰγύπτου κύριε κύριε [53α] τότε ἐλάλησεν Σαλωμων ὑπὲρ τοῦ οἴκου ὡς συνετέλεσεν τοῦ οἰκοδομῆσαι αὐτόν ἥλιον ἐγνώρισεν ἐν οὐρανῷ κύριος εἶπεν τοῦ κατοικεῖν ἐν γνόφῳ οἰκοδόμησον οἶκόν μου οἶκον ἐκπρεπῆ σαυτῷ τοῦ κατοικεῖν ἐπὶ καινότητος οὐκ ἰδοὺ αὕτη γέγραπται ἐν βιβλίῳ τῆς ᾠδῆς.
>
> Because you have set them apart for an inheritance for yourself out of all the nations of the earth just as you spoke by the hand of your servant Moses when you brought our fathers out of the land of Egypt, O Lord God. [53α] Then Solomon said concerning the house when he finished building it: "He manifested the sun in heaven; the Lord said that he would dwell in darkness. Build my house, a beautiful house for yourself in order to dwell in newness." Behold, is this not written in the book of the song?

This addition probably draws—in part—on 1 Kings 8:12–13, which, as it happens, is missing in the LXX. Then again, the differences cannot be accounted for by simple, mechanistic text-critical explanations. Taken together with the other two variations in Solomon's prayer, this points to conscious interpretative work on the part of the Alexandrian translators. A relationship between 3 Kingdoms 8:53α and 1 Kings 8:12–13 (MT) can be readily observed by the following parallel columns:

LXX 3 Kingdoms 8:53α	*MT 1 Kings 8:12–13*
[53α] Then Solomon said concerning the house when he finished building it:	Then Solomon said,
"He manifested the sun in heaven; the Lord said that he would dwell in darkness.	"YHWH has chosen to dwell in a thick cloud:
Build my house, a beautiful house for yourself in order to dwell in newness."	I have now built for You a stately House, a place for you to dwell forever."
Behold, is this not written in the book of the song?	

The reference to the enigmatic "book of the song" is also an alleged source. Concerning this addition, H. Thackeray suggests that this clear editorial revision takes its cue from Exodus 15. He suggests that the reference to ἐν βιβλίῳ τῆς ᾠδῆς "in the book of the song" derives from the opening verse of Exodus 15: "Then sang" (אז ישׁר; cf. Num 21:17). Further, Thackeray suggests that the expression "a place for you to dwell" (v. 17, מכון לשבתך; 1 Kgs 8:13 has מכון לשבתך עולמים, "a place for you to dwell forever") in the concluding verse of the Song of the Sea may be behind the difficult LXX expression "to dwell on newness" (τοῦ κατοικεῖν ἐπὶ καινότητος). The connection which these texts make with the temple may be conditioned by the pun between "a place for you to dwell" and "the place for your Sabbath."[41] It is noteworthy that 4QFlorilegium also cites both Exodus 15:17 and 2 Samuel 7:10 in its *pesher* on the divine temple. The Qumran *pesher* would then be a further development of this exegetical maneuver and suggests that the LXX addition is not a unique exegetical innovation but follows a previously plowed interpretative trajectory. Indeed, the association between Exodus 15:17 and 1 Kings 8:13 became a staple of later rabbinic midrash (e.g., *Mekilta de-Rabbi Ishmael*, Shir. 24–29; Targum Neophyti, Fragment Targum, ad loc.). Although it is difficult to know exactly when the associations were first made between Exodus 15:17 and the temple and between Exodus 15:17 and 1 Kings 8:13, it seems likely that the LXX already reflects something of these interpretative trajectories.

As Brevard Childs points out, the movement of the Song of the Sea is from deliverance at the sea to the planting in the land. YHWH guides Israel into the land (cf. Exod 15:13).[42] In this respect, there is a sharp contrast between the Song of the Sea and 1 Kings 8:12–13. Yet, it is again instructive that the final verse of the Song of the Sea was taken by later interpreters as a reference to the temple (not the land). In this respect, it parallels the shift in the theology of "rest," which also was apparently first associated with the land and only later the temple (see chapter 6). The clearest example is in the Qumran *pesher* 4QFlorilegium; an additional example is the LXX's version of Solomon's Prayer, which appends a lengthy passage (3Kgdms 8:53α) that depends on Exodus 15:17. Once the text of 2 Samuel 7 is assumed, the more significant parallel, however, is to be found with the ancient Song of Moses.

Palestinian Judaisms of the Late Second Temple Period

The late Second Temple period in Palestine was marked by a proliferation of sectarian movements. A common element in the diverse expressions of Judaism in the late Second Temple period was the interpretation of texts. Joseph Blenkinsopp correctly notes that "continuity and discontinuity in Palestinian Judaism were primarily a matter of the interpretation of these texts [i.e., the Hebrew Bible], serving the goal of either affirming existing conceptual and societal structure or authorizing new departures."[43]

The Promise in the Wisdom of Sirach: Pre-Hasmonean Judaism

The Wisdom of Sirach was a priestly work composed in Jerusalem in the early second century BCE, sometime *before* the Hasmonean revolts. It curtails the Promise to David. Indeed, the Promise is stripped of any eternal implications in Sirach 47:11: "The Lord took away his [David's] sins, and exalted his power (τὸ κέρας αὐτοῦ) forever; he gave him a covenant of kingship (διαθήκην βασιλέων) and a glorious throne in Israel." Here, for example, Sirach introduces an ambiguity into the duration of the Promise. Instead of giving David an eternal kingdom, he receives "power forever." This may be understood, on the one hand, as a rationalization of the Promise which could no longer be understood as literally referring to a continuous line of Davidic monarchs. On the other hand, the implication of a "covenant of kingship" is that it is conditional on the observation of the conditions of the covenant. In its brief survey of Solomon and Rehoboam, then Sirach highlights the ultimate forfeiture of the covenant (cf. 47:18–25).

Although the Promise to David is left sterile by Sirach's reading, it is invigorated through its coordination with the high priesthood. The priesthood is the central focus of the historical epilogue of Sirach. Its survey of Israel's history (chapter 44) begins with Enoch and ends with Simon, the high priest. Although the priesthood is a certain theme and the Promise to David is marginalized, nevertheless, the Promise is employed to highlight the eternal covenant for the high priests. Chapter 45 introduces Aaron as Moses' brother and ends by comparing his covenant with the Davidic covenant.

> [6]He exalted Aaron, a holy man like Moses who was his brother, of the tribe of Levi. [7]He made an eternal covenant with him, and gave him the priesthood of the people . . . . [24]Therefore a covenant of friendship was established with him, that he should be leader of the sanctuary and of his people, that he and his descendants should have the dignity of the priesthood forever. [25]Just as a covenant was estab-

lished with David son of Jesse of the tribe of Judah, that the king's heritage passes only from son to son, so the heritage of Aaron is for his descendants alone. [26]And now bless the Lord who has crowned you with glory. May the Lord grant you wisdom of mind to judge his people with justice, so that their prosperity may not vanish, and that their glory may endure through all their generations.

It should not be lost, however, that Aaron's covenant is described here as an "eternal covenant" (διαθήκην αἰῶνος, 45:7), whereas David is given a "covenant of kingship" (διαθήκην βασιλέων, 47:11).[44] On the one hand, it is curious that the Promise to David is introduced at this point. It points to the prestige of the Promise, and it perhaps suggests that the eternal promise to Aaron was derived from Nathan's oracle. Indeed, it is clear that the promise for the temple was derived from Nathan's oracle; consequently, it should hardly be surprising that a promise for the chief guardian of that temple, the high priest, should also derive authority from a particular reading of Nathan's oracle. On the other hand, it is ironic that, while the high priesthood apparently derives an eternal covenant through Nathan's oracle, Sirach's reading limits the application of the Promise to David. As such, it highlights the growing power of the priesthood at the expense of the Davidic monarchy.

Psalms of Solomon 17

The Psalms of Solomon were composed in Jerusalem between 80 and 40 BCE. Chapters 17–18 can actually be placed between 61 and 57 BCE because they mention Pompey's capture of Jerusalem, Aristobolus II's exile, and John Hyrcanus II's rule but make no reference to the revolt of Alexander in 57 BCE. The authorship is a matter of more debate, though the Psalms of Solomon show the closest affinities to the Pharisees.[45] Although our sources for the Pharisees during the late Second Temple period are meager, it is clear that the Pharisees arose and existed primarily as a popular opposition party during the Hasmonean period (ca. 167–63 BCE). Even their name "Pharisees," which means "the separated ones (פרושים; Παρισαῖοι)," suggests their position as outsiders during the Hasmonean period. At times there was a rapprochement between the Hasmoneans and the Pharisees, particularly during the reign of Alexandra (ca. 76–67 BCE). Psalms of Solomon 17 is of particular interest in the present study because it provides an extended reflection on the future emergence of a Davidic monarch.

The Psalms of Solomon derive their name from the similarity between the most prominent psalm of the collection, Psalms of Solomon 17, and the canonical Psalm 72, which is assigned by its superscription to Solomon.[46] R. B. Wright points to some striking similarities between the biblical portrait of Solomon and the anointed one of Psalms of Solomon 17: (1) both are the son of David, (2) they extend boundaries, (3) they restore Jerusalem, (4) they defend Yahwistic worship, (5) they receive tribute from foreign monarchs, and (6) they are wise and just. On the other hand, the future anointed one will not commit the sins of Solomon—namely, the accumulation of wealth and trusting in military (cf. PssSol 17:33; 1 Kgs 10:26–29; Deut 17:16–17). In a way, the pointed association between Solomon and the future anointed one serves as a disjunction in the continuity of the Promise to David; that is, it is for David's *son*, not his *sons*. To be sure, such a pointed association between the Promise and the person of Solomon is already present in the books of Chronicles (see chapter 6). The pointed focus on the person of Solomon allows both Chronicles and the Psalms of Solomon to sidestep the apparent failure of the Promise while still holding on to a hope for the reestablishment of the Davidic line. In this aspect, the Psalms of Solomon follow a well-established interpretative trajectory.

The emphasis on an anointed and specifically *Davidic* leader in the Psalms of Solomon comes as a pointed critique of the Hasmonean dynasty. Indeed, given that the Psalms of Solomon were likely all composed soon after the conquest by Pompey (63 BCE) and the final demise of the Hasmonean dynasty, it is apparent that they were intended to address the issue of Hasmonean legitimacy. The Jewish enemies of the Psalms of Solomon usurped the monarchy, as we may ascertain from 17:6–7a: "With pomp they set up a monarchy because of their arrogance; they despoiled the throne of David with arrogant shouting. But you, O God, overthrew them, and uprooted their descendants from the earth." This can only refer to the Hasmonean dynasty, which the author(s) considered illegitimate, undoubtedly because they were not the rightful heirs of the throne of David.

Throughout Psalms of Solomon 17, we find a loose reflection on the Promise to David. The psalm both recalls the plight of the righteous in the face of both Jewish sinners and the Gentiles and also anticipates deliverance of the Jewish people by a Davidic leader. Psalms of Solomon 17:4 reads,[47] "O Lord, you choose David to be king over Israel, and you swore to him concerning his seed forever so that his kingdom would not fail before you." However, because of Israel's sins (v. 5), the throne of David was destroyed (v. 6). Still, the psalmist awaits deliverance by a promised Davidic monarch. In verse 21, we read, "See, O Lord, and rise up for them their king, the son of David, to rule over your servant Israel in the time known to you, O God." And the psalm continues in verse 32, "And he will be a righteous king over them, taught by God. There will be no unrighteousness among them in his days, for all shall be holy and their king shall be the anointed of the Lord." In these verses we see a dependence of the literary tradition that emanates from the Promise to David, but in no place is there a direct quotation of any of the related texts. It is important to note that the king will be "taught by God" (v. 32) and not the priests. This contrasts with the Temple Scroll from Qumran, where the Davidic king is taught by the priests, and it points to an origin for the Psalms of Solomon both outside priestly circles and in opposition to the Hasmonean kings. In this respect, the proposed Pharisaic origin of the Psalms of Solomon is most plausible. Their aspirations for a future Davidic monarch likely reflects their position as outsiders during most of the tenure of the Hasmonean priest-kings. Given the Pharisees' popularity among the lower classes, it may be argued on the basis of Psalms of Solomon 17 that there were popular aspirations for the restoration of a Davidic monarchy that were justified in part by an appeal to the Promise to David. Such a picture would also be supported by the Gospels (e.g., Matt 21:1–17; Mark 11:1–11; Luke 19:29–44). However, our sources for this early Pharisaic movement are unfortunately meager.

The Qumran Sect

The Qumran community may be described in sociological terms as an anticommunity or antisociety.[48] In other words, the Qumran community set itself in opposition to the perceived establishment. The precise development of the community's history has been a subject of some discussion. The community at Khirbet Qumran should almost certainly be identified with the Essenes.[49] This identification, however, is not critical to the sociopolitical background of the community. There is enough consensus about the sociopolitical background of the community to contextualize their literature and place it within the literary history of the Promise to David.

To begin with, the term "Qumran literature" needs to be clarified. In the present study, the term "Qumran literature" refers to texts *composed* by the residents of Khirbet Qumran. Not everything found in the caves was composed by the inhabitants of Qumran; the most obvious examples are the biblical scrolls. Other scrolls like Jubilees and Enoch also predate the Qumran settlement. Devorah Dimant estimates that 40% of Cave 4 manuscripts should be classified among those "not containing terminology connected to the Qumran Community."[50] Dimant distinguishes between "documents employing terminology connected to the Qumran Community" and "works not containing such terminology." Clusters of terms and ideas concern four areas: (1) practices and organization, (2) history and present situation, (3) theological and metaphysical outlook, and (4) peculiar biblical exegesis. Dimant emphasizes that religious concepts and ideas themselves are not sufficient (e.g., 1 Enoch; Jubilees) except when they are accompanied by distinctive terminology. Likewise, Emanuel Tov has emphasized this distinction by isolating what he describes as Qumran orthography; scrolls not written in the peculiar orthography of the community most likely were not written by the community's scribes.[51] Orthography must be studied in concert with terminology in determining whether each scroll is a sectarian composition.

An additional difficulty with the term "Qumran literature" stems from the fact that the community existed for at least two hundred years. It must be assumed that their ideology evolved over that period.[52] So, for example, an important text like MMT ("Some Torah Precepts"), while seminal in understanding the early history of the Qumran community, predates some of the violent conflicts between the community and the Hasmonean establishment reflected in the *pesher* texts (e.g., 1QpHab; 4QpPs 37; 4QpNah). With these consideration in mind, we may turn to the history of the Qumran community and their literature.

The most obscure part of the Qumran community's history is their origins. What is clear is that the sectarian views of the community were acerbated by a conflict with the Hasmonean rulers beginning in the mid-second century BCE. In the early period of the Hasmonean struggles with the Seleucid kingdom (ca. 167–152 BCE), there was apparently at least a rapprochement between the community and the Hasmoneans in spite of disputes over legal issues. For example, the "Halakhic Letter" (4QMMT) outlines some of the disagreements between the Jerusalem priestly aristocracy and the community.[53] It is clear, however, that the disagreements were still amiable. The disagreements later turned more hostile. I would concur with Devorah Dimant, who writes,

> It is now agreed by most scholars that the Wicked Priest is to be identified by Jonathon the Maccabee and that the sect's opponents, Ephraim and Manasseh, should be identified with the Pharisees and the Sadducees. Most of the other events alluded to by the *Pesharim* fall into the Hasmonaean Period, from the reign of Alexander Janaeus to the conquest of Jerusalem by Pompey (63 B.C.E.). Significantly, no later event is alluded to in the Qumran writings. . . . this means that most of the sectarian literature originated in the early period of the sect, between 150 and 50 B.C.E.[54]

Judging from the archaeological evidence at Khirbet Qumran, the settlement was established sometime between 150 and 125 BCE.[55] The community's literature also includes obvious polemics against the Hasmoneans and their supporters (4Q471), as well as descriptions of the persecutions by the Hasmoneans against the community and their leader, the "Teacher of Righteousness" (cf. 4QpNah; 4QpPs 37). The Damascus Document includes an extended description of the early history of the community, which may be set against this background (CD 1:4–13):

> (4) [God] left a remnant (5) to Israel and give them over to complete destruction. And in the age of wrath, three hundred (6) and ninety years after He handed them over to Nebuchadnezzar, king of Babylon, (7) he visited them and caused to grow from Israel and from Aaron a root of planting to inherit (8) his land and to grow fat on the good produce of his soil. Then they understood their punishment and knew that (9) they were guilty men. They were like the blind and like those groping for the way (10) twenty years. And God considered their deeds, that they had sought Him with a whole heart. (11) So He raised up for them a Teacher of Righteousness to guide them in the way of his heart. He taught (12) to later generations what God did to the generation deserving wrath, a company of traitors, (13) to those departing from the way of his heart.

This description is cryptic. Nevertheless, it suggests that the origins of the Qumran sect belong sometime in the early second century. There is little alternative to understanding the description of "a company of traitors, those departing from the way of his heart," apart from Hasmoneans and their supporters. The self-identity of the community is set against those who betrayed them (e.g., 1QpHab 2:1–5). The strongest opposition with the Jerusalem establishment seems to have been from the rise of the Hasmoneans until Pompey's conquest of Jerusalem (152–63 BCE). This is the period in which the most characteristically sectarian literature was composed (e.g., the Damascus Document, the Community Rule, the Thankgiving Hymns [*Hodayot*], the *Pesherim*). Although the community apparently first welcomed Roman rule (cf. 4QpNah), they later grew antagonistic toward these foreign rulers (cf. 1QM). In the end, the Qumran community probably collaborated in the Jewish Revolt, and as a result their settlement was destroyed by the Romans in 68 CE.

Further evidence for the Qumran community's status as an anticommunity or antisociety is their peculiar language. Qumran Hebrew is an antilanguage. M. A. K.

Halliday explains, "An anti-language is not only parallel to an anti-society; it is in fact generated by it."[56] The creation of socially differentiated language is a reflex of the sectarian group ideology. This new language takes the form of a partial relexicalization and even overlexicalization:

> the [linguistic] code's origin in *counter-societies* is reflected in many aspects of their linguistic form, for instance in their elaboration of lexicon and metaphor relevant to their special activities and their attitudes toward the normative society . . . . Also significant is their conspicuous avoidance and violation of forms recognized as "standard". . . . The anti-language is not, and has never been, anyone's native tongue, nor are all its formal characteristics simply arbitrary. Both functionally and formally it is derived from the normative code, just as its speakers define their social role in opposition to the normative society.[57]

The attempt to form an antilanguage is most apparent in the surface structures of language (e.g., lexicon), while its deep structure (e.g., syntax) is less affected. These sociolinguistic observations are especially apt for understanding the language of the Qumran community.[58] Qumran Hebrew is at the same time a continuation of Late Biblical Hebrew and a reaction against the colloquial languages spoken in Palestine—both Aramaic and Mishnaic Hebrew. As a result, its main difference with colloquial Hebrew and where its language is most exceptional is in lexicon; its syntax is quite predictable.

The ideological role of language in the Qumran community can be illustrated by the numerous references to language in Qumran literature. Chaim Rabin already suggested that the Scrolls allude to Mishnaic Hebrew as "a halting language" (לועג שפה, 1QHod 12:16), "an uncircumcised language" (ערול שפה, 1QHod 10:7, 18–19), and "a blasphemous language" (לשון גדופים, CD 5:11–12).[59] The last example is particularly instructive because it seems to imply that the community's opponents believed in Oral Law: "Also they have corrupted their holy spirit; with blasphemous language they open their mouth against the laws of the covenant of God, saying, "They are not fixed (לא נכונו)." It seems likely that the charge that the laws were "not fixed" refers to the oral law which was necessarily more fluid. Certainly, the legitimacy of the oral law was a hotpoint in the late Second Temple period. Rabin's case is further strengthened by the community's pejorative references to "another language" (לשון אחרת, 1QHod 10:19; 12:16). The ruin of those who do not belong to the community apparently has to do—among other things—with their use of "another language" (note 4QpNah frags. 3–4 2:8). However, the community member was distinguished by his special use of language: "You [have taught me] Your covenant and my language is as one of Your disciples (ולשוני כלמודיך)" (1QHod 15:10). In sum, language served as one of the ways the Qumran community expressed its opposition to the Hasmonean establishment.

The complex status of prophecy in the Qumran scrolls is exemplified by the sect's belief that prophecy did not exist in its time. Yet, they appointed themselves as the living substitute for the defunct office of the prophet. This substitution took the form of the kind of interpretation of Scripture exemplified in the *pesher* literature.[60]

4QFlorilegium (4Q174): A Midrash on 2 Samuel 7

The most extended and direct reflection on the Promise to David in Qumran literature is found in 4QFlorilegium (4Q174 frags. 1–3, 1:1–13),[61] a thematic *pesher* on 2 Samuel 7. This text is one of the most characteristically sectarian documents—from the perspective of genre, terminology, and orthography—in the entire Dead Sea Scrolls corpus. In this text emerges an eschatological interpretation of the Promise to David characteristic of Qumran literature. The preserved fragments can be translated as follows:

> (0) "and I shall set a place for my people Israel and I shall plant him, and he shall dwell on it. (1) The enemy shall not agitate any more, and the son of wickedness shall no longer afflict him as formerly and from the day which (2) I commanded judges over my people Israel" [2 Sam 7:10–11a]. This refers to the house which [he shall build] for [them in] the last days just as it is written in the book of (3) [Moses, "the sanctuary of the Lord] your hand shall establish it; YHWH shall reign forever and ever" [Exod 15:17]. This refers to the temple which (4) [no impure person] shall enter there, neither Ammonite, nor Moabite, nor uncircumcised, nor foreigner, nor alien, forever because my holy ones are there. (5) [. . .] Strangers shall never again destroy it as they formerly (destroyed) (6) the sanctuary of Israel because of its sin. And He said to build for himself a sanctuary of man to offer incense in it to him, (7) before him the works of the law (i.e., Torah). And concerning that which He said to David, "And I [will give] you [rest] from all your enemies" [2 Samuel 7:11a] which means He will give rest to them from all (8) the sons of Belial who cause them to stumble in order to finish them of [. . .] just as they came into the devices of Belial to order to make the sons of light (9) stumble and to devise against them a wicked plot [. . .] (10) "And the Lord declares to you that he will build you a house. And I will raise up your seed after you, and I will establish the throne of his kingdom (11) forever. I will be to him as a father, and he will be to me as a son" [2 Samuel 7:11c–14a]. This one is the Branch of David who will stand with the Interpreter of the Law, who (12) [will rule] in Zion in the latter days as it is written, "And I will raise up the booth of David which is fallen" [Amos 9:11]. This one is the booth of (13) David which was fallen, who shall arise to save Israel.

The top of the fragment is broken, but its continuation is a citation of 2 Samuel 7:10–11a. One can only speculate as to precisely where the citation might have begun, but the *pesher* in line 2, "This is the house," identifies of the "place" (מקום) with the temple, suggesting that the lemma probably began with 2 Samuel 7:10. This identification of the "place" with the temple follows a long exegetical tradition which is reflected in the book of Chronicles and the Septuagint.

The text cites 2 Samuel 7:10–14, along with Exodus 15:17–18, and Amos 9:11. This particular configuration of prooftexts should not surprise us. Amos 9:11 was from its inception part of the literary history of 2 Samuel 7. Its central place in the literary history is underscored by an additional citation in the Damascus Document (CD 7:16; see discussion later). The apparent error in the citation of Amos 9:11—namely, using the converted perfect form "and I shall raise up (והקימותי)" where the MT Amos 9:11 used the simple imperfect "I shall raise up

(אקים)"—undoubtedly arises from a familiarity with 2 Samuel 7:12 which reads, "and I shall raise up your seed (והקימותי את־זרעכה)." This only further suggests how closely Amos 9:11 and 2 Samuel 7 were associated in the Qumran community. Exodus 15:17 is drawn into the literary history of the Promise in the Alexandrian translation of the Prayer of Solomon (3 Kgdms 8:53α; see previous discussion).

In lines 10–11, the text cites selections from 2 Samuel 7:11b–14 that relate to the one who shall build the house for YHWH. It interprets this text as referring to two eschatological figures, "the Branch of David" and "the Interpreter of the Law." The title, Branch of David, is well known in Qumranic literature and is most closely associated with Isaiah 11 (cf. 4QpIs[a] frags. 7–10 3:22; 4Q252 frag. 1 5:3; 4Q285 frag. 5 1:3–4). Particularly interesting is that when the Qumran text continues its further citations of 2 Samuel 7, it omits verse 13a. Why? It cites these verses as though they were a continuous quote from 2 Samuel. Why is verse 13a omitted? I think the answer is obvious. Verse 13a focuses attention on Solomon's temple. This certainly didn't fit into the Qumran reading of the Promise. More than this, however, the very reason that the Qumran readers could leave out verse 13a in their citation was because they recognized it as an interpretation. In previous chapters I pointed out that verse 13a was a doubly marked (by a *Wiederaufnahme* and a deitic pronoun) exegetical comment that directed attention to Solomon as the builder of the legitimate temple and answered the lingering ambiguity of 2 Samuel 7:5. The Qumran community overwrote this Deuteronomic interpretation with their own statement: "this refers to the house which God shall build for them in the last days."

The Qumran translators' *pesher* immediately identifies the appearance of "the Branch of David" with "the Interpreter of the Law." This person can only have been only a priestly figure because the task of interpretation of the law was given first of all to the priests (cf. 2 Chr 15:3; Ezr 7:6; 1QSb 3:22–24). This figure is also known in other Qumran texts (e.g., CD 6:7; 7:18). The immediate introduction of a priestly figure, "the Interpreter of the Law," alongside a royal figure is quite significant. This may be seen as following in the early postexilic tradition exemplified by Zechariah 6:13, which established the parity between the high priest and king (see chapter 6).[62]

The Promise to David provides a pretext for the Qumran community to describe a heavenly temple that will be built in the last days. This eschatological age will be ushered in by "the Branch of David" and "the Interpreter of the Law." These two figures, although not called messiahs, clearly together represent the balance of leadership between monarchy and temple. The monarchy is represented by the messianic figure called "the Branch of David." A messianic figure called "Branch" (צמח) is referred to by the prophets Jeremiah (23:5–6; 33:15–16) and Zechariah (3:8; 6:12). According to the Qumran exegete, this Davidic descendent restores the kingdom of Israel, here referred to as the "booth of David" (סוכת דויד; also see 4QpIs[a] frags. 7–10, column 3 which identifies the figure of Isa 11:1 with "the Branch of David"). Alongside the Davidic ruler arises "the Interpreter of the Law," who undoubtedly represents the interests of the temple. The priestly Interpreter would have his locus in the eschatological temple to be built in the last days. The Qumran exegete comments on 2 Samuel 7:10, the place which God promises for his people: "That is the house which [he will build] for him in the latter days, as it is written in the book of (3) [Moses], 'The sanctuary of the Lord (מקדש אדני) which your hands have established'." (lines 2-3). These two figures then are the eschatological leaders of the divine temple (מקדש אדני) and the Davidic kingdom (סוכת דויד). Thus, 4QFlorilegium confirms that there was a duality in Qumran messianism, although it is also becoming apparent that Qumran messianism was not well-defined or static.[63]

The focus on two individuals in 4QFlor arises from the duality of institutions: kingdom and temple. This dual focus on kingdom and temple is anticipated by DtrH and in the exilic literature, but especially developed in the books of Chronicles. Nowhere, however, do we have a focus on two individuals arising from the Promise to David. Although numerous places in biblical literature emphasize the duality of priestly and royal figures (e.g., Zech 6:11–13) and both priests and kings were "anointed" (√משיח), this structural aspect of ancient Israelite leadership never receives justification by a reading of the Promise to David. The Qumran community appears quite innovative in this particular reading. Yet, it also seems like a forced reading. While it is easy to understand how previous readings of the Promise to David could lead to the Qumran reading's focus on two individuals, it is nevertheless quite a contrived reading. As such, the emphasis on two individuals must have been quite important to the community. It is difficult not to understand this reading as arising in part as a response to the Hasmonean dynasty which fused the offices of king and priest.

Damascus Document

One of the most important documents for the Qumran community was the Damascus Document. Although there are no direct citations of the Promise to David in the Damascus Document, it is clear in many places that the *pesher* is directly or indirectly dependent on the discourse about the Promise to David. The clearest case is CD 7:9–21:

> (9) And all those who despise (the commandments and statutes) when God judges the land to recompense the wicked; (10) it is concerning them that the word of the prophet Isaiah son of Amoz shall come to pass (11) which says, "Days are coming on you and on your people and on your father's house that (12) have never come before, since the departure of Ephraim from Judah" [Isa 7:17], that is, when the two houses of Israel separated, (13) Ephraim departed from Judah. All who backslid were handed over to the sword, but those who held fast (14) escaped to the land of the north. As it says, "I will exile the tents of your king (15) and the foundation of your images beyond the tents of Damascus" [Amos 5:26–27]. The books of the *Torah* are the tents of (16) the king, as it says, "I will re-erect the fallen tent of David" [Amos 9:11]. "The king" is (17) the congregation and the "foundation of your images" is the books of the prophets, (18) whose words Israel despised. The star is the interpreter of the Torah (19) who comes to Damascus, as it is written, "A star has left Jacob, a staff has risen (20) from Israel" [Num 24:17]. This one is the leader of the whole congregation; when he arises, "he will shatter (21) all the sons of Seth" [Num 24:17].

With the exception of Numbers 24:17, the prooftexts cited here—Amos 5:26–27; 9:11; Isaiah 7:17—are known from discussions in earlier chapters. It is difficult to know exactly when Numbers 24:17 becomes part of the discourse, but it is clearly an important text in the Qumran community's messianic expectations (e.g., 1QSb 5:27; 1QM 11:5–7; 4Q175 1:9–13). By contrast, Amos 5:26–27, 9:11, and Isaiah 7:17 are all part of the discourse on the meaning of the Promise to David within the biblical literature itself. Isaiah 7 becomes quite important in the community's ruminations undoubtedly because it was perceived as speaking to the community's own situation—namely, its estrangement from the Jerusalem aristocracy.[64] The *Damascus Document* also reflects the attempt to understand the meaning of the enigmatic Amos 5:26–27 by association with Isaiah 9:11—a procedure which may be justified if, as I have argued, Amos 9:11 was originally composed with Amos 5:26–27 in mind. As I pointed out in chapter 4, Amos 9:11 derives from both a reflection on 2 Samuel 7 and an attempt to understand the 5:26–27. The close association between Amos 9:11 and the Promise to David in the discourse is underscored by its use in 4QFlor where it is used to directly interpret 2 Samuel 7:12–14.

In this place, the Damascus Document emphasizes two individuals who will fulfill the Promise to David.[65] Given the fusion of the royal and priestly roles by the Hasmoneans, it is difficult not to see this emphasis on two individual as a direct response to the Hasmonean dynasty. In this respect, it is quite similar to 4QFlor. On the other hand, 4QFlor is quite explicitly a *pesher* on 2 Samuel 7, whereas the *Damascus Document* only indirectly reflects on it. How can we explain this? The focus on two individuals does not arise easily in a reading of 2 Samuel 7. The fact that such a reading is made at all suggests that dual messianic expectations were quite important to the community. Perhaps the CD *pesher* avoids 2 Samuel 7 precisely because its emphasis on two individuals might seem to be contrived, even by members of the community.

11QTemple: "The Law of the King"

The Promise to David figures in the Temple Scroll's elaboration of the Deuteronomic "law of the king" (cf. Deut 17:14–20; 11QT[a] 56:12–59:21). Unfortunately, a good deal of debate continues to swirl around the date of the Temple Scroll's composition and its precise relationship with the Qumran community. The text is known from two copies labeled 11QT[a] and 11QT[b]. The first is relatively well preserved, and the second is quite fragmentary.[66] Although the Temple Scroll does not seem to have been central to the Qumran community—this is indicated by both the limited number of manuscripts and their location in cave 11—nevertheless, the scrolls are copied in Qumran orthography and should be considered part of the community's literature. It may be that 11QTemple is analogous to the Book of Jubilees—namely, a text probably composed before the sect moved to the site at Khirbet Qumran.

A democratization of the Promise is clear in the Temple Scroll's elaboration of the "law of the king." Although Deuteronomy itself does not cite the Promise in its enumeration of the "law of the king," the Temple Scroll explicitly cites the Promise to David at the conclusion of its lengthy elaboration. The most explicit development of the Promise appears in column 59, lines 13–21:[67]

> [13]And I will be for them (their) God, and they will be for me (my) people. [[*vacat*]] As for the king [14]whose heart and eyes whorishly depart from my commandments, he shall not have a descendent sitting on the throne of [15]his fathers for all time. Indeed, I shall forever cut off his seed from ruling Israel. [16][[*vacat*]] But if he walks in my laws, keeping my commandments, and does [17]the upright and good thing before me, then there shall not be cut off from him one of his sons sitting on the throne of the kingdom [18]of Israel forever. I shall be with him, I shall save him from those who hate him and [19]from those who would seek to take his life. I shall set all his enemies before him so he can rule them [20]as he wishes—they shall not rule him. I shall set him at the top, not the bottom; at the head, [21]not the tail. He will long endure over his kingdom, he and his sons after him.

There is much that paraphrases the Promise here. There are also places that clearly expand it. The most prominent expansion, which has many precedents, is the conditions of the Promise. Where 2 Samuel 7:14 has the quite abbreviated note "when he sins (אשר בהעותו)," the Temple Scroll details the requirement of observing the laws, commandments, and doing good along the lines established by Deuteronomic literature (cf. 1 Kgs 2:4; 8:25; 9:4–6; Ps 89:30–32; 2 Chr 7:17–18).

The citation of the Promise to David in 11QTemple's "laws of the king" brings the issue of a king's Davidic lineage to the forefront. On the one hand, Pomykala points out that "the qualifications for the king in 11QTemple do not include davidic lineage."[68] Lawrence Schiffman, on the other hand, argues that the absence of a requirement that the king be a Davidide resulted from the author's attempt to avoid anachronisms.[69] Certainly, since the text of Deuteronomy seems to have been the basis for the composition of the "law of the king," a Davidic requirement would be entirely out of place. Unless the Temple Scroll is viewed as either an apologetic for a non-Davidic king or a critique of a non-Davidic king, the issue of Davidic lineage would have no place in the Temple Scroll.[70] Even if Davidic lineage were an issue, the literary framework of 11QTemple precluded it from being mentioned. The only way that the issue of Davidic lineage could be introduced was indirectly.

The Temple Scroll here begins with a recitation of the adoption formula known from 2 Samuel 7:14, though it actually refers to the people of Israel (note the use of the plurals) and not the king. The application of the adoption formula to the people of Israel is by no means original to the Temple Scroll; for instance, the adoption formula is first applied to all Israel in exilic literature, especially Jeremiah (cf. Jer 11:4; 24:7; 30:22; 31:1; Ezek 36:28; also note Jub 19:31).[71] The interesting feature of the Temple Scroll is that, following a small space in the manuscript, the text returns to the person of the king. This transition probably was undoubtedly facilitated by the strong association of the adoption formula with the Promise and the Davidide kings. After another small space, beginning at line 16, the manuscript turns to the conditions of the Promise. The column ends with a citation from the blessings and curses in Deuteronomy 28 to highlight the conditional nature of the

Promise. In Deuteronomy 28:13 (also verse 44), we read, "YHWH will set you at the head, not the tail; you will always be at the top and not at the bottom—if only you obey and faithfully observe the commandments of YHWH your God that I command you today to keep and do." The Temple Scroll's incorporation of this Deuteronomic blessing (and curse) calls further attention to the democratization of the Promise. After all, the blessings and curses of the covenant are for all Israel, yet in 11QT^{a} 59:20–21 they are applied specifically to the king: "I shall set *him* at the top, not the bottom; at the head, not the tail." Conversely, the adoption was initially applied to the king, but now it was for all Israel.[72]

The Temple Scroll falls in with some recent studies of collective expectations in the Qumran texts. In particular, Hartmut Stegemann has argued that there was no individual messianism before the mid-second century BCE; rather, the people of Israel saw themselves in a collective messianic role.[73] Stegemann suggested that such a collective lies behind Daniel 7, as well as behind certain passages from the War Scroll (cf. 1QM 11:6–7; 4QM^{a} frg. 11 1:12–18). In a similar manner, Annette Steudel argued that 4Q246 (the "Son of God" text) should be understood.[74] Steudel and Stegemann understand this collective messianism as part of Second Temple Judaism, from which the individual messianic expectations of the Qumran community and later early Christianity would develop.[75] The present study offers some support for Stegemann and Steudel's observations, although the features of this "collective messianism" begins well before the late Second Temple period. The democratization of the Promise to David in texts like Second Isaiah (see chapter 5), for example, may be understood as pointing toward a collective messianism. However, the term "messianism" is a misleading way of describing the collective expectations of texts like Second Isaiah. Furthermore, it seems unlikely that there was any unanimity in Judaism during the early Second Temple period (or at any other time, for that matter). The books of Chronicles, for example, evidence royalist expectations, which would imply individual, and not collective, expectations.

4QpGen^{a} (for Genesis Reworked)

4QpGen^{a} column 5 (4Q252 5) begins with a quote from Genesis 49:10 and alludes to the Promise in the course of its elaboration of the lemma. This fragment of the 4QpGen^{a} scroll was first published by John Allegro in 1956, but all the fragments became available in 1991.[76] Its technical terminology, particularly "men of the *Yahad* (אנשי היחד)", mark it as a sectarian document. Nevertheless, the orthography is not sectarian. Unfortunately, as is so often the case, column 5 is fragmentary, and it is difficult to know what texts and issues may have been raised in its continuation. The text may be translated as follows:

> (1) "A ruler shall [no]t depart from the tribe of Judah [Gen 49:10aα]." When Israel has dominion, (2) there [shall not] be cut off one who sits on the throne of David because "the scepter" is the covenant of the kingdom, (3) [and the clan]s of Israel are the divisions, until the Messiah of Righteousness, the Branch of David, (4) For to him and to his seed the covenant of the kingdom of His people has been given for the eternal generations, because (5) he has kept[. . .] the Law with the men of

> the Yahad. For (6) [. . . the "obedience of the people]s" is the assembly of the men of (7) [. . .] he gave . . . .

The statement "There [shall not] be cut off one who sits on the throne of David ([לוא י]כ̊ר̊ת יושב כס̊א לדויד)" depends on earlier readings of 2 Samuel 7 (cf. 1 Kgs 2:4; 8:25; 9:5; Jer 33:17; 1 Chr 7:18). It is clear from this text that Genesis 49:10 was regarded by the Qumran community as part of the literary horizon of the Promise. The only innovation that *pesher* introduces comes in lines 2 and 4. The expression "the covenant of the kingdom (ברית המלכות)" is heretofore unique in the literary history of the Promise to David. The description of the Promise as a "covenant (ברית)" occurs already in the exilic period, where it arose by the Promise's association with the Mosaic covenant. The expression "covenant of the kingdom" also gives a corporate, rather than individual, focus of the Promise. This was also a feature of the exilic interpretation of 2 Samuel 7. A similar democratization of the Promise to David is a feature of 11QTemple 59:13–21 and most likely the 4Q "Son of God" text (4Q246). These observations bring us back to the question of the sectarian composition of 4QpGen[a].

4QDibHam[a] Fragments 1–2, 4:2–8

4QDibHam[a], "The Words of the Luminaries" (4Q504), was first published by M. Baillet in 1961.[77] The text is written in Qumran orthography and is clearly a sectarian composition.[78] The text seems to be part of a series of prayers for the days of the weeks contained in a larger composition of "Festival Prayers" (cf. 4Q509). Its ruminations on the Promise to David comes from fragments 1–2, column 4:

> (2) in your residence [. . .] rest (3) in Jerusalem [the city which you c]hoose from the whole earth (4) for your Name to be there forever. For you loved (5) Israel more than all the peoples. And you choose the tribe (6) of Judah and established your covenant with David that he might be (7) as a princely shepherd over your people and sit on the throne of Israel before you (8) forever.

The beginning is fragmentary but complete enough so that a clear allusion to the Deuteronomic Prayer of Solomon from 1 Kings 8. The shepherd terminology in 4QDibHam[a] is probably an allusion to 1Samuel 5:2 and Ezekiel 34:23. In 1 Samuel 5:2, God promises David, "You shall shepherd My people Israel; you shall be ruler of Israel." Ezekiel 34:23 apparently develops this promise, "Then I will appoint (והקימתי) a single shepherd over them to tend them—My servant David."

The use of the Prayer of Solomon in 4QDibHam[a] is particularly interesting because of the different versions of 1 Kings 8:16 represented by the MT of Kings, the LXX of 3 Kingdoms 8:16, 4QKgs, and 2 Chronicles 6:5–6 (see the excursus in chapter 4 on "4QKgs for 1 Kings 8:16" and previous discussion of LXX in this chapter). In brief, the MT of 1 Kings 8:16 represents the shortest version that omits the idea that the city of Jerusalem was chosen. The LXX, 2 Chronicles, and 4QKgs all add the statement that God choose Jerusalem as a place for his name to dwell. Second Chronicles and 4QKgs represent the fullest versions in their emphasis (lacking in the LXX and MT of 1 Kings 8:16) that God chose no one except David.

As such, 4QKgs and 2 Chronicles explicitly rule out non-Davidic monarchs like the Hasmoneans. The extent of variation and the sensitive political issues underlying the variations suggest that ideology influenced the textual variation. For example, the LXX highlights the temple and adds nothing concerning David. This surely reflects the Alexandrian community's concern for the temple and lack of concern for the Davidic dynasty. As for 4QDibHam^a, because it is fragmentary, it would be unwise to draw conclusions about what is not there—that is, the temple or priests. What is there, however, testifies to the importance of Jerusalem, which was God's residence, and the Davidic dynasty, from which would come the "princely shepherd." Pomykala argues that 4QDibHam^a directs the covenant toward David and not his descendants.[79] To argue this, however, Pomykala must argue that the expression "all the days (כול הימים)" does not refer to perpetuity. This is an implausible argument because "all the days" occurs in contexts, both in Qumran literature and biblical literature, where it is explicitly parallel to "forever (לעולם)" (cf. 11QT 46:3–4; 59:15; Deut 5:29; Ps 44:9). Moreover, the context of its use elsewhere in Qumran literature suggests perpetuity and not a limited period (e.g., 1QHod 4:14; 7:9; 11QT 29:10). The suggestion that "all the days" is a limited time is certainly a case of special pleading, which Pomykala needs to do to make his argument that the Davidic dynasty tradition was unimportant in early Judaism. It may be the case that the Davidic dynasty was in fact unimportant to certain early Jewish communities. It is not a question of whether the Promise was important, but what was the context of reading.

In the fragmentary beginning of the column, 4QDibHam^a uses the term "rest" (מנוחה). Although an exact reconstruction cannot be made, it is clear from the following lines that the reference points to Jerusalem as the place of God's rest. It will be recalled that the Promise to David suggests that the people will find rest in the land (2 Sam 7:1, 10). Chronicles rewrites the Promise to David here (cf. 1 Chr 17:1, 11); instead, God finds rest in the temple which is actually referred to in one place as "the house of rest (בית מנוחה)" (2 Chr 28:2; see chapter 6). The concluding chapter of Isaiah, by contrast, questioned whether God could find rest on earth (Isa 66:1-2; see chapter 5), and 4QDibHam^a should be seen as continuing in this discourse. In the case of 4QDibHam^a, however, it is not so much the temple as the city of Jerusalem that is considered the place where God rests. This would be in keeping with what we know of the Qumran community's ideology, which held the city of Jerusalem as holy while rejecting the temple as corrupted.[80]

Messianisms in the Late Second Temple Period

The present study would suggest that there was continuous discourse on the Promise to David throughout the Second Temple period and, in fact, throughout the history of the Jewish people. This continuous discourse does not imply a singularity in interpretation, however. Indeed, a premise of the discourse is disagreement. For this reason, it is imperative to isolate each moment in the discourse and every community participating in the discourse. In this respect, I believe that Kenneth

Pomykala misses the point when he argues that "there existed in early Judaism no continuous, widespread, or dominant expectation for a davidic messiah."[81] Perhaps not, but the evidence amassed here suggests a continuous and widespread discourse on the meaning of the Promise to David. In some cases, eschatological messianic expectations emerged from these reflections—more often they did not. Perhaps more to the point is the conclusion of Joachim Becker, who writes,

> It is on the threshold of the New Testament that we first encounter a real messianism. It is not the seamless continuation of the restorative monarchism of the exilic and early postexilic period; it is a new outgrowth of anti-Hasmonean, anti-Roman, and anti-Herodian tendencies. The messiah is aroused by God; although he will be a descendant of David, he has no fixed genealogy. This is not the same thing as royalist fidelity to the royal family in restorative monarchism.[82]

If one defines "real messianism" by its eschatological aspect—in other words, real messianism is apparently to be defined *by its expression in early Christianity* and Qumran literature, then, of course, Becker is certainly right. It may be rightly questioned whether this is the correct framework to address the issue. And with one point we must quibble. Becker adds to his previous statement, "It is both new and characteristic, furthermore, that interpretation of Scripture is influential." The interpretation of Scripture is hardly new, though certainly characteristic of the Promise from its inception. When "real messianism" emerges, it does so by the reinterpretation of the same texts from which a literary discourse of centuries had already grown, developed, and even flourished. The point should be that there was no continuous *eschatological* messianic expectation in the Second Temple period. Its emergence was fresh and relatively sudden—conditioned by new political developments in Palestine in the late Second Temple period.[83] The Qumran community was disenfranchised, first from the Hasmonean Dynasty and then during the Roman administration. Such a social situation is an ideal setting for the development of eschatological expectations. At the same time, eschatological messianism also emerges out of the well-established literary discourse that surrounded the Promise to David.

It should hardly be surprising that the Alexandrian Jewish community developed no such eschatological or messianic expectations. In fact, their interpretation of the Promise to David marginalized the kingdom in favor of the temple. The Jerusalem temple remained an important cornerstone of Jewish identity in Alexandria and throughout the diaspora. This is accomplished initially by making the Promise apply specifically to Solomon. At the same time, the temple became a more central feature of 2 Samuel 7. The Alexandrian translators further develop role of the Jerusalem temple in their additions to the Prayer of Solomon (3 Kgdms 8:16, 53α). Their translation arose from the particular social setting of the Alexandrian Jewish community.

The present study has limited itself to pre-Christian literature, though it has obvious importance to early Christian—particularly New Testament—writings. The choice to exclude the New Testament writings was partially pragmatic, partially programmatic. There are no explicit citations of 2 Samuel 7 in the New

Testament, though there are many citations in various prooftexts.[84] The most relevant New Testament texts for the present study are from the books of Acts (7:49–50; 13:33–37; 15:15–18), 2 Corinthians (6:18) and Hebrews (1:5). All of these books are somewhat later than the Qumran corpus, and most likely post-70 CE—the cut-off point for the present study. The great war with Rome and the destruction of the Jerusalem temple ushered in an entirely new sociopolitical context, which is beyond the scope of the present study. Still, it is noteworthy that many of the prooftexts cited in the New Testament writings are well known from the literary history of the Promise. In other words, the present study should be essential for scholars pursuing the reception of the Promise to David in early Christian writings.

Now that we have reached the end of the present journey, the hermeneutic of *pesher* that characterizes Qumran literature should not be considered so unique. Qumran *pesher* sees the prophetic writings as all applicable to the time of the Qumran community. There is certainly an element of novelty in the particular method but hardly in the hermeneutic conception. There is a certain inevitability to interpretation. The process of reading is ultimately one of interpretation. Moreover, this reading is conditioned by and ultimately conditions society. Interpretation certainly comes into focus as an issue sharply defining identity in the late Second Temple period. Joseph Blenkinsopp, in particular, points to the role of interpretation for Jewish self-definition: "the interpretation or reinterpretation of both the laws and prophecy was carried on as a function of the self-understanding of the postexilic Palestinian Jewish community and the conflicts and divisions which it occasioned."[85] When we closely examine this interpretation, however, it becomes clear that the discussion follows along well-established lines in spite of aspects of discontinuity and originality.

8

The Legacy of the Promise to David

The Promise to David leaves a long literary legacy. Texts that deal with issues of vital importance to the community attract redaction, supplementation, editorial glossing, commentary, and complete rewriting. Part of the measure of a text's ongoing vitality is its ability to coax new readers into fresh interpretations. An example is the interpretation and revision of the covenant code from Exodus in the book of Deuteronomy.[1] The process of redaction and supplementation continues in the Temple Scroll from Qumran, and even after the canon is considered closed in works like the Mekilta de Rabbi Ishmael or in *Sifre Devarim.* Texts of vital importance like the Covenant Code or, in the present case, the Promise to David, invited interpretation and revision from the very moment the text was produced. I would also argue that striking proof for the long development of biblical tradition (in contrast to the recent fashion, which makes it an invention of the Persian or Hellenistic period) comes from the study of inner-biblical discourse. We should hardly be surprised that texts like the Promise to David were continually reworked and reinvented.

By calling attention to the particular historical moments of reading and by tracing a history of interpretations, we piece together an intellectual history of ancient Israel and early Judaism. For the most part, this intellectual history is a history of literary elites—that is, of those who read, interpreted, and passed on the literary traditions of ancient Israel. Through the lens of 2 Samuel 7, the Promise to David, we gain a glimpse into the intellectual history of ancient Israel and early Judaism. Throughout the literary history of the Promise, the symbiotic relationship among text, reader, and society evolves.

The story began in the tenth century BCE, when the settled pastoralists who came to be known as Israel were coalescing into an early state under Saul, David, and Solomon. The transition from semi-nomadic pastoralists to rural agrarians and finally toward an urban state was tumultuous. Radical social changes in culture, religion, and polity accompanied the various stages of the Israel state. The emerging state required a common ideology to hold it together. The Promise to David was this common ideology. By giving divine sanction to the politics of the United Monarchy, it attempted to create an ideology through which the diverse clans and tribes of the central hill country and Galilee could be unified. It was only marginally successful, even according to biblical accounts. Saul's chiefdom quickly disintegrated on his death, and civil war ensued. David finally reunited the tribes, but despite all his military success his rule was plagued by palace intrigues. Solomon tried unsuccessfully to stamp out these factions. After his death, the kingdom quickly divided again. Scarcely a century passed from the first movement toward a centralized state until the chieftain Saul under the disintegration of this tenuous union after the death of Solomon. The precise nature of this early United Monarchy is now shrouded in the literary embellishments of its history as recorded on the pages of the Bible. Yet enough remains in the archaeological record to indicate that the first beginnings of state formation in ancient Palestine are to be found in the tenth century BCE—what would become for later biblical and Jewish historians the golden age of the Jewish people. The Promise to David was a monarchic and dynastic ideology holding together this tenuous union and justifying its particular ruling family.

After the division of the kingdom, the Promise to David became entirely the property of the small, rural Judaean polity. Its importance undoubtedly faded in the isolated, rural Judaean polity. Judah would emerge as a full-blown state only in the eighth century BCE and was spurred on by the rise of the Assyrian empire. In a curious way, the Assyrian destruction of Israel justified the Davidic monarchy and reinvigorated the Promise to David. Israel was castigated as "those who broke away from the house of David" (cf. Isa 7). The deportation of Israel was all the more a kind of poetic justice because of the repeated northern attempts to circumvent traditional Davidic rule in the south. The survival of Judah likely gave rise to the rather unrealistic religious rhetoric that deluded itself into thinking that "YHWH had promised a lamp for David forever" (1 Kgs 11:36; 15:4; 2 Kgs 8:19). Ultimately, such ideology must have been responsible for the rather foolhardy confrontation between Judah and Assyria during Hezekiah's reign.

Isaiah of Jerusalem entered the stage of history at one of Judah's more tumultuous moments. The depiction of the prophet and his ministry in Isaiah 7–11 highlights the importance of the Davidic dynasty in the face of several different challenges. To begin with, the Promise to David was justified by the survival of Judah as opposed to the extinction of long-domineering Samaria. The authority of the Promise empowered the tiny Judaean polity to remake itself. It was used to sanction the incorporation of northern refugees. It was used to justify the political expansionism that marked the days of Hezekiah, who apparently sought to reestablish the legendary kingdom of David. Through the authority of the Davidic monarchy, the government was centralized. Public works (e.g., water systems) and military infrastructure (e.g., fortifications) were undertaken under the authority of the king of "the house of David." The social turmoil of the late eighth century was the catalyst for the first stage in the collection and editing of biblical literature. Indeed, the infrastructure for collecting and editing normally accompanies more developed states, and as such it is unlikely that any large-scale production of literature in Judah began before the late eighth century. An offhand remark we find in Proverbs 25:1, "These also are proverbs of Solomon, which the men of King Hezekiah of Judah copied," indicates that the production and preservation of literature at this time was consciously tied to the golden age of Israel. The social processes of centralization and urbanization created ideal conditions for such literary activity. There was a new need for a common ideology, which they found in their particular reading of the Promise to David.

Much of Judaean literature from this time is marked by its interest in the northern kingdom as interpreted through the lens of the restoration of the Davidic kingdom—that is, the United Monarchy of the north and south. This literature preserves a somewhat nostalgic, yet critical view of the northern kingdom. For example, the depiction of eight northern kings as successful military leaders (compared with only three Judaean kings)—as we have in the books of Kings—may be in keeping with the historical realia of the relative strength of the north and south. Yet, it is hardly in step with the pervasive critique of northern kingship of the Josianic historian, which continues in exilic literature. And the books of Chronicles illustrate what happens to Israel in the hands of a postexilic writer: the northern kingdom of Israel all but disappears. In a rather Pauline way, "Israel" is redefined as only Judah.[2] The only time in history when the *integration* of the north with the south was actually even contemplated was during the late eighth and early seventh centuries BCE, during the reigns of Hezekiah and Manasseh. The sharp division between the Samaritans and the Judaeans only becomes stronger under Hellenistic, Hasmonean, and Roman rule. In this light, the aspirations for a restoration of a golden age that *reintegrates* the northern kingdom fit properly in the period of Hezekiah and Manasseh. The Promise to David was vindicated by the fall of Samaria and sanctioned the vision of a reestablished Davidic kingdom. Ultimately, the vision would be scuttled forever in the violent reaction of the Josianic reformers, and Manasseh would become the scapegoat for the vision.

Another distinguishing feature of the literature of the late eighth century is its allusive use of the Promise to David. This, I would argue, reflects the orality of ancient Judaean culture during this period. The differences between oral and written culture are rarely taken into account in regard to biblical literature. Yet, social anthropological studies would suggest that the transition from an oral culture to a written one would have a profound impact on literature and especially on intertextuality in literature.[3] Reading and writing were restricted to trained scribes in the early Judaean polity. Literature, including the Promise to David, was primarily known orally, not textually. What we mean by "intertextuality" differs dramatically between oral and literate cultures. The dramatic transformation ushered in by literacy begins only in the seventh century. At that time, a panoply of inscriptional evidence, including seal impressions (both public and private), letters and receipts written on ostraca, and graffiti, appears. The most telling example of this emergent literacy is the "Letter of the Literate Soldier" (Lachish Letter 3), in which a junior officer expresses hurt feelings at the mere suggestion that he is unable to read. Literacy was expected. The emergence of literacy explains the orthodoxy of the book reflected in the Josianic reforms and Deuteronomy. It can also account for the changing textuality in the literary history of 2 Samuel 7. Literature created during this period (i.e., Dtr[1] and Ps 89:19–37) makes careful *textual* use of 2 Samuel 7:1–17, as opposed to the allusive use in earlier literature. At the same time, the rapid growth of Jerusalem and the centralization of power changed the sociopolitical dynamic of Judah in the seventh century. With the prominence of the priesthood and the temple support of the youthful monarch Josiah, it was only natural for the Promise to David to be tied to the Jerusalem temple. This was the exclusive dwelling place of YHWH, the God of Israel, where his name alone dwelled.

The exile thrust the Promise into crisis. How could David's sons inherit the throne of an eternal, yet now defunct, kingdom? Where would the physical presence of YHWH dwell, now that his temple had been destroyed? Most important, how could "Israel" still be YHWH's people? The fate of the Jewish people would now be tied to the Promise to David. In the words of Second Isaiah, "I will make with all of you an everlasting covenant, my steadfast, sure love for David" (Isa 55:3). In this union, the seeds for "collective messianism" were born. The exile, however, was short-lived. The return to Zion rekindled aspirations for the restoration of the monarchy. However, it was the priests who wielded the power in the exilic and postexilic Judaean community. As a result, the vision for restoring the Davidic monarchy imagined a curious duality: the Davidic *Branch* "shall build the Temple of YHWH and shall assume majesty, and he shall sit on his throne and rule. And there shall also be a priest seated on his throne, and harmonious understanding shall prevail between them" (Zech 6:13).

The exile forced a relocation of the God of Israel. He could no longer dwell in the destroyed temple. The exilic Deuteronomic theologian reasoned that only his name dwelled there, not the Deity himself. YHWH dwelled in the heavens, not in an earthly temple. How could such a building contain him (cf. Isa 66:1)? The exile provided the context for a universalization of the God of Israel. The exile uprooted both a people and the Promise. When the Jews were allowed to return by Cyrus the Mede (ca. 539 BCE), the exilic rationization of the Promise had added a dramatically new layer to its legacy. Would God now dwell again in a rebuilt Jerusalem temple? Didn't God dwell in heaven? The exile broadened the literary horizons of the Promise, and with it, Judaism itself.

The connection between the social setting of the readers and the interpretation is nowhere clearer than in the various readings of the Promise to David given by different communities in the late Second Temple period. Among Alexandrian Jews, the Davidic kingdom was a mute issue, while the Jerusalem temple remained a touchpoint of their identity. As a result, their reading of the Promise circumvented the Promise to the Davidic dynasty and introduced the temple as the central feature of the Promise. The Qumran sectarians rejected the Jerusalem temple and separated themselves in the desert. Not surprisingly, their reading of the Promise to David envisioned a new temple "not built by human hands." In an apparent reaction to the Hasmonean fusion of the priestly and royal offices, the Qumran community highlighted the two messiahs, both a priest and a king, who would arise in the end of days. It can also hardly be surprising that in the pro-Hasmonean books of Maccabees, the Promise to David disappears completely. After all, the Hasmoneans could claim no part in the Promise. They were not Davidides. More than this, the Promise provided no precedent for the merging of the priestly and royal offices. Such a merger, however, would prove useful to the early Christian community, which made Jesus both king and priest. While the Gospels were at pains to point out Jesus' Davidic lineage, the book of Hebrews was saddled with the more delicate task of explaining how Jesus was also a legitimate priest. The mysterious person of Melchizedek who paved the literary path. Ironically, however, it was only the inclusion of the temple within the Promise that made such an argument—namely, for one royal and priestly messiah—both necessary and possible. In each particular community, the Promise was read differently and reflected a unique discourse between reader and society. The different readings of the Promise are as diverse as the communities that read the text. At the same time, these diverse readers draw on a reading tradition that frames their understanding of the Promise.

At this point in our story, the literary life of the Promise to David has been artificially cut short. The convenient excuse for this termination is the destruction of the Second Temple, which introduces an entirely new set of social contexts. But the story could (and, in fact, should) be continued. For instance, the writings of the early Christian church just alluded to are clearly dependent on the discourse entrenched among the varieties of early Judaism.[4] I leave to others the resuscitation of the story.

Notes

Chapter 1

1. B. Halpern, *The Constitution of the Monarchy in Israel* (Chico, Calif.: Scholars Press, 1981), pp. xx–xxi.

2. The best summary of his approach may be found in Jauss, "Literary History as a Challenge to Literary Theory," *New Literary History* 2 (1970–71), pp. 19–37, and Jauss, *Toward an Aesthetic of Reception*, trans. T. Bahti (Minneapolis: University of Minnesota Press, 1982). See also Jauss, "The Idealist Embarrassment: Observations on Marxist Aesthetics," *New Literary History* 7 (1975), pp. 191–208.

3. Jauss, "Literary History as a Challenge to Literary Theory," p. 19

4. Jauss, *Toward an Aesthetic of Reception*, p. 19.

5. S. Suleiman, "Varieties of Audience-Oriented Criticism," in *The Reader in the Text*, ed. S. Suleiman and I. Corsman (Princeton: Princeton University Press,1980), p. 37.

6. See, for example, J. Blenkinsopp, "Interpretation and the Tendency to Sectarianism: An Aspect of Second Temple History," in *Jewish and Christian Self-Definition.* Volume 2: *Aspects of Judaism in the Graeco-Roman Period*, ed. E. P. Sanders, A. I. Baumgarten, and A. Mendelson (London: SCM, 1981), pp. 1–26; S. Talmon, "The Emergence of Jewish Sectarianism in the Early Second Temple Period," in *Ancient Israelite Religion: Essays in Honor of Frank Moore Cross*, ed. Patrick D. Miller; Paul Hanson, and S. Dean McBride (Philadephia: Fortress, 1987), pp. 587–616 [also published in *King, Cult and Calendar in Ancient Israel* (Jerusalem: Magnes Press, 1986), pp. 165–201].

7. This is, in fact, the direction in which Wolfgang Iser took Jauss's theoretical model; see Iser, *The Act of Reading: A Theory of Aesthetic Response* (Baltimore: Johns Hopkins University Press, 1978).

8. Jauss, *Toward an Aesthetic of Reception*, p. 23.

9. M. Fishbane, *Biblical Interpretation in Ancient Israel* (Oxford: Clarendon, 1985). Fishbane was neither the first nor is only practitioner, yet his work is the most comprehensive and pivotal. Some other important figures include Jon Levenson, Bernhard Levinson, James Kugel, James Sanders, Nahum Sarna, and Yair Zakovitch.

10. Jauss, *Toward an Aesthetic of Reception*, p. 23.

11. Y. Zakovitch, *"And You Shall Tell Your Son . . . ": The Concept of the Exodus in the Bible* (Jerusalem: Magnes Press, 1991). See also A. Shinan and M. Zakovitch, "Midrash on Scripture and Midrash within Scripture," in *Studies in Bible*, ed. S. Japhet (Jerusalem: Magnes Press, 1986), pp. 257–278.

12. L. Eslinger, "Inner-biblical Exegesis and Inner-biblical Allusion: The Question of Category," *VT* 42 (1992), pp. 47–58.

13. Eslinger's characterization of the work of historical criticism in general and Fishbane in particular as literary naiveté is quite unfair. Fishbane in particular is hardly naive in issues of literature; see, for example, *Text and Texture* (New York: Schocken, 1979) and *The Garments of the Torah: Essays in Biblical Hermenutics* (Bloomington: University of Indiana Press, 1988).

14. Eslinger, "Inner-Biblical Exegesis and Inner-Biblical Allusion," p. 49.

15. W. Ong, *Orality and Literacy: The Technologizing of the Word* (reprint; London: Routledge, 1982), p. 173.

16. S. Niditch, *Oral World and Written Word*, Library of Ancient Israel (Louisville: Westminister John Knox, 1996). One weakness in Niditch's work is a lack of serious engagement with the changing social context of the late Judaean monarchy.

17. M. Bakhtin, "From Notes Made in 1970–71," in *Speech Genres and Other Late Essays*, trans. V. McGee (Austin: University of Texas, 1986), p. 140.

18. E.g., R. Alter, *The Art of Biblical Narrative* (New York: Basic Books, 1981), pp. 3–22; R. Polzin, *David and the Deuteronomist: A Literary Study of the Deuteronomistic History, Part Three: 2 Samuel* (Bloomington, Ind.: Indiana University Press, 1993), pp. 71–87.

19. See M. Fishbane, "Use, Authority and Interpretation of Mikra at Qumran," in *Compendia Rerum Iadaicum* (Cambridge: Cambridge University Press, 1989), pp. 339–77.

20. See Brian Peckham, "Writing and Editing," in *Fortunate the Eyes That See: Essays in Honor of David Noel Freedman in Celebration of His Seventieth Birthday*, ed. A. Beck, A. Bartelt, P. Raabe, and C. Franke (Grand Rapids: Eerdmans, 1995), pp. 364–83.

21. These markers are described in Fishbane's *Biblical Interpretation in Ancient Israel*, pp. 44–65, and more recently, B. Levinson's *Deuteronomy and the Hermeneutics of Legal Innovation* (New York: Oxford University Press, 1997).

22. See H. Tadmor and M. Cogan for a critique of the two campaign hypothesis; *II Kings*, Anchor Bible (New York: Doubleday, 1988), pp. 246–51. The expression "at that time" (בעת ההיא) itself is often used as an editorial marker. See, e.g., 2 Chr 16:7, 10; Schniedewind, *The Word of God in Transition: From Prophet to Exegete in the Second Temple Period* (Sheffield: JSOT, 1995), pp. 91–93.

23. Jauss, "Literary History as a Challenge to Literary Theory," p. 29.

24. Ibid., p. 31.

25. This problem is explored by D. LaCapra, *Rethinking Intellectual History: Texts, Contexts, Language* (Ithaca: Cornell, 1983), pp. 23–69.

26. On the "old" biblical archaeology, see W. Dever's essay, "What Remains of the House that Albright Built?" *BA* 56,1 (1993), pp. 25–35.

27. Particularly noteworthy is the book edited by T. Levy, *The Archaeology of Society in the Holy Land* (New York: Facts on File, 1995).

28. An interesting recent book highlighting the role of physical environment in shaping human history is J. Diamond, *Guns, Germs, and Steel: The Fates of Human Societies* (New York: Norton, 1997).

29. G. Smith, *Historical Geography of the Holy Land*, ed. 25th (1931); reprint (Jerusalem: Ariel, 1966), p. 215.

30. Ibid., *Historical Geography of the Holy Land*, p. 216.

31. J. Rosenberg, *King and Kin: Political Allegory in the Hebrew Bible* (Bloomington, Ind.: Indiana University Press, 1986), p. x.

32. Ibid., p. 108.

33. Ibid., p. 109. Rost's study was translated as *The Succession to the Throne of David*, trans. M. Rutter and D. Gunn (Sheffield: Almond, 1982).

34. R. Fogel, " 'Scientific' History and Traditional History," in *Which Road to the Past?* ed. R. Fogel and G. Elton (New Haven: Yale University Press, 1983), p. 15.

35. Jauss, "Literary History as a Challenge to Literary Theory," p. 31.

36. The concept of a "horizon of expectations" in Jauss's work reflects the influence of Karl Popper and Karl Mannheim. See Popper, "Natural Laws and Theoretical Systems," in *Theorie und Realität*, ed. H. Albert (Tübingen: Mohr, 1964), pp. 87–102; and Mannheim, *Mensch und Gesellschaft in Zeitalter des Umbaus* (Darmstadt: Wissenschaftliche Buchgesellschaft, 1958).

37. For a review of functional grammar and its relationship to formal linguistic theory, see Johanna Nichols, "Functional Theories of Grammar," *Annual Review of Anthropology* 13 (1984), pp. 97–117. One of the criticisms of formal and structural linguistics is its tendency

to merely *describe* phenomena and not to *explain* them; cf. T. Givón, *On Understanding Grammar* (New York: Academic, 1979).

38. Jauss, *Toward an Aesthetic of Reception*, p. 14.

39. See I. Finkelstein's critique, *The Archaeology of the Israelite Settlement* (Jerusalem: Israel Exploration Society, 1988), pp. 306–14.

40. See the comments by Frick, "Social Science Methods and Theories of Significance for the Study of the Israelite Monarchy: A Critical Review Essay," *Semeia* 37 (1986), p. 11.

41. See the comments by D. Smith-Christopher, "The Mixed Marriage Crisis in Ezra 9–10 and Nehemiah 13: A Study of the Sociology of the Post-exilic Judaean Community," in *Second Temple Studies. 2. Temple Community in the Persian Period*, ed. T. Eskenazi and K. Richards (Sheffield: JSOT, 1994), p. 246.

42. See, for example, B. Childs, *Introduction to the Old Testament as Scripture* (Philadephia: Fortress, 1979).

43. Prominent examples of this would include Northrop Frye and Robert Alter; see Frye, *The Great Code: The Bible and Literature* (San Diego, Calif.: Harcourt Brace Jovanovich, 1983); Alter, *The Art of Biblical Narrative* (New York: Harper & Row, 1981). Wolfgang Iser takes Reception Theory in a different direction, Reader-Response criticism which emphasizes the individual reader; cf. Iser, *The Act of Reading*.

44. Rost, *The Succession to the Throne of David*; Veijola, *Die Ewige Dynastie. David und die Entstehung seiner Dynastie nach der deuteronomistischen Darstellung* (Helsinki: Suomalainen Tiedeakatemia, 1975); *Das Königtum in der Beurteilung der deuteronomistischen Historiographie: eine redaktionsgeschichtliche Untersuchung* (Helsinki: Suomalainen Tiedeakatemia, 1977); *Verheissung in der Krise: Studien zur Literatur and Theologie der Exilszeit anhand des 89. Psalms* (Helsinki: Suomalainen Tiedeakatemia, 1982).

45. Eslinger, *House of God or House of David : The Rhetoric of 2 Samuel 7* (Sheffield: JSOT, 1994).

46. See, for example, Laato, *Who is Immanuel? The Rise and the Foundering of Isaiah's Messianic Expectations* (Albo: Albo Akademik., 1988); *Josiah and David Redivivus. The Historical Josiah and the Messianic Expectations of Exilic and Postexilic Times* (Stockholm: Almqvist & Wiksell, 1992); *A Star Is Rising: The Historical Development of the Old Testament Royal Ideology and the Rise of the Jewish Messianic Expectations* (Atlanta: Scholars, 1997).

47. K. Pomykala, *The Davidic Dynasty Tradition in Early Judaism: Its History and Significance for Messianism* (Atlanta: Scholars Press, 1995), p. 8. As H. G. M. Williamson points out in a review of Pomykala, "The anchoring of the developments in the tradition in specific social and historical contexts is also a line of investigation which would repay further research" (*IOUDAIOS Review* 3.021 [1995] [electronic journal]).

48. B. Halpern, "Jerusalem and the Lineages in the Seventh Century BCE: Kinship and the Rise of Individual Moral Liability," in *Law and Ideology in Monarchic Israel*, ed. B. Halpern and D. Hobson (Sheffield: JSOT, 1991), pp. 11–107.

49. Ibid., "Jerusalem and the Lineages in the Seventh Century BCE," p. 17.

50. See especially the papers in *Synchronic or Diachronic? A Debate on Method in Old Testament Exegesis*, ed. J. C. de Moor (Leiden: Brill, 1995).

51. The impact of sociology and anthropology on Old Testament scholarship is surveyed in *The World of Ancient Israel: Sociological, Anthropological and Political Perspectives: Essays by Members of the Society for Old Testament Study*, ed. R. E. Clements (Cambridge: Cambridge University Press, 1989).

52. See, for example, recent studies by P. Davies, *In Search of Ancient Israel*, (Sheffield: JSOT, 1992); T. Thompson, *Early History of the Israelite People from the*

Written and Archaeological Sources (Leiden: Brill, 1992); and N. Lemche, "The Old Testament: A Hellenistic Book?" *SJOT* 7 (1993), pp. 163–93.

53. See, for example, devastating critiques by S. Japhet, "Can the Persian Period Bear the Burden? Reflections on the Origins of Biblical History," in *Proceedings of the Twelfth World Congress of Jewish Studies* (Jerusalem: Magnes Press, forthcoming), and A. Hurvitz, "The Historical Quest for 'Ancient Israel' and the Linguistic Evidence of the Hebrew Bible: Some Methodological Observations," *VT* 47 (1997), pp. 310–15.

Chapter 2

1. An excellent summary of recent scholarship on this question may be found in G. Knoppers, "The Vanishing Solomon: The Disappearance of the United Monarchy from Recent Histories of Ancient Israel," *JBL* 116 (1997), pp. 19–44.

2. See essays in *Cambridge Ancient History* on the various regions. For Assyria, see A. K. Grayson, *CAH III/1*, pp. 247–48; for Anatolia, see J. D. Hawkins, *CAH III/1*, pp. 372–75; for Egypt, see J. Černy, *CAH II/2*, pp. 643–57.

3. Although some have questioned the import of this inscription (e.g., G. Ahlström, *Who Were the Israelites?* [Winona Lake, Ind.: Eisenbrauns, 1986], pp. 37–43; Ahlström and D. Edelman, "Merneptah's Israel," *JNES* 44 (1985), pp. 59–61), the reading of Israel as a people is correctly the consensus (Antonio Loprieno helped guide me through the Egyptian here).

4. W. Dever, "Monumental Architecture in Ancient Israel in the Period of the United Monarchy," in *Studies in the Period of David and Solomon and Other Essays*, ed. Tomoo Ishida (Winona Lake, Ind.: Eisenbrauns, 1982), pp. 286–87.

5. R. Cohen and Y. Israel, "The Iron Age Fortresses at 'En Ḥaṣeva," *BA* 58, 4 (1995), p. 232.

6. A moderate position is taken by J. M. Miller, "Solomon: International Potentate or Local King?" *PEQ* 123 (1991), pp. 28–31; see also K. Younger, "The Figurative Aspect and the Contextual Method in the Evaluation of the Solomonic Empire (1 King 1–11)," in *The Bible in Three Dimensions: Essays in Celebration of Forty Years of Biblical Studies in the University of Sheffield*, ed. D. Clines, S. Fowl, and S. Porter (Sheffield: JSOT, 1990), pp. 157–75; L. Herr, "Iron II: Emerging Nations," *BA* 60 (1997), pp. 120–32.

7. See the observations of H. Sader, *Les Etats arameens de Syrie depuis leur fondation jusqu'a leur transformation en provinces assyriennes* (Beirut; Wiesbaden, 1987).

8. Talmon, "Kingship and the Ideology of the State," in *King, Cult, and Calendar in Ancient Israel* (Jerusalem: Magnes Press, 1986), p. 9.

9. An excellent summary may be found in Knoppers, "The Vanishing Solomon," pp. 19–44.

10. See, for example, Ian Young, *Diversity in Pre-Exilic Hebrew* (Tübingen: Mohr, 1993).

11. This evidence is conveniently summarized in a monograph edited by I. Finkelstein and N. Na'aman, *From Nomadism to Monarchy: Archaeological and Historical Aspects of Early Israel* (Jerusalem: Israel Exploration Society, 1994); see also J. Holladay, "The Kingdoms of Israel and Judah: Political and Economic Centralization in the Iron IIA–B (ca. 1000–750 BCE)," in *The Archaeology of Society in the Holy Land*, ed. T. Levy (New York: Facts on File, 1995), pp. 368–98.

12. The chronology of Iron IIA has been questioned by I. Finkelstein, "The Archaeology of the United Monarchy: An Alternative View," *Levant* 28 (1996), pp. 177–87. Finkelstein argues that a later date for the transition is possible (ca. 900 BCE); however, Finkelstein also notes that "all this has nothing to do with the question of the historicity of

the United Monarchy" (p. 185). The campaign of Shishak in 925 BCE, particularly sites like Arad and Taanach, provides a chronological peg militating against Finkelstein's wholesale revisionism; see the point by point rebuttal by A. Mazar, "A Reply to I. Finkelstein," *Levant* 29 (1997).

13. Frank Frick, "Ecology, Agriculture and Patterns of Settlement," in *The World of Ancient Israel: Sociological, Anthropological and Political Perspectives. Essays by Members of the Society for Old Testament Study*, ed. R. E. Clements (Cambridge: Cambridge University Press, 1989), pp. 67–93; L. Stager, "The Archaeology of the Family in Ancient Israel," *BASOR* 260 (1985), pp. 1–35.

14. Na'aman, "The Contribution of the Amarna Letters to the Debate on Jerusalem's Political Position in the Tenth Century B.C.E.," *BASOR* 304 (1996), p. 25; see also Na'aman, "Cow Town or Royal Capital? Evidence for Iron Age Jerusalem," *BAR* 23/4 (1997), pp. 43–47, 67.

15. The role of geography is also highlighted by the *annales* school; for example, F. Braudel, *The Mediterranean and the Mediterranean World in the Age of Philip II*, 2 vols., trans. Sian Reynolds (New York: Harper & Row, 1976).

16. Smith, *A Historical Geography of the Holy Land*, p. 216.

17. I. Finkelstein, "Environmental Archaeology and Social History: Demographic and Economic Aspects of the Monarchic Period," in *Biblical Archaeology Today, 1990: Proceedings of the Second International Congress on Biblical Archaeology* (Jerusalem: Israel Exploration Society, 1993), p. 63.

18. Cf. Y. Shiloh, "Elements in the Development of Town Planning in the Israelite City," *IEJ* 28 (1978), pp. 36–51.

19. Although Ussishkin questioned whether all these gates belong to the tenth century, a consensus still supports this interpretation; cf. Ussishkin, "Was the 'Solomonic' City Gate at Megiddo Built by King Solomon?" *BASOR* 239 (1980), pp. 1–18; A. Mazar, *Archaeology of the Land of the Bible*, (Garden City, N. Y.: Doubleday, 1990), pp. 380–82.

20. See Z. Herzog, "Administrative Structures in the Iron Age," in *The Architecture of Ancient Israel: From the Prehistoic to the Persian Periods*, ed. A. Kempinsky and R. Reich (Jerusalem: Israel Exploration Society, 1992), pp. 223–30.

21. See Dever, "Monumental Architecture in Ancient Israel in the Period of the United Monarchy," pp. 281–86; R. Cohen, "The Iron Age Fortresses in the Central Negev," *BASOR* 236 (1979), pp. 61–79. The recent excavations at Hatzeva (= Tamar; cf. 1Kgs 9:18) add to the list of Negev fortresses established in the tenth century; cf. Cohen and Israel, "The Iron Age Fortresses at 'En Ḥaṣeva," pp. 223–35.

22. See Finkelstein, *Living on the Fringe: the Archaeology and History of the Negev, Sinai and Neighbouring Regions in the Bronze and Iron Ages* (Sheffield: Sheffield Academic Press, 1995), pp. 103–57. Finkelstein argues that we have the sedentarization of desert nomads because of new economic prospects—in this case, the rise of a centralized government in Judah gave rise to mining and caravaneering (p. 156).

23. Elman Service originally divided the process into four stages—bands, tribes, chiefdoms, and states—but later admitted there were no objective criteria for distinguishing between "bands" and "tribes"; see Service, *Primitive Social Organization* (New York: Random House, 1962) and *Origins of the State and Civilization* (New York: W. W. Norton, 1975).

24. Service, *Origins of the State and Civilization*, p. 304.

25. See Frick, "Social Science Methods and Theories of Significance for the Study of the Israelite Monarchy," p. 20. Frick relies on the study by H. Claessen and P. Skalník, "The Early State: Theories and Hypotheses," in *The Early State*, ed. H. Claessen and P. Skalník (The Hague: Mouton, 1978), pp. 3–29.

26. Holladay, "The Kingdoms of Israel and Judah: Political and Economic Centralization in the Iron IIA-B (ca. 1000 to 750 BCE)," pp. 371–75.

27. On the source problems of Samuel, see Halpern, *The Constitution of the Monarchy in Israel*, pp. 149–74, and the literature cited there.

28. The premonarchical period in Israel has been sometimes characterized as a "primitive democracy" owing to the charismatic "election" of its leaders; e.g., C. Wolf, "Traces of Primitive Demoncracy in Israel," *JNES* 6 (1947), pp. 98–108; R. Gordis, "Primitive Democracy in Ancient Israel—The Biblical Edah," in *Alexander Marx Jubilee Volume* (New York, 1950), pp. 369–88. P. A. H. de Boer rightly rejects this claim; "Vive le Roi," *VT* 5 (1955), p. 227.

29. S. Eisenstadt observes that it was critical for a ruler to secure an independent military class during his early rise to power, "Observations and Queries about Sociological Aspects of Power in the Ancient World," in *Power and Propaganda: A Symposium on Ancient Empires* (Copenhagen: Akademisk Forlag, 1979), pp. 14–16.

30. On onomastic evidence see J. Tigay, *You Shall Have No Other Gods: Israelite Religion in the Light of Hebrew Inscriptions* (Atlanta: Scholars Press, 1986).

31. The reading "house of David" is found in the Tel Dan Stela (line 9) and the Mesha Stela (line 33); cf. A. Biran and J. Naveh, "The Tel Dan Inscription: A New Fragment," *IEJ* 45 (1995), pp. 1–18; A. Lemaire, " 'House of David' Restored in Moabite Inscription," *BAR* 20,3 (1994), pp. 30–37. K. A. Kitchen proposes reading *h(y)dbt dwt* in the Sheshonq list as "highlands of David"; cf. Kitchen, "A Possible Mention of David in the Late Tenth Century BCE, and the Deity *Dod as Dead as the Dodo?" *JSOT* 76 (1997), pp. 29-44.

32. See T. Mettinger, *Solomonic State Officials: A Study of the Civil Government Officials of the Israelite Monarchy* (Lund: Gleerups, 1971). Mettinger combines the civil administration of David and Solomon. However, it is clear by comparing the accounts of civil administration and building that the Solomonic period far surpasses the former in the development of civil administration. Additionally, comparing the parallel lists of David's administration in 2 Sam 8:15–18 with 20:23–26, it is clear that the latter has edited the former. In a similar manner, 1 Chr 18:14–17 also redacts 2 Sam 8:15–18.

33. This passage can be interpreted as religious syncretism; e.g., J. A. Soggin, "Der offiziell geförderte Synkretismus in Israel während des 10. Jahr-hunderts," *ZAW* 78 (1966), pp. 179–204. Certainly, it is part of the Deuteronomistic critique of Solomon; cf. M. Brettler, "The Structure of 1 Kings 1–11," *JSOT* 49 (1991), pp. 87–97. I think that it reflects some of the diverse elements of the population that were attacked in the Josianic religious reformation (see chapter 4).

34. D. Jamieson-Drake argues that the archaeological evidence suggests that the Solomonic kingdom never actually attained statehood. In criticizing the consensus he writes, "Some of the features which have been used to characterize Solomon or David as statebuilders in fact appear here as distinguishing lower-order societies from chiefdoms"; *Scribes and Schools in Monarchic Judah* (Sheffield: JSOT, 1991), p. 143. The basic problem is scale: "the levels of production and population were just too small in tenth-century Judah to suggest the presence of the full-scale state" (p. 139). However, these differences in part reflect problems of the archaeological record, a point Jamieson-Drake acknowledges but does not figure in his conclusions. It is also a problem of definition: what is a "state"? At what point the Israelite tribes actually progressed to the status of a state—however one defines it—is immaterial to the present study because it is clear that the process of state formation was under way. It is that sociopolitical process which concerns us.

35. P. Machinist, "Literature as Politics: The Tukulti-Ninurta Epic and the Bible," *CBQ* 38 (1976), p. 478; cf. also J. A. Soggin, *ZAW* 78 (1966), pp. 179–204.

36. Machinist, "Literature as Politics," pp. 478–79.

37. Ibid., p. 479. This explains then the traditions of David as a psalmist and Solomon as a wise sage and author (cf. 1 Kgs 5:9–14 [MT]; e.g., Proverbs, Ecclesiastes).

38. R. Coote and D. Ord present a cogent case for placing the composition of *J* within the sociopolitical context of David's rise to power; cf. *The Bible's First History* (Philadepia: Fortress, 1989). This early dating of *J* has come under attack particularly by John van Seters, Erhard Blum, and others. This debate is outside the purview of the present monograph; however, it is noteworthy that the sociopolitical dimensions involved in the creation of literature and highlighted by Coote and Ord, Machinist, and others are not directly addressed by the critics of the traditional view.

39. Machinist, "Literature as Politics," p. 482.

40. On the rivalry between the Davidides and the Saulides, see J. Flanagan, "Chiefs in Israel," *JSOT* 20 (1981), pp. 47–73.

41. Talmon, "Kingship and the Ideology of the State," pp. 18–20.

42. E. Knauf, "The Cultural Impact of Secondary State Formation: The Cases of the Edomites and Moabites," in *Early Edom and Moab: The Beginning of the Iron Age in Southern Jordan*, ed. P. Bienkowski (Sheffield: Collis, 1992), pp. 47–54.

43. J. Roberts, "The Davidic Origin of the Zion Tradition," *JBL* 92 (1973), pp. 329–44; "Zion in the Theology of the Davidic-Solomonic Empire," in *Studies in the Period of David and Solomon*, pp. 93–108.

44. The first four were described by Edzard Rohland, *Die Bedeutung der Erwählungstraditionen Israels für die Eschatologie der alttestamentlichen Propheten* (Ph.D. dissertation; Heidelberg, 1956), and the fifth supplemented by H. Wildberger, "Die Völkerwallfahrt zum Zion, Jes. II 1–5," *VT* 7 (1957), pp. 62–81.

45. Cf. *CTA*, 2 III 4; 3 E V 14–15; 4 IV 21–22; 6 I 33–34; 17 VI 47–48. M. Pope identifies El's dwelling at *ǵl ll* with Mount Zaphon; *El in the Ugaritic Texts*, p. 102.

46. Given the parallelism, it seems most likely that צפון וימין אתה בראתם should be emended to read, צפון <<וימנה>> אתה בראתם following Song of Songs 4:8; Amana is a mountain in the anti-Lebanon range known from Assyrian sources as ^{KUR}*Am-ma-na-na*. This emendation, however, is in no way necessary to the argument.

47. J. Levenson emphasizes that the Zion and David traditions could be articulated independently without allusion to each other; see Levenson's review in "Zion Traditions," *ABD 6*, pp. 1098–1102, and also Levenson, *Sinai and Zion: An Entry into the Jewish Bible* (San Francisco: Harper & Row, 1985).

48. A. Kapelrud, "Temple Building, A Task for God and Kings," *Orientalia* 32 (1963), pp. 56–62; A. Hurowitz, *I Have Built You an Exalted House: Temple Building in the Bible in Light of Mesopotamian and North-West Semitic Writings* (Sheffield: JSOT, 1992); C. Meyers, "David as Temple Builder," in *Ancient Israelite Religion: Essays in Honor of Frank Moore Cross*, ed. P. D. Miller, P. Hanson, and S. D. McBride (Philadephia: Fortress, 1987), pp. 357–76.

49. See J. Rosenbloom, "Social Science Concepts of Modernization and Biblical History: The Development of the Israelite Monarchy," *JAAR* 40 (1972), pp. 437–44.

50. The classic expression of early Israelite religion is A. Alt's essay, "The God of the Fathers," in *Essays on Old Testament History and Religion*, trans. R. Wilson (Sheffield: JSOT, 1967), pp. 1–67; see also R. Albertz, *A History of Israelte Religion in the Old Testament.* Volume I: *From the Beginnings to the End of the Monarchy*, trans. J. Bowden (Louisville: Westminister John Knox, 1994), pp. 25–39, 95–104.

51. See K. Whitelam, "The Defense of David," *JSOT* 29 (1984), pp. 61–87.

52. A. Mazar, "The 'Bull Site'—an Iron Age I Open Cult Place," *BASOR* 247 (1982), pp. 27–42.

53. Ibid., p. 38.

54. A. Zertal, "An Early Iron Age Cultic Site on Mount Ebal: Excavation Seasons 1982–1987," *TA* 13–14 (1986–87), pp. 105–65.

55. Although the ethnic identity of these early settlements has been questioned (e.g., K. Whitelam, "The Identity of Early Israel: The Realignment and Transformation of Late Bronze Iron Age Palestine," *JSOT* 63 [1994], pp. 57–78), there is strong evidence in the cultural continuity between the Iron I and II that precludes any alternative identification; see W. Dever, "The Identity of Early Israel: A Rejoinder to Keith Whitelam," *JSOT* 72 (1996), pp. 3–24; A. Mazar, "Iron Age I and II Towers at Giloh and the Israelite Settlement," *IEJ* 40 (1990), pp. 77–101.

56. J. Tigay, "Israelite Religion: The Onomastic and Epigraphic Evidence," in *Ancient Israelite Religion: Essays in Honor of Frank Moore Cross*, p. 159.

57. See J. Tigay, *You Shall Have No Other Gods*, and "Israelite Religion: The Onomastic and Epigraphic Evidence," pp. 157–94; J. Fowler, *Theophoric Personal Names in Ancient Hebrew: A Comparative Study* (Sheffield: JSOT, 1988).

58. S. Grosby, "Borders, Territory and Nationality in the Ancient Near East and Armenia," *JESHO* 40 (1997), p. 6.

59. Cf. K. Whitelam, "The Symbols of Power: Aspects of Royal Propaganda in the United Monarchy," *BA* 49 (1986), pp. 166–73.

60. See, for example, B. Birch, *The Rise of the Israelite Monarchy: The Growth and Development of I Samuel 7–15* (Missoula: Scholars Press, 1976); N. Na'aman, "The Pre-Deuteronomistic Story of King Saul and Its Historical Significance," *CBQ* 54 (1992), pp. 638–58; V. Philips Long, *The Reign and Rejection of King Saul: A Case for Literary and Theological Coherence* (Sheffield: JSOT, 1989).

61. First articulated in the classic study by A. Alt, "Das Königtum in den Reichen Israels und Judas," *VT* 1 (1951), pp. 2–22.

62. As R. Coote and D. Ord did in their work, *The Bible's First History* (Philadephia: Fortress, 1989).

63. E.g., M. Noth, "David and Israel in II Samuel VII," in *The Law in the Pentatuch and Other Studies* (ET, Philadelphia: Fortress, 1967), pp. 250–59.

64. N. Sarna, "Psalm 89: A Study in Inner Biblical Exegesis," in *Biblical and Other Studies*, ed. A. Altmann (Cambridge, Mass.: Harvard University Press, 1963), pp. 29–46.

65. Against previous studies by G. W. Ahlström and R. H. Pfeiffer, which assumed axiomatically that liturgy was earlier than prose; cf. Ahlström, *Psalm 89. Eine Liturgie aus dem Ritual des leidenden Königs* (Lund: Gleerups, 1959), pp. 182ff.; Pfeiffer, *An Introduction to the Old Testament*, 2d ed. (New York: Harper, 1948), pp. 368ff.

66. M. Brettler suggested to me (oral communication) that these texts could have developed in the early post-United Monarchy as a justification for the legitimacy of the South over against the North.

67. For bibliography see recent studies by L. Eslinger, *House of God or House of David: The Rhetoric of 2 Samuel 7*; G. Hentschel, *Gott, König, und Tempel. Beobachtungen zu 2 Sam 7,1–17* (Leipzig: St.-Benno, 1992); G. Jones, *The Nathan Narratives* (Sheffield, JSOT, 1990); T. Veijola, *David. Gesammelte Studien zu den Davidüberlieferungen des Alten Testaments* (Helsinki: Finnish Exegetical Society, 1990).

68. J. Wellhausen, *Prolegomena to the History of Israel* (ET, Meridan Paperback edition, 1957; 1883), p. 253.

69. See F. Crüsemann, *Der Widerstand gegen das Königtum. Die antikönigliche Texte des Alten Testementes und der Kampf um den frühe israelitischen Staat* (Neukirchen-Vluyn: Neukirchener Verlag, 1978), pp. 6–8.

70. Cf. H. Tadmor, "Traditional Institutions and the Monarchy: Social and Political Tensions in the Time of David and Solomon," in *Studies in the Period of David and Solomon*, pp. 239–67.

71. Rost, *The Succession to the Throne of David.*

72. S. Mowinckel, "Nataforjettelsen i 2 Sam. kap. 7," *SEA* 12 (1947), pp. 220–29.

73. A. Weiser, "Dei Legitimation des Königs David. Zur Eigenart und Entstehung der sogen. Gechichte von Davids Aufstieg," *VT* 16 (1966), pp. 325–54. Weiser's genre classification followed Herrmann, but the comparision of the Nathan's prophecy with Egyptian models is problematic; cf. Veijola, *Die ewige Dynastie*, pp. 71–72.

74. Görg, *Gott-König-Reden in Israel und Ägypten* (Stuttgart, 1975).

75. A. Loprieno, "The 'King's Novel'," in *Ancient Egyptian Literature: History and Forms*, ed. A. Loprieno (Leiden: Brill, 1996), pp. 277–96.

76. See the critique of the pan–Deuteronomism by R. E. Friedman, "The Deuteronomistic School," in *Fortunate the Eyes That See: Essays in Honor of David Noel Freedman in Celebration of His Seventieth Birthday*, ed. A. Beck, et al. (Grand Rapids: Eerdmans, 1995), pp. 70–80.

77. R. Carlson, *David, the Chosen King* (Stockholm: Almqvist & Wiksell, 1964).

78. D. McCarthy, "II Samuel 7 and the Structure of the Deuteronomic History," *JBL* 84 (1965), p. 131.

79. F. Cross, *Canaanite Myth and Hebrew Epic* (Cambridge, Mass.: Harvard University Press, 1973), pp. 274–90. Although it is often pointed out that Cross's advocacy of a dual redaction was not original, nevertheless Cross deserves credit for a concise, yet compelling articulation of the dual redaction theory.

80. Eslinger, *House of God or House of David*, p. 35.

81. Cf. S. McKenzie, *The Chronicler's Use of the Deuteronomistic History* (Atlanta: Scholars Press, 1985), and more recently A. G. Auld, *Kings Without Privilege. David and Moses in the Story of the Bible's Kings* (Edinburgh: T & T Clark, 1994).

82. See most recently M. Brettler, "Interpretation and Prayer: Notes on the Composition of 1 Kings 8.15–53," in *Minḥah le-Naḥum: Biblical and Other Studies Presented to Nahum M. Sarna in Honour of his 70th Birthday*, ed. M. Brettler and M. Fishbane (Sheffield: JSOT, 1993), pp. 17–35.

83. M. Weinfeld, *Deuteronomy and the Deuteronomic School* (Oxford: Clarendon, 1972), p. 23.

84. The phenomenon was first observed by H. Weiner, *The Composition of Judges II 11–1 Kings II 46* (Leipzig: J. C. Hinrichs, 1929), p. 2; see also C. Kuhl, "Die 'Wiederaufnahme'—ein literarisches Prinzip?" *ZAW* 64 (1952), pp. 1–11; B. O. Long, "Framing Repetitions in Biblical Historiography," *JBL* 106 (1987), pp. 385–99.

85. See R. Nelson, *The Double Redaction of the Deuteronomistic History* (Sheffield: JSOT, 1981), pp. 106–8.

86. Note that a similar understanding of 2 Sam 7 that is evident in 1 Kgs 8:27–53 indicates that 2 Sam 7:13a cannot be considered just a secondary addition.

87. M. Fishbane, "The Qumran Pesher and Traits of Ancient Hermeneutics," *Proceedings of the Sixth World Congress of Jewish Studies*, 1 (Jerusalem: World Union of Jewish Studies, 1979), pp. 97–114; see also his *Biblical Interpretation in Ancient Israel* (Oxford: Clarendon, 1985), pp. 44–46.

88. The text of 4Q174 with transcription and translation was published by J. M. Allegro, *DJD* 5, pp. 53–54, plates 19–20. For the most comprehensive treatment of the text see recently G. Brooke, *Exegesis at Qumran: 4QFlorilegium in Its Jewish Context* (Sheffield: JSOT, 1985).

89. See Weinfeld, *Deuteronomy and the Deuteronomic School*, pp. 324–25, n. 15.

90. Ibid., pp. 170, 343. See also von Rad's classic essay, "There Remain Still a Rest for the People of God: An Investigation of a Biblical Conception," in *The Problem of the Hexateuch and Other Essays*, trans. E. W. Trueman (London: SCM, 1966), pp. 94–102.

91. Further references to the chosen place and name theology may be found in Weinfeld, *Deuteronomy and the Deuteronomic School*, pp. 324–26.

92. Van Seters, *In Search of History* (New Haven: Yale University Press, 1983), p. 273.

93. Ibid., p. 273, n. 116.

94. E.g., Rost, *The Succession to the Throne of David*, pp. 35–56; R. Nelson, *The Double Redaction of the Deuteronomistic History*, pp. 105–8; J. van Seters, *In Search of History*, pp. 271–77; T. Veiola, *Die Ewige Dynastie*, pp. 68–79; J. Levenson, *Sinai and Zion: An Entry into the Jewish Bible*, pp. 97–101; I. L. Seeligmann, "From Historic Reality to Historiosophic Conception in the Bible," *Peraqim* II (1969–74), pp. 282, 301.

95. E.g., J. Fokkelman, *Narrative Art and Poety in the Books of Samuel. Throne and City (II Sam. 2–8 & 21–24)*, vol. 3, trans. L. Waaning-Wardle (Assen: Van Gorcum, 1990); Eslinger, *House of God or House of David: The Rhetoric of 2 Samuel 7.*

96. Mowinckel, "Natansforjettlesen 2 Sam. kap. 7," pp. 220–29.

97. See Polzin, *David and the Deuteronomist*, pp. 77–82.

98. See discussions by S. Paul, "Adoption Formulae: A Study of Cuneiform and Biblical Legal Clauses," *MAARAV* 2 (1980), pp. 173–86; G. Brin, "The History of the Formula 'He Shall be to Me a son and I Will Be to Him a Father," in *Bible and Jewish History Dedicated to the Memory of Jacob Liver* (Tel Aviv: Tel Aviv University, 1972) [Hebrew]; F. Fensham, "Father and Son as Terminology for Treaty and Covenant," in *Near Eastern Studies in Honour of W. F. Albright*, ed. H. Goedicke (Baltimore: Johns Hopkins University Press, 1971), pp. 121–35.

99. For a classic statement on early Israelite religion see A. Alt, "The God of the Fathers"; see also the recent study by Mark Smith, *The Early History of God* (New York: Harper & Row, 1990).

100. See A. Hurvitz, *The Transition Period in Biblical Hebrew* (Jerusalem: Bialik, 1972) [Hebrew].

101. See especially Robertson, *Linguistic Evidence in Dating Early Hebrew Poetry* (Missoula, Mont.: Scholars Press, 1972).

102. On the relationship of nationalism and the development of language see K. Woolard and B. Schieffelin, "Language Ideology," *Annual Review of Anthropology* 23 (1994), pp. 55–88; and J. Irvine, "When Talk Isn't Cheap: Language and Political Economy," *American Ethnologist* 16 (1989), pp. 248–67; V. N. Vološinov, *Marxism and the Philosophy of Language*, trans. L. Matejka and I. R. Titunik (Cambridge, Mass.: Harvard University Press, 1973).

103. Also see E. Lipinski, *Le poème royal du Psaume LXXXIX 1–5, 20–38* (Paris: Gabalda, 1967); Ahlström, *Psalm 89—Eine Liturgie aus dem Ritual des Leidenden Königs*; J. B. Dumortier, "Un rituel d'intronisation: Le Ps. LXXXIX: 2–38," *VT* 22 (1972), pp. 176–96; A. Caquot, "Observations sur le Psaume 89," *Semitica* 41–42 (1991–92), pp. 133–157.

104. See, for example, Hans-Joachim Kraus, *Psalms 60–150: A Commentary* (ET, Minneapolis: Augsburg, 1989), pp. 201–204.

105. M. Brettler, "Ideology, History and Theology in 2 Kings XVII 7–23," *VT* 39 (1989), p. 280.

106. W. F. Albright, *Archaeology and the Religion of Israel* (Baltimore: Johns Hopkins University Press, 1968), pp. 124–25. Kraus accepted Albright's early dating of the hymnic portion of the psalm (cf. Kraus, *Psalms 60–150*, p. 203). The archaic features of the hymn are bolstered by comparions with the *KRT* epic from Ugarit; cf. M. Dahood, *Psalms II*,

Anchor Bible (New York: Doubleday, 1968), pp. 311–15; John Day, *God's Conflict with the Dragon and the Sea* (Cambridge: Cambridge University Press, 1985), pp. 25–28.

107. Y. Avishur, *Studies in Hebrew and Ugaritic Psalms* (Jerusalem: Magnes Press, 1994), p. 231.

108. See ibid., pp. 207–11.

109. Ibid., p. 232.

110. On Rahab, see J. Day, *God's Conflict with the Dragon and the Sea.*

111. R. Hess, "Hebrew Psalms and Amarna Correspondence from Jerusalem: Some Comparisons and Implications," *ZAW* 101 (1989), pp. 249–65. Hess cites a couple parallels with Ps 89 (pp. 253, 258); I suggest further parallels with Ps 89 based on his categories.

112. The special character of the Jerusalem letters was described by W. Moran, "The Syrian Scribe of the Jerusalem Amarna Letters," in *Unity and Diversity*, ed. H. Goedicke and J. Roberts (Baltimore: Johns Hopkins University Press, 1975), pp. 146–66.

113. See, for example, G. Knoppers, *Two Nations Under God: The Deuteronomistic History of Solomon and the Dual Monarchies,* Volume 1*: The Reign of Solomon and the Rise of Jeroboam* (Atlanta: Scholars Press, 1993), pp. 93–109; Brettler, "Interpretation and Prayer: Notes on the Composition of 1 Kings 8.15–53," pp. 17–35; Levenson, "From Temple to Synagogue: 1 Kings 8," in *Traditions in Transformations: Turning Points in Biblical Faith*, ed. B. Halpern and J. Levenson (Winona Lake, Ind.: Eisenbrauns, 1981), pp. 143–66; E. Talstra, *Solomon's Prayer. Synchrony and Diachony in the Composition of I Kings 8,14–61* (Amsterdam, 1987); G. Jones, *The Nathan Narratives*, pp. 59–92.

114. This division has been pointed out by a number of scholars. A clear presentation and detailed presentation of it may be found in Brettler, "Interpretation and Prayer: Notes on the Composition of 1 Kings 8.15–53," pp. 18–19

115. The literature is summarized by V. Hurowitz, *I Have Built You an Exalted House*, pp. 285–87.

116. Weinfeld, *Deuteronomy and the Deuteronomic School*, p. 35.

117. A varietv of assignments have been given ranging from Dahood who places it in the tenth century (*Psalms III*, Anchor Bible [Garden City, N.Y.: Doubleday, 1970], p. 241) to Duhm who puts it in the Maccabean period (*Die Psalmen,* 2d ed. [Tübingen: Mohr, 1922], p. 447). See recent survey by Jean-Marie Auwers, "Le psaaume 132 parmi les graduels," *RB* 103–4 (1996), pp. 553–58.

118. Auwers, "Le psaaume 132 parmi les graduels," pp. 546–560.

119. Weinfeld, "Zion and Jerusalem as Religious and Political Capital," p. 90.

120. See Schniedewind, *The Word of God in Transition*, pp. 153–60.

121. Mettinger, *King and Messiah: The Civil and Sacral Legitimation of the Israelite Kings* (Lund: Gleerups), pp. 22–25.

122. G. Smith, *The Historical Geography of the Holy Land*, p. 38.

123. Marc Brettler has shown how the book of Judges may be read as a political allegory reflecting on the problem of legitimacy, "The Book of Judges: Literature as Politics," *JBL* 108 (1989), pp. 405–28. In another article Brettler demonstrates the close intertextuality between the Deuteronomic "Law of the King" and the assessment of Solomon's reign, "The Structure of 1 Kings 1–11," *JSOT* 49 (1991), pp. 87–97.

124. Tadmor, "Traditional Institutions and the Monarchy," p. 247.

125. See ibid., pp. 239–58.

126. Cf. A. Hurvitz, "Linguistic Observations on the Biblical Usage of the Priestly Term *ᶜEdah*," *Tarbiz* 40 (1970–71), pp. 261–66 [Hebrew]; J. Milgrom, "Priestly Terminiology and the Political Social Structure of the Pre-Monarchic Israel," *JQR* ns 69 (1978), pp, 65–76.

127. Tadmor, "Traditional Institutions and the Monarchy," pp. 241–45.

128. Ibid., p. 256.

129. Hurowitz, *I Have Built You an Exalted House*, pp. 135–67.

Chapter 3

1. Pedersen, *Israel: Its Life and Culture. I–II* (Copenhagen: Møllers; London: Oxford, 1926), p. 24.

2. N. Avigad summarizes this debate, *Discovering Jerusalem* (Jerusalem: Israel Exploration Society, 1980), pp. 26–31; more recently, A. Vaughn, "The Chronicler's Account of Hezekiah: The Relationship of Historical Data to a Theological Interpretation of 2 Chronicles 29–32" (Th.D. thesis, Princeton Theological Seminary, 1996), pp. 87–100. My own understanding of Jerusalem's archaeology owes much to Gabriel Barkay; see especially his dissertation, "Northern and Western Jerusalem in the End of the Iron Age" (Ph.D. dissertation; Tel Aviv University, 1985) [Hebrew].

3. K. Kenyon, *Digging Up Jerusalem* (London: Ernest Benn, 1974), p. 147.

4. Avigad, *Discovering Jerusalem*, pp. 26–31.

5. Numerous biblical texts indicate that Hezekiah, as we would expect, made substantial preparations for Assyrian invasions (e.g., 2 Kgs 20:20; Isa 10:27–34; 11:8b–11; 2 Chr 32:30–31).

6. Summarized by H. Geva, "Twenty-Five Years of Excavations in Jerusalem, 1968–1993: Achievements and Evaluation," in *Ancient Jerusalem Revealed*, ed. H. Geva (Jerusalem: Israel Exploration Society, 1994), pp. 1–29. Other important studies include M. Broshi, "The Expansion of Jerusalem in the Reigns of Hezekiah and Manasseh," *IEJ* 24 (1974), pp. 21–26; H. Geva, "The Western Boundary of Jerusalem at the End of the Monarchy," *IEJ* 29 (1979), pp. 84–91; Ernest-Marie Laperrousaz, "Jérusalem la grande," *EI* [Malamat Volume] 24 (1993), pp. 138*–47*; "Jerusalem," in *The New Encyclopedia of Archaeological Excavations in the Holy Land*, pp. 698–716.

7. Broshi, "The Expansion of Jerusalem," p. 21.

8. Barkay argues for a super-maximalist view of Jerusalem's size which entails an earlier beginning to Jerusalem's growth; cf. Barkay, "Northern and Western Jerusalem," pp. 490–92, followed recently by Vaughn, "The Chronicler's Account of Hezekiah," pp. 94–99. Even if one concedes that some settlement on the western hill began in the ninth century, the overwhelming evidence suggests that the primary growth begins in the late eighth century. Bahat represents a minority position in suggesting that only part of the western hill was walled in the eighth century; cf. Bahat, "Was Jerusalem Really That Large?" in *Biblical Archaeology Today, 1990: Proceedings of the Second International Congress on Biblical Archaeology*, ed. A. Biran and J. Aviram (Jerusalem: Israel Exploration Society, 1993), pp. 581–84.

9. *The New Encyclopedia of Archaeological Excavations in the Holy Land*, pp. 705–9; also Avigad, *Discovering Jerusalem*, pp. 55–56.

10. Shiloh, "Jerusalem," in *The New Encyclopedia of Archaeological Excavations in the Holy Land*, p. 715.

11. Bahat, "Was Jerusalem Really That Large?" p. 583; for a summary of Jerusalem's water systems see Shiloh's contribution on "Water Systems" in *The New Encyclopedia of Archaeological Excavations in the Holy Land*, "Jerusalem," pp. 709–12.

12. Bahat, "Was Jerusalem Really that Large?", p. 583.

13. The suggestion was made to me orally by Gabriel Barkay.

14. Warren's shaft already brought a safe water supply within the City of David so this could not have been the purpose of Hezekiah's Tunnel. Shiloh suggests it took over the

function of the Siloam Channel (*a.k.a.* Siloam Tunnel) bringing water to the central valley; cf. Shiloh, "Jerusalem," p. 711.

15. Wittfogel, *Oriental Despotism* (New Haven: Yale University Press, 1957).

16. For a similar interpretation, see H. G. M. Williamson, *1 and 2 Chronicles* (Grand Rapids: Eerdmans, 1982), p. 361; also note Talmon's interpretation of Hezekiah in his essay, "The Cult and Calendar Reform of Jeroboam I," in *King, Cult, and Calendar in Ancient Israel: Collected Studies* (Jerusalem: Magnes Press, 1986), pp. 123–30.

17. See Schniedewind, "History and Interpretation: The Religion of Ahab and Manasseh in the Book of Kings," *CBQ* 55 (1993), pp. 657–60.

18. Gabriel Barkay (oral communication). Also see N. Na'aman, "Hezekiah's Fortified Cities and the LMLK Stamps," *BASOR* 261 (1986), pp. 5–21.

19. Although the books of Chronicles were composed in the postexilic period and their historicity has often been questioned, more recent trends have highlighted the Chronicler's use of early sources; see Japhet, "The Historical Reliability of Chronicles: The History of the Problem and Its Place in Biblical Research," *JSOT* 33 (1985), pp. 83–107.

20. Finkelstein, "The Archaeology of the Days of Manasseh," in *Scripture and Other Artifacts: Essays on the Bible and Archaeology in Honor of Philip J. King*, ed. M. Coogan, J. Cheryl Exum, and L. Stager (Louisville: Westminister John Knox, 1994), p. 173.

21. Cf. Y. Dagan, "The Shephelah during the Period of the Monarchy in Light of Archaeological Excavations and Surveys," M.A. thesis, Tel Aviv University [Hebrew]. A summary of Dagan's research can be found in Vaughn, "The Chronicler's Account of Hezekiah," pp. 41–54.

22. Although surveys by M. Kochavi and A. Ofer indicated a slight drop in settlement in the Judaean hills between the eighth and sixth centuries, Finkelstein notes these data are suspect; see Finkelstein's review of the data in "The Archaeology of the Days of Manasseh," pp. 174–75. Recent surveys of the Jerusalem area have uncovered a number of settlements from the eighth to sixth centuries; see G. Edelstein and I. Milevski, "The Rural Settlement of Jerusalem Re-evaluated: Surveys and Excavations in the Reph'aim Valley and the Mevasseret Yerushalayim," *PEQ* 126 (1994), pp. 2–11; Z. Ron, "Agricultural Terraces in the Judean Mountains," *IEJ* 16 (1966), pp. 111–22; S. Gibson and G. Edelstein, "Investigating Jerusalem's Rural Landscape," *Levant* 17 (1985), pp. 139–55; A. Zahavi, "Malḥa Hill," *Hadashot Arkheologiyot* 99 (1993), pp. 59–60 [Hebrew]; R. Ovadiah, "Jerusalem, Giv'at Massu'a," *ESI* 12 (1994), pp. 71–76; Nurit Feig, "New Discoveries in the Rephaim Valley, Jerusalem," *PEQ* 128 (1996), pp. 3–7.

23. See J. Pritchard, "Industry and Trade at Biblical Gibeon," *BA* 23 (1960), pp. 23–29. The discovery of eighty-six *lmlk* stamps indicate that Gibeon was an important agricultural center in Hezekiah's administration. Gitin also explains the rapid growth of the city of Ekron by relating it to northern refugees; cf. Gitin, "Incense Altars from Ekron, Israel and Judah: Context and Typology," *EI* 20 (1989), pp. 52*–67*.

24. Ramat Rahel has been a problem for historical geography. It is often identified by Beth–Haccherem (Jer 6:1; Neh 3:14; Josh 15:59a [LXX]). Gabriel Barkay makes a cogent case for its identification with the enigmatic *mmšt* mentioned in the numerous *LMLK* stamps at the site; cf. "Ramat Rahel," in *The New Encyclopedia of Archaeological Excavations in the Holy Land*, pp. 1261–67.

25. Kenyon excavated a wall on the eastern slope of the City of David and attributed it to Hezekiah ("Wall NA"), but it seems more likely that it should be attributed to Manasseh; cf. Dan Bahat, "The Wall of Manasseh in Jerusalem," *IEJ* 31 (1981), pp. 235–36.

26. There was also a sudden expansion of settlement in the more arid regions of the Beersheba valley and the Judaean desert; cf. Finkelstein, "The Archaeology of the Days of

Manasseh," pp. 175–76. The Beersheba region partly replaced the Shephelah as the "breadbasket" of the small Judaean state.

27. Ibid., p. 181.

28. The exact numbers depend on the size of Jerusalem post-701 BCE. Finkelstein takes a conservative estimate of 60 hectares. This still would translate into an almost fourfold increase in Jerusalem's size making Jerusalem 23% of Judah's total population. G. Barkay cogently argues for a much larger Jerusalem of one hundred hectares, which translates into 34% (cf. Barkay, "Northern and Western Jerusalem in the End of the Iron Age"). I follow a mediating position, estimating a total built-up area of eighty hectares. Of course, this does not include the small agricultural villages that had sprung up around Jerusalem.

29. This definition follows R. Tringham, "Introduction: Settlement Patterns and Urbanization," in *Man, Settlement and Urbanism*, ed. P. J. Ucko, R. Tringham, and G. W. Dimbleby (Cambridge, Mass.: Schenkman, 1972), pp. xix–xxviii.

30. See H. Kuhne, "The Urbanization of the Assyrian Provinces," in *Nuove Fondazioni nel Vicino Oriente Antico: Relata e ideologia*, ed. S. Mazzoni (Pisa: Giardini, 1994), p. 55, and the bibliography cited there.

31. I am indebted to recent UCLA dissertations by Bradley Parker (north Assyrian frontier) and Mitchell Allen (Philistine coast) for their work on the administration of the neo-Assyrian empire; Parker, "The Northern Frontier of Assyria as a Case Study in Imperial Dynamics," (Ph.D, UCLA, 1998); Allen, "Contested Peripheries: Philistia in the Neo–Assyrian World–System" (Ph.D., UCLA, 1997). Also see H. Kuhne, "The Urbanization of the Assyrian Provinces," pp. 55–84.

32. G. Sojberg, "The Rise and Fall of Cities: A Theoretical Perspective," in *Urbanism and Urbanization*, p. 8; this essay summarizes some conclusions of Sojberg's classic work, *The Preindustrial City: Past and Present* (Glencoe, Ill.: Free Press, 1960).

33. I. Eph'al, "On Warfare and Military Control in the Ancient Near Eastern Empires: A Research Outline," in *History, Historiography and Interpretation: Studies in Biblical and Cuneiform Literatures*, ed. H. Tadmor and M. Weinfeld (Jerusalem: Magnes Press, 1983), pp. 88–106.

34. Halpern attributes this term from B. F. Liddell Hart; cf. Halpern, "Jerusalem and the Lineages in the Seventh Century BCE," pp. 18–19.

35. Sojberg, *The Preindustrial City: Past and Present*, p. 76.

36. Ibid., p. 77.

37. E.g., ibid., pp. 110–16; D. Dumond, "Population Growth and Cultural Change," *Southwestern Journal of Anthropology* 21 (1965), pp. 302–24; C. Clark, *Population Growth and Land Use* (New York: Macmillan, 1967); G. Lenski, *Power and Privilege: A Theory of Social Stratification* (New York: McGraw-Hill, 1966).

38. N. Anderson, "Aspects of Urbanism and Urbanization," in *Urbanism and Urbanization*, ed. N. Anderson (Leiden: Brill, 1964), p. 2.

39. It is no coincidence that the northern kingdom had closer cultural, religious, and political ties with its neighbors. This was a simple reflex of its geography.

40. Finkelstein, "Environmental Archaeology and Social History," p. 63.

41. Concerning the degree of Assyrian imposition of religion; see M. Cogan, *Imperialism and Religion: Assyria, Judah and Israel in the Eighth and Seventh Centuries B.C.E.* (Missoula, Mont.: Scholars Press, 1974), and J. McKay, *Religion in Judah under the Assyrians* (Naperville, Ill.: Allenson, 1973).

42. D. Hillers, *Micah: A Commentary*, Hermenia (Philadephia: Fortress, 1984), p. 6.

43. For a review of the field, see Schniedewind, "The Problem with Kings: Recent Study of the Deuteronomistic History," *RSR* 22 (1996), pp. 22–27.

44. H. Weippert, "Die 'deuteronomistischen' Beurteilungen der Königen von Israel und Juda und das Problem der Redaktion der Königsbücher," *Bib* 53 (1972), pp. 301–9; I. Provan, *Hezekiah and the Books of Kings* (Berlin: de Gruyter, 1988). The present study is not the place to discuss this hypothesis in detail. A foundation for the approach is the study of the regnal and judgment formulae; as Vanderhooft and Halpern note, "The most obvious barometer of editorial shifts within Kings is fluctuation in its skeletal formulary" ("The Editions of Kings in the 7th-6th Centuries B.C.E.," *HUCA* 62 [1991], p. 183).

45. See van Seters, *In Search of History*, pp. 31–54.

46. This point is argued cogently and at length by Brettler, "Ideology, History and Theology in 2 Kings XVII 7–23," *VT* 39 (1989), pp. 277–79.

47. Provan, *Hezekiah in the Book of Kings*, pp. 116–17. See also Friedman, "From Egypt to Egypt in Dtr 1 and Dtr 2," in *Traditions in Transformations: Turning Points in Biblical Faith*, ed. B. Halpern and J. Levenson (Winona Lake, Ind.: Eisenbrauns, 1981), pp. 171–73.

48. For a discussion of the literary unit see M. Sweeney, *Isaiah 1–39: With an Introduction to Prophetic Literature* (Grand Rapids: Eerdmans, 1996), pp. 114–15.

49. See recently H. G. M. Williamson, *The Book Called Isaiah: Deutero-Isaiah's Role in Composition and Redaction* (Oxford: Clarendon, 1994), pp. 116–55.

50. E.g., O. Steck finds four sources in Isa 11, yet the text coheres quite well. Steck's redactional analysis depends on poorly grounded historical assumptions about what "fits" and his identification of disjunctions that are not apparent to the average reader; cf. Steck, " 'ein kleiner Knabe kann sie Leiten': Beobachtungen zum Tierfrieden in Jesaja 11,6–8 and 65,25," in *Alttestamentlicher Glaube und Biblische Theologie: Festschrift für Hurst Dietrich Preuß*, ed. J. Haumann and H. Zobel (Stuttgart: Kohlhammer, 1992), pp. 105–8.

51. Sweeney, *Isaiah 1–39*, p. 116.

52. E.g., Isa 40:24; this meaning continues in postbiblical Hebrew (cf. *m. B. Bat.* 4:5). See the discussions by Hayes and Irvine, *Isaiah, the Eighth-century Prophet: His Times and His Preaching* (Nashville: Abingdon, 1987), p. 212, and B. Sommer, *A Prophet Reads Scripture: Allusion in Isaiah 40-66* (Palo Alto, Calif.: Stanford University Press, 1998), chapter 3 under subtitle "Reprediction of Royal Prophecies."

53. Anderson and Freedman, *Amos*, Anchor Bible(New York: Doubleday, 1989); S. Paul, *Amos, A Commentary on the Book of Amos*, Hermenia (Philadephia: Fortress, 1991). Similar views are also expressed by J. Hayes, *Amos, the Eighth Century Prophet: His Times and His Preaching* (Nashville: Abingdon, 1991), pp. 223–24; K. Koch, *The Prophets, Volume 1: The Assyrian Period*, trans. M. Kohl (Philadephia: Fortress, 1982), pp. 169–70.

54. It is also noteworthy that Gath is missing from the list of Philistine cities mentioned in Amos 1:6–8. Its fate is apparently summed up in the words of the prophet Micah, "Tell it not in Gath" (Mic 1:10).

55. R. Clements, *Old Testament Prophecy: From Oracles to Canon* (Louisville: Westminister John Knox, 1996), p. 23.

56. E.g., W. Harper, *A Critical and Exegetical Commentary on Amos and Hosea*, ICC (Edinburgh: T & T Clark, 1905), pp. 195–96; Driver, *Amos*, pp. 119–24; Wolff, *Joel and Amos*, Hermeneia (Philadelphia: Fortress, 1977), p. 352; J. Mays, *Amos*, OTL (Philadelphia: Westminister, 1969), p. 163; Coote, *Amos among the Prophets* (Philadephia: Fortress, 1981), pp. 110–34; Pomykala, *Davidic Dynasty Tradition in Early Judaism*, pp. 61–63.

57. Barr writes, "There is no correlation, then, between the spelling tendencies and the date of origin of the books." *The Variable Spelling of the Hebrew Bible* (Oxford: Oxford University Press, 1989), p. 201.

58. The association between Amos 5:26–27 and 9:11 is recognized by the Damascus Document (cf. CD vii, 14–21). See the discussion in chapter 7.

59. Pomykala, *Davidic Dynasty Tradition in Early Judaism*, p. 62.

60. Gunkel, *Die Psalmen*, 4th ed., HKAT 2/2 (Göttingen: Vandenhoeck & Ruprecht, 1926), p. 342.

61. The linguistic dating of biblical texts was pioneered by A. Hurvitz, see *The Transition Period in Biblical Hebrew: A Study of Post–exilic Hebrew and its Implications for Dating the Psalms* (Jerusalem: Bialik, 1972) [Hebrew].

62. Robertson, *Linguistic Evidence in Dating Early Hebrew Poetry*, p. 150.

63. See R. Clifford, "In Zion and David a New Beginning: An Interpretation of Psalm 78," in *Traditions and Transformation: Turning points in Biblical Faith*, ed. B. Halpern and J. D. Levenson (Winona Lake, Ind.: Eisenbrauns, 1981), pp. 121–41.

64. H. G. M. Williamson, "The Concept of Israel in Transitions," in *The World of Ancient Israel: Sociological, Anthropological and Political Perspectives: Essays by Members of the Society for Old Testament Study*, ed. R. E. Clements (Cambridge: Cambridge University Press, 1989), pp. 141–61.

65. Duhm, *Die Psalmen*, KHAT 15 (Freiburg: Mohr, 1899), pp. 201–6.

66. See Brettler, *God is King*, pp. 80–81.

67. See, for example, Kirkpatrick, *The Book of Psalms* (Cambridge: Cambridge University Press, 1901), p. 5.

68. For example, Anderson, *Psalms 1–72* (Grand Rapids: Eerdmans, 1972), pp. 63–64.

Chapter 4

1. See Schniedewind, "The Geopolitical History of Philistine Gath," *BASOR* 307 (1997), pp. 1–9.

2. Mazar, *Archaeology of the Land of the Bible*, p. 437. On family and clan structure, see Stager, "The Archaeology of the Family in Ancient Israel," pp. 1–35.

3. See Halpern, "Jerusalem and the Lineages in the Seventh Century BCE," pp. 49–77.

4. Gitin, "The Effects of Urbanization on a Philistine City-State," pp. 277–84.

5. The ostracon was first published by J. Naveh, "A Hebrew Letter from the Seventh Century B.C.," *IEJ* 10 (1960), pp. 129–39. An archaeological summary may be found in *The New Encyclopedia of Archaeological Excavations in the Holy Land*, pp. 585–86. For further discussion of the judicial aspects of the letter, see I. Yeiven, "The Judicial Petition from Mezad Hashavyahu," *BibOr* 19 (1962), pp. 3–10; and D. Pardee, "The Judicial Plea from Meṣad Ḥashavyahu (Yavneh–Yam): A New Philological Study," *MAARAV* 1 (1978), pp. 33–66. Halpern shows that Na'aman's argument disputing the association of the fortress with Josiah is not tenable; cf. Halpern, "Jerusalem and the Lineages in the Seventh Century BCE," p. 63; Na'aman, "The Kingdom of Judah under Josiah," *TA* 18 (1991), pp. 3–71.

6. See N. Na'aman, "Hezekiah's Fortified Cities and the LMLK Stamps," pp. 5–21; A. F. Rainey, "Wine from the Royal Vineyards," *BASOR* 245 (1982), pp. 57–62.

7. O. Zimhoni, "Two Ceramic Assemblages from Lachish Levels III and II,"*TA* 17 (1990), p. 48.

8. Ibid., p. 49.

9. Weber, "Urbanisation and Social Sturcture in the Ancient World," in *Max Weber: Selections in Translation*, ed. W. G. Runciman (Cambridge: Cambridge University Press, 1978), p. 291. See also Weber, *Economy and Society*, ed. G. Roth and C. Wittich (Berkeley, Calif.: University of California, 1978), pp. 1212–20.

10. See summary by A. Millard, "An Assessment of the Evidence for Writing in Ancient Israel," in *Biblical Archaeology Today: Proceedings of the International Congress on Biblical Archaeology, Jerusalem, April 1984* (Jerusalem: Israel Exploration Society, 1985), pp. 301–12; A. Lemairé, *Les écoles et la formation de la Bible dans l'ancien Israël*

(Fribourg: Editions Universitaires, 1981); and more generally, Susan Niditch, *Oral World and Written Word.*

11. Avigad, *Hebrew Bullae from the Time of Jeremiah: Remnants of a Burnt Archive* (Jerusalem: Israel Exploration Society, 1986), p. 121. For a complete survey of seals see Avigad, *Corpus of West Semitic Stamp Seals*, revised and completed by B. Sass (Jerusalem: Israel Exploration Society, 1997).

12. See Avigad, *Hebrew Bullae from the Time of Jeremiah*, pp. 120–30.

13. The *editio princeps* was done by H. Torczyner, *Lachish I: The Lachish Letters* (Oxford, 1938); Cross raises the issue of literacy in his study, "A Literate Soldier: Lachish Letter III," in *Biblical and Related Studies Presented to Samuel Iwry*, ed. A. Kort and S. Morschauser (Winona Lake, Ind.: Eisenbrauns, 1985), pp. 41–47.

14. Naveh, "A Hebrew Letter from the Seventh Century B. C.," pp. 129–39.

15. Deutsch and Heltzer, *New Epigraphic Evidence from the Biblical Period* (Tel Aviv: Archaeological Center, 1995), pp. 92–103.

16. J. Goody, *The Domestication of the Savage Mind* (Cambridge: Cambridge University Press, 1977), p. 37. A summary of Orality-Literacy theory may be found in Walter Ong, *Orality and Literacy*. Ong highlights the tension between orality and literacy which is obscured in Goody's work. The dialectic in biblical literature is exploited in S. Niditch's recent book, *Oral World and Written Word*. Both these works highlight a continuum between orality and literacy which is overlooked in Goody's early work

17. Goody, *The Domestication of the Savage Mind*, p. 37.

18. Seidel's law is named for its discoverer, M. Seidel, "Parallels between Isaiah and Psalm," *Sinai* 38 (1955–56), pp. 149–72, 229–40, 272–80, 335–55 [Hebrew]; see also P. Beentjes, "Inverted Quotations in the Bible: A Neglected Stylistic Pattern," *Bib* 63 (1982), pp. 506–23.

19. See my earlier study, *The Word of God in Transition* (pp. 130–62), as well as studies by J. Blenkinsopp, particularly *Prophecy and Canon* (South Bend, Ind.: Notre Dame University Press, 1977) and *A History of Prophecy in Israel* (Philadephia: Westminister, 1983).

20. Geller, *Sacred Enigmas: Literary Religion in the Hebrew Bible* (London: Routledge, 1996), p. 5.

21. Isa 24:4 should be corrected to עִם הארץ "with the earth."

22. Other references include Haggai (once), Zechariah (once), Job (once), Daniel (once), and Ezra (once). All six occurrences in the books of Chronicles have exact parallels in the books of Kings.

23. Weber, *Ancient Judaism*, trans. H. Gerth and D. Martindale (Glencoe, Ill.: Free Press, 1952), pp. 25–26; Daiches, "The Meaning of am-haaretz in the O.T.," *JTS* 30 (1929), pp. 245–49; Gordis, "Sectional Rivalry in the Kingdom of Judah," *JQR* n.s. 25 (1934-35), pp. 237–59.

24. Sulzberger, *'am ha'areṣ—the Ancient Hebrew Parliament, a Chapter in the Constitutional History of Ancient Israel* (Philadephia: Greenstone, 1909); Auerbach, "*'Am ha'areṣ*," *Proceedings of the First World Congress of Jewish Studies, 1947* (Jerusalem, 1952), pp. 362–66 [Hebrew].

25. Noth, "Gott, König, Volk in A.T.," *ZThK* 47 (1950), p. 181 [reprinted in *Gesammelte Studien zum A. T.* (Munich, 1950), p. 217]; de Vaux, *Ancient Israel* (ET, New York: McGraw-Hill, 1961), p. 71.

26. Galling calls them "die ärmeren Volkschichten"; see Galling, "Die israelitische Staatsverfassung in ihrer vorderoientalischen Umwelt," *AO* 28 (1929), p. 23; Menes, "Die vorexilischen Gesetze Israels im Zusammenhang seiner kulturgeschichtlichen Entwicklung," *BZAW* 50 (1928), pp. 70–71.

27. H. Reviv, *The Elders in Ancient Israel: A Study of a Biblical Institution* (Jerusalem: Magnes Press, 1989), pp. 113–19.

28. E. Nicholson, "The Meaning of the Expression עם הארץ in the O.T.," *JSS* 10 (1956), p. 56.

29. Contra Reviv who suggests that the city elders of Jerusalem were undoubtedly partners in the cornation of Jehoash (*The Elders in Ancient Israel*, p. 116).

30. Also note v. 15 ,where Nebuchadnezzar is said to have taken the "elite of the land" into exile.

31. Talmon, "The Judaean *'am ha'areṣ* in Historical Perspective," in *King, Cult and Calendar in Ancient Israel: Collected Studies* (Jerusalem: Magnes Press, 1986), p. 75.

32. Ibid., p. 78.

33. The exact derivation of Meshullemeth is unclear. Although in the MT Meshullemeth apparently derives from the idea "restitution," it also might be analyzed as meaning "Mot rules." Her hometown, Jotbah, may be identified with Kerem el–Ras (or Jifat) in Galilee ("Jotbah," in *ABD*, p. 1020; also Cogan and Tadmor, *II Kings*, p. 275).

34. Tigay points out that although the onomastic picture has sometimes been attributed to the Josianic reforms, the evidence does not bear this out; *You Shall Have No Other Gods*, p. 15.

35. See especially the essays in the book edited by J. Beckford, *New Religious Movements and Rapid Social Change* (London: Sage /Unesco, 1986).

36. Beckford, *New Religious Movements and Rapid Social Change*, p. x.

37. E.g., Y. Kaufmann, *The Religion of Israel,* trans. and ed. M. Greenberg (New York: Schoken, 1960), p. 276; J. Bright, *A History of Israel*, 3d ed. (Philadephia: Westminister, 1979), pp. 311–13; B. Oded, "Judah and the Exile," in *Israelite and Judean History*, p. 453.

38. E.g., Ahlström, *The History of Ancient Palestine From the Palaeolithic Period to Alexander's Conquest* (Sheffield: JSOT, 1992), pp. 730–37.

39. G.Ahlström, *Royal Administration and National Religion in Ancient Palestine* (Leiden: Brill, 1982), pp. 75–81.

40. Beckford, *New Religious Movements and Rapid Social Change*, p. xiv. Bernard Levinson underscores this in his analysis of Deuteronomy's legal innovations, *Deuteronomy and the Hermenuetics of Legal Innovation.*

41. Beckford, *New Religious Movements and Rapid Social Change*, p. xv.

42. Noth, *The Deuteronomistic History*, trans. H. G. M. Williamson (Sheffield: JSOT, 1991); see my review of recent literature, "The Problem with Kings," pp. 22–27.

43. For a recent review of "name theology" see Ian Wilson, *Out of the Midst of the Fire: Divine Presence in Deuteronomy* (Atlanta: Scholars Press, 1995).

44. See Weinfeld, *Deuteronomy and the Deuteronomic School*, pp. 191–209, 324–25.

45. See von Rad's third chapter on "Deuteronomy's 'Name' Theology and the Priestly Document's 'Kabod' Theology," in *Studies in Deuteronomy,* trans. D. Stalker (Chicago: Regnery, 1953), pp. 37–44.

46. Von Rad, *Studies in Deuteronomy*, p. 37.

47. Moran, *The Amarna Letters* (Baltimore: Johns Hopkins University Press, 1992), p. 328.

48. Cf. W. von Soden, *Akkadisches Handwörterbuch*, vol. 3 (Wiesbaden: Harrassowitz, 1981), pp. 1274–75.

49. The exilic prologue to Deuteronomy (chaps. 1–4) will articulate this abstraction of God's name (cf. Geller, *Sacred Enigmas*, pp. 30–61), but this is a radical hermeneutical innovation. Ironically, the books of Chronicles hypostatized God's name so that eventually we come full circle in Rabbinic literature where "the Name" (השם) is God.

50. This division has been pointed out by a number of scholars. A clear presentation and detailed presentation of it may be found in Brettler, "Interpretation and Prayer: Notes on the Composition of 1 Kings 8.15–53," pp. 18–19.

51. Knoppers has argued for the literary unity of the entire prayer based on his identification of a ring composition in 1 Kings 8; however, he himself admits there is less than perfect symmetry. The first prayer (vv. 12–13), for example, must be placed outside the analysis. At best, Knoppers's analysis shows that the final editor of the text was adept; see Knoppers, "Prayer and Propaganda: Solomon's Dedication of the Temple and the Deuteronomist's Program," *CBQ* 57 (1995), pp. 229–54. In a similar manner, B. Long suggests that an exilic Deuteronomist brought order into a text with a complicated history of redaction; Long, *1 Kings* (Grand Rapids: Eerdmans, 1980), pp. 94–108.

52. Levenson, "From Temple to Synagogue," p. 154.

53. Wijngaards, "הוציא and העלה: A Twofold Approach to the Exodus," *VT* 15 (1965), pp. 91–102.

54. The law of centralization here is revised by a Josianic redactor—our Dtr^1; see Bernard Levinson, *Deuteronomy and the Hermeneutics of Legal Innovation.*

55. See, conveniently, Weinfeld, *Deuteronomy and the Deuteronomic School*, pp. 324–25, 350, 354. It should be noted, however, that Weinfeld overstates the amount of Deuteronomic phraseology and conflates clearly distinguishable layers of deuteronomic language, e.g., Dtr^1 and Dtr^2.

56. J. Trebolle-Barrera, "A Preliminary Edition of 4QKings *(4Q54)*," in *The Madrid Qumran Congress: Proceedings of the International Congress on the Dead Sea Scrolls, Madrid, 18–21 March, 1991*, ed. J. Trebolle-Barrera and L. Vegas Montaner (Leiden: Brill, 1992), pp. 229–46. Also see *DJD* 14, p. 177.

57. On the Lucianic revisions see P. Lippi, "The Use of the Computerized Data Base for the Study of Septuagint Revisions," *BIOSCS* 17 (1987), pp. 48–62; E. Tov, "Lucian and Proto–Lucian," in *Qumran and the History of the Biblical Text*, ed. F. Cross and S. Talmon (Cambridge, Mass.: Harvard University Press, 1975), pp. 293–305.

58. See S. McKenzie, *The Chronicler's Use of the Deuteronomistic History*; A. Auld, *Kings without Privilege.*

59. See Paul Dion, "The Angel with the Drawn Sword (II Chr 21,16) [sic!]: An Exercise in Restoring the Balance of Text Criticism and Attention to Context," *ZAW* 97 (1985), pp. 114–17; and my article "Textual Criticism and Theological Interpretation: The Pro–Temple *Tendenz* in the Greek Text of Samuel-Kings," *HTR* 87 (1994), pp. 107–16.

60. See E. Tov, "The History and Significance of a Standard Text of the Hebrew Bible," in *Hebrew Bible/Old Testament: the History of Its Intepretation.* Vol. 1: *From the Beginnings to the Middle Ages (Until 1300)*, ed. Magne Sæbø (Göttingen: Vandenhoeck & Ruprecht, 1996), pp. 49–66.

61. Knoppers, "Prayer and Propaganda," p. 243.

62. Ibid., p. 243, n. 54.

63. See McKenzie, *The Chronicler's Use of the Deuteronomistic History*, pp. 41–47; Provan, *Hezekiah and the Books of Kings*, p. 113.

64. The anachronism here is undoubtedly a problem resulting from the narrative arrangement. The Babylonian envoy narrative (2 Kgs 20:12–19) which follows likely points to a coordination of the Babylonian and Judean revolts against Sennacherib and thus would have chronologically preceded the invasion.

65. Many commentators have picked up on this relationship; e.g., Veijola, *Die ewige Dynastie*, pp. 74–75; K. McCarter, *I Samuel* (Garden City: Doubleday, 1980), p. 91.

66. Noth, for example, assigns vv. 29aβb–31, 36abα to an early prophetic source about Ahijah the Shilohite, which was taken over by the Deuteronomistist (cf. *The*

Deuteronomistic History, p. 68). A variety of other scholars have found a primitive layer to Ahijah's oracle (e.g., Weippert, Campbell, and O'Brien); however, there is little agreement as to what exactly makes up this primitive layer (a recent summary of these views can be found in Knoppers, *Two Nations Under God*, vol. 1, pp. 191–97).

67. See particularly vv. 37–38 and the Deuteronomic language compiled by Knoppers, *Two Nations Under God*, vol. 1, p. 195.

68. N. Lohfink argues that the division of the kingdom renders the Davidic promises void, yet the fall of Samaria restores hope in the Davidic promise; cf. Lohfink, "Welches Orakel gab den Daviden Dauer? Ein Textproblem in 2 Kön 8, 19 und des Funktionieren der dynasticischen Orakel im deuteronomistischen Geschichtswerk," in *Lingering over Words: Studies in Ancient Near Eastern Literature in Honor of William L. Moran*, ed. T. Abusch, J. Huehnergard, and P. Steinkeller (Atlanta: Scholars Press, 1990), pp. 349–70.

69. Mettinger, *King and Messiah*, p. 95.

70. Veijola, *Die ewige Dynastie*, p. 15, note 73.

71. McCarter, *I Samuel*, pp. 91–93. A more guarded judgment is made by Weinfeld who notes that the phrase "all the days" (כל הימים) "belongs to the rhetorical clichés of Deuteronomy, but is too common to be considered as peculiarly deuteronomic"; Weinfeld, *Deuteronomy and the Deuteronomic School*, p. 358.

72. See Weinfeld, *Deuteronomy and the Deuteronomic School*, p. 336.

73. See ibid., pp. 191–209.

74. See von Rad, *Studies in Deuteronomy*, pp. 38–39.

Chapter 5

1. See Michael Barkun, *Disaster and the Millennium* (New Haven: Yale University Press, 1974).

2. I follow the periodization of Gabriel Barkay, "The Iron Age II-III," in *The Archaeology of Ancient Israel*, ed. A. Ben-Tor (New Haven: Yale University Press, 1992), pp. 372–73. Also see L. Herr's discussion of the problems of periodization, "Iron II: Emerging Nations," pp. 116–18.

3. See K. Hoglund, "The Achaemenid Context," in *Second Temple Studies. 1. Persian Period,* ed. Philip Davies (Sheffield: JSOT, 1991), pp. 54–72.

4. Barstad, *The Myth of the Empty Land: A Study in the History and Archaeology of Judah during the "Exilic" Period* (Oslo: Scandinavian University Press, 1996).

5. Ibid., pp. 18–19.

6. Ibid., p. 43.

7. Mazar, *Archaeology of the Land of the Bible*, pp. 459–60.

8. D. Smith, *The Religion of the Landless: The Social Context of the Babylonian Exile* (Bloomington, Ind.: Meyer-Stone, 1989), p. 10.

9. See Mary Douglas's classic work, *Purity and Danger: An Analysis of the Concepts of Pollution and Taboo* (London: Routledge & Kegan Paul, 1966).

10. Cited from the foreword to Smith, *The Religion of the Landless*, p. xiv.

11. This observations relies on the study by J. Armstrong, "Mobilized and Proletarian Diasporas," *American Political Science Review* 70 (1976), pp. 393–408.

12. Bregstein, "Seal Use in Fifth Century BE. Nippur, Iraq: A study of seal selection and sealing practices in the Murašû Archive" (Ph.D. dissertation, University of Pennsylvania, 1993), p. 227.

13. Daiches, *The Jews in the Time of Ezra and Nehemiah according to Babylonian Inscriptions* (London, 1912), p. 35. M. Coogan cautiously agrees with Daiches; cf. Coogan,

West Semitic Personal Names in the Murashu Documents (Missoula, Mont.: Scholars Press, 1976), pp. 120–24.

14. Coogan, "Life in the Diaspora: Jews at Nippur in the Fifth Century B.C.," *BA* 37 (1974), p. 12; more generally, N. Cohen, "Jewish Names as Cultural Indicators in Antiquity," *JSJ* 7 (1976–77), pp. 97–128.

15. Daiches, *The Jews in the Time of Ezra and Nehemiah according to Babylonian Inscriptions*, p. 35; Coogan, "Life in the Diaspora," pp. 6–12.

16. H. Reviv argues that the elders in the exile continued and strengthened a preexilic institution; Reviv, *Elders in Ancient Israel*, p. 119.

17. The only occurrence in DtrH is Josh 22:14. The term occurs twenty-four times in Ezra-Nehemiah and Chronicles (e.g., Ezr 2:59; 10:16; Neh 7:61; 10:35; 1 Chr 12:30; 23:24; 2 Chr 17:14; 35:4).

18. Smith, *Religion of the Landless*, p. 115; see also J. Weinberg, *The Citizen-Temple Community*, trans. D. Smith-Christopher (Sheffield: JSOT, 1992), pp. 49–62.

19. The books of Chronicles offer one explicit example of the creation of a fictive kin group: "Jahath was the chief, and Zizah the second; but Jeush and Beriah did not have many sons, so they were enrolled as a single family" (1 Chr 23:11).

20. See P. Briant, "Villages et communautés villageoises d'Asie achéménide et hellénistique," *JESHO* 18 (1975), pp. 176–77.

21. Adams, *Heartland of Cities* (Chicago: University of Chicago Press, 1981), p. 177; see also I. Eph'al, "The Western Minorities in Babylonia in the 6th–5th Centuries B.C.: Maintenance and Cohesion," *Orientalia* 47 (1978), pp. 74–90.

22. Some have argued that we know little about the conditions of the exiles and point to a letter of Jeremiah that suggests the exilic conditions were "easy" (Jer 29:5–7); e.g., I. Zeitlin, *Ancient Judaism* (Oxford: Polity Press, 1984), pp. 258–59. This is a questionable reading of the sources; it is strange to think that the life of any community of forced exiles is easy.

23. See Koehler and Baumgartner, *Hebräisches und Aramäisches Lexikon zum Alten Testament*, 3d ed. (Leiden: Brill, 1995), p. 1597; G. Rendsburg and S. Rendsburg, "Physiological and Philological Notes to Psalm 137," *JQR* 83 (1993), pp. 396–99.

24. See, for example, L. Levine, "The Nature and Origin of the Palestinian Synagogue Reconsidered," *JBL* 115 (1996), pp. 425–48; S. Fine, "Did the Synagogue Replace the Temple?," *Bible Review* 12/2 (1996), pp. 18–26, 41; R. Hachlili, "The Origin of the Synagogue: A Re-assessment," *JSJ* 28 (1997), pp. 34–47; Hilewitz, "The Synagogue: Its Origin and Development," *DD* 14 (1985–86), pp. 71–76; P. Flesher, ed., *Ancient Synagogues: Historical Analysis and Archaeological Discovery* (Leiden: Brill, 1995).

25. E.g., J. Hayes, "The Tradition of Zion's Inviolability," *JBL* 82 (1963), pp. 419–26; J. J. M. Roberts, "The Davidic Origin of the Zion Tradition," pp. 329–44; Roberts, "Zion in the Theology of the Davidic–Solomonic Empire," pp. 93–108; Boyo G. Ockinga, "The Inviolability of Zion—A Pre-Israelite Tradition?" *BN* 44 (1988), pp. 54–60.

26. R. Carroll, *When Prophecy Failed* (New York: Seabury, 1979) p. 150.

27. For the most recent treatment with bibliography see B. Sommer, "Did Prophecy Cease? Evaluating a Reevaluation," *JBL* 115 (1996), pp. 31–47.

28. L. Festinger, *A Theory of Cognitive Dissonance* (Evanston: Peterson, 1957); see also Festinger; Henry Riecken; Stanley Schachter, *When Prophecy Fails* (Minneapolis: University of Minnesota Press, 1956).

29. R. Zajonc, "Cognitive Theories in Social Psychology," in *The Handbook of Social Psychology*, ed. G. Lindzey and E. Aronson, 2d ed. (Reading, Mass.: Addison-Wesley, 1968), p. 359 (quoted by Carroll, *When Prophecy Failed*, p. 86). See also E. McDonagh,

"Attitude Changes and Paradigm Shifts: Social Psychological Foundations of the Kuhnian Thesis," *Social Studies of Science* 6 (1976), pp. 51–76.

30. Aronson, "Back to the Future: Retrospective Review of Leon Festinger's *A Theory of Cognitive Dissonance*," *American Journal of Psychology* 110 (1997), pp. 127–37.

31. Carroll, *When Prophecy Failed*, pp. 87–88.

32. Ibid., p. 151.

33. Ibid., p. 151.

34. Ibid., p. 152.

35. See B. Sommer, *A Prophet Reads Scripture*, chapter 3.

36. My analysis of this third speech follows along similar lines as J. Levenson, "From Temple to Synagogue," pp. 154–57.

37. Levenson, "From Temple to Synagogue," p. 156. The books of Chronicles actually recognize this incongruity and alleviate the problem by making Solomon bow down before he begins to pray; however, the secondary nature of the Chronicler's version is indicated by a *Weideraufnahme*, which marks the insertion (note the repeated phrase "and he spread out his hands (ויפרשכפיו)" in 2 Chr 6:13–14).

38. See the detailed comparison by C. F. Keil, *The Book of Kings* (Grand Rapids, Mich.: Eerdmans, 1950), pp. 128–32, which is cited by Levenson.

39. Levenson, "From Temple to Synagogue," pp. 157–58.

40. Also note that the last chapters of the books of Kings, which depend on Jer 39, are not in the shorter LXX; cf. C. R. Seitz, "The Crisis of Intepretation over the Meaning and Purpose of the Exile. A Redactional Study of Jeremiah XXI–XLII," *VT* (1985), pp. 78–97; H. F. Pohlmann, "Erwägungen zum Schlusskapitel des deuteronomistischen Geschichtswerkes Oder: warum wird der Prophet Jeremia in 2 Kön 22–25 nicht erwähnt?" in *Textgemäss: Aufsätze und Beitrage zur Hermeneutik des Alten Testaments. Festschrift für Ernst Wurthwein zum 70. Geburtstag*, ed. A. H. J. von Gunneweg and O. Kaiser (Göttingen: Vanderhöeck & Ruprecht, 1979), pp. 94–109.

41. See specifically Johan Lust, "The Diverse Text Forms of Jeremiah and History Writing with Jer 33 as a Test Case," *JNWSL* 20 (1994), pp. 31–48.

42. For this classification see already Gunkel, *The Psalms: A Form-Critical Introduction* Philadephia: Fortress, 1967), p. 32, translation from *Die Religion in Geschichte und Gegenwart*, volume 1, 2d ed. (Tübingen, 1930).

43. See S. Mowinkel, *The Psalms in Israel's Worship* (Oxford: Blackwell, 1962), p. 194–95.

44. Sarna, "Psalm 89: A Study in Inner Biblical Exegesis," p. 45.

45. Weiser, *The Psalms*, Old Testament Library, translated from 5th German ed. (1959) (Philadephia: Westminister, 1962), p. 591.

46. Johnson, *Sacral Kingship in Ancient Israel*, pp. 103–4. For a convenient summary and bibliography of the *akitu* festival, see Jacob Klein, "Akitu," *ABD* 1:138–40.

47. See, for example, Schniedewind, "Are We His People or Not? Biblical Interpretation during Crisis," *Bib* 76 (1995), pp. 540–550.

48. Most recently, Sommer, *A Prophet Reads Scripture*.

49. See, for example, H. G. M. Williamson, *The Book Called Isaiah: Deutero-Isaiah's Role in Composition and Redaction*; R. Rendtorff, "The Book of Isaiah: A Complex Unity. Synchronic and Diachronic Reading," in *SBL Seminar Papers, 1991*, ed. Eugene Lovering, Jr. (Atlanta: Scholars Press, 1991), pp. 8–20; Odil Steck, *Bereitete Heimkehr: Jesaja 35 als redaktionelle Brücke zwischen dem Ersten und Zeiten Jesaja* (Stuttgart: Katholisches Bibelwerk, 1985); David Carr, "Reaching for Unity in Isaiah," *JSOT* 57 (1993), pp. 61–81.

50. Sweeney, *Isaiah 1–39*, p. 41.

51. Seitz, *Zion's Final Destiny: The Development of the Book of Isaiah: A Reassessment of Isaiah 36–39* (Minneapolis: Fortress, 1992), p. 206.

52. E.g., O. Eissfeldt, "The Promise of Grace to David in Isaiah 55:1–5," in *Israel's Prophetic Heritage. Essays in Honor of J. Muilenburg*, ed. B. W. Anderson and W. Harrelson (New York: Harper, 1962), pp. 196–207; M. Weinfeld, "Bond [הברית] and Grace [החסד]—Covenantal Expressions in the Bible and in the Ancient World: A Common Heritage," *Leshonenu* 36 (1971-72), pp. 86–105 [Hebrew]; A. Coquot, "Les grâces de David," *Semitica* 15 (1965), pp. 45–59; W. Brueggemann, "Isaiah 55 and Deuteronomic Theology," *ZAW* 80 (1968), pp. 191–203.

53. See most recently Gordon Clark, *The Word Hesed in the Hebrew Bible* (Sheffield: JSOT, 1993), and the literature cited there.

54. A quite different type of democratization may be envisioned by Ezekiel. This exilic prophet sees a vision of the ideal temple, which is described in detail in chapters 40-48. This ideal temple is also closely associated with the Davidic Promise in Ezek 37:24-28 . Alluding to the Promise in a prophetic vision, we read that "my servant David will be their prince forever . . . and I will set my sanctuary among them forever" (ונתתי את־מקדשי בתוכם לעולם, vv. 25-26). The latter phrase could be an allusion to 2 Sam 7:10 "I shall set a place (מקום ושׂמתי) for my people." In any event, it is clear that David is the vehicle through which God establishes his eternal presence in the sanctuary with his people Israel.

Chapter 6

1. This represents a broad consensus and is forcefully argued by K. Hoglund, *Achaemenid Imperial Administration in Syria-Palestine and the Missions of Ezra and Nehemiah* (Atlanta: Scholars Press, 1992), pp. 51–96.

2. See ibid., pp. 86–96, and literature cited there. See also A. F. Rainey, "The Satrapy 'Beyond the River,' " *Austrialian Journal of Biblical Archaeology* 1 (1969), pp. 51–78.

3. E. Meyers, "The Shelomith Seal and the Judean Restoration: Some Additional Considerations," *EI* 18 (1985), pp. 33*–38*.

4. C. Carter, "The Province of Yehud in the Post-Exilic Period: Soundings in Site Distribution and Demography," in *Second Temple Studies. 2. Temple Community in the Persian Period*, ed. T. Eskenazi and K. Richards (Sheffield: JSOT, 1994), pp. 121–22.

5. Kochavi, *Judaea, Samaria, and the Golan: Archaeological Survey 1967–1968*, p. 23. A revision of the data for Judaea is currently being undertaken by Avi Ofer in a Ph.D. dissertation at Tel Aviv University, and some of the results for the earlier period are summarized in Ofer's article, " 'All the Hill Country of Judah': From a Settlement Fringe to a Prosperous Monarchy," in *From Nomadism to Monarchy*, pp. 92–121.

6. Those who emphasize continuity, for example, in the ceramic repertoire, tend to construct the argument from sites that had continuous settlement from the Iron II through Persian period—i.e., at sites whose settlement history lends itself toward continuity (e.g., Lachish).

7. Hoglund, "The Achaemenid Context," p. 58.

8. Ibid., p. 59.

9. As, for example, by Morton Smith, *Palestinian Parties and Politics* (New York: Columbia University Press, 1971), pp. 99–125.

10. See Carter, "The Province of Yehud in the Post–Exilic Period," pp. 106–45.

11. Although A. Alt and K. Galling had argued that Yehud was under the administration of Samaria, Kenneth Hoglund points out that, as a policy, the Assyrians and Babylonians kept conquered geopolitical entities intact as administrative subunits; cf. Hoglund, *Achaemenid Imperial Administration*, pp. 21–23; Alt, "Die Rolle Samarias bei der

Entstehung des Judentums," in *Kleine Schriften zur Geschichte des Volkes Israel, II*, 2d ed. (Munich: Beck, 1959), pp. 316–37; Galling, *Studien zur Geschichte Israels im persischen Zeitalter* (Tübingen: Mohr, 1964).

12. There is much debate concerning the dating of Ezra and Nehemiah primarily because there are three Artaxerxes with whom their missions can be associated. I follow the general consensus, which would place Ezra and Nehemiah within the reign of Artaxerxes I (465–423 BCE). For a survey of the literature, see H. G. M. Williamson, *Ezra and Nehemiah* (Sheffield, JSOT, 1987), pp. 55–69.

13. Hoglund, "The Achaemenid Context," p. 60.

14. E. Stern, *The Material Culture of the Land of the Bible in the Persian Period 538–332 BC* (Warminster: Aris & Phillips, 1982), pp. 109–110.

15. Summaries for all these sites can be found in *The New Encyclopedia of Archaeological Excavations in the Holy Land.*

16. The fortresses are usually square, measuring about 30 x 30 meters; cf. Hoglund, "The Achaemenid Context," p. 63. Hoglund rightly criticizes Stern's interpretation of the fortresses as constituting "a clear line of border fortresses"; cf. Stern, *Material Culture*, p. 250.

17. Stern, "Between Persia and Greece: Trade, Administration and Warfare in the Persian and Hellenistic Periods (539-63 BCE)," in *The Archaeology of Society*, ed. T. Levy, pp. 435-437.

18. Ibid., p. 66.

19. See Williamson, "The Concept of Israel in Transition," in *The World of Ancient Israel: Sociological, Anthropological and Political Perspectives: Essays by Members of the Society for Old Testament Study*, ed. R. E. Clements (Cambridge: Cambridge University Press, 1989), pp. 141–61; P. Davies, "Sociology and the Second Temple," in *Second Temple Studies. 1. Persian Period*, p. 16.

20. Barkay, "The Iron II–III," p. 373. Hoglund cites Barkay approvingly here but contends further that there is no significant break even in the late sixth century; Hoglund, "The Archaeology of Silence: Recent Treatments of the Persian Period," *Archaeology in the Biblical World* 3 (1995), pp. 37–38. Helga Weippert's treatment see also the major cultural break in the Hellenistic period; Weippert, *Palästina in vorhellenistischer Zeit* (Munich: Beck, 1988).

21. This is argued persuasively by Berquist, *Judaism in Persia's Shadow.*

22. Recent surveys of this question can be found in Japhet, *I & II Chronicles* (Philadelphia: Westminister, 1993), pp. 23–28.

23. Pomykala, *The Davidic Dynasty Tradition in Early Judaism*, p. 102. Pomykala sweeps Davidic references under the proverbial carpet as possible textual problems or unimportant to the Chronicler's perspective. Once, however, one realizes that the Chronicler's work was intended primarily to speak to his postexilic community and not merely as an antiquarian exercise, the import of the references to the Davidic covenant looms much larger. See my essay, "History or Homily: Toward Understanding the Chronicler's Purpose," in *Proceedings of the Eleventh World Congress of Jewish Studies: Division A: The Bible and Its World* (Jerusalem: Magnes Press, 1994), pp. 91–97.

24. Japhet, *Ideology*, p. 459.

25. Williamson, "Eschatology in Chronicles," *TynBul* 28 (1977), pp. 115–54; "The Dynastic Oracle in the Books of Chronicles," in *Leo Isaac Seeligman Anniversary Volume*, vol. 3 (Jerusalem, 1983), pp. 305–18. A strong argument for the importance of the Davidic dynasty tradition to Chronicles is made by D. N. Freedman, "The Chronicler's Purpose," *CBQ* 23 (1961), pp. 436–42.

26. Japhet, *Chronicles*, p. 25. Williamson also argues Persian loanwords point to a later dating of Chronicles to provide time to allow for the anachronism, but this assumes modern conventions about what would be anachronistic; see Williamson's review (*VT* 37 [1987], pp. 107–14) of McKenzie, who argued for an early date in *The Chronicler's Use of the Deuteronomistic History.*

27. For an introduction to the dating of Ezra-Nehemiah and bibliography see H. G. M. Williamson, *Ezra and Nehemiah*, pp. 37–47. Williamson places the final redaction around 300 BCE. I concur with his arguments rejecting the late date for the mission of Ezra.

28. Cf. Kutscher, *A History of the Hebrew Language* (Jerusalem: Magnes Press, 1982), p. 137.

29. See, for example, W. Ruldoph, *Chronikbücher* (Tübingen: Mohr, 1955), pp. 26–29.

30. See Japhet's detailed comments (though she regards the entire geneaology as original), *Chronicles*, pp. 93–94, 99–102.

31. Ibid., p. 102.

32. Cross, "A Reconstruction of the Judean Restoration," *JBL* 94 (1975), pp. 11–14.

33. Williamson is undoubtedly correct in seeing editorial hands at work in 1 Chronicles 22–27; see his studies "The Origins of the Twenty-Four Priestly Courses," *VTSup* 30 (1979), pp. 251–68, "Sources and Redaction in the Chronicler's Genealogy of Judah," *JBL* 98 (1979), pp. 351–59, and "The Composition of Ezra i–vi," *JTS* ns 34 (1983), pp. 1–30.

34. It should now be clear that by "the Chronicler" I refer only to the early Persian stage of the work before it was joined to Ezra-Nehemiah.

35. Freedman, "The Chronicler's Purpose," pp. 440–41. See also J. Newsome, "Toward a New Understanding of the Chronicler and his Purposes," *JBL* 94 (1975), pp. 201–17; this article summarizes some of the conclusions of his doctoral thesis, "The Chronicler's View of Prophecy" (Ph.D. dissertation, Vanderbilt University, 1973).

36. S. de Vries, "Moses and David as Cult Founders in Chronicles," *JBL* 107 (1988), pp. 631–32. R. Braun argues that the Chronicler's central concern is the legitimacy of Solomon and the first temple, "The Message of Chronicles: Rally 'Round the Temple," *CTM* 42 (1971), pp. 508–9.

37. Other studies on the Promise to David in Chronicles have focused on the Chronicler's supposed messianic tendencies (e.g., R. Mosis, *Untersuchungen zur Theologie des chronistischen Geschichtswerkes* [Freiburg: Herder, 1973], pp. 89–94; T. S. Im, *Das Davidbild in den Chronikbuchern. David als Idealbild des theokratischen Messianismus* [Frankfurt, 1985], pp. 145–63). However, Williamson rightly argues that Chronicles' perspective is more royalist than messianic, "The Promise to David in the Books of Chronicles," pp. 305–18.

38. Steven McKenzie, for example, argued, "The notion that [the] Chr[onicler] has tendentiously and extensively rewritten his S[amuel] source must be abandoned. The available textual evidence points in the opposite direction, that Chr has generally followed his S[amuel] *Vorlage* quite closely in the synoptic passages." McKenzie, *The Chronicler's Use of the Deuteronomistic History*, p. 72.

39. See, for example, P. Dion, "The Angel with the Drawn Sword (II [*sic*] Chr. 21,16), pp. 114–17; Schniedewind, "Textual Criticism and Theological Interpretation," pp. 107–116.

40. Williamson, *Chronicles*, p. 134. R. Mosis thinks that Solomon's temple is a "typisierte Darstellung" of the post-exilic temple and he writes, "so ist auch der Erwarb der Tenne Ornans nicht nur eine technisch-materielle Bereitstellung des Bauplatzes für den Tempel, sondern als Konstitutierung eines kultores für Israel . . . " (*Untersuchungen zur Theologie des chronistischen Geschichtswerkes*, p. 124); see also S. Japhet, " 'History' and 'Literature' in the Persian Period," pp. 174–88.

41. See von Rad, "There Remain Still a Rest for the People of God," pp. 94–102.

42. The close association of rest with YHWH and the ark's rest in the temple is indicated in the exegesis in 1 Chr 23:24–27 (cp. 2 Chr 35:3). Psalm 132 emphasizes that YHWH himself was present in the temple and not just his name (contra the Deuteronomist). The emphasis on the real presence of YHWH in the temple highlights the importance of the temple, whereas the Deuteronomic emphasis on the name of YHWH residing in the temple undermines the importance of the temple. This hints at a fundamental difference between the concept of rest in Chronicles and DtrH. From the Deuteronomic perspective, Israel finds rest *in the land* from their enemies, e.g., 2 Sam 7:1, 11. However, the Chronicler emphasizes that YHWH finds rest *in the temple* from his wanderings (1 Chr 23:24–27; 28:2; 2 Chr 6:41–42).

43. In contrast to Isa 66:1, "What house could serve as my resting place?" Beuken notes the "remarkable" similarity between 1 Chr 28:2–3 and Isa 66:1, "Does Trito-Isaiah Reject the Temple? An Intertextual Inquiry into Isa. 66:1–6," in *Intertextuality in Biblical Writings: Essays in Honor of Bas van Iersel*, ed. S. Draisma (Kampen: Uitgeversmaat-schappij J. K. Kok, 1989), pp. 56–57.

44. Eslinger, *House of God or House of David*, p. 33. At this juncture, Eslinger's study would have profited from the observations in the seminal study by Gerhard von Rad on the concept of rest in biblical literature, which both presage Eslinger and place his comments in a broader context; cf. "There Remain Still a Rest for the People of God," pp. 79–93. It is difficult to say whether Eslinger was unaware of von Rad's study or just dismissed it because of its traditional approach, which according to him does not read the text "closely."

45. Braun develops this in a series of articles, "The Message of Chronicles: Rally 'Round the Temple," "Solomonic Apologetic in Chronicles," *JBL* 92 (1973), pp. 503–16, and "Solomon, The Chosen Temple Builder: The Significance of 1 Chronicles 22, 28, and 29 for the Theology of Chronicles," *JBL* 95 (1976), pp. 581–90. Also see R. Dillard, "The Chronicler's Solomon," *WTJ* 43 (1980), pp. 289–300, and H. G. M. Williamson, "The Accession of Solomon in the Books of Chronicles," *VT* 26 (1976), pp. 351–61.

46. Williamson, *Chronicles*, 134.

47. See R. Braun, *1 Chronicles* (Waco, Tex.: Word, 1986), pp. 195–99. Braun emphasizes the difference by translating הבית as "this house." However, we must be careful not to overinterpret the verse.

48. The MT, לפניך, makes no sense must be emended to לפני. It resulted from dittography and was influenced by the other pronominal suffixes in v. 16, ביתך, ממלכך, and כסאך.

49. See most recently Williamson, *Chronicles*, p. 136; Braun, *1 Chronicles*, pp. 199–200.

50. Curtis and Madsen, *A Critical and Exegetical Commentary on the Books of Chronicles* (Edinburgh: T & T Clark, 1910), p. 228.

51. R. Braun in particular has emphasized the ideology of the chosen temple builder in his article, "Solomon, The Chosen Temple Builder." Braun, Williamson, and Dillard have also pointed out that the Chronicler uses types or models after which he patterns the role of Solomon; see Williamson, "The Accession of Solomon in the Books of Chronicles," pp. 351–61; Dillard, "The Chronicler's Solomon," pp. 289–300.

52. ברוח cannot be understood as "the plan David had in mind." One cannot be unduly influenced by the tabernacle narrative as Braun contends (against Rothstein, Rudolph), (*1 Chronicles*, 266). The Chronicler was clearly influenced by these traditions at many junctures in his narratives. See S. de Vries, "Moses and David as Cult Founders," pp. 619–39; Dillard, "The Chronicler's Solomon," pp. 296–99.

53. S. de Vries, "Moses and David as Cult Founders," pp. 619–39.

54. David's temple supersedes Moses' tabernacle because it is founded on a site that dates back to Abraham (2 Chr 3:1; note also 2 Chr 8:12–15, where Mosaic legislation is placed side by side with David's commands).

55. The dual commissioning of Zerubbabel and Joshua, the priest, finds a parallel with the dual anointing of Solomon and Zadok in 1 Chr 29:22. Also see Zech 4:6–10; 6:9–13. See further my article "King and Priest in the Book of Chronicles and the Duality of Qumran Messianism," *JJS* 94 (1994), pp. 71–78.

56. See A. Brunet, "Le Chroniste et ses Sources," *RB* 61 (1954), pp. 349–86.

57. Williamson, "Eschatology," p. 149.

58. Williamson argues that the reference to חסדי דוד alludes to Isa 55:3. He believes that the Chronicler's use of this phrase emphasizes a royalist interpretation of the phrase, as opposed to Isaiah, which applies the Davidic covenant to Israel as a whole; O. Eissfeldt, "The Promises of Grace to David in Isaiah 55:1–5," pp. 196–207.

59. Williamson, *Chronicles*, p. 10.

60. B. Kelly, *Retribution and Eschatology in Chronicles* (Sheffield: JSOT, 1996), p. 23.

61. See E. Tov, *Textual Criticism of the Hebrew Bible* (Minneapolis: Fortress, 1992), pp. 319–27.

62. See the argument of Fishbane, *Biblical Interpretation in Ancient Israel*, pp. 471–74.

63. Duhm had suggested that the Hasmoneans saw themselves as Davidides, but this is unlikely, as William McKane has pointed out. McKane sees the insertion of the Levitical priesthood into an oracle whose original subject was the Davidic king as pointing to the early postexilic age; McKane, *A Critical and Exegetical Commentary on Jeremiah*, vol. 2 (Edinburgh: T & T Clark, 1996), p. clxiii.

64. Most recently, Y. Goldman has argued that this addition must be associated with the early returnees and Zerubabbel; cf. *Prophétie et royauté au retour de l'exil. Les origines littéraires de la forme massorétique du livre de Jéremie* (Freiburg: Universitätsverlag; Göttingen: Vandenhoeck & Ruprecht, 1992), p. 226.

65. McKane points out that early translators (i.e., *Vulgate* and *Peshitta*) were perplexed by the change and attempt to revise back to a Davidic emphasis; McKane, *Jeremiah*, vol. 2, pp. 861–62. These attempts should undoubtedly be understood within the context of early Christianity with its emphasis on messianic prooftexts and marginalization of Jerusalem's importance.

66. Weinfeld, "Zion and Jerusalem as Religious and Political Capital," p. 90. Ezekiel 37:24-28 also suggests that YHWH's presence will dwell "in his sanctuary." Most significant is the juxtaposition of this idea with the Promise that David's sons will shepherd Israel as "their prince forever." While the text at best alludes to 2 Sam 7, the juxtaposition on the Davidic kingship with the temple clearly draws upon the developing discourse about the Promise to David.

67. See my book, *The Word of God in Transition*, pp. 153–60.

68. David Flusser has emphasized that the critique and even opposition to the temple was not only a development of early Christianity but also one tendency of Jewish thought in the Second Temple period, which was already present in the Old Testament; see Flusser, "Two Notes on the Midrash on 2 Sam. VII" and "No Temple in the City," both republished in the collection *Judaism and the Origins of Christianity* (Jerusalem: Magnes Press, 1988), pp. 88–98, 454–65. Flusser even argues that "the lack of consensus about the value of the Jerusalem Temple made it easier for the Jew to overcome the terrible crisis caused by its destruction and contributed to the survival of Judaism after this catastrophe" ("No Temple," p. 456).

69. See C. Newsom, *Songs of the Sabbath Sacrifice* (Atlanta: Scholars Press, 1985), pp. 55–58. 5Q15, "The New Jerusalem," also models itself after Ezekiel 40–48 in its description of the eschatological temple in the New Jerusalem (*DJD*, 3, pp. 184–93); also J. Licht, "An Ideal Town Plan from Qumran—The Description of the New Jerusalem," *IEJ* 29 (1979), pp. 45–59.

70. See Tob 14:5; Enoch 90:28–29; 4QFlor 1, 3.

71. The image of the sacrifice being consumed by fire in 2 Macc 1:23 was undoubtedly meant to recall the dedication of Moses' tabernacle (Lev 9:24) and Solomon's temple (2 Chr 7:1–3). Jonathan Goldstein emphasizes, "Many other Jews—indeed, entire sects—held the Second Temple to be incompletely holy or even completely unfit for the offering of sacrifices" ("How the Authors of 1 and 2 Maccabees Treated the 'Messianic' Promises," in *Judaisms and Their Messiahs at the Turn of the Christian Era*, ed. J. Neusner, et al. [Cambridge: Cambridge University Press, 1987], p. 70).

72. This purpose does not necessarily support either an early (ca. 515 BCE) or later (ca. 400 BCE) date for the authorship of Chronicles because the debate over the role and authority of the Jerusalem temple began long before the writing of Chronicles, already in 2 Samuel 7, and continued long after the writing of the book of Chronicles.

Chapter 7

1. The paradigm shift that now obligates us to speak of Judaism*s* also suggests that we need to speak of the diaspora*s*. For the present work, this is particularly important because the literature I speak of was produced in a specific diaspora; see S. Cohen and E. Frerichs, eds., *Diasporas in Antiquity* (Atlanta: Scholars Press, 1993).

2. See D. Goodblatt, *The Monarchic Principle: Studies in Jewish Self-Government in Antiquity* (Tübingen: Mohr, 1994), pp. 6–56.

3. J. Goldstein, "How the Authors of 1 and 2 Maccabees Treated the 'Messianic' Promises," p. 73.

4. J. Barclay, *Jews in the Mediterranean Diaspora: From Alexander to Trajan (323 BCE – 117 CE)* (Edinburgh: T & T Clark, 1996), p. 22.

5. J. Collins, "Messianism in the Maccabean Period," in *Judaisms and Their Messiahs*, pp. 98–101.

6. See G. Sterling, " 'Thus Are Israel': Jewish Self-Definition in Alexandria," in *The Studia Philonica Annual: Studies in Hellenistic Judaism*, vol. 7, ed. D. Runia (Atlanta: Scholars Press, 1995), pp. 1–18.

7. Ibid., p. 18.

8. Barclay, *Jews in the Mediterranean Diaspora*, pp. 1–4. Even Flavius Josephus acknowledges that ancestral customs were crucial to maintaining social distinction (cf. *Ant.* 1.192; 4.114).

9. Ibid., pp. 29–30.

10. Ibid., pp. 93, 95.

11. Ibid., pp. 96–98.

12. Although it is difficult to define "Hellenism," we may begin with the term ἑλληνιζειν itself, which originally meant "to speak Greek." I follow the definition of Barclay, which views Hellenism as a common urban culture founded on the Greek language and reflected in political and educational institutions; see Barclay, *Jews in the Mediterranean Diaspora*, pp. 88–102.

13. Ibid., p. 31.

14. Lust, "Messianism and Septuagint," p. 190.

15. Ibid., p. 190, n. 58.

16. The colophon to Greek translation of the book of Esther states that the book was translated in Jerusalem and brought to Egypt. Although some books such as Esther may have been translated in Jerusalem, they clearly circulated in Alexandria. On the problem of the term "Septuagint" see E. Tov, "The Septuagint," in *Mikra: Text, Translation, Reading and Interpretation of the Hebrew Bible in Ancient Judaism and Early Christianity*, ed. M. Mulder

(Assen: van Gorcum; Philadephia: Fortress, 1988), pp. 161–88; M. K. H. Peters, "Septuagint," *ABD*, vol. 5, pp. 1093–1104.

17. In his "Explanation of Holy Writ." See E. Schürer, *The History of the Jewish People in the Age of Jesus Christ*, rev. and ed. G. Vermes, F. Millar, and M. Goodman (Edinburgh: T & T Clark, 1987), pp. 474–93.

18. See E. Bickerman, "The Septuagint as a Translation," in *Studies in Jewish and Christian History, Part 1* (Leiden: Brill, 1976), pp. 167–71.

19. I will use the generic term LXX rather than the OG (Old Greek) because in one case I cite from what has come to be termed "the kaige recension." Cross argues that the kaige recension is "an early Jewish attempt to revise the standard Septuagint into conformity with a Proto–Massoretic Hebrew text" ("The History of the Biblical Text in Light of the Discoveries in the Judaean Desert," *HTR* 57 [1964], p. 283).

20. Seeligman, "Problems and Perspectives in Modern Septuagint Research," *Textus* 15 (1990), p. 226. Seeligmann further observes that "the origin of the LXX was in the synagogue, and its use in synagogal homilies and sermons allows us to qualify it as a Targum; its exegesis is that of the midrash and the very essence of true midrash is actualization" (p. 232).

21. Bickerman, "The Septuagint as a Translation," p. 197. Elsewhere Bickerman notes that "the paradox remains that the Septuagint version is literal and free at the same time. It often follows the original slavishly as to wording, syntax and style, but changes the meaning of the original" (p. 198).

22. Jellicoe, *The Septuagint and Modern Study* (Oxford: Clarendon, 1969), p. 283. The books of Samuel have received particularly close attention as a result of the finds in the Qumran Cave 4. Note especially the work of F. M. Cross' students; see J. Shenkel, *Chronology and Recensional Development in the Greek Text of Kings* (Cambridge, Mass.: Harvard University Press, 1968); E. Ulrich, *The Qumran Text of Samuel and Josephus* (Atlanta: Scholars Press, 1979); K. McCarter, *I Samuel* (Garden City, N.Y.: Doubleday, 1980), and S. McKenzie, *The Chronicler's Use of the Deuteronomistic History*. M. Goshen-Gottstein provides an analysis of the history of research, "The Book of Samuel—Hebrew and Greek—Hindsight of a Century," *Textus* 14 (1988), pp. 147–62; also McCarter, *I Samuel*, pp. 5–11.

23. D. Gooding, *Relics of Ancient Exegesis: A Study of the Miscellanies in 3 Reigns 2* (Cambridge: Cambridge University Press, 1976), p. 111.

24. See Schniedewind, "Textual Criticism and Theological Interpretation," pp. 107–116. The LXX's "omission" of MT Jer 33:15–18 (see chapter 6) would be significant if it were a conscious decision by the Alexandrian translators; however, it seems to reflect their *Vorlage*; cf. J. Lust, "The diverse text forms of Jeremiah and history writing with Jer 33 as a test case," pp. 31–48.

25. J. Coppens, *Le messianisme royal* (Paris: Editions du Cerf, 1968), p. 119; see also Coppens, *Le messianisme et sa relève prophétique* (Gembloux: Duculot, 1974).

26. Lust gives a list of the important references and bibliography, "Messianism and Septuagint," *SVT* 36 [*Congress Volume, Salamanca, 1983*, ed. John Emerton] (Leiden: Brill, 1985), p. 174, n. 2.

27. Note, for example, that παρθένος is also used as a translation of עלמה in Gen 24:43.

28. Lust, "Messianism and Septuagint," p. 175.

29. Ibid., p. 176.

30. Chronicles shows some variation, but the meaning is essentially the same as the MT of 2 Sam 7:11: ואגד לך ובית יבנה־לך יהוה, "And I [Yahweh] promise you [David] and Yahweh shall build a house for you" (1 Chr 17:10).

31. In Samuel, יעשה has sometimes been emended on the basis of the LXX to either «תבנה» or «יבנה», because the Greek verb οικοδομειν usually translates the Hebrew verb בנה (cf. McCarter, *II Samuel*, pp. 193–94). McCarter's reconstruction relies upon the LXX^{L}, where manuscripts read οἰκοδομήσει (= יבנה). However, the Hebrew phrase לעשות בית occurs elsewhere in the Hebrew Bible; for instance, in Abigail's blessing of David, she says that God will "build" (יעשה) David's house (1 Sam 25:28; also note 1 Kgs 7:8; 2 Kgs 2:24; 12:14). It is noteworthy that at least one other time οικοδομειν translates the Hebrew verb עשה, cf. 2 Chr 32:29.

32. McCarter suggests that יהוה in the MT of Samuel is a corruption ofוהיה (*II Samuel*, pp. 193–94). However, this emendation is based on the LXX, which is itself tendentious.

33. The problem of naming David instead of Solomon as temple builder in 2 Kgdms 7:11 is more apparent than real. In the books of Chronicles, David and Solomon are thought of as co-temple builders (cf. Braun, "Solomonic Apologetic in Chronicles," pp. 503–16), and a similar notion may underlie the LXX's translation of 2 Sam 7:11.

34. McCarter, *II Samuel*, p. 194.

35. It is clear that v. 13 is secondary to the original oracle (see chapter 2).

36. Chronicles presents a radically altered version in which God promises David that he will establish Solomon in "my house and my kingdom." In this reference to "my house and my kingdom," Chronicles reflects a tendentious theological change (cp. 2 Chr 1:18 and 2:11; contra McKenzie, *The Chronicler's Use of the Deuteronomistic History*, p. 65). Cf. Rudolph, *Chronikbücher*, p. 135; Brunet, "Le Chroniste et ses sources," p. 505.

37. See discussion in chapter 2; already A. B. Ehrlich, *Randglossen zur Hebräischen Bibel*, vol. 3 (Leipzig: Hinrichs, 1910), p. 289.

38. E.g., m. Aboth 3:4 (citing Isa 28:8); cf. A. Cowley, "The Meaning of מקום in Hebrew," *JTS* 17 (1916), pp. 174–76. Already we find the use of מקום for temple in the books of Chronicles (see 1 Chr 21:22, 25 and discussion in chapter 6).

29. Cf. McCarter, *I Samuel*, p. 155. McCarter makes no text-critical judgment.

30. D. Mendels, *The Rise and Fall of Jewish Nationalism*, 2d ed. (Grand Rapids, Mich.: Eerdmans, 1992).

31. Cf. Thackeray, *Some Aspects of the Greek Old Testament* (London: George Allen & Unwin, 1927), pp. 46–51.

32. See B. Childs, *Exodus, A Commentary* (Philadephia: Westminister, 1974), pp. 243–52.

33. J. Blenkinsopp, "Interpretation and the Tendency to Sectarianism," pp. 3–4.

34. Ironically, the expression "eternal covenant" occurs only once in the Hebrew Bible in 2 Sam 23:5, referring to David.

35. See Pomykala, *Davidic Dynasty Tradition in Early Judaism*, pp. 159–60; J. Schüpphaus, *Die Psalmen Salomos: Ein Zeugnis Jerusalemer Theologie und Frömmigkeit in der Mitte des vorchristlichen Jahrhunderts* (Leiden: Brill, 1977). R. B. Wright argues for an Essene origin, "The Psalms, the Pharisees, and the Essenes," in *1972 Proceedings for the International Organization for Septuagint and Cognate Studies and the Society of Biblical Literature Pseudepigrapha Seminar*, ed. R. Kraft (Missoula, Mont.: Scholars Press, 1972). M. de Jonge points out that sectarian tendencies of Qumran are not present in Psalms of Solomon in "Psalms of Solomon," in *Outside the Old Testament*, ed. M. de Jonge (Cambridge: Cambridge University Press, 1985), p. 160.

36. See R. Wright, "Psalms of Solomon," in *The Old Testament Pseudepigrapha*, vol. 2, ed. J. Charlesworth (Garden City, N.Y.: Doubleday, 1985), p. 641.

37. The Psalms of Solomon were probably originally written in Hebrew and then translated into Greek, which becomes their main textual witness; cf. Wright, "Psalms of Solomon," p. 640.

38. A. Baumgarten tries to apply sociological studies of rapid urbanization to the Hasmonean period (cf. "City Lights: Urbanization and Sectarianism in Hasmonean Jerusalem," in *The Centrality of Jerusalem: Historical Perspectives*, ed. M. Poorthuis and Ch. Safrai [Kampen: Kok Pharos, 1996], pp. 50–64]; however, the archaeological evidence does not support a thesis of rapid urbanization in the second century BCE. Better cases can be made for the late eighth through early seventh centuries BCE, although certainly a remarkable social change also accompanied the waves of returning Judaean exiles in the late sixth through fifh centuries BCE.

39. A concise argument for this hypothesis may be found in Vermes, *The Dead Sea Scrolls in English*, 4th ed. (New York: Penguin, 1995), pp. 20–22; see also Vermes and Goodman, eds., *The Essenes according to the Classical Sources* (Sheffield: JSOT, 1989).

40. D. Dimant, "The Qumran Manuscripts: Contents and Significance," in *"Time to Prepare the Way in the Wilderness": Papers on the Qumran Scrolls by Fellows of the Institute for Advanced Studies of the Hebrew University, Jerusalem, 1989–90*, ed. D. Dimant and L. Schiffman (Leiden: Brill, 1994), p. 32. H. Stegemann even more narrowly defines the community's literary corpus by requiring connection with the Teacher of Righteousness; cf. Stegemann, "Die Bedeutung der Qumranfund für die Erforschung der Apokalyptik," in *Apocalypticism in the Mediterranean World and the Near East*, 2d ed., ed. D. Hellholm (Tübingen: Mohr, 1989), p. 511.

41. E. Tov, "The Orthography and Language of the Hebrew Scrolls Found at Qumran and the Origin of These Scrolls," *Textus* 13 (1986), pp. 31–57; Tov, "Hebrew Biblical Manuscripts from the Judaean Desert: Their Contribution to Textual Criticism," *JJS* 39 (1988), pp. 5–37. Tov's observations effectively demolish Norman Golb's objections to the scrolls' association with the site of Khirbet Qumran.

42. Murtonen, "A Historico-Philological Survey of the Main Dead Sea Scrolls and Related Documents," pp. 56–95.

43. For the *edito precepts*, see Qimron, Strugnell, and Sussmann, *Qumran Cave 4. V. MIQṢAT MAʾASE HA-TORAH*, DJD, 10 (Oxford: Clarendon, 1994).

44. Dimant, "Qumran Sectarian Literature," p. 543.

45. See J. Humbert, "L'espace sacré à Qumran. Propositions pour l'archéologie (Planches I–III)," *RB* 101 (1994), pp. 161–214; R. de Vaux, *Archaeology and the Dead Sea Scrolls* (London: Oxford, 1973).

46. M. Halliday, "Anti-languages," *American Anthropologist* 78 (1976), p. 570.

47. J. Irvine, "When Talk Isn't Cheap: Language and Political Economy," *American Ethnologist* 16 (1989), p. 253.

48. See my article, "Qumran Hebrew as an Antilanguage" *JBL*, forthcoming (1999).

49. Rabin, "The Historical Background of Qumran Hebrew," p. 146.

50. See, for example, Gershon Brin, "Biblical Prophecy in the Qumran Scrolls," in *"Sha'arei Talmon": Studies in Bible, Qumran, and the Ancient Near East Presented to Shemaryahu Talmon*, ed. M. Fishbane, et al. (Winona Lake, Ill.: Eisenbrauns, 1992), pp. 101*–112* [Hebrew].

51. My readings are indebted to the host of scholars who have examined these fragments. In particular, see the *editio precepts* by J. M. Allegro, *DJD* 5, pp. 53–57 (Pl. 19–20). A scathing critique of Allegro's volume was published by John Strugnell, "Notes en marge du volume V des 'Discoveries in the Judean Desert of Jordan'," *RQ* 7 (1970), pp. 163–276. Annette Steudel has argued that 4Q174 and 4Q177 are copies of the same composition, although they do not overlap; Steudel, "4QMidrEschat: <<A Midrash on Eschatology>> (4Q*174* + 4Q*177*)," in *The Madrid Congress. Proceedings of the International Congress on the Dead Sea Scrolls. Madrid 18–21 March, 1991*, ed. J. Barrera and L. V. Montaner (Leiden: Brill, 1992), pp. 531–41.

52. On the biblical antecedents for the Qumran community's balance between eschatological priest and king, see Talmon, "Types of Messianic Expectation at the Turn of the Era," pp. 202–24; Schniedewind, "King and Priest in the Book of Chronicles and the Duality of Qumran Messianism," pp. 71–78; "Structural Aspects of Qumran Messianism in the Damascus Document," in *The Provo International Conference on the Dead Sea Scrolls New Text, Reformulated Issues, and Technological Innovations* (Leiden: Brill, 1998), pp. 523-536.

53. Ever since J. Starcky's article, "Les quatres étapes du messiasme à Qumran," *RB* 70 (1963), pp. 481–505, it has been common to speak of a development in messianic thought at Qumran; however, it is difficult to posit a linear development.

54. Isa 7:17 is cited again in CD 13:22–14:2; also 4QD[b] frag. 11 2:1–5 [*olim* 4QD[d]].

55. On the issue of two messiahs in the *Damascus Document*, see my paper, "Structural Aspects of Qumran Messianism in the Damascus Document."

56. See Qimron, *The Temple Scroll: a Critical Edition with Extensive Reconstructions* (Beersheba: Ben-Gurion; Jerusalem: Israel Exploration Society, 1996), pp. 1–8.

57. The translation follows the reconstruction by Qimron, *The Temple Scroll.*

58. Pomykala, *The Davidic Dynasty Tradition in Early Judaism*, p. 237.

59. Schiffman, "The King, His Guard, and the Royal Council in the *Temple Scroll*," in *Proceedings of the American Academy for Jewish Research* (New York: American Academy for Jewish Research), p. 256.

60. For recent interpretations of the Temple Scroll, see George Brooke's introduction to *Temple Scroll Studies. Papers Presented at the International Symposium on the Temple Scroll, Manchester, December 1987*, ed. G. Brooke (Sheffield: JSOT, 1989).

61. The use of the adoption formula in exilic literature may be interpreted as an oblique attempt to democratize the Promise just as we saw in Second Isaiah (see chapter 5).

62. A subtle, but similar type of interpretative maneuver may have gone on in the editing of Isa 9, particularly the positioning of vv. 8–21, which also allude to Deut 23:13. The juxtaposition of the position for a "Davidic son" (9:1–7) with vv. 8–21, which allude to Deut 23:13, probably should attributed to an exilic editor. See, for example, Clements, *Isaiah 1–39*, pp. 66–70.

63. Stegemann, "Some Remarks to 1QSa, to 1QSb, and to Qumran Messianism," *RQ* 65–68 (1996), pp. 479–505.

64. Steudel, "The Eternal Reign of the People of God—Collective Expectations in Qumran Texts (4Q246 and 1QM)," *RQ* 65–68 (1996), pp. 507–25.

65. Steudel locates these texts quite specifically: "During the period of the Maccabaen revolt there was a tendency in certain—priestly and non-priestly—circles to speak about the eschatological reign of the people of God" ("The Eternal Reign of the People of God," p. 524).

66. See J. Allegro, "Further Messianic References in Qumran Literature," *JBL* 75 (1956), pp. 172–76; M. Bernstein, "4Q252: From Re-Written Bible to Biblical Commentary," *JJS* (1994) 1–27; I. Fröhlich, "The Biblical Narratives in Qumran Exegetical Works (4Q252; 4Q180; the Damascus Document)," in *Qumranstudien: Vorträge und Beiträge der Teilnehmer des Qumranseminars auf dem internationalen Treffen der Society of Biblical Literature, Münster, 25.–26. Juli 1993*, ed. Heinz-Josef Fabry and A. Lange (Göttingen: Vandenhoeck & Ruprecht, 1996), pp. 111–24; G. Brooke, "The Genre of 4Q252: From Poetry to Pesher," *DSD* 1 (1994), pp. 160–79; Brooke, "The Deuteronomic Character of 4Q252," in *Pursuing the Text. Studies in Honor of Ben Zion Wacholder on the Occasion of his Seventieth Birthday*, ed. Reeves and Kampen (Sheffield: Academic Press, 1994), pp. 121–35; Brooke, "4Q252 as Early Jewish Commentary," *RQ* 17 (1996), pp. 385–401.

67. Cf. Baillet, “Un recueil liturgique de Qumrân, grotte 4: ‘Les paroles des luminaries’,” *RB* 68 (1961), pp. 195–250. For the official publication, see Baillet, *Qumran Grotte 4: III (4Q482–4Q520)*, DJD 7 (Oxford: Clarendon, 1982), pp. 137–68.

68. On the use of Qumran orthography for determining sectarian compositions in the Qumran corpus, see Tov, “The Orthography and Language of the Hebrew Scrolls Found at Qumran and the Origin of these Scrolls,” *Textus* 13 (1986), pp. 31–57. Orthography should be examined, together with terminology, to distinguish sectarian compositions; on use of terminology, see Chazon, “Is *Divrei Ha-Me'orot* a Sectarian Prayer?” in *The Dead Sea Scrolls: Forty Years of Research*, ed. D. Dimant and U. Rappaport (Leiden: Brill, 1992), pp. 3–17.

68. Pomykala, *The Davidic Dynasty Tradition in Early Judaism*, p. 174.

69. Cf. Schiffman, “Jerusalem in the Dead Sea Scrolls,” pp. 73–88.

70. Pomykala, *Davidic Dynasty Tradition in Early Judaism*, p. 270.

71. Becker, *Messianic Expectation in the Old Testament*, trans. D. Green (Edinburgh: T & T Clark; Philadelphia: Fortress, 1980), p. 87.

72. My analysis here is indebted to H. G. M. Williamson's incisive review of Pomykala in the online electronic journal *IOUDAIOS Review*, vol. 5.016 (1995) [ftp://ftp.lehigh.edu/pub/listserv/ioudaios–review/5.1995/pomykala.williamson.016].

73. See Goldsmith, “Acts 13:33–37: A Pesher on 2 Samuel 7,” *JBL* 87 (1968), pp. 321–24; M. Strauss, *The Davidic Messiah in Luke-Acts: The Promise and Its Fulfillment in Lukan Christology* (Sheffield: Sheffield Academic Press, 1995); D. Juel, *Messianic Exegesis: Christological Interpretation of the Old Testament in Early Christianity* (Philadephia: Fortress, 1987).

74. Blenkinsopp, “Interpretation and the Tendency to Sectarianism,” p. 14.

Chapter 8

1. See Levinson, *Deuteronomy and the Hermeneutics of Legal Innovation.*

2. See H. G. M. Williamson, “The Concept of Israel in Transitions,” in *The World of Ancient Israel: Sociological, Anthropological and Political Perspectives: Essays by Members of the Society for Old Testament Study*, ed. R. E. Clements (Cambridge: Cambridge University Press, 1989), pp. 141–61.

3. The import of this problem to the field of biblical studies is noted in a classic work of linguistic anthropology by W. Ong, *Orality and Literacy*, pp. 172–74.

4. For example, D. Juel, *Messianic Exegesis*; G. Scholem, *The Messianic Idea in Judaism* (New York: Schocken, 1971).

Bibliography

Abel, F. M. *Géographie de la Palestine: Tome II. Géographie politique*. Paris: Gabalda, 1938.

Ackroyd, Peter R. "Historians and Prophets," *SEA* 33 (1954), pp. 18–54.

Ackroyd, Peter R. *Exile and Restoration: A Study of Hebrew Thought in the Sixth Century*. OTL. Philadephia: Westminister, 1968.

Adams, Robert. *The Evolution of Urban Society*. Chicago: Aldine, 1966.

Adams, Robert. *Heartland of Cities*. Chicago: University of Chicago Press, 1981.

Aejmelaeus, Anneli, "Translation Technique and the Intention of the Translator," in *VII Congress of the International Organization for Septuagint and Cognate Studies. Septuagint and Cognate Studies Series* 31. Atlanta: Scholars Press, 1991.

Aharoni, Y. *The Land of the Bible*. Trans., rev., and ed. A. F. Rainey. Philadephia: Westminister, 1979.

Ahlström, G. W. *Psalm 89—Eine Liturgie aus dem Ritual des Leidenden Königs*. Lund: Gleerups, 1959.

Ahlström, G. W. *Who Were the Israelites?* Winona Lake, Ind.: Eisenbrauns, 1986.

Ahlström, G. W. *The History of Ancient Palestine From the Palaeolithic Period to Alexander's Conquest*. *JSOTSS*, 146. Sheffield: JSOT Press, 1992.

Albertz, Rainer. *A History of Israelte Religion in the Old Testament. Volume I: From the Beginnings to the End of the Monarchy*. Trans. John Bowden. Louisville: Westminister John Knox, 1994.

Albright, William F. *Archaeology and the Religion of Israel*. Baltimore: Johns Hopkins University Press, 1968.

Alexander, Philip S. "The Redaction History of Serekh Ha-Yahad: A Proposal," *RQ* 65–68 (1996), pp. 375–84.

Allegro, J. M. "Further Messianic References in Qumran Literature," *JBL* 75 (1956), pp. 174–87.

Allegro, J. M. "Fragments of a Qumran Scroll of Eschatological Midrâshîm," *JBL* 77 (1958), pp. 350–54.

Alt, A. "Die Rolle Samarias bei der Entstehung des Judentums," in *Kleine Schriften zur Geschichte des Volkes Israel, II*. 2nd ed. Munich: Beck, 1959, pp. 316–37.

Alt, A. "The God of the Fathers," in *Essays on Old Testament History and Religion*. Trans. R. Wilson. Sheffield: JSOT Press, 1967, pp. 1–67.

Alt, A. "The Settlement of the Israelites in Palestine," in *Essays on Old Testament History and Religion*. Trans. R. Wilson. Sheffield: JSOT Press, 1967, pp. 133–70.

Alt, A. "The Formation of the Israelite State in Palestine," in *Essays on Old Testament History and Religion*. Trans. R. Wilson. Sheffield: JSOT Press, 1967, pp. 171–239.

Alt, A. "The Monarchy in Israel and Judah," in *Essays on Old Testament History and Religion*. Trans. R. Wilson. Sheffield: JSOT Press, 1967, pp. 239–60.

Auld, A. Graeme. *Kings Without Privilege. David and Moses in the Story of the Bible's Kings*. Edinburgh: T & T Clark, 1994.

Auwers, Jean-Marie. "Le psaaume 132 parmi les graduels," *RB* 103–4 (1996), pp. 546–560.

Avigad, Nahman. *Hebrew Bullae from the Time of Jeremiah: Remnants of a Burnt Archive*. Jerusalem: Israel Exploration Society, 1986.

Avishur, Yitzhak. *Studies in Hebrew and Ugaritic Psalms*. Jerusalem: Magnes, 1994.

Bahat, Dan. "Was Jerusalem Really That Large?", in *Biblical Archaeology Today, 1990: Proceedings of the Second International Congress on Biblical Archaeology*. Ed. Avraham Biran and Joseph Aviram. Jerusalem: Israel Exploration Society/Israel Academy of Sciences and Humanities, 1993, pp. 581–84.

Barclay, John M. G., *Jews in the Mediterranean Diaspora: From Alexander to Trajan (323 BCE–117 CE)*. Edinburgh: T & T Clark, 1996.

Barkay, Gabriel. "Northern and Western Jerusalem in the End of the Iron Age," Ph.D. diss. Tel Aviv University, 1985. Hebrew.

Barkay, Gabriel. "The Iron Age II–III," in *The Archaeology of Ancient Israel*. Ed. Amnon Ben-Tor. New Haven: Yale University Press, 1992, pp. 302–373.

Barkay, Gabriel. "Excavations at Ketef Hinnom in Jerusalem," in *Ancient Jerusalem Revealed*. Ed. Hillel Geva. Jerusalem: Israel Exploration Society, 1994, pp. 85–106.

Barkay, Gabriel. Kloner, Amos. and Mazar, Amihai. "The Northern Necropolis of Jerualem During the First Temple Period," in *Ancient Jerusalem Revealed*. Ed. Hillel Geva. Jerusalem: Israel Exploration Society, 1994, pp. 119–127.

Barkun, Michael. *Disaster and the Millenium*. New Haven: Yale University Press, 1974.

Barstad, Hans M. *The Myth of the Empty Land: A Study in the History and Archaeology of Judah During the "Exilic" Period*. Oslo: Scandinavian University Press, 1996.

Barton, John. *Oracles of God: Perceptions of Ancient Prophecy in Israel after the Exile*. New York: Oxford University Press, 1986.

Baumgarten, Albert I. "City Lights: Urbanization and Sectarianism in Hasmonean Jerusalem," in *The Centrality of Jerusalem: Historical Perspectives*. Ed. M. Poorthuis and Ch. Safrai. Kampen: Pharos, 1996, pp. 50–64.

Baumarten, Albert I. "Invented Traditions of the Maccabean Era," in *Geschichte-Tradition-Reflexion. Festschrift für Martin Hengel zum 70. Gesburtstag. Band I: Judentum*. Ed. Peter Schäfer. Tübingen: J.C.B. Mohr, 1996, pp. 197–210.

Becker, Joachim. *Messianic Expectation in the Old Testament*. Trans. D. Green. Edinburgh: T & T Clark; Philadelphia: Fortress, 1980.

Beckford, James A., ed. *New Religious Movements and Rapid Social Change*. London: Sage, 1986.

Beentjes, P. "Inverted Quotations in the Bible: A Neglected Stylistic Pattern," *Bib* 63 (1982), pp. 506–523.

Ben Zvi, Ehud. "The Authority of 1–2 Chronicles in the Late Second Temple Period," *JSP* 3 (1988), pp. 59–88.

Berlin, Adele, ed. *Religion and Politics in the Ancient Near East*. Bethesda: University of Maryland Press, 1996.

Bernstein, Moshe J. "4Q252: From Re-Written Bible to Biblical Commentary," *JJS* (1994), pp. 1–27.

Berquist, Jon L. *Judaism in Persia's Shadow: A Social and Historical Approach*. Minneapolis: Augsburg, 1995.

Beuken, Wim. " Does Trito-Isaiah Reject the Temple? An Intertextual Inquiry into Isa. 66.1–6," in *Intertextuality in Biblical Writings: Essays in Honor of Bas van Iersel*. Ed. Sipke Draisma. Kampen: Uitgeversmaatschappij J. H. Kok, 1989, pp. 53–66.

Bickerman, Elias. "The Septuagint as a Translation," in *Studies in Jewish and Christian History, Part 1. Arbeiten zur Geschichte des antiken Judentums und des Urchristentums*, 9 Leiden: Brill, 1976, pp. 167–200.

Blenkinsopp, Joseph. *Prophecy and Canon*. South Bend, Ind.: Notre Dame University Press, 1977.

Blenkinsopp, Joseph. "Interpretation and the Tendency to Sectarianism: An Aspect of Second Temple History," in *Jewish and Christian Self-Definition. Volume 2: Aspects of Judaism in the Graeco-Roman Period.* Ed. E. P. Sanders, A. I. Baumgarten, and Alan Mendelson. London: SCM, 1981, pp. 1–26.

Blenkinsopp, Joseph. *A History of Prophecy in Israel.* Rev. and enl. Louisville, Ky.: Westminster John Knox Press, 1996.

Blenkensopp, Joseph. "Temple and Society in Achaemenid Judah," in *Second Temple Studies. 1. Persian Period.* Ed. P. Davies. Sheffield: JSOT Press, 1991, pp. 22–53.

Boccaccini, Gabriele. *Middle Judaism: Jewish Thought, 300 B.C.E. to 200 C.E.* Minneapolis: Fortress, 1991.

Braudel, Fernand. *The Mediterranean and the Mediterranean World in the Age of Philip II.* 2 vols. Trans. Sian Reynolds. New York: Harper & Row, 1976.

Braudel, Fernand. *On History.* Trans. Sarah Matthews. Chicago: University of Chicago Press, 1980.

Braun, Roddy. "The Message of Chronicles: Rally 'Round the Temple," *CTM* 42 (1971), pp. 502–14.

Braun, Roddy. "Solomonic Apologetic in Chronicles." *JBL* 92 (1973), pp. 503–16.

Braun, Roddy. "Solomon, The Chosen Temple Builder: The Significance of 1 Chronicles 22, 28, and 29 for the Theology of Chronicles." *JBL* 95 (1976), pp. 581–90.

Bregstein, Linda. "Seal Use in Fifth Century BC. Nippur, Iraq: A Study of Seal Selection and Sealing Practices in the Murašû Archive," Ph.D. diss. University of Pennsylvania, 1993.

Brettler, Marc Z. *God Is King: Understanding an Israelite Metaphor.* Sheffield: JSOT Press, 1989.

Brettler, Marc Z. "Ideology, History and Theology in 2 Kings XVII 7–23," *VT* 39 (1989), pp. 268–82.

Brettler, Marc Z. "The Book of Judges: Literature as Politics," *JBL* 108 (1989), pp. 405–28.

Brettler, Marc Z. "The Structure of 1–11," *JSOT* 49 (1991), pp. 87–97.

Brettler, Marc Z. "Interpretation and Prayer: Notes on the Composition of 8.15–53," in *Minḥah le-Naḥum: Biblical and Other Studies Presented to Nahum M. Sarna in Honour of his 70th Birthday.* Ed. Marc Brettler and Michael Fishbane. *JSOTSS,* 154. Sheffield: JSOT Press, 1993, pp. 17–35.

Brettler, Marc Z. *The Creation of History in Ancient Israel.* London: Routledge, 1995.

Bright, John. *Covenant and Promise.* London: SCM, 1977.

Brin, Gershon. "Biblical Prophecy in the Qumran Scrolls," in *Sha'arei Talmon : Studies in Bible, Qumran, and the Ancient Near East Presented to Shemaryahu Talmon.* Ed. M. Fishbane. Winona Lake, Ind.: Eisenbrauns, 1992, pp. 101*–112*, [Hebrew].

Brin, Gershon. "The History of the Formula 'He Shall be to Me a Son and I Will Be to Him a Father," in *Bible and Jewish History Dedicated to the Memory of Jacob Liver.* Tel Aviv: Tel Aviv University, 1971. Hebrew.

Brooke, George J. "The Amos-Numbers Midrash (CD 7 13b–8 1a) and Messianic Expectation," *ZAW* 92 (1980), pp. 397–404.

Brooke, George J. "Qumran Pesher: Towards the Redefinition of a Genre," *RQ* 10 (1981), pp. 483–503.

Brooke, George J. *Exegesis at Qumran: 4QFlorilegium in its Jewish Context.* Sheffield: JSOT Press, 1985.

Broshi, Magen. "The Expansion of Jerusalem in the Reigns of Hezekiah and Manasseh," *IEJ* 24 (1974), pp. 21–28.

Broshi, Magen. "Estimating the Population of Ancient Jerusalem," *BAR* 4 (1978), pp. 10–15.

Broshi, Magen. "The Archaeology of Qumran: A Reconsideration," in *The Dead Sea Scrolls: Forty Years of Research.* Ed. Devorah Dimant and Uriel Rappaport. Jerusalem: Magnes, 1992, pp. 101–2.

Broshi, Magen. "The Damascus Document Reconsidered," in *The Damascus Document Reconsidered.* Ed. M. Broshi. Jerusalem: Israel Exploration Society, 1992), pp. 5–8.

Broshi, Magen and Finkelstein, Israel. "The Population of Palestine in Iron Age II," *BASOR* 287 (1992), pp. 47–60.

Bruce, F. F. "Prophetic Interpretation in the Septuagint," *BIOSCS* 12 (1979), pp. 17–26.

Brueggemann, W. "Isaiah 55 and Deuteronomic Theology," *ZAW* 80 (1968), pp. 191–203.

Buccellati, Giorgio. *Cities and Nations of Ancient Syria.* Studi Semitici, 26. Rome: Instituto di Studi del Vicino Oriente, 1967.

Bunimovitz, Shlomo. "Socio-Political Transformations in the Central Hill Country in the Late Bronze-Iron I Transition," in *From Nomadism to Monarchy: Archaeological and Historical Aspects of Early Israel.* Ed. Israel Finkelstein and Nadav Na'aman. Jerusalem: Israel Exploration Society; Washington: BAS, 1994, pp. 179–202.

Callaway, Phillip R. "Qumran Origins: From the Doresh to the Moreh," *RQ* 56 (1990), pp. 637–50.

Coquot, A. "Les grâces de David," *Semitica* 15 (1965), pp. 45–59.

Caquot, A. "Observations sur le Psaume 89," *Semitica* 41–42 (1991–1992), pp. 133–157.

Carlson, R. *David, the Chosen King.* Stockholm: Almqvist & Wiksell, 1964.

Carneiro, Robert. "A Theory of the Origin of State," *Science* 169 (1970), pp. 733–38.

Carroll, Robert P. "Rebellion and Dissent in Ancient Israelite Society," *ZAW* 89 (1977), pp. 176–204.

Carroll, Robert P. *When Prophecy Failed.* New York: Seabury, 1979.

Carroll, Robert P. "Inventing the Prophets," *Irish Biblical Studies* 10 (1988), pp. 24–36.

Carroll, Robert P. "Prophecy and Society," in *The World of Ancient Israel: Sociological, Anthropological and Political Perspectives: Essays by Members of the Society for Old Testament Study.* Ed. R. E. Clements. Cambridge: Cambridge University Press, 1989, pp. 203–225.

Carroll, Robert P. "Textual Strategies and Ideology in the Second Temple Period," in *Second Temple Studies. 1. Persian Period.* Ed. P. Davies. *JSOTSS,* 117. Sheffield: JSOT Press, 1991, pp. 108–124.

Carter, Charles. "The Province of Yehud in the Post-Exilic Period: Soundings in Site Distribution and Demography," in *Second Temple Studies. 2. Temple Community in the Persian Period.* Ed. T. Eskenazi and K. Richards. *JSOTSS,* 175. Sheffield: JSOT Press, 1994, pp. 106–145.

Chaney, Marvin. "Ancient Palestinian Peasant Movements and the Formation of Premonarchial Israel," in *Palestine in Transition: Ther Emergence of Ancient Israel.* Ed. D. N. Freedman and D. F. Graf. *SWBAS*, 2. Sheffield: Almond Press, 1983.

Chaney, Marvin. "Systemic Study of the Israelite Monarchy," *Semeia* 37 (1986), pp. 53–76.

Claessen, Henri J. M. and Skalník, Peter. "The Early State: Theories and Hypotheses," in *The Early State.* Ed. H. Claessen and P. Skalník. The Hague: Mouton, 1978, pp. 3–29.

Claessen, Henri J. M. and Skalník, Peter. *The Study of the State*. The Hague: Mouton, 1981.

Clements, R. E. *Isaiah and the Deliverance of Jerusalem: a Study of the Interpretation of Prophecy in the Old Testament. JSOTSS,* 13. Sheffield: JSOT Press, 1980.

Clements, R. E., ed. *The World of Ancient Israel: Sociological, Anthropological and Political Perspectives*. Cambridge: Cambridge University Press, 1989.

Clifford, Richard. "In Zion and David a New Beginning: An Interpretation of Psalm 78," in *Traditions and Transformation: Turning points in Biblical Faith*. Ed. B. Halpern and J. D. Levenson. Winona Lake, Ind.: Eisenbrauns, 1981, pp. 121–41.

Cohen, Chaim. "Elements Of Peshat in Traditional Jewish Bible Exegesis," *Immanuel* 21 (1987), pp. 30–42.

Cohen, Naomi. "Jewish Names as Cultural Indicators in Antiquity," *JSJ* 7 (1976–77), pp. 97–128.

Cohen, Rudolph. "The Iron Age Fortresses in the Central Negev," *BASOR* 236 (1979), pp. 61–79.

Cohen, Rudolph and Yisrael, Yigal. "The Iron Age Fortresses at 'En Ḥaṣeva." *BA* 58, 4 (1995), pp. 223–35.

Collins, John J. "Messianism in the Maccabean Period," in *Judaisms and Their Messiahs at the Turn of the Christian Era*. Ed. J. Neusner, et. al. Cambridge: Cambridge University Press, 1986, pp. 97–109.

Collins, John J. *The Apocalyptic Imagination: An Introduction to the Jewish Matrix of Christianity*. New York: Crossroad, 1987.

Collins, John J. *The Scepter and the Star: The Messiahs of the Dead Sea Scrolls and Other Ancient Literature.* New York: Doubleday, 1995.

Coogan, Michael David. "Life in the Diaspora: Jews at Nippur in the Fifth Century B.C.," *BA* 37 (1974), pp. 6–12.

Coogan, Michael David. *West Semitic Personal Names in the Murashu Documents. HSM*, 7. Missoula: Scholars, 1976.

Cook, Edward M. "4Q246," *BBR* 5 (1995), pp. 43–66.

Coote, Robert B. and Keith W. Whitelam. *The Emergence of Early Israel in Historical Perspective. SWBAS*, 4. Sheffield: Almond, 1987.

Coppens, J. *Le messianisme royal.* Paris: Editions du Cerf, 1968.

Coppens, J. *Le messianisme et sa relève prophétique.* Gembloux: Duculot, 1974.

Cowley, A. "The Meaning of מקום in Hebrew," *JTS* 17 (1916), pp. 174–76.

Cross, Frank Moore. *Canaanite Myth and Hebrew Epic.* Cambridge, Mass.: Harvard, 1973.

Cross, Frank Moore and Freedman, David Noel. "Josiah's Revolt Against Assyria," *JNES* 12 (1953), pp. 56–58.

Crüsemann, Frank. *Der Widerstand gegen das Königtum. Die antikönigliche Texte des Alten Testementes und der Kampf um den frühe israelitischen Staat.* Neukirchen–Vluyn: Neukirchener Verlag, 1978.

Daiches, Samuel. *The Jews in the Time of Ezra and Nehemiah according to Babylonian Inscriptions.* London: Oxford, 1912.

Dandamaev, M. A. *A Political History of the Achaemenid Empire*. Trans. W.J. Vogelsang. Leiden: Brill, 1989.

Davies, Philip. *In Search of Ancient Israel. JSOTSS,* 148. Sheffield: JSOT Press, 1992.

Dever, William G. "Monumental Architecture in Ancient Israel in the Period of the United Monarchy," in *Studies in the Period of David and Solomon and Other Essays*. Ed. Tomoo Ishida. Tokyo, 1982, pp. 269–306.

Dever, William G. "The Contribution of Archaeology to the Study of Canaanite and

Early Israelite Religion." In *Ancient Israelite Religion: Essays in Honor of Frank Moore Cross*. Ed. Patrick D. Miller, Paul Hanson and S. Dean McBride. Philadephia: Fortress, 1987, pp. 209–248.

Dever, William G. "A Case-Study in Biblical Archaeology: The Earthquake of Ca. 760 BCE," *EI* 23 (1992), pp. 27–35.

Dever, William G. "Cultural Continuity, Ethnicity in the Archaeological Record, and the Question of Israelite Origins," *EI [Malamat Volume]* 24 (1993), pp. 22*–33*.

Dever, William G. "Archaeology and the Religions of Israel," *BASOR* 301 (1996), pp. 83–91.

Dever, William G. "Archaeology, Urbanism and the Rise of the Israelite State," in *Aspects of Urbanism in Antiquity: From Mesopotamia to Crete*. Ed. W.E. Aufrecht, N.A. Mirau and S.W. Gauley. Sheffield: JSOT Press, 1997.

Dever, William G. "Philology, Theology, and Archaeology: What Kind of History Do We Want, and What Is Possible?" in *The Archaeology of Israel: Constructing the Past, Interpreting the Present*. Ed. Niel Asher Silberman and David B. Small. Sheffield: JSOT Press, 1997, pp. 290–310.

Dever, William G. "Social Structure in Palestine in the Iron II Period on the Eve of Destruction," in *The Archaeology of Society in the Holy Land*. Ed. T. Levy. New York: Facts on File, 1995, pp. 416–431.

Dever, William G. ""Will the Real Israel Please Stand Up?" Archaeology and Israelite Historiography: Part I." *BASOR* 297 (1995), pp. 61–80.

Dever, William G. ""Will the Real Israel Please Stand Up?" Part II: Archaeology and the Religions of Ancient Israel." *BASOR* 298 (1995), pp. 37–58.

Dillard, Raymond. "The Chronicler's Solomon," *WTJ* 43 (1980), pp. 289–300.

Dion, Paul. "The Angel with the Drawn Sword (II Chr 21,16) [sic!]: An Exercise in Restoring the Balance of Text Criticism and Attention to Context," *ZAW* 97 (1985), pp. 114–117.

Douglas, Mary. *Purity and Danger: An Analysis of the Concepts of Pollution and Taboo*. London: Routledge & Kegan Paul, 1966.

Dumortier, J. B. "Un rituel d'intronisation: Le Ps. LXXXIX: 2–38," *VT* 22 (1972), pp. 176–96.

Eisenstadt, S. N. "Observations and Queries about Sociological Apects of Imperialism in the Ancient World," in *Power and Propaganda: A Symposium on Ancient Empires*. Ed. Morgens Trolle Larsen. *Mesopotamia*, 7. Copenhagen: Akademisk Forlag, 1979, pp. 7–46.

Eissfeldt, Otto. "The Promise of Grace to David in Isaiah 55:1–5," in *Israel's Prophetic Heritage. Essays in Honor of J. Muilenburg*. Ed. B. W. Anderson and W. Harrelson. New York: Harper, 1962, pp. 196–207.

Eph'al, Israel. "The Western Minorities in Babylonia in the 6th–5th Centuries B.C.: Maintenance and Cohesion," *Orientalia* 47 (1978), pp. 74–90.

Eph'al, Israel. "On Warfare and Military Control in the Ancient Near Eastern Empires: A Research Outline," in *History, Historiography and Interpretation: Studies in Biblical and Cuneiform Literatures*. Ed. H. Tadmor and M. Weinfeld. Jerusalem: Magnes, 1983, pp. 88–106.

Eslinger, Lyle. "Inner-biblical Exegesis and Inner-biblical Allusion: The Question of Category," *VT* 42 (1992), pp. 47–58.

Fensham, F. "Father and Son as Terminology for Treaty and Covenant," in *Near Eastern Studies in Honour of W. F. Albright*. Ed. H. Goedicke. Baltimore: Johns Hopkins University Press, 1971, pp. 121–35.

Festinger, Leon. *A Theory of Cognitive Dissonance*. Evanston, Ill.: Peterson, 1957.

Finkelstein, Israel. *The Archaeology of the Israelite Settlement*. Jerusalem: Israel Exploration Society, 1988.

Finkelstein, Israel. "Arabian Trade and Socio-Political Conditions in the Negev in the 12–11th Centuries BCE," *JNES* 47 (1988), pp. 241–52.

Finkelstein, Israel. "The Emergence of the Monarchy in Israel: The Enviromental and Socio-Economic Aspects," *JSOT* 44 (1989) 43–74.

Finkelstein, Israel, "Environmental Archaeology and Social History: Demographic and Economic Aspects of the Monarchic Period," in *Biblical Archaeology Today, 1990: Proceedings of the Second International Congress on Biblical Archaeology*. Ed. A. Biran and J. Aviram. Jerusalem: Israel Exploration Society, 1993.

Finkelstein, Israel. *Living on the Fringe: the Archaeology and History of the Negev, Sinai and Neighbouring Regions in the Bronze and Iron Ages. Monographs in Mediterranean Archaeology*, 6. Sheffield: Sheffield Academic Press, 1995.

Finkelstein, Israel. "The Archaeology of the United Monarchy: an Alternative View," *Levant* 28 (1996), pp. 177–87.

Finkelstein, Israel and Na'aman, Nadav, ed. *From Nomadism to Monarchy: Archaeological and Historical Aspects of Early Israel*. Jerusalem: Israel Exploration Society, 1994.

Finnegan, Ruth. *Literacy and Orality*. Oxford: Basil Blackwell, 1988.

Fishbane, Michael. *Biblical Interpretation in Ancient Israel*. Oxford: Clarendon, 1985.

Fishbane, Michael. "Use, Authority and Interpretation of Mikra at Qumran." In *Compendia Rerum Iadaicum*. Cambridge: Cambridge University Press, 1989, pp. 339–77.

Flanagan, James W. "Chiefs in Israel," *JSOT* 20 (1981), pp. 47–73.

Flanagan, James W. *David's Social Drama: a Hologram of Israel's Early Iron Age*. *SWBAS*, 7. Sheffield: Almond, 1988.

Flesher, Paul, ed. *Ancient Synagogues: Historical Analysis and Archaeological Discovery*. Leiden: Brill, 1995.

Flusser, David. "Two Notes on the Midrash on 2 Sam. vii," *IEJ* 9 (1959), pp. 99–109.

Flusser, David. *Judaism and the Origins of Christianity*. Jerusalem: Magnes, 1988.

Fogel, R. and Elton, G. *Which Road to the Past?* London: Yale University Press, 1983.

Fokkelman, Jan. *Narrative Art and Poety in the Books of Samuel. Throne and City (II Sam. 2–8 & 21–24)*. Trans. L. Waaning-Wardle. Assen: Van Gorcum, 1990.

Frankfort, Henri. *Kingship and the Gods*. Chicago: University of Chicago, 1948. Reprinted, 1978.

Freedman, David N. "The Chronicler's Purpose," *CBQ* 23 (1961), pp. 436–42.

Frick, Frank. *The Formation of the State in Ancient Israel*. *SWBAS*, 4. Sheffield: Almond, 1985.

Frick, Frank S. "Social Science Methods and Theories of Significance for the Study of the Israelite Monarchy: A Critical Review Essay," *Semeia* 37 (1986), pp. 9–52.

Frick, Frank. "Ecology, Agriculture and Patterns of Settlement," in *The World of Ancient Israel: Sociological, Anthropological and Political Perspectives: Essays by Members of the Society for Old Testament Study*. Ed. R. E. Clements. Cambridge: Cambridge University Press, 1989, pp. 67–93.

Galling, Kurt. *Studien zur Geschichte Israels im persischen Zeitalter*. Tübingen: Mohr, 1964.

Garbini, Giovanni. *History and Ideology in Ancient Israel*. London: SCM, 1988.

Geller, Steven. *Sacred Enigmas: Literary Religion in the Hebrew Bible*. London: Routledge, 1996.

Geva, Hillel. "Twenty-Five Years of Excavations in Jerusalem, 1968–1993: Achievements and Evaluation," in *Ancient Jerusalem Revealed.* Ed. H. Geva. Jerusalem: Israel Exploration Society, 1994, pp. 1–29.

Geva, Hillel. "The Western Boundary of Jerusalem at the End of the Monarchy," *IEJ* 29 (1979), pp. 84–91.

Goldsmith, D. "Acts 13:33-37: A Pesher on 2 Samuel 7," *JBL* 87 (1968), pp. 321–24.

Goldstein, Jonathon A. "How the Authors of 1 and 2 Maccabees Treated the 'Messianic' Promises, in *Judaisms and Their Messiahs at the Turn of the Christian Era.*" Ed. J. Neusner, et. al.. Cambridge: Cambridge University Press, 1987, pp. 69–96.

Gooding, David W. *Relics of Ancient Exegesis: A Study of the Miscellanies in 3 Reigns 2.* Cambridge: Cambridge University Press, 1976.

Goody, Jack. *The Domestication of the Savage Mind.* Cambridge: Cambridge University Press, 1977.

Goody, Jack. *The Logic of Writing and the Organization of Society.* Cambridge: Cambridge University Press, 1986.

Goody, Jack, and Watt, Ian. "The Consequences of Literacy," *Comparative Studies in Society and History* 5 (1963), pp. 304–345.

Görg, M. *Gott-König-Reden in Israel und Ägypten. BWANT*, 105. Stuttgart, 1975.

Gottwald, Norman. *The Tribes of Yahweh.* London: SCM, 1979.

Grosby, Steven. "Borders, Territory and Nationality in the Ancient Near East and Armenia." *JESHO* 40 (1997), pp. 1–29.

Hachlili, Rachel. "The Origin of the Synagogue: A Re-assessment," *JSJ* 28 (1997), pp. 34–47.

Halpern, Baruch. *The Constitution of the Monarchy in Israel. HSM*, 25. Chico, Calif.: Scholars Press, 1981.

Halpern, Baruch. "The Uneasy Compromise: Israel between League and Monarchy," *Traditions in Transformations.* Ed. B. Halpern and J. D. Levenson. Winona Lake, Ind.: Eisenbrauns, 1981, pp. 59–96.

Halpern, Baruch. "Jerusalem and the Lineages in the Seventh Century BCE: Kinship and the Rise of Individual Moral Liability," in *Law and Ideology in Monarchic Israel.* Ed. Baruch Halpern and Deborah W. Hobson. *JSOTSS*, 124. Sheffield: JSOT Press, 1991, pp. 11–107.

Halpern, Baruch and David S. Vanderhooft. "The Editions of Kings in the 7th-6th Centuries B.C.E." *HUCA* 62 (1991), pp. 179–244.

Hauer, Chris. "From Alt to Anthropology: The Rise of the Israelite State," *JSOT* 36 (1986), pp. 3–15.

Hayes, John H. "The Tradition of Zion's Inviolability," *JBL* 82 (1963), pp. 419–26.

Hentschel, Georg. *Gott, König, und Tempel. Beobachtungen zu 2 Sam 7,1–17. Erfurter Theologische Schriften*, 22. Leipzig: St.-Benno, 1992.

Herr, Larry. "Iron II: Emerging Nations," *BA* 60 (1997), pp. 120–132.

Hess, Richard. "Hebrew Psalms and Amarna Correspondence from Jerusalem: Some Comparisons and Implications," *ZAW* 101 (1989), pp. 249–65.

Hoffman, H. D. *Reform und Reformen. ATANT*, 66. Zürich: Theologischer Verlag, 1980.

Hoglund, Kenneth. "The Achaemenid Context," in *Second Temple Studies. 1. Persian Period.* Ed. Philip Davies. *JSOTSS*, 117. Sheffield: JSOT Press, 1991, pp. 54–72.

Hoglund, Kenneth. *Achaemenid Imperial Administration in Syria-Palestine and the Missions of Ezra and Nehemiah. SBLDS*, 125. Atlanta: Scholars, 1992.

Holladay, John. "The Kingdoms of Israel and Judah: Political and Economic Centralization in the Iron IIA-B (ca. 1000–750 BCE)," in *The Archaeology of*

Society in the Holy Land. Ed. T. Levy. New York: Facts on File, 1995, pp. 368–398.

Humbert, Jean Baptiste. "L'espace sacré à Qumran. Propositions pour l'archéologie (Planches I–III)," *RB* 101 (1994), pp. 161–214.

Hurowitz, Avigdor. *I Have Built You An Exalted House: Temple Building in the Bible in Light of Mesopotamian and North-west Semitic Writings. JSOTSS*, 115. Sheffield: JSOT Press, 1992.

Hurvitz, Avi. *The Transition Period in Biblical Hebrew: A Study of Post-exilic Hebrew and its Implications for Dating the Psalms.* Jerusalem: Bialik, 1972. [Hebrew]

Hurvitz, Avi. "The Historical Quest for 'Ancient Israel' and the Linguistic Evidence of the Hebrew Bible: Some Methodological Observations," *VT* 47 (1997), pp. 310–315.

Iser, W. *The Act of Reading: A Theory of Aesthetic Response.* Baltimore: Johns Hopkins University Press, 1978.

Ishida, T. *The Royal Dynasties in Ancient Israel: A Study on the Formation and Development of Royal-Dynastic Ideology. BZAW*, 142. Berlin: de Gruyter, 1977.

Ishida, T., ed. *Studies in the Period of David and Solomon and Other Essays.* Winona Lake, Ind.: Eisenbrauns, 1982.

Jacobsen, T. "Early Political Development in Mesopotamia," *ZA* 52 (1957), pp. 91–140. [=*Toward the Image of Tammuz and other Essays.* Ed. W. L. Moran. Cambridge, MA, 1970].

Jamieson-Drake, D. W. *Scribes and Schools in Monarchic Judah. JSOTSS*, 109. Sheffield: JSOT Press, 1991.

Japhet, Sara. *The Ideology of the Book of Chronicles and Its Place in Biblical Thought.* Trans. A. Barber. Frankfurt: Lang, 1989.

Japhet, Sara. " 'History' and 'Literature' in the Persian Period: The Restoration of the Temple," *ScrHier* 33 [Tadmor Festschrift] (1991), pp. 174–88.

Jauss, Hans Robert. "Literary History as a Challenge to Literary Theory," *New Literary History* 2 (1970), pp. 7–37.

Jauss, Hans Robert. "The Idealist Embarrassment: Observations on Marxist Aesthetics," *New Literary History* 7 (1975), pp. 191–208.

Jauss, Hans Robert. *Toward an Aesthetic of Reception.* Trans. Timothy Bahti. Minneapolis: University of Minnesota Press, 1982.

Jones, Gwilym H. *The Nathan Narratives. JSOTSS,* 80. Sheffield, JSOT Press, 1990.

Juel, Donald. *Messianic Exegesis: Christological Interpretation of the Old Testament in Early Christianity.* Philadephia: Fortress, 1987.

Kapelrud, Arvid. "Temple Building, A Task for God and Kings," *Orientalia* 32 (1963), pp. 56–62.

Kelly, Brian. *Retribution and Eschatology in Chronicles. JSOTSS,* 211. Sheffield: JSOT Press, 1996.

Kempinski, Aharon, and Ronny Reich. *The Architecture of Ancient Israel: From the Prehistoric to the Persian Periods.* Jerusalem: Israel Exploration Society, 1992.

Kenyon, Kathleen. *Digging Up Jerusalem.* London: Ernest Benn, 1974.

Knauf, Ernst Axel. "The Cultural Impact of Secondary State Formation: The Cases of the Edomites and Moabites," in *Early Edom and Moab: The Beginning of the Iron Age in Southern Jordan.* Ed. P. Bienkowski. *Sheffield Archaeological Monographs*, 7. Sheffield: Collis, 1992, pp. 47–54.

Knauf-Belleri, Ernst Axel. "Edom: The Social and Economic History." In *You Shall Not Abhor an Edomite For He is Your Brother: Edom and Seir in History and*

Tradition. Ed. D. Edelman. Atlanta: Scholars, 1995, pp. 93–118.

Knoppers, Gary. *Two Nations Under God: The Deuteronomistic History of Solomon and the Dual Monarchies, volume 1: The Reign of Solomon and the Rise of Jeroboam*. *HSM* 52. Atlanta: Scholars, 1993.

Knoppers, Gary. "The Vanishing Solomon: The Disappearance of the United Monarchy from Recent Histories of Ancient Israel," *JBL* 116 (1997), pp. 19–44.

Laato, Annti. "Hezekiah and the Assyrian Crisis in 701 B.C.," *SJOT* 2 (1987), pp. 49–68.

Laato, Antti. *Who Is Immanuel? The Rise and the Foundering of Isaiah's Messianic Expectations*. Albo: Albo Akademik Förl., 1988.

Laato, Antti. "The Composition of Isaiah 40–55," *JBL* 109 (1990), pp. 207–28.

Laato, Antti. *Josiah and David Redivivus. The Historical Josiah and the Messianic Expectations of Exilic and Postexilic Times*. Stockholm: Almqvist & Wiksell, 1992.

Laato, Antti. *The Servant of YHWH and Cyrus. A Reinterpretation of the Exilic Messianic Programme in Isaiah 40–55*. Stockholm: Almqvist & Wiksell, 1992.

Laato, Antti. "Psalm 132 and the Development of the Jerusalemite/Israelite Royal Ideology," *CBQ* 54 (1992), pp. 49–66.

Laato, Antti. "Second Samuel 7 and Ancient Near Eastern Royal Ideology." *CBQ* 59 (1997), pp. 244–269.

Laato, Antti. *A Star Is Rising: The Historical Development of the Old Testament Royal Ideology and the Rise of the Jewish Messianic Expectations*. Atlanta: Scholars, 1997.

Lemairé, Andre. *Les écoles et la formation de la Bible dans l'ancien Israël*. *OBO* 39. Fribourg: Editions Universitaires; Göttingen: Vandenhoeck & Ruprecht, 1981.

Lemche, Niels P. "The Old Testament—A Hellenistic Book?" *SJOT* 7 (1993), pp. 163–193.

Levenson, Jon D. "From Temple to Synagogue: 8," in *Traditions in Transformations: Turning Points in Biblical Faith*. Ed. B. Halpern and J. D. Levenson. Winona Lake, Ind.: Eisenbrauns, 1981, pp. 143–166.

Levenson, Jon D. *Sinai & Zion: An Entry into the Jewish Bible*. San Francisco: Harper & Row, 1985.

Levine, Lee. "The Nature and Origin of the Palestinian Synagogue Reconsidered," *JBL* 115 (1996), pp. 425–448.

Levinson, Bernhard. *Deuteronomy and the Hermeneutics of Legal Innovation*. New York: Oxford University Press, 1997.

Levy, Thomas E., ed. *The Archaeology of Society in the Holy Land*. New York: Facts on File, 1995.

Lipinski, E. *Le poème royal du Psaume LXXXIX 1–5, 20–38*. Paris: Gabalda, 1967.

Lippi, Paul. "The Use of the Computerized Data Base for the Study of Septuagint Revisions," *BIOSCS* 17 (1987), pp. 48–62.

Lohfink, Norbert. "Welches Orakel gab den Daviden Dauer? Ein Textproblem in 2 Kön 8, 19 und des Funktionieren der dynasticischen Orakel im deuteronomistischen Geschichtswerk," in *Lingering over Words: Studies in Ancient Near Eastern Literature in Honor of William L. Moran*. Ed. T. Abusch, J. Huehnergard, and P. Steinkeller. *HSS*, 37. Atlanta: Scholars, 1990, pp. 349–70.

Loprieno, Antonio. "The 'King's Novel'," in *Ancient Egyptian Literature: History and Forms*. Ed. A. Loprieno. Leiden: Brill, 1996, pp. 277–96.

Lust, Johan. "Messianism and Septuagint," in *Congress Volume, Salamanca, 1983*. Ed. J. Emerton. Leiden: Brill, 1985, pp. 174–91.

Lust, Johan. "The Diverse Text Forms of Jeremiah and History Writing with Jer 33 as a Test Case," *JNWSL* 20 (1994), pp. 31–48.

Machinist, Peter. "Literature as Politics: The Tukulti-Ninurta Epic and the Bible," *CBQ* 38 (1976), pp. 455–482.

Matthews, Victor and Don Benjamin. *Social World of Ancient Israel, 1250–587* BCE. Peabody, Mass.: Hendrickson, 1993.

Mazar, Amihai. "The 'Bull Site'—An Iron Age I Open Cult Place," *BASOR* 247 (1982), pp. 27–42.

Mazar, Amihai. "Iron Age I and II Towers at Giloh and the Israelite Settlement." *IEJ* 40 (1990), pp. 77–101.

Mazar, Amihai. *Archaeology of the Land of the Bible*. Garden City, N.Y.: Doubleday, 1990.

Mazar, Amihai. "A Reply to I. Finkelstein," *Levant* 29 (1997), pp. 000–000.

McCarthy, Dennis. "II Samuel 7 and the Structure of the Deuteronomic History," *JBL* 84 (1965), pp. 131–38.

McKenzie, Steven L. *The Chronicler's Use of the Deuteronomistic History*. *HSM*, 33. Atlanta: Scholars, 1985.

Mettinger, Tryggve N. D. "'The Last Words of David': A Study of Structure and Meaning in II Samuel 23:1–7," *SEA* 41–42 (1976–1977), pp. 147–56.

Mettinger, Tryggve N. D. *King and Messiah: the Civil and Sacral Legitimation of the Israelite Kings*. Lund: CWK Gleerup, 1976.

Meyers, Carol. "David as Temple Builder," in *Ancient Israelite Religion: Essays in Honor of Frank Moore Cross*. Ed. P. D. Miller, P. Hanson, and S. D. McBride. Philadephia: Fortress, 1987, pp. 357–376.

Meyers, Eric. "The Shelomith Seal and the Judean Restoration: Some Additional Considerations," *EI* 18 (1985), pp. 33*–38*.

Milgrom, Jacob. "Priestly Terminiology and the Political Social Structure of the Pre-Monarchic Israel," *JQR* ns 69 (1978), pp, 65–76.

Millard, Allan R. "An Assessment of the Evidence for Writing in Ancient Israel," in *Biblical Archaeology Today: Proceedings of the International Congress on Biblical Archaeology Jerusalem, April 1984*. Jerusalem: Israel Exploration Society, 1985), pp. 301–12.

Miller, J. M. "Solomon: International Potentate or Local King?" *PEQ* 123 (1991), pp. 28–31.

de Moor, J. C., ed. *Synchronic or Diachronic? A Debate on Method in Old Testament Exegesis*. Leiden: Brill, 1995.

Moran, William L. "The Syrian Scribe of the Jerusalem Amarna Letters," in *Unity and Diversity*. Ed. H. Goedicke and J. Roberts. Baltimore: Johns Hopkins University Press, 1975, pp. 146–166.

Mowinckel, Sigmund. "Nataforjettelsen i 2 Sam. kap. 7," *SEA* 12 (1947), pp. 220–29.

Na'aman, Nadav. "Hezekiah's Fortified Cities and the LMLK Stamps," *BASOR* 261 (1986), pp. 5–21.

Na'aman, Nadav. "The Negev in the Last Days of the Kingdom of Judah," *Cathedra* 42 (1987), pp. 5–21.

Na'aman, Nadav. "The Kingdom of Judah under Josiah," *TA* 18 (1991), pp. 3–71.

Na'aman, Nadav. "The Contribution of the Amarna Letters to the Debate on Jerusalem's Political Position in the Tenth Century B.C.E." *BASOR* 304 (1996), pp. 17–28.

Na'aman, Nadav. "Cow Town or Royal Capital? Evidence for Iron Age Jerusalem." *BAR* 23/4 (1997), pp. 43–47, 67.

Neusner, Jacob, editor. *Judaisms and Their Messiahs at the Turn of the Christian Era.*

Cambridge: Cambridge University Press, 1987.

Newsome, James. "Toward a New Understanding of the Chronicler and his Purposes," *JBL* 94 (1975), pp. 201–17.

Niditch, Susan. *Oral World and Written Word.* Library of Ancient Israel. Louisville: Westminister John Knox, 1996.

Noth, Martin. *Das System der zwölf Stämme Israels.* Stuttgart: Kohlhammer, 1930.

Noth, Martin. *The Deuteronomistic History.* Trans. H. Williamson. Sheffield: JSOT Press, 1991.

Ockinga, Boyo G. "The Inviolability of Zion—A Pre-Israelite Tradition?" *BN* 44 (1988), pp. 54–60.

Ong, Walter J. *Orality and Literacy: The Technologizing of the Word.* London: Routledge, 1982.

Paul, Shalom. "Adoption Formulae: A Study of Cuneiform and Biblical Legal Clauses," *MAARAV* 2 (1980), pp. 173–86.

Peckham, Brian. "Writing and Editing," in *Fortunate the Eyes That See: Essays in Honor of David Noel Freedman in Celebration of His Seventieth Birthday.* Ed. A. Beck. A. Bartelt. P. Raabe. C. Franke. Grand Rapids, Mich.: Eerdmans, 1995, pp. 364–383.

Pedersen, Johannes. *Israel: Its Life and Culture. I–II.* Copenhagen: Møllers; London: Oxford, 1926.

Pohlmann, H. F. "Erwägungen zum Schlusskapitel des deuteronomistischen Geschichtswerkes Oder: warum wird der Prophet Jeremia in 2 Kön 22–25 nicht erwähnt?" in *Textgemäss: Aufsätze und Beitrage zur Hermeneutik des Alten Testaments. Festschrift für Ernst Wurthwein zum 70. Geburtstag.* Ed. A. H. J. von Gunneweg and Otto Kaiser. Göttingen: Vanderhöeck & Ruprecht, 1979, pp. 94–109.

Polzin, Robert. *David and the Deuteronomist: A Literary Study of the Deuteronomistic History: Part Three: 2 Samuel.* Bloomington, Ind.: Indiana University Press, 1993.

Pomykala, Kenneth E. *The Davidic Dynasty Tradition in Early Judaism: Its History and Significance for Messianism. EJL*, 7. Atlanta: Scholars Press, 1995.

Provan, Ian. *Hezekiah and the Books of Kings. BZAW*, 172. Berlin: de Gruyter, 1988.

Von Rad, Gerhard. "The Promised Land and Yahweh's Land in the Hexateuch," in *The Problem of the Hexateuch and Other Essays.* Trans. E. W. Trueman. London: SCM, 1966, pp. 79–93.

Von Rad, Gerhard. "There Remain Still a Rest for the People of God: An Investigation of a Biblical Conception," in *The Problem of the Hexateuch and Other Essays.* Trans. E. W. Trueman. London: SCM, 1966, pp. 94–102.

Rainey, Anson F. "The Satrapy 'Beyond the River'," *Austrialian Journal of Biblical Archaeology* 1 (1969), pp. 51–78.

Reviv, Hanoch. *The Elders in Ancient Israel: a Study of a Biblical Institution.* Jerusalem: Magnes, 1989.

Roberts, J. J. "The Davidic Origin of the Zion Tradition," *JBL* 92 (1973), pp. 329–44.

Roberts, J. J. "Zion in the Theology of the Davidic–Solomonic Empire," in *Studies in the Period of David and Solomon.* Ed. T. Ishida Winona Lake, Ind.: Eisenbrauns, 1982, pp. 93–108.

Rosenberg, Joel. *King and Kin: Political Allegory in the Hebrew Bible.* Bloomington: Indiana University Press, 1986.

Rosenbloom, J. "Social Science Concepts of Modernization and Biblical History: The Development of the Israelite Monarchy," *JAAR* 40 (1972), pp. 437–444.

Rost, L. *The Succession to the Throne of David.* Trans. Michael D. Rutter and David M. Gunn. Sheffield: Almond, 1982.

Sarna, Nahum. "Psalm 89: A Study in Innerbiblical Exegesis," in *Biblical and Other Studies*. Ed. A.Altmann. Cambridge: Harvard, 1963, pp. 29–46.

Schiffman, Lawrence H. "The Concept of the Messiah in Second Temple and Rabbinic Literature." *The Review and Expositor* 84 (1987), pp. 235–246.

Schiffman, Lawrence H. "Jerusalem in the Dead Sea Scrolls," in *The Centrality of Jerusalem: Historical Perspectives*. Ed. M. Poorthuis and Ch. Safrai. Kampen: Kok Pharos, 1996, pp. 29–49.

Schniedewind, William M. "History and Interpretation: The Religion of Ahab and Manasseh in the Book of Kings," *CBQ* 55 (1993), pp. 649–661.

Schniedewind, William M. *The Word of God in Transition: From Prophet to Exegete in the Second Temple Period. JSOTSS*, 197. Sheffield: JSOT Press, 1995.

Schniedewind, William M. "King and Priest in the Book of Chronicles and the Duality of Qumran Messianism," *JJS* (1994), pp.

Schniedewind, William M. "History or Homily: Toward Understand the Chronicler's Purpose," in *Eleventh World Congress of Jewish Studies: Division A: The Bible and Its World.* Jerusalem: Magnes, 1994, pp. 91–97

Schniedewind, William M. "Textual Criticism and Theological Interpretation: The Pro-Temple Tendenz in the Greek Text of Samuel-Kings," *HTR* 87 (1994), pp. 107–116.

Schniedewind, William M. "The Problem with Kings: Recent Study of the Deuteronomistic History," *RSR* 22,1 (1995), pp. 22–27.

Schniedewind, William M. "Are We His People or Not? Biblical Interpretation During Crisis," *Bib* 76 (1995), pp. 540–550.

Schüpphaus, J. *Die Psalmen Salomos: Ein Zeugnis Jerusalemer Theologie und Frömmigkeit in der Mitte des vorchristlichen Jahrhunderts.* Leiden: Brill, 1977.

Seeligmann, I. L. "The Beginnings of Midrash in the Book of Chronicles," *Tarbiz* 49 (1979/80), pp. 14–32. Hebrew.

Seeligmann, I. L. "Hebräische Erzählung und biblische Geschichtsschreibung," *Theologische Zeitschrift* 18 (1962), pp. 305–25.

Seeligmann, I. L. "Problems and Perspectives in Modern Septuagint Research," *Textus* 15 (1990), pp. 169–232.

Seidel, Moshe. "Parallels between Isaiah and Psalm," *Sinai* 38 (1955–56), pp. 149–72, 229–40, 272–80, 335–55. Hebrew.

Seitz, Christopher R. "The crisis of intepretation over the meaning and purpose of the exile. A redactional study of Jeremiah XXI–XLII," *VT* (1985), pp. 78–97.

Service, Elman R. *Primitive Social Organization.* New York: Random House, 1962.

Service, Elman R. *Origins of the States and Civilization.* New York: Norton, 1975.

Shanks, H., editor. *Recent Archaeology in the Land of Israel.* Washington, DC: Biblical Archaeology Society, 1988.

Sharvit, Baruch. "Leadership of the Judaean Desert Sect," *Beth-Mikra* 24 (1979), pp. 295–304. Hebrew.

Shiloh, Yigael. "Elements in the Development of Town Planning in the Israelite City," *IEJ* 28 (1978), pp. 36–51.

Shiloh, Yigael. "Judah and Jerusalem in the Eighth-Sixth Centuries B.C.," in *Recent Excavations in Israel: Studies in Iron Age Archaeology*. Ed. S. Gitin and W. G. Dever. Winona Lake, Ind.: Eisenbrauns, 1989, pp. 97–105.

Silver, M. *Prophets and Markets: the Political Economy of Ancient Israel.* Boston: Kluwer-Nijhoff Publishing, 1983.

Smith, Daniel L. *The Religion of the Landless: The Social Context of the Babylonian*

Exile. Bloomington, Ind.: Meyer-Stone Books, 1989.

Smith, Daniel L. "The Politics of Ezra: Sociological Indicators of Postexilic Judaean Society," in *Second Temple Studies. 1. Persian Period*. Ed. P. Davies. *JSOTSS*, 109. Sheffield: JSOT Press, 1991, pp. 73–97.

Smith-Christopher, Daniel L. "The Mixed Marriage Crisis in Ezra 9–10 and Nehemiah 13: A Study of the Sociology of the Post-exilic Judaean Community," in *Second Temple Studies. 2. Temple Community in the Persian Period*. Ed. T. Eskenazi and K. Richards. *JSOTSS*, 175. Sheffield: JSOT Press, 1994.

Smith-Christopher, Daniel L. "Reassessing the Historical and Sociological Impact of the Babylonian Exile (597/587-539 BCE)," in *Exile: Old Testament, Jewish, and Christian Conceptions*. Ed. J. M. Scott. *SJSJ*, 56. Leiden: Brill, 1997, pp. 7-36.

Smith, George Adam. *Historical Geography of the Holy Land*. Reprint. Jerusalem: Ariel, 1966.

Smith, Morton. "God's Begetting the Messiah in 1QSa," *JTS* 5 (1959), pp. 218–224.

Smith, Morton. *Palestinian Parties and Politics*. New York: Columbia University Press, 1971.

Sojberg, Gideon. *The Preindustrial City: Past and Present*. Glencoe, Ill.: Free Press, 1960.

Sommer, Ben. *A Prophet Reads Scripture: Allusion in Isaiah 40–66*. Palo Alto, CA: Stanford University Press, forthcoming.

Stager, Lawrence E. "The Archaeology of the Family in Ancient Israel," *BASOR* 260 (1985), pp. 1–35.

Stegemann, Hartmut. "Some Remarks to 1QSa, to 1QSb, and to Qumran Messianism," *RQ* 65–68 (1996), pp. 479–505.

Sterling, Gregory. " 'Thus are Israel': Jewish Self-Definition in Alexandria," in *The Studia Philonica Annual: Studies in Hellenistic Judaism, Volume 7*. Ed. David T. Runia. *BJS*, 305. Atlanta: Scholars Press, 1995, pp. 1–18.

Stern, Ephraim. "The Province of Yehud: the Vision and the Reality," *The Jerusalem Cathedra* 1 (1981), pp. 9–21.

Stern, Ephraim. *The Material Culture of the Land of the Bible in the Persian Period 538–332 BC*. Warminster: Aris & Phillips, 1982.

Stern, Philip. "The Eighth Century Dating of Psalm 78 Re-argued," *HUCA* 66 (1995), pp. 41–65.

Steudel, Annette, "4QMidrEschat: <<A Midrash on Eschatology>> (4Q*174* + 4Q*177*)," in *The Madrid Congress. Proceedings of the International Congress on the Dead Sea Scrolls. Madrid 18–21 March, 1991*. Ed. J. Trebolle Barrera and L. Vegas Montaner. Leiden: Brill, 1992.

Steudel, Annette. "The Eternal Reign of the People of God Collective Expectations in Qumran Texts (4Q246 and 1QM)," *RQ* 65–68 (1996), pp. 507–525.

Strauss, Mark L. *The Davidic Messiah in Luke-Acts: The Promise and Its Fulfillment in Lukan Christology*. *JSNTSS*, 110. Sheffield: Sheffield Academic Press, 1995.

Strickert, Frederick M. "Damascus Document VII, 10–20 and Qumran Messianic Expectation," *RQ* 12 (1986), pp. 327–49.

Suleiman, Susan and Corsman, Inge, ed. *The Reader in the Text: Essays on Audience and Interpretation*. Princeton: Princeton University Press, 1980.

Tadmor, H. "Traditional Institutions and the Monarchy: Social and Political Tensions in the Time of David and Solomon," in *Studies in the Period of David and Solomon and Other Essays*. Ed. T. Ishida. Winona Lake, Ind.: Eisenbrauns, 1982, pp. 239–58.

Talmon, S. "Kingship and the Ideology of the State," in *King, Cult and Calendar in*

Ancient Israel. Jerusalem: Magnes, 1986, pp. 9–38.

Talmon, S. "Waiting for the Messiah: The Spiritual Universe of the Qumran Covenanters," in *Judaisms and their Messiahs at the Turn of the Christian Era*. Ed. J. Neusner. Cambridge: Cambridge University Press, 1987, pp. 111-37.

Talmon, S. "Qumran Studies: Past, Present, and Future," *JQR* 85 (1994), pp. 1–31.

Talmon, S. "The Emergence of Jewish Sectarianism in the Early Second Temple Period," in *Ancient Israelite Religion: Essays in Honor of Frank Moore Cross*. Ed. Patrick D. Miller. Paul Hanson. and S. Dean McBride. Philadephia: Fortress, 1987), pp. 587–616. Also published in *King, Cult and Calendar in Ancient Israel*. Jerusalem: Magnes, 1986, pp. 165–201.

Talmon, S. "The Judean ^{c}am ha$^{\supset}$aretṣ in Historical Perspective," in *King, Cult and Calendar in Ancient Israel*. Jerusalem: Magnes, 1986, pp. 68–78.

Talstra, Eep. *Solomon's Prayer. Synchrony and Diachony in the Composition of I Kings 8,14–61*. Amsterdam, 1987.

Thompson, T. L. *Early History of the Israelite People From the Written and Archaeological Sources*. Leiden: Brill, 1992.

Tigay, Jeffrey. *You Shall Have No Other Gods*. Atlanta: Scholars, 1986.

Tigay, Jeffrey. "Israelite Religion: The Onomastic and Epigraphic Evidence," in *Ancient Israelite Religion: Essays in Honor of Frank Moore Cross*. Ed. Patrick D. Miller, Paul Hanson. and S. Dean McBride. Philadephia: Fortress, 1987, pp. 157–194.

Tov, Emanuel. "A Modern Textual Outlook Based on the Dead Sea Scrolls," *HUCA* 10 (1982), pp. 11–27.

Tov, Emanuel. "History and Significance of a Standard Text of the Hebrew Bible," in *Hebrew Bible/Old Testament: The History of Its Interpretation. Volume 1: From the Beginnings to the Middle Ages (Until 1300)*. Ed. Magne Sabø. Göttingen: Vandenhoeck & Ruprecht, 1996, pp. 49–66.

Tov, Emanuel. "The Literary History of the Book of Jeremiah in the Light of its Textual History," in *Empirical Models for Biblical Criticism*. Ed. J. Tigay. Philadephia: University of Pennsylvania Press, 1985, pp. 211–237.

Trebolle Barrera, Julio. "A Preliminary Edition of 4QKings (4Q54)," in *The Madrid Qumran Congress: Proceedings of the International Congress on the Dead Sea Scrolls Madrid 18–21 march, 1991*. Ed. J. Trebolle Barrera and L. Vegas Montaner. Leiden: Brill, 1992, pp. 229–246.

Trebolle-Barerra, Julio, "The Text-Critical Use of the Septuagint in the Books of Kings," in *VII Congress of the International Organization for Septuagint and Cognate Studies*. Ed. Claude E. Cox. Atlanta: Scholars Press, 1991.

Trebolle-Barerra, Julio. "Light from 4QJudg^{a} and 4QKgs on the Text of Judges and Kings," in *The Dead Sea Scrolls: Forty Years of Research*. Ed. D. Dimant and U. Rapport. Jerusalem: Magnes Press; Leiden: Brill, 1992, pp. 315–23.

Tsevat, Matitiahu. "The House of David in Nathan's Prophecy," *Bib* 46 (1965), pp. 353–56.

Tsevat, Matitiahu. "The Steadfast House: What Was David Promised in 2 Samuel 7?" in *The Meaning of the Book of Job and Other Biblical Studies*. New York: Ktav, 1980, pp. 101–117.

Van der Toorn, Karel and Houtman, Cees. "David and the Ark," *JBL* 113 (1994), pp. 209–231.

VanderKam, James C. "Jubilees and the Priestly Messiah of Qumran," *RQ* 13 (1988), pp. 352–65.

Van Seters, J. *In Search of History: Historiography in the Ancient World and the Origins of Biblical History*. New Haven: Yale, 1983.

Vaughn, Andrew. "The Chronicler's Account of Hezekiah: The Relationship of Historical Data to a Theological Interpretation of 2 Chronicles 29–32," Th.D. diss., Princeton Theological Seminary, 1996.

de Vaux, Roland. *Ancient Israel*. New York: McGraw-Hill, 1961.

Veijola, Timo. *Die Ewige Dynastie. David und die Entstehung seiner Dynastie nach der deuteronomistischen Darstellung*. Helsinki, 1975.

Veijola, Timo. "Davidverheissung und Staatsvertrag. Beobachtungen zum Einfluss altorientalischer Staatsverträge auf die biblische Sprache am Beispeil von Psalm 89," *ZAW* 95 (1983), pp. 9–31.

Veijola, Timo. *David. Gesammelte Studien zu den Davidüberlieferungen des Alten Testaments. Schriften der Finnischen Exegetischen*, 52. Helsinki: Finnish Exegetical Society, 1990.

Vermes, Geza. "Bible Interpretation at Qumran," *EI* 20 (1989), pp. 184*–191*.

Vermes, Geza. "The So–Called King Jonathon Fragment (4Q448)," *JJS* 44 (1993), pp. 294–300.

Vries, Simon de. "Moses and David as Cult Founders in Chronicles." *JBL* 107 (1988), pp. 619–39.

Weber, Max. *Ancient Judaism*. Trans. H. Gerth and D. Martindale. Glencoe, Ill.: Free Press, 1952.

Weber, Max. *Economy and Society*. Ed. G. Roth and C. Wittich. Berkeley: University of California Press, 1978.

Weinberg, Joel P. *The Citizen-Temple Community*. Trans. D. Smith-Christopher. *JSOTSS*, 151. Sheffield: JSOT Press, 1992.

Weinfeld, Moshe. "Jeremiah and the Spiritual Metamorphosis of Israel," *ZAW* 88 (1976), pp. 17–56.

Weinfeld, Moshe. "Zion and Jerusalem as Religious and Political Capital: Ideology and Utopia," in *The Poet and the Historian: Essays in Literary and Historical Biblical Criticism*. Ed. R. E. Friedman. Chico, CA: Scholars Press, 1983, pp. 75–116.

Weinfeld, Moshe. *Deuteronomy and the Deuteronomic School*. Reprint. Winona Lake, IN: Eisenbrauns, 1992. Oxford: Clarendon Press, 1972.

Weinfeld, Moshe. "Bond [הברית] and Grace [החסד]–Covenantal Expressions in the Bible and in the Ancient World: A Common Heritage," *Leshonenu* 36 (1971/72), pp. 86–105 [Hebrew].

Weippert, Helga. "Die 'deuteronomistischen' Beurteilungen der Königen von Israel und Juda und das Problem der Redaktion der Königsbücher," *Bib* 53 (1972), pp. 301–9.

Weippert, Helga. *Palästina in vorhellenistischer Zeit*. Handbuch der Archäologie. Vorderasien 2. Band 1. Munich: Beck, 1988.

Weiser, Artur. "Dei Legitimation des Königs David. Zur Eigenart und Entstehung der sogen. Gechichte von Davids Aufstieg," *VT* 16 (1966), pp. 325–54.

Whitelam, Keith W. "The Defense of David," *JSOT* 29 (1984), pp. 61–87.

Whitelam, Keith W. "Recreating the History of Israel," *JSOT* 35 (1986), pp. 45–70.

Whitelam, Keith W. "The Symbols of Power: Aspects of Royal Propaganda in the United Monarchy," *BA* 49 (1986), pp. 166–73.

Whitelam, Keith W. "Israelite Kingship. The Royal Ideology and its Opponents," in *The World of Ancient Israel: Sociological, Anthropological and Political Perspectives: Essays by Members of the Society for Old Testament Study*. Ed. R. E. Clements. Cambridge: Cambridge University Press, 1989, pp. 119–139.

Wildberger, Hans. "Die Völkerwallfahrt zum Zion, Jes. II 1–5," *VT* 7 (1957), pp. 62–81.

Williamson, H. G. M. "The Accession of Solomon in the Books of Chronicles," *VT* 26 (1976), pp. 351–61.
Williamson, H. G. M. "Eschatology in Chronicles," *TynBul* 28 (1977), pp. 115–54.
Williamson, H. G. M. "Sources and Redaction in the Chronicler's Genealogy of Judah," *JBL* 98 (1979), pp. 351–59.
Williamson, H. G. M. "The Dynastic Oracle in the Books of Chronicles," in *Leo Isaac Seeligman Anniversity Volume, volume 3*. Jerusalem, 1983, pp. 305–18.
Williamson, H. G. M. "The Temple in the Books of Chronicles," in *Templum Amicitiae: Essays on the Second Temple presented to Ernst Bammel. JSNTSS*, 41. Sheffield: Almond, 1991, pp. 15–31.
Williamson, H. G. M. *The Book Called Isaiah: Deutero–Isaiah's Role in Composition and Redaction*. Oxford: Clarendon Press, 1994.
Williamson, H. G. M. "Hezekiah and the Temple," in *Texts, Temples, and Traditions: a Tribute to Menahem Haran*. Ed. Michael V. Fox, et. al. Winona Lake, Ind.: Eisenbrauns, 1996, pp. 47–52.
Wise, Michael O. "4QFlorilegium and the Temple of Adam," *RQ* 15 (1991), pp. 103–32.
Wise, Michael O. and Tabor, James D. "The Messiah at Qumran," *BAR* 18(6) (1992), pp. 60–65.
Yadin, Yigael. "A Midrash on 2 Sam. vii and Ps. i–ii (4Q Florilegium)," *IEJ* 9 (1959), pp. 95–98.
Younger, K. L. "The Figurative Aspect and the Contextual Method in the Evaluation of the Solomonic Empire (1 King 1–11)," in *The Bible in Three Dimensions: Essays in Celebration of Forty Years of Biblical Studies in the University of Sheffield*. Ed. D. Clines, S. Fowl, and S. Porter. *JSOTSS*, 87. Sheffield: JSOT Press, 1990, pp. 157–175.
Zakovitch, Yair. *"And You Shall Tell Your Son . . . ": The Concept of the Exodus in the Bible*. Jerusalem: Magnes, 1991.
Zakovitch, Yair. and A. Shinan. "Midrash on Scripture and Midrash within Scripture," in *Studies in Bible*. Ed. S. Japhet. Jerusalem: Magnes, 1986, pp. 257–278.
Zertal, Adam. "An Early Iron Age Cultic Site on Mount Ebal: Excavation Seasons 1982–1987," *TA* 13–14 (1986–87), pp. 105–165.
Zertal, Adam. "The Israelite Settlement in the Hill Country of Manasseh," Ph.D. diss., Tel Aviv University, 1986. Hebrew.
Zimhoni, O. "Two Ceramic Assemblages from Lachish Levels III and II," *TA* 17 (1990), pp. 3–52.

General Index

Adams, R. 103, 193
adoption 39, 70, 95, 162-163, 182, 205
Ahlström, G. 176, 180, 190
Albright, W.F. 42, 183
Alt, A. 179, 180, 182, 196
Alter, R. 174, 175
Amarna Letters 20, 40, 42-43, 85
Anderson, N. 57, 186
Auerbach, E. 77, 189
Auwers, J.-M. 44, 183
Avigad, N. 52, 184, 189
Avishur, Y. 42, 183
Babylonian exile 4, 84-85, 98-106, 117-118, 119-121
Bahat, D. 184, 186
Baillet, M. 164
Bakhtin, M. 8, 174
Barclay, J. 141-143, 144, 200
Barkay, G. 124, 184, 185, 186, 192, 196
Barr, J. 64, 188
Barstad, H. 99-100, 192
Becker, J. 166, 205
Beckford, J. 72, 80, 81, 82, 190
Benjamin, D.
Bickerman, E. 144, 201
Blenkinsopp, J. 173, 189, 202
Bliss, F. 52
Braun, R. 197, 198
Bregstein, L. 102, 193
Brettler, M. 24, 42, 180, 181, 182, 183, 187, 188, 191
Bright, J. 190
Broshi, M. 53, 57, 184
Bruggemann, W. 195
Carlson, R. 31
Carroll, R. 105, 106, 193, 194
Carter, C. 121, 195, 196
centralization 17-18, 36, 49-60, 73, 89, 96-97, 118, 170
Childs, B. 14, 151, 175, 202
Clements, R.E. 63, 65, 187
Clifford, R. 67, 68, 188
Collins, J. 200
conditional Promise 4, 89, 94-96, 97, 106, 109-110, 116, 118, 133-134, 152
Coogan, Michael
Coppens, J. 145, 201
Cross, F. M. 32, 83, 126, 127, 181, 189, 197, 201
Cyrus 98, 106, 114, 119, 142
Dagan, Y. 54
Daiches, S. 77, 89, 102, 189, 193
Davies, P. 176
de Vaux, R. 77
de Vries, S. 128, 132, 197, 199
de Wette, W.M.L. 84
deitic particles 9, 35-36, 77, 83, 159
demographics 20-21
Dever, W. 18, 174, 176, 177
Dickie, A.C. 52
Dimant, D. 155, 156, 203
Dion, P. 191
Douglas, M. 101, 192
Driver, S.R. 144
Duhm, B. 67, 114, 136, 188, 199
Edelman, D. 176
Eisenstadt, S. 178
Eissfeldt, O. 195
Enuma Elish 26, 28
Eslinger, L. 8, 32-33, 131, 173, 175, 180, 198
Fall of Samaria 41-42, 51-52, 57-61, 65-66, 71, 91-92, 193
Festinger, L. 105, 194
Finkelstein, I. 20, 54, 55, 57, 175, 176-77, 185, 186
Fishbane, M. 7-8, 30, 35, 173, 174, 199
Flusser, D. 199
Fogel, R. 12, 174
Frankfort, H. 24

Freedman, D. 63, 128, 187, 197
Frick, F. 175, 177
Friedman, R. 181, 187
Galling, K. 77, 190, 196
Geller, S. 189, 191
Geva, H. 184
Gitin, S. 185, 188
Gooding, D. 145, 201
Goody, J. 76, 189
Gordis, R. 77, 189
Görg, M. 31
Gottwald, N. 13, 101
Gunkel, H. 66, 188, 194
Halliday, M.A.K. 156, 203
Halpern, B. 15, 56, 59, 173, 175, 178, 186, 187, 188
Haran, M. 114
Hart, B.F.
Hess, R. 42, 43, 183
Hillers, D. 57, 187
Hoglund, K. 121, 122, 123, 124, 192, 195, 196
Hurowitz, V. 49, 179, 183
Hurvitz, A. 40, 176, 188
Iser, W. 173, 175
J 25, 29
Jamieson-Drake, D. 178
Japhet, S. 125, 126, 127, 176, 185
Jauss, Hans Robert 5-15, 173, 174
Jellicoe, S. 144, 201
Johnson, A. 113, 194
Kaufmann, Y. 190
Kelly, B. 134, 199
Kenyon, Kathleen
Knoppers, Gary
Königsnovelle 31
Kraus, H. 112
Kugel, J. 8
Kuhne, H. 30, 186
Laato, A. 14-15, 175
LaCapra, D. 174
lamp 45-46, 91-92, 104, 137, 169
Levenson, J. 87, 104, 108, 173
Levinson, B. 174, 191, 205
linguistic dating 16, 40, 42, 44, 64, 66-67, 176
literacy 8, 74-77, 170
liturgy 18, 29, 33, 40-46, 69-70, 115
Lohfink, N. 192
Loprieno, A. 31
Lust, J. 143, 145, 194, 201
Machinist, P. 24, 25, 179
Mazar, A. 73, 99, 177, 180, 188, 192
McCarter, K. 93, 146, 192, 201, 202
McCarthy, D. 31-32
McKane, W. 139, 199
McKenzie, S. 32, 119, 197, 201, 202
Mendenhall, G. 13
Menes, A. 77
Mettinger, T. 92, 178, 192
Meyers, E. 195
Millard, A. 189
Miller, M. 176
Mosiac covenant 109-110, 113, 133, 164
Mowinckel, S. 31, 38, 194
Na'aman, N. 20, 176, 177, 185, 188
name theology 32-33, 35-36, 38, 42-46, 72, 83-89, 91, 96-97, 110-111, 138, 150, 171
Nelson, R. 32
Nicholson, E.W. 77, 190
Niditch, S. 8, 173
Noth, M. 31-32, 59, 77, 82, 84, 190, 192
Ong, W. 8, 173, 189, 205
Orality 8, 62, 74-75
Paul, S. 63, 182
Peckham, B. 174
Pedersen, J. 51, 184
place (מקום) 4, 35-37, 84, 96, 108, 117, 148, 150, 158
Polzin, R. 39, 174, 182
Pomykala, K. 15, 64-65, 125, 162, 165-166, 175, 187, 188, 196, 202, 204, 205
Pritchard, J. 185
Provan, I. 59, 60, 187
Rainey, A. 195
Reader-Response Criticism 7
rest 4, 36, 38, 45-46, 85-86, 108, 130-131, 137-138, 165
Reviv, H. 77, 190, 193
Roberts, J.J.M. 25, 26, 179, 193
Robertson, D. 66, 188
Rosenberg, J. 11-12, 174
Rost, L. 11, 14, 30-31, 175, 182
Rudolph, W. 197, 198, 202

Sarna, N. 29-30, 112, 180, 194
Schiffman, L. 162, 204
Seeligmann, I.L. 144, 201
Seidel, M. 190
Seidel's Law 9, 76, 86, 190
Seitz, C. 194, 195
Sennacherib 53-55
Service, E. 22, 177
shepherd 39, 47, 69, 164
Shiloh 66-69, 92, 104
Sjoberg, G. 56, 186
Smith(-Christopher), D. 100-3, 175, 192, 193
Smith, George Adam 11, 20, 47, 174, 177
Smith, Mark 182
Smith, Morton 195
Sommer, B. 114, 187, 193
Stegemann, H. 163, 204
Sterling, G. 142
Stern, E. 196
Steudel, A. 163, 204
Suleiman, S. 6, 173
Sulzberger, M. 77, 189
"sure house" 92-93
synagogue 103-104, 183
Sweeney, M. 61-62, 114, 187, 195
Tadmor, H. 48-49, 174, 190
Talmon, S. 19, 25, 79, 173, 176, 190, 204
Thompson, T. 176
Tigay, J. 27, 180, 190
Torrey, C.C. 99
Tov, E. 155, 191, 199, 201, 202, 205
Trebolle-Barrera, J. 89-90, 149
universalization 118, 119, 138, 171
urbanization 52-58
United States Constitution 5
Ussishkin, D. 177
van Seters, J. 37, 187
Vaughn, A. 184, 185
Veijola, T. 14, 92, 175, 190, 191, 192
von Rad, G. 84, 182, 190, 198
Weber, M. 74, 77, 188, 189
Weinfeld, M. 34, 36, 43, 45, 84, 137, 183, 190, 191, 195, 199
Weippert, H. 59, 187, 196
Weiser, A. 31, 112, 181, 194
Wellhausen, J. 29-31, 180
Whitelam, K. 179, 180
Wiederaufnahme 9, 35-36, 76, 83, 159, 181
Wijngaards, J. 87, 191
Williamson, H. 67, 114, 125, 127, 131, 133-134, 187, 188, 194, 196, 197, 198, 199, 205
Wittfogel, K. 53-54, 185
Zakovitch, Y. 7, 173
Zertal, A. 27, 180
Zimhoni, O. 73-74
Zion tradition 4, 25-26, 69, 104-106, 114

Index of Passages

Hebrew Bible
Gen
22 26
23:7, 12, 13 77
26:24 77
35:11 32
36:31-39 88
42:6 25
49:10 84, 163, 164
Exod
5:5 79
5:5 77
15:1-17 37
15:1 151
15:13 151
15:16b 68
15:17 68, 151-52, 158, 159
32:8 49
Lev
4:27 77
20:2, 4 77
26:14-45 108
Numb
14:9 77, 79
21:7 151
23:9 142
24:17 162
Deut
3:14 85
3:20 36, 85
5:29 165
5:31 95
6:1 95
7:9 119
7:11 95
12 91, 128, 150
12:2 49
12:5 36, 88
12:5, 21 64
12:10 36, 85
12:11 84
13 76
14:23 84
16:2, 6, 11 84
17:14-20 47, 161
17:16-17 154
17:18-20 97
25:19 36, 85
26:2 84
28:13 163
28:15-68 108
Josh
1:8 97
1:11-15 30
1:13, 15 36
12 30
21:44 36
23 30
23:1 36
Judg
2:11-23 30
3:10 23
6:25 27
6:34 23
8:22 47
8:23 47
9:7-20 47
11:8 48
11:29 23
13:25 23
1 Sam
2:35 92
2:36 93
4:4
5:2 164
7-12 30
7:2-8:22
8:4-22 47
8:5, 20 24
8:11-18 25
8:18 150
9:1-10:16 23, 30
10:17-27 23, 30
10:27b-11:15 23
10:6, 10 23
11:1-2 25
11:6 23
12 31
12:12 23
14:50 23
16:13 23
18:20
20:25 23
25:28
25:44 92
31 23
2 Sam
3:1 29
5-6 27
5:1-5 29
5:9 85
6:2 84
8:18 23
10:1 25
12:28 84
15:7-12 48
16:5-8 29
16:5 25, 29
16:15 48
17:3-4 48
19:11 48
19:41 48
20:1-2 25, 29
20:24 20, 25
21:1-6 29
23:2 23
23:8-39 23
1 Kgs
2:4 162, 164

3:2 32, 84
3:7 24
4:6 20
5:1-12
5:3 30
5:3-4 36, 38
5:12-18 24
5:13 25
5:16-19
5:17-18
5:17 84, 147
5:18 36
5:19
5:27-28 20
5:27
9:3 32, 84
9:4-6 162
9:5 134, 164
9:7 32, 84
9:15-19 24
9:15-17 21, 26
9:15 20, 21
9:26-28 24
10:26-29 153
11:1-8 24
11:9-13 60
11:11-13 34
11:12 138
11:13 104
11:28 20
11:29-40 92
11:36 45, 84, 104, 169
11:37-38 28
11:38 92
12:1-19 25
12:16 47
12:19 60, 71
12:25-31 27, 49
12:28 49
12:3-14,18 20
13:1-2 60
13:2 92
14:7-14 28
14:7 63
14:21 84, 91
15:4 46, 91, 104, 169
16:2 63
16:3-12 28
16:5, 27 59
16:16 49
22:45 59

2 Kgs
6-7 59
8:19 45, 91, 104, 133, 138, 169
9:9 28
10:30-31 28
10:34 59
11:1-12
11:13-20 78
13:12
13:14-21 59
13:8 59
14:28 59
16:4 49
17 42, 60
17:20-21a 60, 66, 71
17:7-23 31
17:10 49
17:37 95
18:3-5 81
18:13-15 19
18:13 55
18:16-37 19
18:16 19
19:34 91, 104, 138
20:6 91
20:20 50
21:1-9 80
21:3 54
21:4, 7 37, 84, 104
21:7-7 110-111
21:7 36, 91, 96
21:19 54, 80
21:23-24 80
23:9 54
23:21-23 61
23:24
23:27 32, 84
24:3-4 81
24:4 99
24:14 79
25:3 99
25:12 79, 95
25:19 78

1 Chr
1:43 25
3:19-24 120, 126
7:18 164
12:19 132
18-20 132
18:17 23
19:1-2 25
22-28 48
22:7-8 33, 132, 137
22:8 38, 130, 132
22:9 38
24:3 136
24:19 136
26:18 125
28:2 46, 130, 132, 137
28:3 33, 137, 147
28:10 133
28:11 125
28:12 132
29:1, 19 125
29:7 125
29:16 133
29:19 125, 133

2 Chr
1:18 131
2:1, 4 33
2:11 131
3:1 26
6:2 117
6:5-6 89
6:7, 8, 9, 10 33
6:41-42 44, 45, 128
6:41 130
6:42 133
7:17-18 162
13:5 133
15:1 132
15:3 159
16:9 126
21:7 133
23:3 133
28:2 165

30:1 54
33:14 55
33:17 82
35:1-19 61
36:22-23 127, 128
Ezra
1-6 128, 135
1:1-4 116, 128
3:8 133
3:12-13 138
4:4 79, 99, 100
6:12 84
7:6-73 128
7:6 159
Neh
1:9 84
2:8 123
5:1-5 122-23
5:6-12 123
7:2 123
13:16 123
Ps
2 58, 69-70, 95
2:7-9 70
44:9 165
49:12 84
72 153
74 42
74:9 42, 105
78:44-55 68
78:67-72 58, 66-69, 70
78:68 26
80:2 96
84-89 111
89 29-30
89: 3-18 40-43
89:19-37 93-96
89:38-51 111-114
105:43 114
106:5 25
121 115
125:1 26
132 26, 40, 44-46, 108, 130, 136-38
137 103
Prov
25:1 58, 74, 169
Job
42:8 32
Isa
1:8 64
4:1 84
5:1-30 61
6:1-9:6 61
7-11 169
7:2-3 62
7:17 61, 62, 160
9:1-7 54, 62
9:1 71
9:7-12:6 61
11:1 159
11:6-9 61
11:6 62
11:12 61
22:10, 11 53
36:1 19
38:6 91
41:8 32
43:20 114
44:1 32
45:4 114, 116
47:6 104
55 118
55:3 171
56:3-8 117
65:22 114
66:1-2 116-117, 171
66:1 85, 138, 165
Jer
1:10 37
2:21 37
7:1-15 67
7:10 84
7:12 63, 84, 104-105
7:13-14 104
11:4 162
18:9 37
23:5-6 135-36, 159
24:6 37
24:7 162
25:9 84
25:29 32
26:1-24 67
27:6 32
29:1 103
30:22 162
31:1 162
31:28 37
32:24 84
32:41 37
33:14-22 135-36
33:15-16 159
33:17 109
34:15 84
42:10 37
45:4 37
52:28-30 99
Lam
2:14 105
Ezek
8:1 103
20:3 103
21:30-32 143
28:11-19 143
34:23 164
34:27 103
36:28 162
37:25 1
40-48 138
Hos
1:7 65
3:4-5 65-66
8:4 65
Amos
5:2 63
5:26-27 64, 160-161
6:2 63
7:8, 15 63
8:2 63
9 15, 37
9:11-15 63-65
9:11 61
9:15 37
Mic
1:13 58
3:9-12 54, 58, 104
Zech
3:8 159

4:10 126
6:11-13 171
6:12-13 134-135, 159
7:5 99
Hag
2:4 99, 133
2:23 133

Septuagint
2 Kgdms
7:1-17 146-147
3 Kgdms
8:12-53 149
8:16 26, 89-91, 149, 164, 166
8:42 149, 150
8:53 149-152, 159, 166
Tobit
1:4 140
14:5 138
Sirach
45:7 153
47:11 152-153
47:18-25 152
50:25
2 Macc
1:18-19 139

New Testament
Matt
21:1-17 154
Mark
11:1-11 154
Luke
19:29-44 154
Acts
7:49-50 167
13:33-37 167
15:15-18 167
2 Corith
6:18 167
Hebrews
1:5 167

Mishnah
Aboth
2:6
3:4
3:11 79

Dead Sea Scrolls
Genesis Apocryphon
1QHod
4:14 165
7:9 165
10:7, 18-19 157
10:19 157
12:16 157
15:10 157
1QpHab
2:1-5 156
1QM
11:5-7 161
11:6-7 163
11 1:12-18 163
1QSb
3:22-24
5:27 161
4Q174 (Flor) 35, 117, 148, 151, 158-160
4Q175 1:9-13 157, 161
4Q246 163, 164
4Q252 159
4Q285 159
4Q471 156
4Q504 164-165
4Q509 164
4QKgs 89-91, 149-150, 164
4QMMT 155
4QpGen[a] 163-164
4QpIs[a] 159
4QpPs 37 155, 156
11QT (Temple Scroll)
29:10 165
46:3-4 165
56:12-59:21 161
59:13-21 161-163, 164
59:15 165
59:20-21 163
CD (Damascus Doc.)
1:4-13 156
5:11-12 157
6:7 159
7:9-21 160-161
7:16 158
7:18 159

Other Ancient Sources
Jubilees
19:31 162
Psalms of Solomon
17 153-154
Josephus
Ant 13.62-73
Bell 2.488
Bell 7.421-436
Philo
Legat., 308 141
Mos 2.41-43 143
Letter of Aristeas
12-27 141-142